The Jacobite Risings
in Britain 1689–1746

'Bruce Lenman has chosen a subject about which he has strong opinions and he has written about it with zest . . . a very readable and entertaining book.'
English Historical Review

'For anyone interested in Jacobitism, Mr Bruce Lenman has written a book which cannot be ignored.'
The Scottish Historical Review

'It is written with style and learning, based on an intimate knowledge of the sources (especially the Scottish sources) both in public and private muniments. As an account of the risings and the gentlemen involved in them it will be quite indispensable for anyone working subsequently on the Jacobites in either country; that in itself makes it a substantial scholarly achievement.'
Social History

'He shows, with a thorough command of the primary sources and a trenchant and stimulating style, how complex were the various elements, political, social, religious and economic, that lay behind the Jacobite movement . . .'
Royal Stuart Review

'This is a valuable and very readable contribution to Jacobite studies.'
The Times Higher Educational Supplement

The Jacobite Risings
in Britain 1689–1746

BRUCE LENMAN

Reader in Modern History,
University of St Andrews

METHUEN

A METHUEN PAPERBACK

First published in 1980
by Eyre Methuen Ltd
This paperback edition first published 1984
by Methuen London Ltd
11 New Fetter Lane, London EC4P 4EE
Set and printed in Great Britain
by Richard Clay (The Chaucer Press) Ltd, Bungay, Suffolk

Copyright © 1980 Bruce Lenman

ISBN 0 413 56210 7

For G. O. Sayles

Contents

Preface

While I have always respected the view that it is one of the misfortunes of Scottish history that far too much attention is focused on a limited number of personalities and episodes, such as Mary Queen of Scots and Jacobitism, I make no apologies for what I would like to think was at least to some extent a fresh interpretation of a major theme in late seventeenth and early eighteenth-century British history. In so far as the subject permits such a course, I have consciously tried to write British rather than purely Scottish history, and to indicate, where appropriate, the European context of the events I analyse. I am an economic and social historian, so my vision of Jacobitism is primarily from the grass roots upwards. My main concern is with the factors and motives which made men active Jacobites, rather than with a detailed narrative of events which have often been narrated before, and by more skilled pens than my own. Jacobite sentiment is for me important only in so far as it led to Jacobite deeds. It is perfectly legitimate for other historians to study those expressions of Jacobite sentiment which were confined to private correspondence and which never governed a man's outward behaviour. Such sentiment is, however, not the object of this study. I have tried to set my particular contribution in a general framework which makes the course of events comprehensible to the general reader, but he or she will have to bear with the particular emphases which mark a work committed to the difficult task of combining in unequal measure political, social, and economic history.

In the course of the dozen or more years during which I have worked on this topic, I have accumulated many debts of gratitude which can only be very inadequately expressed here. To the staffs of the British Museum (latterly British Library) Reading Room and Manuscripts Department I owe a debt of very long standing, as I do to the staff and resources of the Institute of Historical Research of the University of London. In Edinburgh the Keeper of the Records of Scotland, Mr John Imrie, and his staff at Register House and West Register House have shown great courtesy and patience in the face of my requests and enquiries. Dr Ian Rae of the Department of Manuscripts of the National Library of Scotland and his colleagues have also helped to confirm my view that Edinburgh must be one of the pleasantest centres for the historical researcher in the world. The Chief Librarian of the Customs and Excise service, Mr Carson, gave me access to customs archives temporarily deposited in Dundee, where the staff at the Customs and Excise office were extremely helpful. Gateshead Central Public Library, and university libraries in Aberdeen, Dundee, St Andrews and Newcastle all furnished important assistance. For assistance with illustrations I am much beholden to Dr Rosalind Marshal of the National Portrait Gallery of Scotland. Mrs Marjorie Nield coped with the task of typing my manuscript in her usual efficient way. None of the above should be held responsible for the shortcomings of this work, which like its eccentricities are entirely my responsibility. Even less must those who, like Dr Joyce Ellis, drew my attention to relevant sources, or who, like Dr Eveline Cruickshanks, allowed me to see unpublished work, be blamed for the use I have made of these materials. The final product I dedicate in gratitude to a scholar to whom I owe much.

St Andrews, March 1979   Bruce Lenman

Acknowledgement to the paperback edition

I am grateful to several friends for pointing out slips in my text. Above all I owe a debt in this field to the eagle eye of the Historiographer Royal for Scotland, Professor Gordon Donaldson. I have tried to correct such errors for the paperback edition, though I must add that any remaining ones are my own responsibility.

B.P.L.

1 *The Pre-History of Jacobitism*

Jacobitism is a term derived from the Latin word *Jacobus* which means James. It is also a creed and a memory which can still inspire passionate admiration. Jacobites were opposed to the Glorious Revolution of 1688 which thrust James VII and II from the thrones of Scotland, England and Ireland. They showed their loyalty to the exiled senior line of the royal house of Stewart by a series of plots and risings which have left imperishable memories of self-sacrificing heroism on the battlefield and the scaffold. That ultimately Jacobitism failed in its central objective of reversing the decision of 1688 has not, at least since the rise of Romanticism as an intellectual style and popular culture, dimmed its glamour. On the contrary it possesses all the attractions of a Lost Cause, and in the English-speaking world perhaps only the story of the Confederates in the American Civil War, or of Mary Queen of Scots can match its perennial attraction.

That Mary was the ancestress of all the Jacobite Pretenders is a reminder of how ancient was the kingship of the Stewarts. Kings of Scotland since 1371, they had in the bizarre person of James VI united Scotland and England in 1603 in a purely personal union. After the execution of Charles I in 1649 by the English New Model Army, Charles II spent the best part of a decade in dreary exile, but in 1660 in the words of an eye-witness, the diarist John Evelyn, Charles II returned in triumph to London, restored 'by that very army which rebelled against him: but it was the Lord's doing, for such a restoration was never mentioned in any history, ancient or modern.'[1] It is in the Restoration era, and especially the reign of Charles II from 1660 to 1685, that the intellectual roots of post-1688 Jacobitism must be sought.

The Stewarts' return from exile in 1660 was a fact not easily forgotten after 1690. It is one explanation, though not the only one, for the tendency of leading soldiers and politicians to keep up an intermittent and ambiguous correspondence with the exiled dynasty after 1690, even when actively engaged in serving those who had supplanted it. Such contacts were a natural form of political fire insurance. Nevertheless, we must not exaggerate in retrospect the role of either the royal house of Stewart, or of militant Royalists in the return of the dynasty in 1660. The restoration of

Charles II to the thrones of his father was a response to incipient anarchy.

Royalist plots and risings against the English republican regime had been, under both the Commonwealth and then the Cromwellian Protectorate, uniformly unsuccessful. When Richard Cromwell succeeded his father Oliver late in 1658 not a mouse stirred. The French ambassador in London reported that even professed Royalists were only too glad to persuade themselves that honour no longer required them to resist a *de facto* government so consistently favoured by Providence. It was the collapse of the Protectorate from within which brought the king into his own again.[2] The main instrument of the Restoration proved to be George Monck, the Cromwellian Commander-in-Chief in Scotland. Edward Hyde, Earl of Clarendon, the historian and statesman, was convinced that Monck had jumped on an irresistible Royalist bandwagon just in time to receive excessive rewards from Charles II. Such an interpretation smacks too much of the rivalry between the two men after 1660. There is no evidence that Monck was in any way committed to the Stewarts when he first led his army into England in January 1660.[3]

The ruling classes of England, of which Monck was a member, seem to have become converts to ardent monarchism when, during Monck's intervention, it became clear that ordered government had collapsed, and that only on the old monarchical foundations could the rule of law be reestablished. What the dynasty thought of itself was therefore of little consequence compared with what the 'natural rulers' of the three kingdoms chose to think of it. In the last analysis it was the nobility, gentry and urban élites who decided the fate of regimes. The only political capital of any value to the exiled Stewarts after they had again been driven abroad in 1688 was an ability to play on the heart-strings and convictions of these same aristocratic groups. Undoubtedly their ability to do this can largely be explained in terms of circumstances existing or arising after 1690, but not entirely. In at least two areas of thought the period before 1690 contributed substantially to the living Jacobite creed of the late seventeenth and early eighteenth centuries. One was the theory of indefeasible hereditary right and the providential sanctions which it implied, and the other was the cult of martyrdom and loyalty in the Stewart cause. It is time to turn to the first of these.

It is important to recognize that because of the tenuousness of their links with reality, there was never very much independent vitality in the theories of royal absolutism which were so ill-advisedly bandied about by the dynasty and its hangers-on from the late sixteenth century onwards.[4] James VI of Scotland published in 1598 his *Trew Law of Free Monarchies*, in which he sought to teach his subjects their duty towards their monarch. In simple, lucid and forceful language James preached on the themes of the absolute power of kings, the necessity of passive obedience on the part of subjects, and the accountability of kings to God alone. There is no reason to doubt the sincerity of James in making the last point. He was convinced that anyone abusing the sacred trust of kingship would be punished far more severely by God than any ordinary sinner 'for the highest bench is sliddriest to sit upon'.

By 1603 James was James I of England as well as James VI of Scotland and a revised version of a book he had published secretly in 1599 had become, by contemporary standards, a best-seller in his new realm. This was *Basilikon Doron*, a manual of instruction for his son Prince Henry. It is imbued with the same patriarchal view of kingship which had character-ized the *Trew Law*, but seems to have been appreciated by contemporaries mainly for its brilliant combination of trenchant prose and uplifting moral platitudes. It may be doubted whether *Basilikon Doron* had any greater effect on the underlying attitudes of its readers than James's *Counterblaste to Tobacco*, another splendid piece of prose published in 1604 with a view to saving his subjects from slavery to that vile weed. In the last analysis, James was a successful monarch mainly because his practice in kingship bore relatively little relationship to his theory. In Scotland in particular he functioned as the last great medieval monarch, cajoling and flattering the magnates so as to keep a consensus of those who mattered behind him until the end of the reign.

If Charles I, the younger son who became heir to the throne on the premature death of Prince Henry, proved only too receptive to some of his father's less realistic ideas, this did not, in the long run, endow them with any greater substance. The lack of connection between the artificial world of the court, where Charles could act out in elaborate masques the wise, beneficent, all-powerful kingship of his dreams, and the harsh realities of the outside world, was a major factor in precipitating crisis and civil war. Charles died heroic but intransigent, asserting on the scaffold itself that the liberty of the subject 'is not for having a share in government, Sir, that is nothing pertaining to them. A subject and a sovereign are clean different things . . .'. The Restoration of 1660 was no tribute to that viewpoint, as the political balance established by the Restoration Settlement rapidly showed. However, it was a tribute to an earlier insight which had guided the dead king through the elaborate negotiations which followed his mili-tary defeat. This was the insight which told Charles that the traditional ruling classes found it almost impossible to operate a stable political system without the principle of monarchy as its central pivot.[5]

Divine right was never, then, a particularly potent creed, even among Anglicans, if by divine right is meant royal absolutism. Outside court circles it tended to be held with some violence only by clerics. One of the strongest pre-civil war statements of divine right absolutism is contained in the Constitutions and Canons Ecclesiastical Concerning Royal Power, adopted by Convocation in 1640. However 1660 did see a massive and self-conscious surge in support for another version of royal right in the shape of indefeasible hereditary right, as a guarantor of the monarchical principle itself. Both in Scotland and in England, the traditional rulers of society had experienced very severe psychological traumas during the civil wars and the Interregnum. In England the 'moral revolution' which the politicians of both the Commonwealth and the Protectorate sought to enforce had often to be forced through by men alien to the close-knit local societies in which the vast majority of the population lived. Instead of the traditional élites, carpetbaggers of no substance or real local standing, or Cromwell's Major-Generals, often became the agents of deeply-resented policies. In Scotland equally drastic experiences had befallen the tightly-knit hierarchies of magnates, lords, lairds and burghal patriciates who had led a confident and militant, but socially very conservative, nation into direct confrontation with the royal power in the late 1630s.

By 1641 the Scottish Revolution seemed complete. It was radical, enshrined in parliamentary form, and even acknowledged by a reluctant Charles when he visited Scotland in the autumn of 1641, looking for possible allies in the conflict which was clearly looming in England. Despite his ultimate defeat, the repeated and brilliant victories of the Royalist Lieutenant-General in Scotland, the Marquis of Montrose, fatally shook the prestige of the revolutionary Covenanting regime in the years 1644–5. Increasing radicalism in England deeply disturbed the Scottish aristocracy, so that by 1647 the great bulk of them were anxious to come to terms with the Crown. The Duke of Hamilton, the leading court Scot of his generation, who had repeatedly been placed in the most invidious of positions, as he tried to build bridges between a resentful and suspicious Scottish aristocracy and an unrealistic and shifty king, was able to forge the agreement known as the Engagement which led to an invasion of England by a Scottish army.[6]

The upshot was cataclysmatic defeat in Lancashire at the hands of Oliver Cromwell. Worse still, from the point of view of the nobles, was that the Marquis of Argyll, paramount chief of Clan Campbell and one of the few nobles to grasp the folly of the Engagement, was left to govern Scotland as best he could with such allies as he could find. Sadly, he had to turn to the Kirk and for a brief period what had started out as a rather anti-clerical revolution led by the nobility and gentry became something suspiciously like a theocracy presided over by an unhappy Argyll, forced to govern with 'extremists' because so many 'moderates' had committed military and political suicide through the unrealistic nature of the Engagement. If the execution of Charles I early in 1649 removed a major source of instability in English politics, it inevitably destroyed the fragile stability of the Argyll regime in Scotland, where even the most militant Covenanters were also convinced monarchists. The proclamation of Charles II in Edinburgh was followed by another spasm of Anglo-Scottish war which ended with Scotland prostrate by 1651 under an English army of occupation.

Both in England and in Scotland the Restoration was as much a restoration of the traditional ruling classes as a restoration of the king. Therein lay its strength. In both countries the restoration of an episcopal regime in the established church secured for the crown a devoted and vocal group of ecclesiastical supporters, who not only controlled pulpits which were much the most effective contemporary means of communicating with large numbers of people, but also dominated the universities. Both the Church of England and the newly-restored episcopal order in the Church of Scotland knew that they were surrounded by enemies, recently triumphant. The inevitable result was that the established clergy clung tenaciously to the restored dynasty and its rights as the supreme bulwark of their own position. The University of Oxford, that great centre of Royalism and seminary of the Church of England, excelled itself in extravagant support for the concepts of divine right and passive obedience during the Restoration period. Its views were expressed in most trenchant form in July 1683, during the aftermath of the so-called Rye House Plot against the life of Charles II, when Convocation of the University of Oxford solemnly anathemized 'certain pernicious books and damnable doctrines destructive to the sacred persons of princes', and called upon all teachers in the university to inculcate into their pupils the doctrine of passive obedience, 'which in a manner is the badge and character of the Church of England'.[7]

Afterwards the Vice-Chancellor and Bishop led a solemn procession of doctors and masters of the university 'into the School quadrangle, where a bonfier being prepared in the middle thereof, were severall books, out of which those damnable tenets and propositions were extracted, committed to the flames by Gigur, the Universitie bedell of beggars. The scholars of all degrees and qualities in the meane time surrounding the fier, gave severall hums whilst they were burning.' And well they might, for the list of authors was an interesting one. It included, inevitably, such paladins of the king-killing English republic as John Milton, John Goodwin and John Owen. Sixteenth-century exponents of Protestant theories of the right of resistance to ungodly rulers formed another category which included Christopher Goodman and Stephen Junius Brutus, the pseudonym used by the Frenchman who published in 1579 the *Vindiciae contra tyrannos*. A very substantial proportion of the books burned were of Scottish provenance. These included works by champions of the Covenanting revolution of the 1630s and 1640s, notably the *Lex Rex* of Samuel Rutherford, but also earlier works by such Fathers of the Scottish Reformation as John Knox and

George Buchanan. Some of these books were very cautious, but the bonfire was for any theory of resistance to royal authority, however circumscribed.

That the performance would have gladdened the heart of his late sacred majesty King James VI and I is clear. It included his pet aversions such as his tutor Buchanan's theory of justifiable tyrannicide by the people (in very unusual circumstances only, be it said), and the Jesuit Robert Bellarmine's *De potestate summi pontificis* (1610), which had upheld the right of the Pope to depose a heretical ruler.[8] Not much wonder that Charles II, in the last years of his life, was able to create a new kind of personal rule based, in the words of David Ogg, 'not on parliament, whose criticism he resented, but on the Church of England, in the tenets of which he did not believe'.[9] Yet soon after his own succession to the throne in 1685 James VII and II discovered that in practice the predominantly clerical dons of Oxford were not prepared humbly to accept whatever orders their sovereign chose to issue to them, and neither were their academic colleagues at Cambridge. When he wished to insert Roman Catholics into high positions in those institutions by royal fiat in 1687, James had to overrule stubborn opposition from the academic community. The simple truth was that no established church which adopted an Erastian or submissive attitude towards the state could afford to see state power in the hands of someone like James, who was clearly actively hostile to the church which acknowledged him its Supreme Governor. The Church of England in a sense started off the crisis which led to the revolution of 1688 and the exile of James. The fact that Archbishop Sancroft, who led the crucially important episcopal opposition to the policies of James in 1688, refused later to accept the displacement of James from the throne must not be allowed to obscure this fact.

If theories of royal absolutism struck no deep roots in the Restoration era, it was a different story when it came to the concept of indefeasible hereditary right. After all, a ruling class which consisted mainly of landed proprietors who had inherited the bulk of their wealth under a system of primogeniture was likely to be aggressively in favour of the right to inherit property, be it an estate or a kingdom. The most extreme development of the sort of dynasty-worship implicit in the concept of indefeasible hereditary right was to be found in Scotland. In a sense this was odd, because it was no secret that the Stewarts were originally a cadet branch of the English Fitzalan family, and their very name showed that these Anglo-Norman magnates had once exercised a specific function in the household of the medieval Scottish kings. An attempt by the patriotic poet Barbour to manufacture an illustrious Trojan descent for the Stewarts when they reached the Scottish throne in the late fourteenth century was unacceptable even in that age, and was promptly demolished by the equally patriotic Walter Bower, Abbot of Inchcolm.[10] What the Scots could and did do was to fit the Stewarts into a (largely bogus) succession of kings reaching back into the mists of antiquity. When the Scots parliament in 1685 granted James VII the excise in perpetuity, it accompanied its fiscal generosity with a solemn declaration that:

> This nation hath continued now upwards of two thousand years in the unalterable form of our monarchical government, under the uninterrupted line of one hundred and eleven kings, whose sacred authority and power hath been upon all signal occasions so owned and assisted by Almighty God that our kingdom hath been protected from conquest, our possessions defended from strangers, our civil commotions brought into wished events, our laws vigorously executed.[11]

The declaration went on to mention the 'solid, absolute authority of the Crown', but in fact the Restoration in Scotland was a compromise. Indeed the word 'restoration' is probably misleading when applied to the politics of Scotland after 1660. The governance of church and state were returned to the institutional patterns characteristic of the later reign of James VI, but the essentials of the revolt against Charles I, in so far as that revolt was anti-clerical and aristocratic, were maintained after the Restoration, for the new regime rested on a tacit but fundamental assumption that the king would govern through, and in a manner acceptable to, the nobility and gentry. No distinction was drawn between noble houses with a history of active support for the Covenanting revolution, and the others. The nobles, as a class, came into their own again. In exchange, they loyally upheld the rights and antiquity of the royal house. Partly this was pure self-interest, for they had learned to identify the hereditary right of the ruling dynasty with the stability of the social hierarchy of which they were the apex. There was, however, more to the pride of the leaders of the Scottish nation in the supposed antiquity of their monarchy than mere self-interest.

The technique of flattering the Stewarts about the number of their predecessors on the throne was easily acquired. Shakespeare seems to have artfully linked it with retrospective prophecy in *Macbeth*, where Macbeth in Act IV is duly awed by the procession of supposed royal ancestors of James VI conjured up by the witches, and depressed by the prospect of an indefinite future extension of a line of kings 'That twofold balls and treble sceptres carry'. All this was incorporated into a play probably written for performance at the royal court in 1604. It has the marks of a piece tailored to the taste of the new king, from its emphasis on witchcraft, in which James was known to be interested, to its brevity which might make it possible for a notorious fidget like him to sit out the performance.[12] It may be doubted if Shakespeare's personal identity was in any vital way bound up with Act IV of *Macbeth*, where he was surely laying on flattery with a trowel. Yet the identity of the most intelligent of late seventeenth-century Scots could be bound up in the defence of the supposed antiquity of Scottish kingship. It was a matter of patriotic pride. Even the relatively radical George Buchanan in the sixteenth century had accepted in his ambitious *History of Scotland* the existence of sixty-eight monarchs before Kenneth Macalpine ascended the throne in 843 A.D. When the learned English Bishop Lloyd of St Asaph had the temerity to try to lop off forty-four of these mythical creatures (which, incidentally, still left a fair clutch of phantom monarchs on the accepted Scottish regnal list), his criticism evoked a furious Scottish response. No less a person than Sir George Mackenzie of Rosehaugh, Lord Advocate of Scotland and friend of the poet John Dryden, led the counter-attack. Early in 1685 Mackenzie published his *A Defence of the Antiquity of the Royal Line of Scotland*, with a dedication to the new king, James VII. With approval and assistance from contemporary Scots antiquaries, Mackenzie bent his lucid intelligence to defending the indefensible nonsense of Scotland's mythical sovereigns, not to mention the descent of the royal house of Stewart from Fleance, son of the Banquo who had featured so conspicuously in *Macbeth*. Mackenzie was no fool. He was a central figure in the Scottish political and social establishment, and he saw Bishop Lloyd of St Asaph as a man wantonly undermining one of the foundations of the Scottish social hierarchy, and of Scottish identity.[13]

There is every reason to regard Mackenzie's views as representative of at least the basic instincts of those who mattered in Scotland between 1660 and 1688. His father, Simon Mackenzie of Lochslin, was a brother of the Earl of Seaforth, the chief of Clan Mackenzie and a great power in the north-western Highlands. His mother was Elizabeth, daughter of the Reverend Peter Bruce, Principal of St Leonard's College in the University of St Andrews. When another learned Englishman, Dr Stillingfleet, had the temerity to defend the critical views of the Bishop of St Asaph on the antiquity of the royal line of Scotland, Mackenzie promptly launched a reply to Stillingfleet into print. This pamphlet was in fact produced in London in 1686 (a Latin translation appeared in Utrecht in 1689), but its distribution in Edinburgh appears to have been jointly financed by the author and Dr Alexander Monro, Principal of the University of Edinburgh and Minister of the Second Charge of St Giles, the High Kirk of Edinburgh.[14] Although the devotion of both Mackenzie and Monro to the legitimate Stewart succession was undoubtedly given edge by their deep-seated Scottish patriotism, it would be quite wrong to think that either man was not at home in a more general British context. After the 1688 revolution both retired to England; Monro to London, and Sir George Mackenzie to the congenial atmosphere of that loyal and learned university

of Oxford which had consigned such a substantial proportion of contemporary political thought to the flames in 1683.

What made the widespread respect for the theory of indefeasible hereditary right so potentially useful to the exiled dynasty after 1690 was the
fact that virtually everyone in later seventeenth-century England and
Scotland believed implicitly in the doctrine of Providences. This was the
belief that the judgement of God was expressed, in this mortal world, by
the events of history. Even for so intellectually radical an Elizabethan as
Sir Walter Raleigh, history was the theatre of God's judgements. His
History of the World showed evil actions inevitably producing, in the long
run, evil consequences for the sinner, albeit in a way dependent on a logical
analysis of cause and effect. If anything subsequent writing tended to
minimize the incipient rationalism of Raleigh. Thus Oliver Cromwell's
schoolmaster, Dr Thomas Beard, in his *Theatre of God's Judgements*
(1597) saw God intervening directly in human affairs to smite erring
princes.[15] We have seen that the diarist John Evelyn regarded the Restoration of 1660 as a manifest act of Providence.

During the first fine rapture of release from the rule of James VII and
II, it was natural to regard the 'Glorious Revolution' as itself an example
of God's judgement. Mr James Nimmo, a Scot who had joined a rebellion
against the government of Charles II and who had had to flee to the
Netherlands in consequence refers in his diary to the events of 1688 in the
following terms:

> But it pleased the Lord to open that wonderfull door of deliverance
> himself, by the glorious providence of the Prince of Orange landing in
> England about 4th November that year, which freely loosed all our
> bonds . . . let that day never be forgotten by all fearers of God and good
> protestants, for that was a day of the rejoicing of their hearts.[16]

There was, however, no reason why the doctrine of Providences should not
prove two-edged, especially when coupled with the doctrine of indefeasible
hereditary right. It was a very natural and persuasive Jacobite argument
after 1690 that the misfortunes which were afflicting Scotland and England were the direct consequences of the heinous sin committed by both
nations in setting aside the hereditary succession to the crown. The more
discontented the bulk of the political nation in either country was, the more
widely this point of view was likely to be held.

Widespread discontent by itself, however, is not usually enough to topple
a government. The exiled Stewarts needed to overthrow a regime which,
though weak and unpopular at times, never looked like repeating the
history of the later Cromwellian Protectorate to the point of crumbling
from within. This meant that force was indispensable to the Jacobite cause.

It could come in two forms: intervention by a foreign power on behalf of the exiled dynasty, or internal rebellion on behalf of the cause. Ideally, the Jacobites wanted the simultaneous occurrence of a formidable rebellion or rebellions and massive foreign intervention. In practice they were usually dependent on the willingness of a small number of noblemen or gentlemen in England or Scotland to raise the standard of rebellion, and to some extent the culture of the Restoration left a heritage of ideas which helped to nerve men to take the difficult decision to plunge into Jacobite rebellion.

The themes of sacrifice and loyalty were carefully woven into the fabric of the Restoration regime. The supreme example was naturally Charles, King and Martyr, whose sacrifice for his people and loyalty to the Church of England was celebrated in the very year of his execution by perhaps the most successful piece of royalist propaganda of the seventeenth century – the book called *Eikon Basilike*. It went through fifty editions in its first year in print, remaining in steady demand for decades thereafter, whereas John Milton's attempted counterblast, the *Eikonoklastes*, fell flat with two English editions and one in French.[17] There were, however, other possible royalist martyr cults, and in Scotland the state went to great lengths to establish one of these after 1660. In death James Graham, Marquis of Montrose, served the interests of the royal house of Stewart just as he had in life.

Few historical characters can have enjoyed so consistently favourable a treatment at the hands of their twentieth-century biographers as this Scots nobleman born in 1612 who was still a young man in May 1650 when he was executed by hanging in Edinburgh. His last campaign had culminated in crushing defeat at Carbisdale less than a month earlier. Charles II promptly and cynically came to terms with his executioners, the Covenanting government of the Estates of Scotland. Cut down from a thirty-foot gallows after three hours, the body of Montrose was dismembered. The head was placed on a spike on the west face of Edinburgh tollbooth. The limbs were distributed for grisly display amongst the principal burghs of Scotland: Stirling, Glasgow, Perth and Aberdeen. The trunk found ignominious burial beside the common gallows on the Boroughmuir. It was a violent end to an extremely violent life.[18] The two great objects of Montrose's jealous rivalry, James first Duke of Hamilton, and Archibald eighth Earl and first Marquis of Argyll, also died on the scaffold; Hamilton before him in 1649, and Argyll after the Restoration. It is ironic that the brilliantly-written biography of Montrose published by John Buchan in 1928 should have established a tradition of interpretation which turned this baroque personality into a patron saint of the liberal-conservative 'moderates' of twentieth-century British politics.[19]

Like modern historians, the Restoration regime used Montrose as a vehicle for values which it wished to propagate. Early in January 1661 the Scots Parliament resolved:

> *an honourable reparation* for that horrid and monstrous barbarity *fixed on royal authority*, in the person of the great Marquis of Montrose, his Majesty's Captain General, and Lord High Commissioner; namely, that his body, (together with that of the Baron of Dalgetty, murdered on the same account, and buried in the same place) head, and other his divided and scattered members, may be gathered together and interred with all honour imaginable.

The next Monday a solemn procession set out for the public gibbet to recover the body. It was headed by 'The Lord Marquis of Montrose, with his friends of the name of Graham, the whole nobility and gentry, with Provost, Bailies and Council . . .'. The Provost of Edinburgh, Sir Robert Murray, must have reflected grimly on the fate of his immediate predecessor Sir James Stewart, who at the Restoration had been made a state prisoner along with his cousin Sir John Chiesly, and narrowly escaped execution. However, it is clear if one examines the list of nobles participating in the ceremony that no distinction was drawn between houses which had helped and houses which had hindered Montrose. The canopy over the coffin into which the exhumed trunk of the martyr was placed was held by, among others, George, Lord Strathnaver, eldest son of John, thirteenth Earl of Sutherland, and James, second Lord Rollo. Sutherland had held the north of Scotland against Montrose at the time of Carbisdale, while Rollo was another former ally of Argyll, having literally been in the same boat as Argyll on the day of the battle of Inverlochy, when Montrose defeated and massacred Clan Campbell.

It was the same story at Aberdeen where the dismembered arm of 'the Great Montrose' had already been taken down from its place of public exposure and decently interred in the burial place of the Marquis of Huntly. The burghers of Aberdeen had more cause than most to detest the memory of Montrose. As a Covenanter he had bullied, fined and occupied their town and finally stormed their gates in 1639. As a Royalist in 1644 he again stormed Aberdeen, this time to add the horrors of sack and massacre to those of battle. Nevertheless, in 1661 civic and university dignitaries stood reverently by while Henry Graham, son of Graham of Morphie, solemnly raised the arm and deposited it in a box covered in crimson velvet – the colour of flame, conviction, and martyrdom.[20]

After lying in state in the Abbey of Holyrood, the re-assembled remains of Montrose were given a spectacular public funeral in May 1661, 'at his Majesty's own expense'. For all that Charles II had sent Montrose to his death, it would be naïve to think that remorse rather than policy stimulated the royal generosity. The state funeral was directed by Lyon King of Arms Sir Alexander Durham of Largo. The Lord Lyon was not only a minister of the Crown but also a judge of the realm. His position was a political appointment, and Sir Alexander Durham had succeeded Sir James Campbell of Lawers, purged at the Restoration because of the twin handicaps of being a Campbell and of having been appointed Lyon by Oliver Cromwell. Durham had a Covenanting background but like his brother-in-law General John Middleton he had rallied to the cause of the Crown at the time of the Engagement. By 1661 Middleton was an earl and King's Commissioner to the Scots Parliament, before which Durham was duly crowned with a gold circlet symbolic of his rank as King of Arms.[21] His accounts for the funeral ceremony survive, showing that he disbursed the substantial sum of £802 sterling.[22]

Throughout these extraordinary proceedings there was a heavy emphasis on the solidarity of the Graham 'name'. This was clearly identified with the concepts of loyalty to the Crown and of gentility. Originally the 'name' in the Lowlands of Scotland was not very different from the concept denoted by the word 'clan' in the Highlands. Both concepts were extremely vague in practice, covering a myriad of widely differing social structures, but in the sixteenth century a big Lowland 'name', like the Hamiltons, could mobilize several thousand fighting men at surprisingly short notice, usually to confront the government. By 1661 there was no question of such behaviour, at least in the Lowlands. At the funeral ceremonies of Montrose his heir presided over a band of noble kinsmen all serving a cult of loyalty. In Edinburgh the ceremony of lifting the head of the martyr from the tollbooth spike was led by Lord Napier, the son of a nephew of Montrose, attended by Graham lairds such as Graham of Morphie, Graham of Inchbrakie, Graham of Orchill, and Graham of Gorthie. The last named lifted the head from the pinnacle of the tollbooth and kissed it before it was placed in the coffin which was crowned with the coronet of a marquis. Gorthie died the same night, his son taking as crest a crowned skull between two hands with the motto '*Sepulto viresco*'. It was an ironic reference to growing green by the place of burial, for the colour green was long deemed fatal to the Grahams.[23]

Obviously the restored Stewart regime was exploiting an already established Royalist cult of Montrose. As early as 1650 his kinswoman Lady Napier of Merchiston had rescued his heart from his dishonoured body, embalmed it, and sent it to his son and heir in Flanders. Equally, the enhanced aristocratic self-consciousness and conviction that crown and nobility stood or fell together in Scotland dated from the Engagement, but was assiduously cultivated by the Restoration regime, which really rested on that conviction. The cult of gentility was given strong state backing after 1660. By 1663 Sir Charles Erskine of Cambo had been appointed Lord

Lyon and was quarrelling heartily with his predecessor's clerk who was refusing to hand over the registers and records of the Lord Lyon unless he was himself confirmed in office.[24] However, in 1672 the Scots Parliament passed legislation establishing a Public Register of All Arms and Bearings in Scotland with which all armigerous families were to register not only their arms but also a certificate of descent from 'persons of honour, noblemen, or gentlemen of quality'. The Lord Lyon and the heralds assiduously exercised their powers of visitation and reform of arms throughout Scotland until in the year of Sir Charles Erskine of Cambo's death, 1677, the first volume of the great Register was bound up in the sight of Lyon-Depute Robert Innes of Blairton. This gentleman had to supervise proceedings since Sir Alexander Erskine second Baronet of Cambo, who had legal right by royal patent to succeed his late father as Lyon, was fourteen years old and was only crowned in 1681 at the regal age of eighteen.[25] Early seventeenth-century Scotland was dominated by its nobility and gentry but their strength lay in the closeness of the links between the many levels of a complex hierarchical society. Social revolution was inconceivable to the nobility of Covenanting Scotland. The nobility of Restoration Scotland were haunted by fear of just such a revolution. Their heightened class-consciousness was itself an index of that fear.

It is no exaggeration to say that all the major aspects of the Restoration in Scotland bear the imprint of aristocratic reaction. This was certainly true of the settlement of the Kirk. When in April 1662 the recently-created Archbishop Sharp of St Andrews made a formal entry into that ancient city he came accompanied by 600 horsemen including most of the nobility and gentry of Fife. He rode between the Earl of Rothes and the Earl of Kellie while the Earl of Leven and the Earl of Newark rode behind with a host of Fife lairds. In the parish kirk of the Holy Trinity, which was Sharp's cathedral, they listened while he preached an edifying discourse on the need and utility of episcopacy.[26] It was the supreme guarantee of order and deference in matters ecclesiastic. Nor did Restoration bishops threaten to assume too many airs in the presence of the nobility. When a group of bishops were created in Scotland in 1662 they were specifically warned not to presume to encroach upon the privileges and status of the nobles. Restoration prelates in Scotland were indeed partakers of Glory, but in a very humble way. All the prejudices of the Fife lairds were inevitably confirmed and strengthened when in 1679 a group of political and religious dissidents brutally murdered Sharp on Magus Muir outside St Andrews. This crime seemed to confirm that religious dissent and social disruption marched hand in hand. In Kilrenny the Anstruther family, with whom Sharp had spent the night before he moved on to his death, obtained a cast of the relief of the murder scene from Sharp's great baroque tomb in

Holy Trinity and displayed it in their home, a perpetual reminder of the perils of radicalism.[27]

It was in this fertile soil of the ideas and prejudices of the Restoration that the ideological roots of latter-day Jacobitism lay. The first man to raise the standard of the exiled dynasty in Britain was John Graham of Claverhouse, Viscount Dundee. In April 1689 on Dundee Law he thus defied in arms the authority of the Convention of the Estates of Scotland sitting in Edinburgh. Now the compulsion of circumstances alone does not explain Dundee's decision. He had been a pillar of the regime of James VII and II, with a long record of high-handed police duties in the south-west of Scotland, but men with similar records and bloodier hands, like the Fife laird Bruce of Earlshall, were allowed to retire peacefully into private life after 1689. When it had been proposed that five Scotsmen, the Duke of Queensberry, Viscount Tarbat, Sir George Mackenzie, Viscount Dundee and Lord Balcarres, 'be for ever incapacitated from all public employment', William of Orange had specifically rejected the idea 'being resolved to put nobody in Despair, till once he know how they intended to behave for his Interest'.[28]

Dundee was very self-consciously a Graham. He had at one stage in his career proposed to marry Helen Graham, the heiress to William Graham eighth Earl of Menteith. This nobleman was burdened with debt, and the object of the marriage seems to have been to place Claverhouse in a position to obtain a royal grant of the title after Menteith's demise. The Marquis of Montrose, the officially recognized head of the Graham 'name', may well have sensed in this attempt to secure the devolution of an ancient title a challenge to his own primacy, for he intervened in the marriage negotiations in such a way as to frustrate Claverhouse's suit.[29] In the long run the favours of the Duke of York and Albany, the heir to the throne, proved more valuable than those of Helen Graham. Claverhouse became a lieutenant-general and built up a great territorial holding north of Dundee. Cadet branches of the Grahams like Graham of Fintry and Graham of Duntrune were closely associated with his complex of interests. When, as Viscount Dundee, Claverhouse rode out of Edinburgh to raise the Jacobite standard, he conversed briefly on the Castle Rock of Edinburgh with the Duke of Gordon who was holding that great fortress in the name of King James. Asked by the duke whither he was going Dundee replied 'Wherever the spirit of Montrose shall lead me.' Here was the spiritual heir, perhaps not of the Great Marquis as he was in life, but certainly of the Royalist saint whose corporeal remains had been enshrined with such splendour in 1661.

Specific themes recur over and over again in the records which tell us how participants in Jacobite rebellions sought to justify their behaviour at the time of the rising. Indefeasible hereditary right is here the outstanding example. Thus Robert Patten, curate of Allendale, who became chaplain to Thomas Foster, the leader of the English Jacobite rising in 1715, and who turned King's evidence to save his skin after being captured, has left us an interesting account of one of his own sermons during the rebellion:

> Next Day being Sunday the 23rd of October, my Lord Kenmure, having the chief Command in Scotland, ordered me to preach at the Great Kirk of Kelso, and not at the Episcopal Meeting-House, and gave further Orders that all the Men should attend Divine Service. Mr. Buxton read Prayers, and I preached on these Words, Deut. xxi. 17, the latter part of the Verse, The Right of the First-born is his . . .[30]

Fuller versions of the Jacobite creed were in circulation further north during the same rebellion. From a contemporary note we know that Angus Jacobites sent a statement of principles to Aberdeen, but the Aberdonians preferred their own version which was duly preached from a local pulpit. It begins:

> The great corruption of all ranks and degrees both in Church and in State within this kingdom, during a long course of prosperity, peace, and plenty, under the auspicious reign of Charles the Second of happy memory, and that of his Royal brother James the Seventh, did provoke God in his just judgement to punish us with an unhappy, (dismal) Revolution, which has proved a fruitful mother of many miseries, and calamities under which this nation has groaned this twenty-seven years last past.

The statement goes on to claim that as a result of the violation of the hereditary succession 'the fundamental laws and constitution' of the realm were subverted and the miseries of God's judgement guaranteed as long as the exiled Stewarts survived and were denied their just rights.[31]

The author of this creed appears to have been James Garden, Professor of Divinity in King's College, the University of Old Aberdeen (Marischal College, the University of New Aberdeen, was a quite distinct institution). In 1690 the Scots Parliament passed an act which decreed that no Principal, Professor or Regent should be allowed to bear office in any college or university unless he subscribed the Westminster Confession of Faith, took the oath of allegiance to William and Mary, and acknowledged the Presbyterian government of the established church. Garden was the only teacher in a college which must have been full of Jacobite sympathizers who could not bring himself to take these oaths. Yet his beliefs were not simply the theories of an excessively scrupulous and unworldly academic. They were basic Jacobite convictions. On the scaffold, facing the horrible and obscene death which English law dealt out to treason, Mr James Bradshaw, an Anglican merchant from Manchester, said at the very end of the Jacobite adventure in November 1746:

> I am convinced that these nations are inevitably ruined unless the royal family be restored, which I hope will soon happen. For I love my country, and with my parting breath I pray God to bless it.[32]

In this he echoed those who had suffered before him such as David Morgan, a Welsh gentleman from Monmouthshire who led the devotions of the first batch of Jacobite prisoners executed on Kennington Common in July 1746. Morgan ascribed to the accession of the House of Hanover 'all our present ills'.[33] To the Englishman and the Welshman may be added a Scottish example in the shape of the dauntless Arthur, Lord Balmerino, a man in his late fifties who, after being 'out' in the Jacobite ranks during the '15, was beheaded, as befitted a peer, in August 1746 for his part in the '45. His dying speech began with an assertion that he stood firm 'in true loyal Anti-Revolution principles'[34] in which he had been brought up. Balmerino, a Scots Episcopalian, died after communicating in the Church of England.

Not everyone who took up arms on behalf of the exiled dynasty shared this quasi-mystical political religion. Nevertheless, its influence was real, if not decisive. A political faith which could sustain men in the face of the gallows, the burning faggots and the disembowelling knife may have been misguided, but it cannot be regarded as of no consequence. The dying speeches of martyrs to the Jacobite cause not only testified to their own convictions, but also gave those convictions the added dignity of association with the heights of human courage and selflessness. Written down as they were spoken at the foot of the gallows, their words were promptly printed and circulated in broadsheet form. Even households whose commitment to Jacobitism was less than firm could be avid collectors of such statements. Thus the archives at Blair Castle, the seat of the Dukes of Atholl, a dynasty which balanced precariously but successfully between the Jacobite and the Hanoverian camps, contain a fine contemporary collection of the last speeches before execution in 1746 of such Jacobite worthies as Lord Balmerino and James Bradshaw. Also represented at Blair are the speeches of Major Donald Macdonald of Tiendrish who was executed at Carlisle and who had been the first Jacobite commander to draw blood in the '45 when he successfully ambushed two companies of Guise's regiment near Fort William; Thomas Theodore Deacon, eldest son of Dr Thomas Deacon, the non-jurant Anglican Bishop in Manchester, and the second son of that staunchly anti-Revolution prelate to give his life for the Stewarts (his brother Robert had died in prison); and James Dawson, of

St John's College, Cambridge, who had run away to join the Jacobite Manchester Regiment, and who was executed on Kennington Common. The chaplain of that regiment, the English clergyman Thomas Coppoch, briefly Jacobite Bishop of Carlisle, is also represented in the collection by his dying speech at his execution at Carlisle.[35]

Understandably, the Hanoverian government became anxious to suppress the circulation of such defiantly treasonable matter. The last Jacobite to be executed for his beliefs was Dr Archibald Cameron, the brother of Cameron of Lochiel of the '45. Considerable efforts were made to deprive Archibald Cameron of writing materials and the chance to deliver any set speech at the gallows. This was a very late execution, for he had been arrested in March 1753 in his own country in the Highlands, was sent to London, arraigned under his old attainder for treason during the '45, and sentenced to be hanged and quartered. The Hanoverian regime graciously dispensed with disembowelling in his case, though it did rip the heart out of his body after it had been cut down from the gallows. Ironically, despite all precautions, the prisoner managed to write in pencil on a few slips of paper a fragmentary but moving confession of faith which he left in the hands of his wife. In it this staunch Scots Episcopalian affirmed that the testimony of both religion and reason had but confirmed in his mind 'the principles of Christian loyalty' in which he had had the happiness to be educated. That phrase was shorthand for the whole complex of beliefs we have just examined. Predictably, he ended with a prayer for the restoration of the exiled dynasty, as the only way in which an erring people could regain peace and happiness.[36] It was magnificent, but by the summer of 1753 when Dr Archibald Cameron suffered death it was also very unconvincing. It was a great asset to the exiled Stewarts that they possessed an ideology which awoke deep-seated responses in the ruling classes of England and Scotland. However, that ideology was only one of several currently on offer. It had not sufficed to save the thrones of James VII and II, let alone raise an immediate rebellion capable of restoring him. Only when set against a background of otherwise favourable circumstances could the ideology wax potent. In that sense the Glorious Revolution, if the end of the main line of the Stewarts as a ruling dynasty, was indeed the beginning of the Jacobite story, for like all revolutions it was followed by disillusionment and disenchantment.

2 *The Glorious Revolution and the First Jacobite Rebellion*

The Glorious Revolution and the Revolution Settlement which followed it have always generated more heat and enthusiasm than understanding. Ireland is the extreme example of this. There in the twentieth century folk memory still cherished, depending on its religious bias, images such as the heroism of Patrick Sarsfield, last champion in arms of the Catholic gentry of Ireland, or the successful resistance of the Protestant garrison at the siege of Londonderry. Admittedly, the Irish scene in 1688–91 did possess, at one level, a stark simplicity, for Ireland, a kingdom still firm in its allegiance to its hereditary monarch James II and VII, was invaded and conquered by William of Orange and his largely mercenary army. Even so, the course of events in Ireland showed that there were profound differences in outlook between William and his Protestant Irish supporters. William went to Ireland as part of an inevitable sequence of moves in a game of power politics. He fought the Battle of the Boyne against a Franco-Irish army with a host compounded of Englishmen, Ulstermen, Dutchmen, Scots, French Huguenots, Danes, Swedes and Prussians. Such a polyglot army was perfectly satisfactory as an instrument of power, and unlikely to develop a mind of its own.[1]

In Scotland the situation was fundamentally different. Though the bulk of the political nation was slow to commit itself, the flight of James from England in December 1688 was rapidly followed by the expulsion of his known supporters from control of the executive government of the kingdom of Scotland. James had called the Scottish army into England, thereby depriving his deeply unpopular Scottish Privy Council of the main prop of its authority. Increasingly, the magnates, who were the traditional leaders of the loose association of regional societies which made up Scotland, had withdrawn from association with the regime, leaving James dependent on a strange mixture of rogues and converts to Roman Catholicism. In the first category lay such notably unprincipled politicians as the Earl of Breadalbane, Mackenzie of Tarbat, and Sir John Dalrymple. Prominent in the second category was James Drummond, fourth Earl of Perth and Lord Chancellor of Scotland 1684–8. This scion of a noble but impoverished house undoubtedly entered politics with a view to the pickings, being inspired by the profits which friends had derived from serving the crown. Yet there is no reason to doubt his underlying deep conservatism, reinforced in his case, as with his father and grandfather, by firsthand experience of the aristocratic culture of Bourbon France. It is also true that his conversion to Roman Catholicism assisted his career. The seventeenth and indeed the early eighteenth centuries were eras of aggressive proselytism in Europe when a man who rejected his sovereign's religious creed risked forfeiting vital royal patronage. Nevertheless, it is quite clear from his correspondence with the good Bishop Bossuet of Meaux, that ornament of the court of Louis XIV of France, that Perth's conversion was perfectly sincere.[2] Bossuet rather specialized in this kind of courtly convert, having for example assisted the transition to Roman Catholicism of the Dane Nicholas Steno (1631–87), court physician to Grand Duke Ferdinand II of Tuscany and later Bishop of Heliopolis and Vicar Apostolic to the north of Europe.[3]

Alas, not all convenient conversions turned out so well, as the career of Perth's cynical and opportunistic brother John Drummond, Viscount Melfort, Secretary of State 1684–8, demonstrated. In him the categories of rascal and convert came together. Nor did all converted court physicians progress to an apostolic vicarate. The amiable and scholarly Sir Robert Sibbald, founder of the Royal College of Physicians of Edinburgh, had the misfortune before 1688 to be both Perth's family doctor and a major object of the Chancellor's relentless zeal for fresh conversions. Converting for the sake of minimal peace and quiet, surely the least a man can ask for, Sibbald quite reasonably de-converted himself after the Revolution.[4] The exercise underlined how slender was the basis on which the clique which governed Scotland in 1688 stood. The Duke of Gordon held the virtually impregnable fortress of Edinburgh Castle for King James as late as June 1689, but elsewhere the authority of those appointed by James was rapidly swept away in Scotland. There were anti-Catholic riots in Edinburgh, and a systematic expulsion of parish ministers identified with the collapsing regime in the south-west of Scotland. Yet the remarkable aspect of affairs was the relatively peaceful way in which the authority of King James's Scottish Privy Council (the day-to-day government of the realm) was simply appropriated by what has been described as 'a camarilla' of magnates and politicians headed by the Earl of Crawford, the Earl of Glencairn, and Sir James Montgomerie of Skelmorlie. When a Convention Parliament met in Edinburgh in March 1689 to try to settle the fate of Scotland, it was not in any way committed to oppose James, but James had lost control of the machinery of government in the ancient kingdom of the Stewarts.[5]

Whatever chance he may have had of regaining Scotland was thrown away by the almost unbelievable arrogance and ineptitude of James himself. On 16 March letters from the rival claimants to the throne were read to the Convention. That of William was conciliatory and ambiguous in all points of substance save a heavy emphasis on the security of the Protestant religion. That of James, by now at the head of an army in Ireland, was a crude essay in the politics of enraged absolutism, rendered all the more counter-productive by threats against those who refused to render instant obedience. In the words of a contemporary periodical 'this Letter, instead of encouraging King James's Friends, put them out of Countenance'.[6] Thereafter the committed Jacobites were an isolated minority in the Convention, and their most active leader, John Graham of Claverhouse, Viscount Dundee, was increasingly concerned simply to secure a propaganda advantage in his exchanges with the Convention prior to inevitable appeal to the judgement of battle. Nothing else can explain, for example, his request to the Convention that he be granted a safe-conduct to Ireland, where it was clear that he would promptly join the army of King James.[7] The Scottish Convention Parliament was nothing if not obsessed by fear of invasion by a Roman Catholic army from Ireland, and it followed minutely the desperate struggles of the embattled Protestants of Ulster to hold off the blows aimed at them by James and his lord-lieutenant Richard Talbot, earl of Tyrconnel.[8] The Scots had a long history of contact with Ulster. In the midst of their own revolution in the 1640s they had maintained a surprisingly large Scottish army in north-east Ulster between 1642 and 1649, in order to succour the Protestant interest there.[9] Dundee's request for a Pass for Ireland must be placed on a par with his subsequent insistence that after quitting Edinburgh for his castle of Dudhope his sole objective was to live in peace at home.

When, then, he raised the standard of King James on Dundee Law in April 1689, there was no reason to regard him as other than a rebel against the *de facto* government of Scotland. He himself argued that the Convention, or Estates as it was commonly called, had made it impossible for him to live at peace under their rule, but it is fairly clear that he never intended to accept any rule other than that of King James. 'The Heralds who denounced the Viscount of Dundee at the Market Cross of Forfar, Head-Burgh of the Sheriffdom, wherein the Viscount dwells,' as a rebel against the Estates of Scotland were making a fair point.[10] It was the first Jacobite rebellion. Unlike the campaigns of Montrose, it had no roots in complex magnate rivalries and subtle political theory. Rather was it a straightforward rising led by a simple, if ambitious, soldier, with a view to asserting the hereditary rights of the displaced dynasty.

This heroic simplicity continued to characterize Dundee's actions in the brief span of life left to him. The original nucleus of his force was a small band of professional cavalry from the Scots army, of whose horse Dundee had been the commander. Retreating into the Highlands to gather recruits,

Dundee manoeuvred through the hills on the edge of the Lowlands with a rapidity worthy of Montrose. After him plodded the Williamite army commanded by that brave pious and slightly uninspired officer, General Hugh Mackay of Scourie, a Gael from the northern parts of Scotland who had spent long years in the service of the United Netherlands. The climax of the campaign was matchless in drama and setting. The rival hosts were both anxious to control Blair Castle in Perthshire, the seat of the Atholl dynasty and a crucial strategic point controlling north-south routes within the central area of the Grampian Mountains. As Mackay's troops debouched from the Pass of Killiecrankie, which lies a few miles south of Blair, and found themselves still severely cramped by the narrowness of the path which follows the eastern bank of the River Garry, they saw Dundee's men massed on the commanding slopes above them. Both generals tried to outflank their opponent by extending their line. In a career hitherto more marked by the qualities of a conscientious political policeman than by those of a master of tactics, Dundee suddenly had the first and last flash of pure inspiration. His was the attacking force. It also had the advantage of the slope. It did not need a centre. Mackay's thin line was shattered and rolled up by the impact of a Highland charge. Given his position, defeat was bound to be total, though he did manage to fight his way off the field with a remnant of his regiments.[11]

Dundee was favoured by the God of Battles that day and never more so than in his own death. At sunset, leading his handful of cavalry in a charge over a scene of unimaginable triumph, he fell to a solitary bullet, passing from history to immortality with untarnished laurels. Extraordinarily enough, the second scene in the rising he had led was almost a mirror image of the first. Led by Colonel Alexander Cannon, the triumphant Jacobite army moved south towards the Lowlands by the valley of the Tay. At the small 'frontier' trading and episcopal burgh of Dunkeld, on the verge of open country, it was met by a regiment of Cameronians, Presbyterian enthusiasts of the most uncompromising kind. Entrenched in and around the cathedral of Dunkeld these men fought with a determination worthy of their militant creed until they had shot, stabbed and hacked the Highlanders to a standstill. The garrison's young commander, Colonel Cleland, died like Dundee in the hour of victory. The military drama was all a stark antithesis of black and white, as striking in its contrasts as the white water of the rapids against the normal dark course of the Garry.

In practice this simplicity was entirely confined to the surface of events. When analysed in any depth the picture of a straight clash between Good and Evil, black and white (the ascription of shade depending on the observer's prejudice), dissolves not so much into the greys so beloved of modern intellectuals as into the deep peaty brown of the pools where Highland trout lie deep. The Revolution in any one of the three kingdoms ruled by James VII and II was a complex phenomenon, rendered all the more so by the usually neglected connections between events in that specific kingdom, and events in the other two. Ultimately events in England were the determinants of what happened in Ireland or Scotland. The Glorious Revolution was made in England. It was exported to Ireland by force of arms. In Scotland there was indeed a distinct political upheaval comparable to the English one, but it only occurred because James lost control of England.

From the start Englishmen were hopelessly and bitterly divided over the significance of the Glorious Revolution. Though virtually the entire political nation could agree in 1688 that the principal policies of James II constituted a threat to property rights and the Protestant religion, and as such must be reversed, it proved much more difficult to reconcile the deepest prejudices of the ruling classes with a course of events which included the actual removal of a king. Left-wing political thought had fallen into absolute disrepute as a result of the social and political traumas of the English mid seventeenth-century revolution.[12] Deference was the keynote of Restoration society and the Church of England preached, with sustained and fanatical enthusiasm, the doctrine that deference was only safe when universally respected. A master who wanted his servants to defer to him; a husband who expected his wife and children to defer to him; a gentleman who demanded of his tenants the deference he himself showed towards the nobility – all must ultimately, through the great chain of human ranks, defer to the king, the supreme guarantor of deference and social order. Only a small minority of hard-line Whigs were willing to argue that James II had been deposed for breaching a fundamental social contract with his subjects. Their doctrine of the right of resistance horrified the bulk of the articulate ruling class, and ensured that Whigs fared very badly in peace-time elections in England between 1688 and 1713. They were a minority, and they exercised influence mainly during wars, when their high political motivation and belligerent instincts made them useful to government. The Tories, who in the last analysis made the Revolution, were able to insist that it be interpreted minimally. An attempt to argue that the Revolution was a divinely-ordained miracle, not to be questioned by mere mortals never gained widespread support.[13] Rather was it generally maintained that the Revolution had involved neither resistance nor deposition and even then many were convinced that the only decent attitude was to accept the Revolution but worry continually whether it was right to have done so.

The element of intellectual infantilism inherent in this sort of position was, of course, massive. It involved for a start accepting William of Orange's less than convincing argument that the 14,000 troops who accompanied him on his trip to England in 1688 were simply a personal bodyguard. For all that, it was this minimalist interpretation which dictated the terms of the English Revolution Settlement. From resolutions of the House of Commons to the Declaration of Rights, all official pronouncements in England after the flight of James insisted that the monarch had abdicated. Those with a taste for the niceties of politics might add that his precise gesture of abdication had been the throwing of the Great Seal of the Realm into the Thames. The suggestion was quite fatuous. James threw away the Great Seal in the hope of paralysing what he regarded as a usurping regime. On the other hand, the concept of abdication not only helped the nobility and gentry of England over an appalling psychological hurdle, but also chimed in with the preferences of William of Orange. That astute politician knew full well the depths of conservative loyalty on which a Stewart king of England could call. William had watched in 1685 when two desperate men used Holland as the springboard for an attempt to overthrow James. The Duke of Monmouth, illegitimate son of Charles II, invaded south-west England, using slogans curiously reminiscent of the radical strain in the 'Puritan' revolution of the 1640s and 1650s, and went down to total defeat at Sedgemoor because the aristocracy and gentry refused to support him. In Scotland Archibald, ninth Earl of Argyll, found some support amongst his Campbell clansmen in Argyll but so little in the Lowlands that he bitterly remarked in prison after his defeat that 'in this country I see no great party that desire to be relieved'.[14] William of Orange naturally bent over backwards in 1688 to avoid any overt hostility towards the person of James, or any statement of political philosophy other than the most conservative and ambiguous which was compatible with his military operations.

In a profound sense William, an autocrat by nature, and a Stewart by birth and marriage, did not come to save England, Scotland and Ireland from Stewart monarchy. He came to save as much as he could of Stewart monarchy and its vital prerogative from the dangers created by the clumsy and inept reign of James. Of course there was no way of managing the Revolution which did not involve a relative decline in the personal power of the monarch himself, and William fought much harder to minimize this in the field of foreign affairs, his central interest, than elsewhere. Yet the Revolution in England left the principle of absolutism which lay at the heart of the political creed of James VII and II untouched. At least one distinguished French historian, Roland Mousnier, has argued that in seventeenth-century Europe absolutism was 'indispensable to any state wishing to retain its independence, to grow, indeed to exist'. There were obviously exceptions to this generalization. The United Netherlands, for example, were a loose confederation of sovereign provinces in which a centralized absolute authority was inconceivable. However, Mousnier was right in arguing that England was no exception to the triumph of

absolutism among the great powers of Europe.[15] After 1688 absolute, un-
bridled authority checked by no institutional safeguards for provincial, or
corporate, let alone individual liberties was exercised by that very English
beast the King in Parliament. Many a moderate Tory found no difficulty
in transferring his belief in the duty of passive obedience from the person
of the monarch to the corporate sovereign composed of King, Lords and
Commons. The simple fact is that the Whigs were unable to establish the
English revolution of 1688 as a revolutionary act, and from the start were
incapable of framing an acceptable definition of their own favourite shib-
boleth – 'Revolution Principles'.[16]

On the other hand, many people, even in England, thought that there
was more substance to the Glorious Revolution than was in fact the case.
A great deal of confusion and ambiguity arose precisely because it was
possible to hold such very different views of the significance of the Revolution Settlement. The same problem existed in Ireland and Scotland,
infinitely exacerbated by the fact that the executive governments of both
these kingdoms were, in the last analysis, controlled from England. When
an early eighteenth-century English Lord-Lieutenant of Ireland rose at a
banquet in Dublin Castle to propose, to the strains of 'Lillibullero' the
toasts of 'the Glorious Memory of King William' and 'the first of July,
1690', he was not doing anything even remotely radical. When Protestant
artisans in Londonderry celebrated 'the Glorious Memory' they also reminded themselves that in the face of the armies of King James their
leaders had tried to betray them. The implication, incidentally an exceed-
ingly wise one, was that it would probably happen again and that crude
populist initiative rather than deference was the key to survival when the
chips were down.

The full potential for mutual incomprehension inherent in these diver-
gent mentalities was only to appear in the nineteenth and twentieth
centuries but the problem of different interpretations of the Revolution
arose almost at once in an Anglo-Scottish context, because the Scottish
Revolution settlement was totally different in nature and ideology from
the English one. It was radical with little trace of the elaborate pussy-
footing and intellectual dishonesty which found favour at Westminster.
The Convention Parliament in Edinburgh resolved with only five dissenting votes on 4 April 1689 that James VII had forfeited the crown. The
suggestion that the word 'abdicate' be used was scorned, and the implication was clearly that a King of Scots held his throne contractually. On
11 April the Convention accepted the document known as the Claim of
Right, which spelled out the fact that James, a professed Papist, had not
only sought to undermine the Protestant faith, but had also attacked 'the
fundamental constitution of this Kingdom, and altered it from a legal
limited monarchy, to an arbitrary despotic power'. A great many Scots

regarded the Claim of Right as a statement of basic constitutional principles, and the Convention certainly thought of its offer of the crown of Scotland to William and Mary as conditional on acceptance of those principles. Furthermore the Revolution Settlement in Scotland did involve a massive shift in the balance of political power between the king and the Scots Parliament (which was organized in three Estates sitting together as one body). The Lords of the Articles, a committee which had engrossed most of the business of Parliament and had been completely under royal control, were abolished. An executive still nominated from London had to face an unleashed Scots Parliament working on very different basic assumptions from Westminster.

If the Anglo-Scottish dimension be ignored, all this seems to confirm the straightforward simplicity of the Revolution within Scotland. In fact, the very starkness of the political justification officially advanced for the Revolution is evidence of a complex and peculiar situation within the kingdom. Even within the ruling classes, the activist element, on either the Jacobite or the Williamite side, was a tiny minority. Most people of any consequence were, to use a relevant modern phrase 'on strike'. It was remarkable how few men turned out to fight for James VII. Here was the main line of Scotland's ancient dynasty being forcibly expelled from its thrones, yet not a single magnate of any consequence stirred a little finger to stay the process.

It was not as if the Restoration regime had been unable to mobilize armed support amongst its Scottish subjects in previous decades. On the contrary, that regime, which lacked the financial resources to maintain more than a small standing army and which faced continual if sub-critical resistance to its rule, relied all the time on support from loyal regions against disloyal ones. Thus James Lord Ogilvie (from 1666 the second Earl of Airlie) was ordered into Fife in April 1667 with a strong military force. The Second Dutch War between England and the United Netherlands was still raging. Its outbreak in 1665 had owed much to a spirit of naval and commercial aggression in court circles in London. The Duke of York, the future James VII, had been in the van of this maritime imperialism both as Lord High Admiral and as a hater of the Protestant and republican Dutch. The war was far from successful and the Scots, dragged in on the heels of the English by their joint monarch, suffered considerably from the breach with the Dutch who were, after all, by far their most important overseas trading partners. No towns were harder hit than the maritime burghs of Fife and Ogilvie's troops were quartered in the country primarily to ensure that a section of its inhabitants did not make common cause with any Dutch force which landed.[17] The interests of the office-holding nobility and those of the trading classes of Scotland were simply not compatible during the Dutch wars of the Restoration. The Third Dutch War of 1672, for example, was blatantly provoked by the English court, which failed to win the quick victory it had hoped for, and which had to face bitter criticism even in England.[18] Yet in Scotland Lord Lyon Sir Charles Erskine can be found in 1672 trying to catch up on £300 arrears in his salary by cadging the gift of one of two Dutch prizes loaded with coal which had been taken into Leith harbour.[19]

The south-west of Scotland was an area which bred endemic radical Presbyterian opposition to the Scottish government after 1660. Just why an area almost as remote and conservative as the notoriously royalist 'Conservative North-East' should have inclined so sharply towards radical religion is a nice question. One part of the answer may lie in the proximity of Ulster, with its pockets of obstreperous Presbyterians as given to taking temporary refuge on the Scottish side of the North Channel as Scottish militants were to slipping over to the Irish side. Be that as it may, James Ogilvy, second Earl of Airlie, next served in the west and south-west, first in Renfrewshire, then Ayrshire, and finally for two years in Galloway.[20] It was in this area that the most notorious example of the Stewart regime's penchant for pursuing the inhabitants of one Scottish region with the warriors of another occurred in the shape of the somewhat misnamed Highland Host of 1678.

This was not strictly a Highland force, being raised by order of Charles II by men who were not primarily chiefs of clans such as the Marquis of Atholl and the Earls of Mar, Moray, Perth, Strathmore, Airlie and Caithness. Its commander was the Earl of Linlithgow and regular militia and crown troops were part of it. The Earl of Caithness was in fact Campbell of Breadalbane, who maintained a debatable claim to the northern earldom by virtue of the sword, and it is amusing that no sooner had he led his contingent into the south-western parts than he was demanding release to return to defend his Breadalbane lands against the ravages of the men of adjacent Lochaber and Glencoe.[21] Even more striking is the fact that the Irish executive decided not to transfer to Scotland troops massed under Viscount Granard in eastern Ulster. The reason given was, in effect, that there was little to choose between the rebellious temper of south-west Scotland and that of north-east Ulster, so the royal forces in Ireland could not be spared.[22] The Ulster Scots were almost as antipathetic to the Restoration regime as some Lowland Scots. In both cases the standard technique of government was to move troops from loyal parts of the kingdom into disloyal areas.

This remained a characteristic response of the government of Scotland to any serious regional military threat well into the 1680s. In the years before the Revolution, for example, Argyll had been effectively occupied and administered by officials and militia forces drawn mainly from Perthshire. This was an aftermath of the troubles of the years 1684–5, when the

Earl of Argyll, the great local magnate and paramount chief of the Campbells, had fled to Holland from whence he returned to lead his unsuccessful
revolt against James VII. The Marquis of Atholl held a commission from
August 1684 as Lord-Lieutenant of Argyll, Tarbert and the adjacent
islands.

The behaviour of the Atholl family during the Revolution is therefore a
peculiarly revealing index of the mentality of a typical loyal magnate house
at the end of the reign of James VII. The winter of 1688–9 was a particularly bleak one with great storms and much hardship amongst the poor
because of soaring grain prices. The grain shortage was partly the result of
the freezing of rivers and streams, which prevented mills from grinding
corn. Lady John Murray, the wife of the heir to the Atholl estates, was in
Falkland in Fife, grieved by the suffering around her, and showing her
Presbyterian sympathies by remarking that she saw no reason why the
Presbyterians should not be forward in petitioning the Prince of Orange,
as they had suffered most under James.[23] The Marchioness of Atholl
showed staunch Protestant sympathies but a good deal of political disillusionment allied to fear of social upheaval. She was convinced that her
husband's influence alone had ensured that 'the rabble' on his estates did
not seize the opportunity to riot and plunder. She was pleased that the
Marquis did not wish for office but rather aspired 'to get leave to live
peaceably at home and to enjoy his religion', though she did hope that a
young nobleman like Lord John Murray would secure a post under the
new regime.[24]

There was a conspicuous lack of zeal in all this, though it is clear that the
senior members of the house were convinced that James VII must go. In
this, they seem to reflect a widespread attitude amongst the Scots nobility.
The third Duke of Hamilton is a good illustration of the point. He was the
father-in-law of Lord John Murray, and destined to act as William of
Orange's Commissioner to the Scots Convention Parliament. In the spring
and early summer of 1689 he can be found writing to his son-in-law to the
effect that Dundee's rebellion was ultimately bound to be futile because it
suffered from a chronic shortage of provisions and ammunition. Any
attempt to remedy deficiencies by living off the countryside, Hamilton
argued, would simply alienate people.[25] Not surprisingly, Hamilton was in
favour of sparing Scotland a civil war by shipping Dundee and his army
to Ireland. The Duke's own Roman Catholic upbringing* may explain his
lack of violent feelings with regard to the affairs of Ireland, but he was
both a practising Protestant and a pro-Revolution magnate, so his distinct
lack of enthusiasm for any kind of conflict in Scotland is striking.[26]

---

* He was Lord William Douglas, Earl of Selkirk, and the Hamilton dukedom was
a title bestowed on him for life in 1660 after his marriage in 1656 to Anne, Duchess
of Hamilton in her own right.

This attitude was very general, even amongst noblemen who had been very active indeed in defence of the throne of the Stewarts in Scotland in the early 1680s. The second Earl of Airlie had personal as well as public reasons for supporting the Revolution. Neither Charles II nor James II were at all prompt at paying him for the military service they were so ready to demand. His private affairs were neglected and his petitions for arrears ignored.[27] The Earl of Strathmore, who had been created a member of the Scottish Privy Council in 1682, and an Extraordinary Lord of Session in 1686, had led militia forces westwards as part of the moves against Argyll's rebellion. In theory he would like to have opposed the Revolution. In practice he persuaded himself that it would be futile to act, because events were conspiring entirely in favour of William of Orange, and somehow or other he squared his conscience with taking the oath of allegiance to the new sovereign. Mostly he just sulked in his fortress, Castle Huntly, in the Carse of Gowrie outside Dundee.[28]

Men who actually fought alongside Dundee in the rising were prepared to admit that there was virtually no enthusiasm for either side amongst large sections of the population. Here again the Atholl dynasty provides a good example. It was predominantly in favour of the Revolution, but careful to cover all possible angles. Notoriously, as Mackay and Dundee converged at Killiecrankie something suspiciously like a family pantomime was going on around Blair. That strategic castle was being held, for King James, by Patrick Steuart of Ballechin, factor to the Marquis of Atholl. He was being besieged, not very vigorously, by the Williamite heir Lord John Murray. The Marquis himself, most thoughtfully, had retired to Bath to 'pump his head'. This was very sensible, for Atholl was a regional prince whose duty to his people, rationally considered, involved staying out of trouble. However, a younger son of the Marquis, Lord James Murray, joined the Jacobite army, partly from conviction and partly to take out yet another political insurance policy on his father's estates. By the end of August 1689, when the Jacobite cause had obviously lost any chance of success, Lord James was writing apologetically to his family saying that he had meant well and had hoped that his actions would endanger only himself. He added casually, as an accepted fact, that the men of Atholl had no particular prejudices, either way, in the conflict.[29]

This seems a very likely state of affairs. James VII had alienated the governing élites of late seventeenth-century Scotland to a great degree, but because of their continuing acceptance of an outlook which made it almost impossible to initiate a rebellion, the upshot on their part was a sullen refusal to act. It would be surprising if the classes below the nobility and gentry showed a more positive attitude to the crisis than their natural leaders. The whole Restoration Settlement had rested on a deal between the throne and the nobility. James had shattered that compact beyond repair. It is now fashionable to stress how 'modern' James was, with his sincere zeal for religious toleration,[30] but his tolerance was not that of the indifferent, secular state. James intended, rapidly, to man all the commanding heights of social, political, and military power with Roman Catholics before throwing the prestige, pressure and power at his disposal behind a drive for mass conversions. His policy was based on the delusion that mass conversion would be easy. Had the entire royal programme been successfully implemented there is no doubt that society would have been in some ways even more hierarchical than before. The green ribbon which features conspicuously in so many Scottish Jacobite portraits of the exiled Stewarts is a reminder that James VII founded the Order of the Thistle in 1687, with the creation of eight original knights of that order including Atholl, Perth, and Melfort. In James's dream world an absolute King of Scots was to be surrounded by a deferential and strictly graded nobility while a hierarchical Kirk buttressed both throne and social order. The snag was that the transition to this blessed state was quite impractical. In February 1688 Perth was reporting gloomily that there had been very few conversions to add to the tiny minority of Scottish Roman Catholics. He was particularly unhappy about the Scots army 'the hundredth man in which is not a Catholic, and we have scarce any officers of that persuasion'.[31] As a result James was forced to rely on men who were not the natural leaders of the nobility and gentry, and worse still, his high-handed methods seemed to challenge the sacred right of the aristocracy to control the pattern of life in the regions of Scotland. In the countryside stunned disbelief was a common response to the royal policies.

In the towns hostility to James VII's policies was if anything sharper. The royal burghs of Scotland had a tradition of self-government stretching back almost to their origins as chartered bodies in the twelfth century. No medieval king of Scots had dreamed of attacking the autonomy of such loyal bodies where he collected a substantial proportion of his revenue. The town councils were, of course, self-perpetuating oligarchies with an internal balance of power between merchants and craftsmen, heavily weighted towards the merchants. Once again, it was James's inability to find amongst existing élites willing tools prepared to execute his unpopular policies which drove him to arbitrary government through non-traditional agents. The royal burgh of Dundee is here an intriguing example, for the estates of John Graham of Claverhouse, Viscount Dundee, lay immediately adjacent to it, and it featured in the whirlwind campaign which culminated at Killiecrankie. That campaign started when the scarlet-coated Graham raised his standard on the Law, a hill of volcanic origin which then lay outside the walls of the burgh. Almost immediately the tiny Jacobite force moved off northward to recruit in the safety of the Highlands. However, it returned a few weeks later when Claverhouse swooped over the Sidlaws, fully expecting to meet signs of sympathy from the burgh and its garrison. After driving in the garrison scouts, he rode the circuit of the town's defences, finding the walls guarded and the gates firmly closed against him. Admittedly Claverhouse was probably counting more on defection to the Jacobite cause by the small regular garrison than on popular sympathy, but the stony hostility of the townsfolk was scarcely surprising.

High above the seventeenth-century town of Dundee lay the severe pile of Dudhope Castle, seat of the Scrymgeour family who claimed the hereditary Constableship of Dundee, and with it certain rights over the burgh. Needless to say, that ancient burgh, with a record of loyalty to the throne sealed in the blood of General Monck's assault and sack of 1651, furiously resisted these pretensions. In 1668 the last of the Dudhope Scrymgeours, who had progressed via the Viscounty of Dudhope to the Earldom of Dundee, died without heir. King Charles II granted the estates to Charles Maitland, Lord Hatton, brother to the most powerful of all Scottish Restoration politicians, John Maitland, first Duke of Lauderdale. Hatton was Master of the Mint and an extreme case of that cynical corruption which was only too common in those holding public office in Restoration Scotland. As Constable of Dundee Hatton maintained claims to jurisdiction over the clergy, fairs, and governance of the burgh. By 1683, however, Hatton's malpractices with the public funds had pulled down on him exposure and a heavy fine. The ravens in favour with the king gathered for the pickings. Characteristically, they squabbled over the carcass and it was only in 1684 that Graham of Claverhouse emerged with Dudhope Castle and the Constableship, thus inheriting a standing quarrel with the burgh.

The Town Council of Dundee had naturally hoped to take advantage of Lord Hatton's fall to clear up the jurisdictional disputes by buying out the Constable's rights in and claims over Dundee. In the meantime the civic fathers kept their political noses very clean, arranging promptly for the royal proclamations issued against Argyll in 1684 to be read about the town cross by tuck of drum.[32] The negotiations with Hatton, who had succeeded his elder brother as Earl of Lauderdale in 1682, proved difficult, for the burgh wished only to buy out his property in the town, as well as certain specific rights which he claimed there, and it showed no interest in the Dudhope estate as a whole, though it did want a small piece of it – the lands of Logie – which lay close to the municipal boundary.[33] Lauderdale, as he now was, was playing a disreputable game in collusion with George, Earl of Aberdeen, Chancellor of Scotland and a rogue of some stature. The objective was the exaction of a large price from Claverhouse for Dudhope. Reluctantly Claverhouse, who had at one stage hoped to receive Dudhope for nothing as a royal gift, accepted the need to pay stiffly for it.

At this point the burgh of Dundee was in deeper trouble over the Constableship than it realized. Graham of Claverhouse was a man after his monarch's heart. Though a devout son of the Church of Scotland and a staunch upholder of its Protestant theology and episcopal form of government, he was primarily a very unimaginative soldier for whom the arrival of an order from a superior terminated all speculative thought, if indeed he ever indulged in such. Firm in maintaining the claims of the Constable, he was an even firmer prop of the regime of James VII. Thus, when James decided to replace the traditional burghal authorities in Dundee, as elsewhere, by a direct nominee of his own, it was possible for him to do it with the help of a legal fig leaf. On 22 June 1685 the Provost of Dundee read to the Town Council an extract from the record of the proceedings of the Privy Council of Scotland. It was a transcript of a letter from James VII saying that having pondered the problem of the relationship between the town and the Constable, he was of a mind to enforce the opinion of his late royal brother Charles II, and insist that the Constable be recognized as the first magistrate of the burgh.[34] In 1679 the Court of Session had in fact ruled on the problem of the relationship of the Constable to the Town Council of Dundee. The case was brought at the instance of the Lord Chancellor and the verdict must have pleased that dignitary, for it was that the Constable enjoyed full criminal jurisdiction over the burgh both in capital and in lesser crimes. In practice Lord Hatton does not seem to have enforced his full rights. He soon had other problems to worry about, and the 1679 Court of Session ruling was mainly important as the precedent which made legal resistance by the burgh impractical in 1686. In that year the Town Council consulted leading Edinburgh counsel but were warned that, although the 1679 ruling obviously implied absurd consequences, for it left the Town Council of an ancient and important royal burgh with a mere shadow of jurisdiction, it was futile to challenge it.[35] From the position of first magistrate of the burgh, it was but a step for Claverhouse in March 1688 to become Provost of Dundee. The Act of the Privy Council of Scotland nominating Major-General John Graham of Claverhouse as Provost represented only the last twist to a screw which had been progressively tightened since 1685. Since 1686 all the officials of the burgh had been nominated by royal missive.[36] It would be quite wrong to suggest that Claverhouse's reign as Provost of Dundee was at all remarkable. He did not by any means preside over every meeting of the Town Council, and day-to-day life in the burgh probably went on exactly as before.

It would be equally wrong to suggest that James VII did not deeply shock and alienate burghal opinion in Scotland by his unprecedented attack on the right of self-government. That the instruments of his aggression were often not the natural rulers of Scottish urban communities made his offence worse. Dundee was an extreme case in that James subordinated the burgh to a Constable whom the townsfolk had learned, rightly, to regard as the hereditary enemy of their liberties. Such episodes go far to explain the ease with which the Revolution was accepted in a burgh with a history of almost extravagant loyalty, such as Aberdeen. A black pall had draped the market cross of Aberdeen in 1685 when news was received of the death of Charles II. The next morning it was replaced by cheerful tapestry to celebrate the accession of James VII, while toasts, instrumental music, cannon salutes, and peals of bells were the order of the day. At night the loyal revelry continued, the ships in the harbour being illuminated with lanterns on their topmasts. Yet by early 1689 it was possible to proclaim William of Orange at that same market cross, without even a hint of opposition.[37]

Not all urban communities were as instinctively loyal as such ancient royal burghs as Dundee and Aberdeen. The Fife burgh of Inverkeithing, for example, was a small trading community with a harbour prosperous enough in the early 1680s for its pier to require a major extension in 1683. It had a tradition of radicalism in religion, being a centre for those conventicles or unauthorized meetings for worship at which dissenting Presbyterians defied the Restoration episcopacy. Such famous religious malcontents as John Blackadder of Troqueer (a parish outside Dumfries) were assured of a warm welcome at Inverkeithing when they left the south-west of Scotland to assist at conventicles in Fife. Troops were quartered on Inverkeithing by the royal government which also heavily fined the parish to the tune of £15,000 Scots (there were £12 Scots to £1 sterling). From 1686 the Provost and Town Council of Inverkeithing were nominated by royal letters communicated and enforced by the Scottish Privy Council. Needless to say, the Revolution was greeted with a great deal of enthusiasm in Inverkeithing, the Kirk Session of the parish kirk of St Peter resolving that a solemn Thanksgiving 'be given to the Lord for delivering us from popery and arbitrary power'. The Town Council, restored on the old basis, made very substantial sacrifices to forward the Revolution, providing fifty men and sixty stands of arms for the period of the civil war and accepting with good grace the obligation to find quarters for a period for a Williamite regiment.[38]

Socially Fife was an odd county, with its more-than-loyal gentry, and its less-than-loyal trading burghs. Elsewhere Scottish society tended to display a much greater degree of regional solidarity. One of the reasons why the Restoration government had such problems in dealing with the south-west of Scotland, for example, was that the nobility and gentry of those parts contained a high proportion of men who were at least passively unsympathetic towards the religious policies of the regime. The merchant class of Glasgow, the most rapidly-expanding burgh in late seventeenth-century Scotland, was very often recruited from younger sons of nearby lairds. Provost Walter Gibson was the son of a laird who apprenticed him to malt-making. From that base Walter Gibson expanded his activities until he was the richest merchant in Glasgow in the 1680s, with his own landed estate and a mansion designed by Sir William Bruce, the favourite architect of the government and nobility of Restoration Scotland. Much of Gibson's wealth was based on the systematic violation of the English Navigation Acts, which aimed at excluding, in so far as was practical, the ships of third countries like Scotland from the direct trade between England and her colonies. Gibson brazenly disguised his ships as English vessels and brought St Nevis sugar across the Atlantic to refineries on the Clyde.[39] It is easy to find prominent Glasgow merchant dynasties whose record during the Restoration period was a good deal more subversive. George Buchanan, younger son of Andrew Buchanan, laird of Gartacharan, near Drymen north of Glasgow, was a militant Covenanter, so hostile to the Restoration regime that he fought against it in the rebellion which culminated in the battle of Bothwell Bridge, and earned a price on his head. After the Revolution he re-emerges as a prosperous Glasgow maltster and in 1691, 1692 and 1694 Deacon-Convener and Visitor of that trade. His son Andrew Buchanan of Drumpellier, born in 1690, was to be a pioneer of the Glasgow Virginia trade.[40]

It is therefore clear that a somewhat ambiguous attitude towards constituted authority was not uncommon amongst the merchants and tradesmen of Glasgow, socially conservative though they all were in day-to-day living. Glasgow prided itself on being the first city in Scotland to publish, with solemn rejoicing, the declaration issued by the Prince of Orange to justify his invasion. In January 1689 the Provost and Town Council of Glasgow petitioned the Prince for a free parliament to secure their lives, liberties and property against the assaults of arbitrary power and the Court of Rome.[41] The last point was distinctly hard on the Papacy which, if it shared the same ultimate objectives for England and Scotland as James II and VII, had the gravest reservations about the wisdom of his timing and tactics. However, the main point is that there was no effective urban support for the first Jacobite rebellion anywhere in Scotland, nor was this surprising. It was not difficult for James to alienate opinion in burghs with traditions of religious radicalism, like Inverkeithing and Glasgow. What was really remarkable was the extent to which he had dissipated the colossal reserves of royalist sympathies and prejudices in the other burghs. Claverhouse did collect public revenues from Perth, but only by occupying it with a raiding party. There was no other way of compensating for the disastrous political ineptitude of his royal master.

If then we return to the battlefield of Killiecrankie, the most significant political fact about the triumphant Jacobite army was its smallness due to the absence of any major regional magnates in its ranks. The whole campaign was described in suitably heroic Latin verse by Claverhouse's standard bearer James Philip (or Philp) of Almerieclose in his poem *The Grameid*, written after the events which it records, but with all the benefits of first-hand knowledge. James Philip was a relative of Claverhouse. His mother was Margaret Graham, a daughter of Graham of Duntrune, and second cousin to the hero of *The Grameid*. On his father's side the poet came of a line of clergymen and lairds, all of a staunchly episcopal persuasion. The family estate lay near and in the burgh of Arbroath, being centred on the Almonry premises of the ruined medieval Arbroath Abbey. After his adventure in arms in 1689 James Philip reappears in history in August 1692 when he was in trouble for publicly cursing the Town Council of Arbroath (since 1689 once more elected and not just a body of royal nominees), as base and unworthy rascals. It was a very Jacobite and very conservative view, but then the poet was obviously an extremely conservative man. His literary culture, with its old-fashioned Latin emphasis, showed this.[42] Fortunately, it was not an inappropriate style in which to salute Highland chiefs whose life-styles and egos were perhaps not all that different from those of Ajax and Achilles. It certainly led him to include a roll-call of the chiefs and other prominent men of the Jacobite army in his poem, in a manner at once Homeric and historically valuable.[43]

The figures he gives for their followers are palpable exaggerations. Claverhouse appears to have had less than 2,000 men under his command on the day of the battle. From the Lowlands he drew pathetically little support and even his Highland allies were a very mixed bag. One significant segment of support was derived from groups which were at best marginal and at worst positively criminal within the context of the society of the Gaelic-speaking Highlands. Here the prize example is Coll Macdonald of Keppoch, known all too accurately as 'Coll of the cows'. Inhabiting as they did a remote fastness on the western seaboard of mainland Scotland, the Macdonalds of Keppoch were effectively immune from the attention of regular troops. In the course of a lengthy feud with the Mackintosh of Mackintosh they emerged victorious from the last big inter-clan battle, at Mulroy in 1688. Coll Macdonald tried to plunder Inverness whilst on his way to join Claverhouse. The specious excuses advanced for this piece of banditry ranged from debts due to Coll to the farcial argument that Inverness was a Mackintosh town. Bought off with 4,000 merks (a merk was 13s. 4d. Scots) after mediation by Claverhouse, the Macdonalds of Keppoch then embarked on an orgy of cattle thieving which acutely distressed the Jacobite general. Coll fought bravely enough at Killiecrankie, though he abandoned the Jacobite army before the final battle of the campaign. No doubt he was of a conservative and Jacobite disposition, but this had not stopped him from engaging the troops of James VII in open battle not very long before the Revolution. Coll and his Macdonalds were professional thieves and a rebellion, any rebellion, was a Heaven-sent opportunity for plunder to them.

Another group scarcely less notorious, though less numerous than the Keppoch Macdonalds, were the Macdonalds or MacIans of Glencoe. They rallied to Claverhouse under their gigantic chief Alasdair Macdonald, twelfth of Glencoe. Even the brass blunderbuss which he brandished as he led his men in review past Claverhouse had been looted from Strathspey, and it was perhaps not inappropriate that this regal figure whose manners had been polished in Paris in his youth sought a wife from the Keppoch Macdonalds. The latter were the constant companions and allies of the Glencoe men in enterprises which seldom boded well for third parties.

More deserving, though in many ways even more marginal, were the MacGregors. There probably never was a truly stable Highland clan, and the very word clan is full of ambiguities, but the MacGregors were conspicuously lacking in stability, even by Highland standards. A long time before the Revolution they lost their ancestral lands in Glenorchy in Argyllshire to the expanding Campbells. In 1603 they fell foul of the Stewart dynasty so gravely that James VI banned their very name and sought to extirpate the clan. Montrose, as part of the price of their support, had promised to restore to their chief some part of their ancient estates. In 1661 Charles II lifted the penal statutes against the MacGregors. They were given the right to their name again, but not the land which alone could partially stabilize these dispersed, alienated and warlike people. The very chieftainship of the clan was much debated. Individual MacGregors had survived by being 'resett' by neighbouring communities between 1603 and 1661. This meant that they were given shelter and succour on the understanding that they adopted the name of their host simply to avoid the penalty of death, which was the punishment for the use of their own. Clan Gregor joined the Jacobites too late for Killiecrankie. Under MacGregor of Roro and MacGregor of Glengyle they came in time to fight at Dunkeld, ironically thereby once again losing their name and civil rights when the penal laws against them were re-imposed in 1693.[44]

One group of MacGregors held, or rather occupied by force, lands around the Moor of Rannoch, that thieves' kitchen of the southern Grampians, admirably placed to receive stolen cattle and desperate men. Subsequently the MacGregors tended to drift further south, concentrating in areas to the east of Loch Lomond which were easily defensible but close to the temptingly richer lands of the Lowlands. However, the MacGregor settlements around Loch Rannoch are interesting for they placed many of that name close to the territory ruled, if that be the word, by Robertson of

Struan, chief of the Clan Donnachaidh. Alexander Robertson, thirteenth of Struan, started an incredible career when, against the furious protests of his mother, he led his Robertsons to join Claverhouse's army. Too late for Killiecrankie, he was harrying retreating Williamite troops two days later. As the greatest harbourer of stolen animals in Scotland, it was perhaps appropriate that he ended up recognizing no government whatsoever. King James did not recover his crowns and the 'Elector of Struan' as Alexander Robertson came to be known, did not deign to acknowledge any other sovereign. Attempts to alter his outlook by stationing troops in Rannoch proved futile. His brother Duncan summed up the family attitude when he beat up military outposts which had had the impudence to interfere in a family quarrel by trying, unsuccessfully, to stop him laying waste lands belonging to his mother and sister.[45]

The Jacobite army also contained men of upright life and proven honour attracted to its standard by a loyalty rooted in firm conviction. The outstanding example here is Sir Ewan Cameron of Lochiel, the sixty-year-old beau ideal of Highland chieftainship, who had fought for the royal house of Stewart since the 1650s. Active in Glencairn's rising against the Cromwellian occupation forces in Scotland, Lochiel had once bitten out the throat of an English officer rash enough to grapple with him during the aftermath of that rising. Clan Cameron was an unusually cohesive and compact unit, partly because it was continually hammered together by attacks from outside, notably by the Macintosh of Macintosh. Formed for defence, and deliberately eschewing claims to marginal areas of dubious loyalty on the fringe of the Cameron heartland, this could never be a large clan. All the big, expanding ones, in defiance of the solid blocks of colour ascribed to their names by modern tourist maps, had to incorporate many smaller peoples. By the side of Lochiel at Killiecrankie there fought several chiefs of not dissimilar status and outlook. Sir Donald Macdonald of Sleat, a man of notably upright life and the head of one of the many independent branches of the long-divided Clan Donald, brought a contingent to the battle, where he lost five close relatives. The Macdonalds of Clanranald also formed part of the Jacobite line of battle. Allan Macdonald, twelfth of Clanranald, was a minor in his teens and although he was in attendance on Claverhouse during the campaign and went into temporary exile in France afterwards, command of the clan regiment went to his guardian Donald Macdonald of Benbecula, Tutor of Clanranald. Another very young chief involved in the campaign was Sir John Maclean of Duart, a youth of nineteen whose seat, Duart Castle, and principal territorial interests were concentrated in the island of Mull. There the Macleans were under heavy pressure from the expanding Argyll Campbells.

This pattern of smallish clans, often with very young chiefs, was common in the Jacobite ranks. At Killiecrankie the Stewarts of Appin were led by their chief, Robert Stewart, a mere lad who had hurried from college to join the force being assembled by his guardian, John Stewart of Ardsheal, Tutor of Appin. Among the smaller island chiefs who joined the Jacobite Army were the MacNeill of Barra and Macleod of Raasay (a small island off the east shore of Skye). It was much the same story with the odd Angus or Morayshire laird who joined Claverhouse. They were all men of limited consequence like Fullerton of Fullerton, an Angus laird from the vicinity of Meigle, or Kinnaird of Culbin whose estate, which bordered the Moray Firth, was chiefly remarkable for being almost entirely overwhelmed by drifting sand. Sir Alexander Innes of Coxton, a Morayshire baronet of ancient lineage, was the proud owner of a reputation for probity which was acknowledged even by Whigs. His castle, constructed in 1644, was one of the last classic tower houses built in Scotland. It contained accommodation no greater than that of a substantial cottage. Sir Alexander somehow managed to avoid any penalty for his role in the Jacobite rebellion and died in 1707. However, by 1715 a tide of debt finally overwhelmed the family, and the estate broke up.

There just was not enough political, military, or social weight behind the rebellion for it to have any serious chance of effecting a counter-revolution in Scotland. Apart from the usual 'tail' of enterprising rascals attracted to any Highland rising, Claverhouse was supported only by a limited number of chiefs and gentlemen, none of them of the first importance. The most important single motive in his ranks seems to have been straightforward loyalty to the dynasty. It is fashionable to argue that many Highlanders fought for the Stewarts primarily because they hated the Campbells, at once the staunchest of Whigs, and the most aggressive of clans. In fact the latter title could be hotly contested by the Mackenzies or Gordons, and the hostility of many Jacobites to the Campbells can be grossly exaggerated. Lochiel's mother was a Campbell of Glenorchy and he had been brought up by 'Gillespie Grumach', the great eighth Earl of Argyll. Although he rejected his guardian's Covenanting politics, Lochiel remained on social terms with the house of Argyll during the Restoration. Alasdair Macdonald of Glencoe married his second son to a daughter of Campbell of Lochnell, and guarded himself against a surprise attack from the south along Glen Etive by means of a formal bond of alliance, signed in 1669 and renewed in 1679, with the proprietor of Loch Etiveside, Campbell of Inverawe.[46] Alexander Drummond of Balhadie, who fought with distinction for the Jacobites at Killiecrankie, was in fact a MacGregor and in 1715 claimed to be chief of his clan, but it is naïve to see him as pursuing an hereditary feud with the Campbells of Breadalbane. Clan Gregor had lost that war generations earlier, and the most significant relationship in Balhadie's life was undoubtedly his marriage to Lochiel's daughter in 1688.

Several fiercely Jacobite groups had rather good personal relations with the Argyll Campbells. The Robertsons of Struan, for example, had earned Campbell gratitude by being very unenthusiastic when ordered to participate in Atholl's occupation of Argyll in 1685. As a result Campbell influence was exerted to make it easier for the Robertsons to avoid serious repercussions after their participation in Claverhouse's army.[47] Maclean of Duart did not need to join Claverhouse in order to save his lands in Mull. On the contrary, he gravely weakened his grip on those lands by the obstinacy with which he held to the cause of James VII. That obstinacy was formidable, for in the virtually inaccessible fortified islet of Cairn na Burg Mor in the Treshnish Isles off the west coast of Mull a Maclean garrison held out for King James until 1691. In 1692 Maclean of Duart was allowed a safe-conduct to the court of William of Orange, in exchange for acknowledging the new regime and surrendering Castle Duart to the Earl of Argyll. At this stage of the political game Maclean was far from finished because he made an excellent impression at court, being openly favoured by Queen Mary, and rather admired by King William. The essence of the latter's policy in Scotland was to make it easy for any Jacobite, regardless of his record, to come to terms with the new regime. Drummond of Balhadie, for example, crypto-MacGregor, son-in-law of Lochiel and leading Jacobite conspirator and soldier that he was, found no difficulty in adjusting himself to the new state of affairs once he had taken the oath of allegiance to William, which he did quite early after the failure of the rebellion. It was the decision of Maclean of Duart to desert from William's army in Flanders to join the French forces on his way to the exiled court of James VII which ultimately conveyed his Mull lands into Campbell hands.

In short, clan feuds were real and never wholly at rest, even between the ranks of a Jacobite army, but it is possible to carry the concept of all Jacobite risings as anti-Campbell crusades much too far. Most men of standing who supported Claverhouse seem to have done so out of genuine attachment to James VII. Some, of course, had particular reasons for doing so. Lochiel had been knighted by James, then Duke of York, in 1682, and James both appreciated Lochiel's outstanding loyalty and gave his appreciation concrete expression. In order to buy off the persistent claims of the Macintosh of Macintosh, Lochiel borrowed money from Argyll, agreeing to hold Glen Loy and Loch Arkaigside from Argyll as his feudal superior. This involved only the rendering of a token annual feu duty, and an obligation to furnish a hundred men in arms when required. This last provision was never enforced, so when Argyll was temporarily eliminated by his flight and rebellion in 1684–5, no great burden was lifted from Lochiel's shoulders. On the contrary, the eclipse of Argyll tempted the Duke of Gordon to advance claims of feudal superiority over Lochiel. At this point James VII intervened in person to protect the interests of the Camerons. However, it would be quite wrong to conclude from such episodes, as some historians have,[48] that James was a particular friend of the Gael, a king who turned his back on the traditional hostility of his house to Celtic civilization. This is to make James a far more unusual person than he was. His religious views apart, that monarch's prejudices were in virtually every respect those of a typical, patriotic and insular Anglo-Saxon Briton, with all the dislike and distrust of the Gael which that implies. In exile in 1692 he drew up 'Instructions' for his son which recognized indeed, the loyalty of Scotland north of the Forth, but were full of warnings about the dangers of Gaelic separatism in Ireland, with remedies ranging from an educational programme designed to extirpate the Gaelic tongue to a firm exclusion of all 'natives' from the highest civil and military posts in Ireland.[49] Whatever else he was, James was no lover of the Celt.

James II and VII in many ways deserved no more support than he received in Britain in 1688–90. In England there was virtually no effective support for his cause. In Scotland there was very little. The first Jacobite rebellion ended in fiasco. Colonel Cannon, who had brought 300 very indifferent infantry from Ireland to reinforce Claverhouse, succeeded him in command, failed in his assault on Dunkeld, and was superseded by General Buchan who was surprised and disgracefully routed by Mackay's cavalry in an action on the Haughs of Cromdale. The Jacobite ballad commemorating the battle has to introduce the ghost of Montrose in order to reverse the real result. As a feat of impudent legerdemain this has few equals, even in the shameless history of propaganda, but the whole rising, in retrospect, became a feat of legerdemain. It showed how unpopular James VII was and ended in defeat and humiliation. However, the ghost of Montrose did well, deriving strength, like the shade of a classical hero, from libations of blood poured out by a Jacobite army in which many had the name of Montrose continually on their lips. Above all, Montrose's kinsman, James Graham of Claverhouse Viscount Dundee, added another striking figure to the list of martyrs for the Stewart concept of kingship.

It should not have mattered. Even in Scotland where the bulk of the nobility and gentry hung back from commitment to the Revolution, good, acceptable government after 1690 would have gradually won them over without intellectual trauma. This was the normal pattern of Scottish history. To it some of those in the Jacobite army duly conformed. Young Lord James Murray of Dowally, for example, the Jacobite member of the Atholl family in 1689, received an indemnity for his actions, became in 1696 a captain in the regiment raised by a brother for William of Orange, and was by 1699 Depute Bailie of the Regality of Atholl, the biggest of the family jurisdictions. From that position he advanced to being Member of

Parliament for Perthshire in 1708–9, 1710, 1710–13, and 1713–15. Before he died in 1719 he had enjoyed his share of office, being at one stage Receiver General of the Customs in Scotland.[50] Late in 1689 when Lord James was apologizing to his family for his actions and reporting that he and other Atholl men were taking advantage of the Act of Indemnity, he added that all the Highlanders who had supported Claverhouse were dispersing and that he did not believe they would ever 'draw to a body' again.[51]

It needed a long spell of bad or unlucky government after 1690 to make Jacobitism a viable political movement in Scotland. Few contemporaries expected ever to see another rising. Indeed some of the most radical supporters of the Revolution in Scotland, such as the stern patriot laird Andrew Fletcher of Saltoun, were inclined to agree with the suggestion advanced by William of Orange, that the surest way to safeguard the Revolution would be by a political union between Scotland and England. Fletcher assumed, of course, that the English constitution was about to be reconstructed on a radical basis. He soon realized how wrong he was.[52] The proposals for union came to nothing, and William of Orange proved to be an authoritarian, an unlucky, and in many ways a thoroughly bad King of Scots.

3 The Growth of Jacobite Sentiment from the Revolution to 1704

After his defeat on the Boyne north of Dublin in the summer of 1690 James II and VII returned to France. He may have reckoned that French victories, such as the battle of Fleurus in the Netherlands, and above all the naval victory at Beachy Head over an English fleet, had opened the Channel route for an invasion of England. That Louis XIV of France would not regard his restoration to the English throne as the first priority of French policy probably never occurred to James.[1] In practice the main French military effort continued to be placed in Flanders. Shortage of troops and transports ruled out any immediate invasion across the Channel. When in 1692 a French invasion force was concentrated in the Cotentin Peninsula of Normandy, and James joined it, ready to embark for England, the fortunes of the naval war swung decisively against France. Outnumbered and outgunned, the French Channel fleet faced an aggressive English force under Admiral Russell, later Earl of Orford, a committed Whig who had been one of the 'Immortal Seven' signatories of the invitation to the Prince of Orange to invade England. Russell won a smashing victory at the battle of Barfleur or La Hogue, and France never recovered command of the seas. James was doomed to be a perpetual guest of France, living in the palace of St Germain, which Louis XIV had, with characteristic grace, placed at his disposal when he first reached France as a fugitive very early in 1689.

This exile was by no means an unmitigated disaster from the point of view of the Jacobite cause. Indeed there is a sense in which it was essential to it. It was much easier to work up sentimental enthusiasm for James when he was a pathetic and powerless exile, than when he was in power and giving regular demonstrations of his rare knack for offending and alienating people. Once he was safely in exile, it was possible for him to act as a symbol of resistance to all sorts of policies, including ones which he himself had pursued with characteristic zeal and rigour. To take a particularly blatant example: a great deal of Jacobite support derived from regional hostility to central government, yet James was himself a militant centralizer, as befitted a man of profoundly autocratic temper. This paradox by no means entirely escaped the notice of contemporaries. James as

Duke of York, or rather Duke of Albany as he was normally known in Scotland, had been virtually viceroy of Scotland in 1681–2, when political pressures in England were such that Charles II preferred to have his Roman Catholic brother and heir out of the way in Edinburgh. As ruler of Scotland James was in a position to test many of his absolutist theories, ranging from a high degree of state-sponsored and regulated protectionism in the Scottish economy, to the drawing up of plans for the improvement and beautification of the capital city of Edinburgh, so as to make it an appropriate setting for the court of its divinely-appointed ruler. The new Edinburgh was a long time in coming and when it came it came in the form of the New Town, the 'Heavenly City' of the eighteenth-century Scots philosophers, based on designs submitted by the architect James Craig. However, when in 1763 the foundation stone of the first stage in this development, the North Bridge, was laid by Provost George Drummond, that worthy remarked that 'he was only beginning to execute what the Duke of York (afterwards James II) had suggested so far back as 1681 when residing at Holyrood'. From a Hanoverian Whig and staunch Protestant it was a singularly fair-minded remark.[2]

Politically, James was a mature imperialist who wished to rationalize his inherited complex of kingdoms and colonies and to strengthen the grip of the central royal administration over them. The Restoration government after the collapse of English parliamentary opposition in 1681 mounted a sustained offensive against the chartered rights of its subjects. English towns, Scottish burghs, and American colonies all felt this pressure. During the reign of James even the recalcitrant New England colonies were grouped together into a Dominion of New England under a royal Governor-General.[3] The basic units of James's ideal empire seem, in his mind, to have been either the three kingdoms in the British Isles, or collections of colonies comparable in status to the large territorial divisions of the contemporary Spanish empire in Latin America, which were legally kingdoms. He did not during his short reign countenance schemes for the union of England and Scotland, as Charles II had at various times. In exile he was quite clear, as his Instructions of 1692 for his son show, that it was in the interest of the monarch to uphold the separate status of Scotland. Such distinctiveness could only enhance the power of the royal administration which acted as the vital link between these kingdoms and dominions. However, James as a dogmatic administrator was all for standardizing governmental procedures. Most Scots regarded the absence in Scotland of the rigorous English Customs and Excise administration as a major blessing. James could see no reason why the Scottish Excise should not be collected in exactly the same manner as the English, though he realized that it would be necessary to create in Scotland a cadre of salaried disciplined officers of the state to do this.[4]

The Revolution was bound to involve a reaction in favour of the local power of the traditional rulers of society. Yet since William of Orange was very much the heir of James, he was bound to inherit the tension between central and local power, not to mention the ongoing quarrel as to how central power should be exercised and controlled. The shape of the future was revealed in the extraordinary aftermath to the Highland rebellion. Even after Cromdale a loose confederacy of Jacobite chiefs, led by Lochiel, stood together and bargained with the government as if two sovereign bodies were arranging a settlement. This situation was only possible because of the extreme weakness of the Revolution government in the Highlands. From the very start of his great adventure in 1688 William of Orange was operating with inadequate forces, which could not be indefinitely withdrawn from Continental battlefields. Had the invasion of England led to serious warfare, William's position would have been impossible. Scotland he neither cared for, nor was interested in, except in so far as it was a source of taxes and troops. The latter were to be used in Continental Europe, and the diversion of significant forces to cope with the Highland problem, after the defeat of the Jacobite field army, was simply unthinkable. A stronghold, appropriately named Fort William, was constructed at the southern end of the strategic Great Glen which divides the Highlands into two. An elderly former Cromwellian officer, Colonel John Hill, was brought back from Ireland to command it. At this point the energy and will-power of the government largely terminated. It was perfectly reasonable for Sir John Campbell of Glenorchy, Earl of Breadalbane, to propose that, given the feeble nature of the military resources available to the government, the recalcitrant Jacobite chiefs should be offered a full indemnity, bribed with cash to make peace, and allowed to salve their inflated self-conceit by asking the permission of James VII to settle with William III. At a meeting with the Jacobite chiefs at Achallader in Argyll in the summer of 1691, Breadalbane laid the basis of just such a settlement.[5]

Tragically, the details of the pacification became a subject of dispute between different factions in the Scottish government. Its *amour propre* was damaged by the independent air of the chiefs (itself largely the product of William's refusal to make a serious effort in the Highlands). Sir John Dalrymple, Master of (i.e. heir to) Stair, led the hard-liners in the administration, which was perhaps a congenial role for a former ornament of the Scottish regime of James VII. Even he had to accept the limitations imposed by a gross shortage of troops and funds, so where he could not control he sought to terrorize. Taking advantage of an accidental failure by Macdonald of Glencoe to swear the oath of allegiance to William by the deadline of 1 January 1692 set by the government, he organized the disgraceful and ghastly episode of the massacre of Glencoe.

Captain Robert Campbell of Glenlyon, who commanded the detachment of Argyll's Regiment which perpetrated the deed, was a Campbell laird ruined by the depredations of the Macdonalds of Glencoe, but it would be wrong to see the massacre as a tribal conflict between Campbells and Macdonalds. Very few members of Glenlyon's company bore the name of Campbell, as muster rolls of 1691 attest.[6] Indeed, strikingly few of the common people of Argyll as a whole in the late seventeenth century bore the Campbell name. Surnames in the Highlands were originally only used by landed and chiefly families. A clan really consisted of the chief and the clan gentry, or tacksmen, who were often relatives of the chief, and holders of substantial grants of land from him at very low rents in exchange for acting as officers to their own sub-tenants in the clan army. The records of the Justice Court of Argyll show that in 1699, seven years after the massacre, two Macdonalds of Glencoe were perfectly willing to join with four Kilmartin Campbells and a Cameron to commit robberies in mid Argyll.[7] The massacre is best seen as a symptom of that combination of ruthlessness and weakness which was the hallmark of the Revolution government's style in the Highlands and which earned for it a richly merited combination of contempt and dislike.

It would, however, be quite wrong to think that William was by 1693 on conspicuously good terms with the political class in Lowland Scotland. Quite the reverse was the case. William was so convinced of his own mission to protect the liberties of Europe from France that he was liable to ride roughshod over the liberties of small nations which he saw as obstructing his own larger purposes. He retained the much-resented Restoration practice of keeping the Secretary for Scotland in London. The Claim of Right, that fundamental document of the Scottish Revolution, had demanded the frequent calling of Parliament, but William recalled the Convention which offered him the crown, renaming it a Parliament, and kept it for the rest of his reign in nine consecutive sessions. The same document called for the abrogation of all oaths save a new oath of allegiance, but in 1693 William demanded that all civil, military and church office-bearers should swear an 'Assurance' recognizing him as king '*de jure*' as well as '*de facto*'. In appointing to office William displayed a disturbing willingness to choose men tarnished by association with the regime of James VII. Here the Dalrymples were the classic case. The father, Sir James, was appointed Lord President of the Court of Session, Scotland's highest civil court, as one of a series of appointments made by William without consultation with Parliament. The son, the sinister Sir John, later the prime mover in the massacre of Glencoe, was at the same time re-appointed Lord Advocate of Scotland, a post he had held under James. There was nothing peculiar to Scotland in such appointments. Given William's outlook, last-minute deserters from James often proved more congenial to him than ardent champions of the Revolution, especially if they tended to be radical in their view of the significance of the events of 1688. Thus Henry Compton, Bishop of London and sole clerical representative among the seven signatories of the famous letter inviting William of Orange to England, was twice passed over for the archbishopric of Canterbury, in favour each time of a clergyman from his own diocese not even in episcopal orders.

One result of these events was that by 1692 Henry Compton was inclining towards anti-court views and was increasingly identified with 'Tory' rather than 'Whig' factions in politics. He did not, of course, abandon his loyalty to William or the Revolution.[8] Some English 'Tories' were Jacobites but the two terms were not synonymous. In Scotland in the period 1690–1707 there was a much greater likelihood that a disgruntled and conservative laird or nobleman would carry his opposition to the policies of the executive to the point of entering, at least in his heart, the Jacobite camp. Such serious alienation from the existing regime was the product of a social crisis within Scotland which really had no parallel in contemporary England, at least in terms of its gravity. In Scotland William's government was not only unsatisfactory, but also desperately unlucky.

It proved impossible to arrange an ecclesiastical settlement which commanded general support in Scotland. William had in the Netherlands naturally seen a great deal of Scottish Presbyterian exiles, such as William Carstares, his close confidant and chaplain. Once in London, with representatives of the Scots nobility and gentry flocking to his court, William realized that the maintenance of an episcopal order in the Kirk by law established was a policy which commanded widespread support among the upper clases, if only as a guarantee of order and social deference. Nor could William ignore the usefulness of the Scottish bishops to his Stewart predecessors as instruments of royal control, not just over the Kirk, but also over Parliament. Bishop Alexander Rose of Edinburgh was therefore granted a formal audience with William and told beforehand that the new monarch was anxious to sustain the Scottish bishops. William minced no words. He approached Rose and expressed the hope that the order he represented would 'be kind to me and follow the example of England'. Rose's reply sounds ambiguous only to modern ears: 'I will serve you Sir, as far as law, reason, or conscience shall allow.' William recognized it for the rank Jacobitism it was, turned his back, and accepted the brutal fact that there was now no possible basis for an ecclesiastical settlement in Scotland other than a Presbyterian one.[9]

The implications of this situation verged on the horrendous. More than half the established clergy of Scotland refused to accept the abolition of episcopacy. The deposition of over 500 men might be, indeed was, carried through in theory, but in practice their replacement by adequate ministers of staunchly Presbyterian persuasion was impractical, save in the very long run. Although attempts have been made to weigh the relative mass support for Episcopacy and Presbyterianism in 1690 in Scotland, such endeavours are doubly misguided. There were never two large and distinct churches in seventeenth-century Scotland: rather were there two groups of men struggling for control of the Church of Scotland. Liturgical and theological differences between the two sides were minimal. The debate was about governance in church and state. Secondly, what mattered was not a non-existent 'popular opinion' but the attitudes of the traditional ruling élites. Here those clergymen keen to eliminate episcopacy very often showed a lack of respect for social rank which could only give them a bad name in gentry circles. The united parishes of Daviot and Dunlichty in the Nairn valley, east of Inverness, furnish a good example. The area had an early and strong Protestant tradition, but had accepted the Restoration episcopate. The Minister, the Reverend Alexander Fraser, became increasingly restive under this dispensation. He also fell foul of the local gentry, having had the courage of his principles to the point of censuring John Mackintosh, brother to the laird of Aberarder, for moral lapses. The application of ecclesiastical discipline to the upper classes was invariably fraught with difficulty, so there must have been rejoicing in the best circles when Alexander Fraser finally quit his charge in 1672 and the bishop nominated Mr Michael Fraser. Sir Hugh Campbell of Cawdor was less enthusiastic, for he claimed the patronage of the parish for himself, but the bishop most tactfully accepted his claim, and Cawdor then very gracefully nominated the same Michael Fraser.

During the fifty-four long and often troubled years of his incumbence the Reverend Michael Fraser was sustained by his amiable relationship with 'the gentlemen and elders of the parish'. Fraser was an uncompromising Jacobite. His parish was declared vacant on this score by a Committee of Assembly of the Kirk in 1694, but Fraser contrived to remain in possession until his death in 1726, despite his active role in the rising of 1715, when he carried threatening letters from local Jacobite forces to Lady Culloden, the staunchly Hanoverian defender of Culloden House. Attempts by the Presbytery to take control of the parish in late 1721 were rendered impractical by physical violence. Fraser's parishioners simply stoned the visitation away. The local landowners, led by Farquhar Macgillivray of Dumnaglass and the Mackintosh of Mackintosh appealed to Presbytery to leave Fraser in peace, promising that there would be no trouble after the old man's death. This promise was not honoured. When in 1726 the Reverend Lachlan Shaw of Cawdor, the future historian of the Province of Moray, went to declare Daviot and Dunlichty vacant after Michael Fraser's death, he met with systematic and violent obstruction.[10]

The interesting point is not the sequence of events, which can be found in hundreds of similar cases, but the fact that Michael Fraser can be shown to have been a conspicuously careless and unenthusiastic pastor. His bishop repeatedly rebuked and censured him for non-residence; neglect of duty, including failure to celebrate the Eucharist; and above all for his tendency to take long holidays in order to indulge in his ruling passion for 'limning' or painting. Michael Fraser survived the Revolution not because he was a faithful shepherd, but because he was acceptable to the lairds. Nor can one doubt that the violence mentioned above could only have occurred with their support and approval.

This is not to say that there was never a warm current of affection amongst parishioners for a devoted minister of Episcopal and Jacobite persuasion. Hundreds of such cases can be found. Indeed it was one of the main difficulties facing the Presbyterian establishment after 1690 that it was often committed to removing exemplary pastors from their charges. In practice many good and devout men who kept their heads down after the Revolution were left untroubled in their parishes despite their continuing theoretical commitment to both bishops and the exiled dynasty. An outstanding example here is the Reverend Robert Kirk, incumbent first of Balquidder and then of Aberfoyle (a parish to which his father had ministered for many years). Living on the very margin of the Highlands, Robert Kirk was naturally interested in the Gaelic tongue, and came to be deeply concerned about the lack of adequate translations of the Scriptures into the Gaelic. This concern brought Kirk into contact with James Kirkwood, a native of Dunbar who, when acting as chaplain to Sir John Campbell of Glenorchy (later first Earl of Breadalbane), had been distressed by the spiritual destitution of the Highlands. Kirkwood established contact with that great Irish chemist and Christian philanthropist Robert Boyle, and it was Boyle who originally financed a series of schemes designed to provide the Scottish Highlands with Bibles and catechisms in their own tongue, or perhaps more accurately in archaic literary Irish which was at least comprehensible in the Highlands, as English was not.

Robert Kirk began by distributing, very selectively, a couple of hundred copies of a complete Bible printed as a quarto volume in Irish type at Boyle's expense and comprising Nehemiah Donellan's translation of the New Testament into Irish and Bishop Bedell of Kilmore's Irish version of the Old Testament. Boyle also financed the printing of 3,000 copies of a catechism produced by Professor Charteris and translated into Gaelic by Sir Hugh Campbell of Cawdor. These ventures are all the more remarkable in that they occurred about the time of the turmoil associated with the Revolution. 'Boyle's' Bible was distributed in Scotland in 1688 and Kirk then buckled down to the huge task of transcribing Bedell's Old Testament and Donellan's New Testament into roman characters, and seeing this new version, revised as well as transcribed, through the press. This he did in 1689, to the accompaniment of some good-humoured asides on the contemporary storm in church and state, asides which reveal what an extraordinarily engaging personality Kirk was. His greatest literary enterprise came to fruition after his death in 1692, but not for nothing is he described on his tomb as 'Linguae Hiberniae Lumen' – light of the Irish language.[11]

Of course, True Believers are aware that Kirk did not really die. He sank down into the earth while walking across a Fairy Hill behind his manse at Aberfoyle. There is nothing inherently improbable about the idea. The worthy minister of Aberfoyle was a great authority on the Wee Folk, being the author of a strange but powerful and impressive work entitled *The Secret Commonwealth – of Elves, Faunes, and Fairies* (first published in 1815 in a version edited by Sir Walter Scott). Written seemingly around 1691, this work rounded off a literary life which had started in 1684 when Kirk published an edition of the Psalter in Gaelic. Throughout this varied career Kirk was a man of businesslike habits. He was Presbytery Clerk between 1667 and 1688, and the Presbytery minutes, kept in his neat and lucid hand, are still a pleasure to read. Withall, he was an intensely human character. His parishioners long remembered his anguish at the death of his first wife Isabel, daughter of Sir Colin Campbell of Mochaster. His second wife was also a Campbell. She was Margaret, daughter of John Campbell of Glendaruel. When Kirk died she was pregnant, and it was at the christening of Kirk's posthumous child (a future parish minister of Dornoch), that Graham of Duchray saw a vision of Kirk, but failed to throw his dirk over the vision's head, thereby dooming Kirk to perpetual residence in Fairyland.[12]

Mention of Duchray and of Kirk's wives makes it clear that Robert Kirk lived in a world of lairds. He married into their families, and lent money to not a few. The latter activity must have come very naturally to Kirk. His marriage to Isabel Campbell had involved a substantial tocher or dowry, paid by his future brother-in-law Colin Campbell of Carwhin, an Edinburgh Writer to the Signet (i.e. a lawyer of considerable standing). To this sum of a thousand merks (£666 13s. 4d. Scots) Kirk had to add a similar sum, so that the life-rent of two thousand merks could be settled on the marriage, its survivor, and eventually the lawful offspring of the match. It was a very sensible form of social insurance, though one only open to the relatively well-off, and Kirk and Colin Campbell were still adjusting the terms of the marriage settlement, to enable the capital to be used to maximum advantage, as late as 1691. Campbell of Glendaruel cheerfully borrowed money from his new son-in-law, but Kirk discovered that lending to lairds was easier than collecting from them. Colin Campbell and Kirk remained close allies in the network of legal problems created by Kirk's financial dealings. In 1688 the correspondence between the two men was an extraordinary mixture of assurances that, God willing, Kirk would undertake the transcription of the Irish Bible, and discussions as to the best means of screwing payment of debt out of Campbell of Lawers. It was Robert Kirk's disillusioned but no doubt realistic view that Lawers would only pay this debt (due originally to Glendaruel) when driven to the last legal ditch.[13]

However much Kirk dealt with Campbells, the connection to which he belonged politically was undoubtedly a Graham one. Graham of Duchray was his kinsman, and a man with a record of passionate royalism during the civil wars. The patron of the parish of Aberfoyle, the Earl of Menteith, was the representative of a very old Graham stock which had been unjustly deprived of the ancient earldom of Strathearn by James I in the early fifteenth century. Sadly, an attempt to recover the historic title incurred the wrath of Charles I, as the result of foolish talk about the debatable legitimacy of the main Stewart line and the superior claims of the Earls of Strathearn to the Scottish succession. The Earl of Menteith was very firmly put in his place by having the earldom of Airth, a dignity no greater than his existing one and emphatically not the longed-for honour of Strathearn, wished upon him in 1633. Despite these events, the Earl of Airth and Menteith staunchly upheld the royalist cause against both Scottish Covenanters and English Cromwellians during the civil wars. His son was killed while serving with Montrose and his grandson succeeded to a financially crippled inheritance. Apart from severe fines, the estate had suffered a great deal of deliberate devastation at the hands of English troops commanded by General Monck. William Graham, second Earl of Airth and Menteith, failed to secure any significant compensation for his sufferings from Charles II. He seems to have had difficulty in paying Robert Kirk the full stipend he was entitled to, though he did his best to oblige the minister by furnishing him with timber and hewn stone for his manse at Aberfoyle in 1687. Relations between Kirk and the earl appear to have been consistently cordial. In a letter to Campbell of Carwhin of 1691 in which he expressed his disgust at the sustained refusal of Campbell of Glendaruel to honour his debts to his own son-in-law, Robert Kirk remarked that he was no longer willing to waste time and money year after year pursuing debts in Edinburgh courts 'all the Ministers of the late times being neglected'. Yet it is difficult to see how a clergyman like Kirk, himself well-connected with the gentry, and solidly supported by his noble patron, could possibly have been ejected from his parish.

At the same time it is worth emphasizing that this learned, devout, and assiduous pastor was, in theory, intransigently hostile to both the Revolution and the Presbyterian settlement in the ecclesiastical sphere. By chance a notebook containing Kirk's thoughts and reflections on a great range of subjects has survived, and from it we can cull succinct statements of his position on the major political issues of his time. Kirk was of the school of that most saintly of Restoration bishops, Robert Leighton, with all that such discipleship implies in terms of spiritual grace and political pusil-lanimity. Kirk was as attached to the doctrine of non-resistance to legiti-mate royal authority as he was to the concept of episcopacy in the church. Indeed, he must have felt that the events of 1688–90 proved that the divine right of the Stewarts and the cause of episcopacy were one. It was a highly dubious interpretation of events, but a widespread one. Fortunately for Robert Kirk's peace of mind the Earl of Menteith came to terms with the new regime only in 1693, after the gentle Jacobite incumbent of Aberfoyle had passed from mortal ken.[14]

If all patrons had been like the Earl of Menteith, and all Jacobite clergy like Robert Kirk, the transition from the old order to the new would have been relatively painless, albeit slow, for not every incumbent of Jacobite views could be relied upon to die, like Kirk, in his late forties. In practice the transition was protracted and extremely bitter almost everywhere north of the Tay. In Dundee, for example, Robert Norrie and Robert Rait, Ministers of the Second and Third Charges of the City Kirk, were deprived by the Scottish Privy Council in 1689, as inimical to the Revolu-tion, while Henry Scrymgeour of the First Charge chose to demit office and retire. Not until 1699 was it possible to find a reliable Presbyterian clergy-man for the normally very attractive and much sought-after First Charge. There was nothing unusual in this delay. Arbroath experienced a very similar hiatus between 1694 and 1699 when the first Presbyterian incum-bent assumed his duties. In April 1696 the Presbytery of Montrose com-plained that two Episcopal meeting houses were kept up, one in Dundee and one in Montrose; that they were ministered to by clergy who refused to take the oath of allegiance to the government; and that these meeting houses were seducing people from the ordinances of the Establishment. The Presbytery went on to say that Mr William Sympson, who had been deprived of his previous charge by due process of law, and who was not qualified by having taken the oath of allegiance to the government, was preaching regularly in the Montrose meeting house, with the open coun-tenance of two magistrates and the effective support of the bulk of the Town Council.

All these places were in the diocese of Brechin and outwith what is generally considered to have been the heartland of Lowland Jacobitism – the north-east. Brechin itself, with its noble cathedral attached to which is one of the two surviving Celtic ecclesiastical towers of refuge in Scotland, was an even more extreme example of the difficulties involved in enforcing the Revolution Settlement in the Kirk. In 1702 a Committee of the General Assembly of the Church of Scotland reported that Brechin Cathedral (which was, of course, a parish kirk) had been technically 'vacant since the Revolution'. The underlying reason for this was hostility on the part of the local notables to the 'planting' of Brechin by a sound Presbyterian. The elders of the cathedral refused to cooperate when the Assembly dispatched its Moderator to Brechin to remedy the situation. Despite hopes expressed in the General Assembly that the Earl of Panmure and the Tutors (i.e. trustees) of the Earl of Southesk might cooperate in the establishment of a Presbyterian incumbent, there was no effective local support for such a policy, and the Episcopalian Jacobite John Skinner, who had never lost control of the cathedral, despite his technical disqualification, resumed his ministry as soon as the Moderator departed.[15]

In the north-east proper – Aberdeenshire and Banffshire – the new Presbyterian order was fighting against almost hopeless odds. In some parts of Aberdeenshire there was a virtually unanimous refusal by parish clergy to accept the new post-1690 dispensation. In the Presbytery of Ellon, for example, only two incumbents were willing to conform, and one of them was a man of low character. For twelve years there was no Presbytery of Ellon. Only by November 1701 had sufficient change occurred for a nominal Presbytery of that name to be revived, but even then there were so few Presbyterian ministers within its bounds that it was necessary to reinforce the reconstituted Presbytery with outside ministers, to give it sufficient weight. A glance at events in the coastal parish of Cruden goes far to explain these circumstances. The dominant figure in the life of the parish was John, twelfth Earl of Erroll, Hereditary Lord High Constable of Scotland, and brother-in-law (by marriage to the Lady Anne Drummond) of James Earl of Perth, Chancellor of Scotland in the latter days of James VII. Unlike his brother-in-law Erroll remained staunchly Protestant to the point where John Barclay, Minister of Cruden, could dedicate to him and his countess a poem he published in 1689 vindicating the Church of Scotland as against Roman Catholicism. To this parish retired in 1689 the extruded Bishop of Brechin, Dr James Drummond. As his name suggests, this saintly prelate, ordained to Brechin in 1684, was a distant relative of the Countess of Buchan. He was also possessed of more spirit than most Restoration bishops, for when the King had at an earlier date informed him that he intended to dismiss the Bishop of Dunkeld out of hand like an unsatisfactory postillion, and had offered him the reversion of the see, Drummond had expressed his disgust in a short reply to the effect that he was unaware of any vacancy in Dunkeld. A successful Minister of Muthil (and after 1682 a Doctor of Divinity of his own university of St Andrews), Drummond undoubtedly owed the see of Brechin to his former parishioner James Earl of Perth. At Cruden he ended his days with great dignity and ensured the succession of Episcopalian ministers in the parish by ordaining on 21 December 1692 at Slains Castle (the seat of Lord Erroll) Barclay's successor, William Dunbar.

Dunbar was a sensible man who cooperated with the Presbytery, while that august but tenuous body had more sense than to challenge a man ordained 'apud capellam illustrissimi comitis Errollii in palatio suo'* until 1708, and even then they did not drive their charges home.[16]

The social realities of late seventeenth-century Scotland were such that only a very foolish man would have wanted to impose himself as incumbent on a parish or burghal kirk if he knew that the local landowners or patricians were likely to be bitterly hostile to him. It is true that, as part of the Revolution Settlement in the Kirk, lay patronage had been abolished in July 1690. On payment by the heritors or principal landowners of compensation of 600 merks to the patron, the right to present ministers to vacant charges devolved on the heritors and elders of the parish, under the supervision of the relevant presbytery. First, it must be stressed that over much of Scotland all this act did was to confirm nobles and lairds in an intransigent Episcopalianism whose main content was a grim determination to keep their ministers in their kirk, if necessary by violence. Riots in early modern Scotland were seldom spontaneous. The lower orders only broke into violence, unless circumstances were very odd, with the active approval of their superiors. Secondly, it must be recognized that the act abolishing lay patronage could not possibly deprive a great territorial lord of massive, often decisive, influence over the appointment of clergymen within his sphere of influence. In many parishes there was only one heritor, and he might well be the landlord or employer of virtually every member of the kirk session.

All this can be easily illustrated from a plethora of ecclesiastical sources, but the records of the Presbytery of Dunkeld happen to be unusually blunt about the realities of the struggle in the parishes. The first Duke of Atholl (created Duke in 1703) was a ruling elder, as well as the principal landowner, within the bounds of Dunkeld Presbytery. In January 1707 the members of the Presbytery nominated His Grace, along with two clergymen, as their Commissioners to the General Assembly of the Church of Scotland,[17] a body to which His Grace was to be the sovereign's Lord High Commissioner in 1712, 1713 and 1714. There was no question as to the devotion of the Duke of Atholl to Presbyterianism. However, many other noblemen in the area ruled by Dunkeld Presbytery were less than enthusiastic about the Kirk by law established after 1690. Thus a minute of the Presbytery for February 1707 records the sad story of the Reverend Mr Gow, Minister of Cargill, but possessor of neither a manse nor a kirk session there. In the manse of Cargill sat, firmly ensconced, the former Episcopalian incumbent William Rattray, and most of the parishioners appear to have attended the services which he regularly conducted in the

* 'in the chapel of the illustrious Earl of Erroll, within his palace (i.e. castle)'.

manse. Part of the complaint raised by Mr Gow about this position was in the form of slightly vague references to the presence of numbers of Papists in the parish. This was not standard Protestant hysteria on the subject of Roman Catholicism. On the contrary, it was a rather delicate reference to the real power behind the opposition to an effective Presbyterian settlement. The parish of Cargill contains Stobhall House, a remarkable and attractive complex of structures perched on a bluff formed by a meander of the Tay. Stobhall was, indeed is, the seat of the Drummonds whose principal representative in the reign of James VII had been James Drummond, fourth Earl of Perth and Chancellor of Scotland. Viscount Cargill was one of the numerous subordinate titles accorded by the exiled James when probably in 1701 he raised his faithful follower in exile and co-religionist to the titular rank of Duke of Perth. Since titles cost nothing the exiled court dispensed them freely. Throughout their vain attempts to gain control of Cargill, the Presbytery of Dunkeld were continually being met by one Lord Drummond. When the usual Scottish legal device (of claiming that misappropriated property had been the subject of a little-known sale in the past) was used to stop the Presbytery taking possession of the manse, it was Lord Drummond who was on hand, smoothly suggesting that no rash steps should be taken in the face of such legal complexities. There were no Roman Catholics in the area other than members of the Drummond entourage (who had been converted with their lord) and Lord Drummond was, of course, the Jacobite Marquis of Drummond, heir to the Jacobite Dukedom of Perth, and Master of the Horse to the exiled Stewart.[18]

Faced with an astute Roman Catholic nobleman, whose estates were perfectly secure despite his father's flight, there was little that the Presbyterians could do. Their confrontations with the Episcopalian incumbent were little better than shadow-boxing. Without ever blatantly breaking the law it was possible for Lord Drummond to postpone almost indefinitely the planting of a secure Presbyterian ministry in Cargill. Presumably the suavity with which his lordship handled the situation was a tribute to the education he had received at a leading seminary of the Counter-Reformation, the Scots College in Paris. Yet he was only an extreme case of a fairly general phenomenon. In the parish of Auchtergaven, where the Presbytery of Dunkeld was facing another protracted squabble over the filling of the incumbency, the key to the conflict was the determination of a group of landowners, headed by Lord Nairn, to have their own nominee, and none other, as minister. Members of the Presbytery believed, after visitation of the parish, that the man proposed by the lairds was not really acceptable to the bulk of his proposed parishioners.[19] In this particular case the Presbytery could at least think of a way of trying to put effective pressure on William Murray, Lord Nairn. They appealed to the Duke of Atholl to speak to Lord Nairn, who was his brother, about Auchtergaven, with a view to bringing Nairn into a more reasonable frame of mind.[20] All this was coming to a head in 1708, and it must be said that Nairn's temper had not been improved by the passage of the Act of Union in 1707. As a staunch Scottish patriot he was disgusted and enraged by what he saw as the sale of his country.

It is significant that the Reverend Brethren of the Presbytery of Dunkeld were at such pains to try to carry the Duke of Atholl with them. There was at times not much to choose between the somewhat unctuous tone in which they addressed His Grace and, say, the obsequious way in which Archbishop Sharp can be found writing to David, second Earl of Wemyss, in the 1660s, assuring him that the archiepiscopal patronage in Fife would ever be used in a way acceptable to the Wemyss interest. Both Presbytery and Archbishop were simply facing up to the facts of life.[21] Regardless of the formal frame of ecclesiastical authority, a great noble could not be ignored in his own region. The first Duke of Atholl appears to have been genuinely interested in increasing the efficiency of the parochial ministry in the Highlands. He was actively interested in the introduction of the Irish Bible and he shared the concern of the Presbytery of Dunkeld to secure and advance clergymen who were fluent speakers of the Gaelic tongue. At the same time, the Duke was determined to keep a firm control of events within his territories. When the Presbytery wished to launch proceedings against 'the scandalous behaviour of an Episcopal Incumbent', they were firmly warned by His Grace to proceed with care and caution.[22] The price of acting in a manner of which His Grace did not approve was complete paralysis. This was demonstrated in no uncertain fashion in connection with an attempt to plant a Presbyterian incumbent in the kirk of Dull. More by accident than design, there would appear to have been a certain lack of agreement between the Duke and the Presbytery on this issue. However, the lack of positive ducal backing had dramatic results, for when the Presbytery tried to enter the kirk in order to formally 'call' a new incumbent, they were seen off, blandly but inflexibly, by one Neil Mc-Glashan, a member of the ducal household, who thoughtfully reinforced his words with the presence of a large number of men armed with swords, targets, pistols, dirks and guns[23]

Beneath all the local crises over the settlement of Presbyterian ministers lay the brutal economic fact that there was just not enough money available to pension off displaced Episcopal clergymen, on a generous basis. The Reformation crisis in mid sixteenth-century Scotland had developed with extraordinary little *odium theologicum* in the parishes mainly because those clergymen who could not conscientiously transfer to the new dispensation (as many did) were allowed to draw the great bulk of their stipends for the rest of their lives. The position of clergymen expelled from their living after the Glorious Revolution was quite different. At the worst they and their families could be cast penniless on the mercy of an unfriendly society. In practice they tended to cling very tightly to any aristocratic patron willing to look after them, and to reinforce, in conversation and in exhortation, the Jacobite convictions of their patron.

An interesting example of this process is provided by three Fife ministers, Robert Edward, minister of Murroes, and his two sons Charles, who was also minister of Murroes, and Alexander, who became minister of another Fife parish, Kemback. In 1687 this particular Levitical dynasty must have seemed very well entrenched. They were all graduates of the local University of St Andrews. The father had secured the incumbency of Murroes as early as 1648, through the patronage of the Earl of Panmure. In 1682 his son Alexander had been admitted minister of Kemback, a charming parish whose kirk perches high above the deep wooded gash of Dura Den in north Fife. In 1684 Charles was admitted as colleague to his father in Murroes, in a fashion which was very common in those days before retirement pensions were heard of, and which guaranteed him the succession on his father's demise. Then came the trauma of the Revolution. Alexander Edward was deprived of his living for refusing to read the revolutionary proclamation of the Estates of Scotland. His old father was also deposed for similar contumacy. Fife was just too close to Edinburgh for intransigently Jacobite clergymen to escape the consequences of their views. In any case, if the Fife gentry tended to the conservative, there was an undercurrent of aggressive radicalism amongst the lower orders in the county, as Alexander Edward found out in 1691 when his house was attacked at midnight, fortunately in his absence, by armed men who threatened his life.[24]

Robert, the father, simply fades from the scene. We know that he died in Edinburgh in 1696. His son and colleague Charles clearly left the parish with him and is last heard of in 1692. The parish itself, incidentally, stood vacant for over six years after the extrusion of its joint pastors. Alexander Edward, however, we know more about, for he was a man of quite outstanding talent and enterprise. After expulsion from Kemback he went to work for Sir William Bruce, the aristocratic architect to the Restoration gentry, and can be found acting as draughtsman to Sir William in 1699, working on Hopetoun House, the great mansion of the Hope family near Queensferry on the south shore of the Firth of Forth. The simple fact that Sir William offered him employment was not without political significance. Bruce had been an important Restoration politician, as well as a gentleman-architect. He was Surveyor to the King's Works and a Baronet of Nova Scotia, taking his territorial title from Balcaskie in Fife, though he later bought the estate of Kinross. An intimate of the Duke of Albany (later James VII), he became, partly through the Duke's influence, a member of the Scots Parliament, and High Sheriff of 'Kinrosher'. The survival of the small county of Kinross, ringed by hills and with Loch Leven at its heart, probably owes a good deal to the political weight of Sir William Bruce, who obviously would not want to see it absorbed, as it so easily could have been, by neighbouring Fife. After the Revolution it soon became apparent that Sir William was less than reconciled to the new regime. Indeed he was imprisoned no less than three times by it, and it was into this militantly Jacobite entourage that Alexander Edward moved.[25]

Sir William Bruce obviously liked intransigently Jacobite clergy, though he lived too close to the government to be able to sustain them in the parish ministry when they nailed their colours provocatively to the mast. Henry Christie, the incumbent of Kinross, for example, was deprived by the Scots Privy Council as early as August 1689 on the not unreasonable grounds that as well as refusing to read official proclamations or pray for William and Mary, he was praying publicly for the restoration of King James and 'confusion to his enemies'. If the patron of the parish, Sir William, could not save Christie, he could as High Sheriff of the county make it extremely difficult for any Presbyterian minister to be settled in Kinross in his stead. The unfortunate Mr William Spens was forced in 1691 to take Sir William in person before the Scots Privy Council to complain that Sir William refused to admit that he, a Presbyterian, had a legitimate call to the parish of Kinross and was refusing to pay him the ministerial stipend, or admit him to either the kirk or the manse. To add insult to injury Sir William as Sheriff was, on the bench, a rabid partisan of Sir William the aggrieved patron. The Lords of his Majesty's Privy Council saw fit on this occasion to order Sir William to be reasonable. He was told to stop using his power as Sheriff to make life difficult for William Spens and to open the kirk to any minister appointed by the Presbytery of Dunfermline, pending a permanent settlement of the parish.[26] The degree of cooperation which the Privy Council secured from Sir William may be deduced from the fact that Spens eventually gave up in despair and returned to Glendevon, whence he had come, while Kinross remained without a settled Presbyterian ministry until 1699. Sir William Bruce started the first of his three spells in prison in 1693.

Alexander Edward clearly used his time with Sir William to build up experience and contacts which enabled him to branch out into architectural practice in his own right. The Edward family seems to have come originally from Angus. Old Robert Edward was a native of Dundee and sufficient of an Angus patriot to have published in 1678 a large map of that county along with *A Description of the County of Angus* (in Latin), which survives in an eighteenth-century translation,[27] and which demonstrates that he was a shrewd intelligent observer. It is hardly surprising that Alexander Edward, after leaving Sir William Bruce, reappears in the historical record working for the noble house of Panmure, to whose patronage his father owed the incumbency of Murroes. In the 1690s Alexander Edward presented the fourth Earl of Panmure with plans for a totally reconstructed Brechin Castle. Completed after Edward's death in 1709, the castle stands just outside the city of Brechin. It is not a fortification but the palace of a great magnate. Its three-storeyed western front, symmetrical around a classical pedimented centre, and balanced with a tower at each end is, in its meticulous detail and shallow relief, not unworthy of the hand of Sir William Bruce himself. Needless to say, the fourth Earl of Panmure was a staunch Jacobite, hostile to the accession of William and Mary. In 1715 he proclaimed James VIII as King of Great Britain at the market cross of Brechin and escaped abroad, though he was attainted of treason and deprived of his lands and titles. He died in exile in Paris in 1723 after refusing to take the oath of allegiance to the Hanoverian dynasty, which would have led to the restoration of his property.[28]

The problem of ejected or recalcitrant Episcopalian clergymen after the Glorious Revolution in Scotland was therefore a very serious one. These men were not like the bulk of English Non-Jurors, whose inability to accept the Revolution Settlement did not necessarily imply that they were politically dangerous to the new regime. The saintly Archbishop Sancroft, for example, was prepared to see James deprived of all effective regal power and reduced to the status of a mere figurehead. It was throwing the figurehead overboard that was too much. Even when an Anglican clergyman enjoyed the reputation of being a Jacobite, it was often the case that his Jacobitism was of a curiously insubstantial nature. The classic case here is William King (1685–1763), Principal of St Mary's Hall Oxford, and for long leader of the Jacobite party in that university. His politics were really compounded of dislike of certain trends in the England of his day, and a determination to express his hostility towards them in the way best calculated to engender shock and gain publicity. This happened to take the form of heavy hints as to his Jacobite sympathies carefully dropped in the middle of his public orations. Then in the early 1750s he actually met Bonnie Prince Charlie (who drank tea at his lodgings during a surreptitious visit to England). He later developed a dislike of the prince.[29] Scottish clergymen of an Episcopal persuasion after 1690 tended to be made of sterner stuff politically. Their Jacobitism was unambiguous. They preached the divine right of the exiled dynasty to real power. Furthermore, they tended to preach their politico-religious doctrines into the ears of people who mattered. The bulk of the Episcopal clergy who survived in Scotland after 1690 did so in close association with a noble household. Only a limited number could find alternative clerical employment, though some Scottish Episcopal ministers were placed in parishes in England and in the American Plantations (especially Virginia) through the kindness and patronage of Henry Compton, Bishop of London.[30] Most others lived in perpetual fear and resentment of the two commissions (one for the north of Scotland, one for the south) set up by the vengeful Presbyterians with the express purpose of harrying the Episcopalian clergy who had for so long harried them. No situation could be better calculated to breed a spirit of uncompromising Jacobitism.

One of the reasons why the Scottish government found it difficult to replace anti-Revolution ministers was that the training of ministers was a slow process. Scottish clergymen were university products, and not only did it take many years to complete the necessary courses, but it was also the case that the Scottish universities were deeply penetrated by Jacobite views. The Restoration had seen the re-establishment of the principle that the bishop or archbishop of the diocese in which a Scottish university was situated should normally be its chancellor. At St Andrews, still the aristocratic university, the Archbishop of St Andrews was more than just an academic and ecclesiastical dignitary to the clergymen who dominated the teaching staff. In this small and rather isolated burgh, perched on a headland battered by the North Sea, the Archbishop was the most significant local employer and fount of patronage. Naturally the Revolution, which abolished episcopacy in the end, seemed far from glorious to many university teachers in St Andrews.

On 4 July 1690 the Scottish Parliament passed an act requiring professors, principals, and regents in the universities, and all schoolmasters teaching Latin in Scotland to swear an oath of allegiance to William and Mary and also to subscribe the Confession of Faith approved a month before by the same Parliament. Anyone refusing thus to adhere to the Revolution and the Presbyterian Kirk was to be expelled from office as a university teacher or grammar-school master. The opportunity was taken to order a full visitation of each university, with special reference to its administration, subjects taught, teaching materials and teaching methods. Parliament set up a general commission of visitation which delegated the inspection of each specific university to a sub-committee which also examined schools in the area around its university. The records show that the process was far from being a simple political purge. On the contrary, a very serious attempt was made to investigate and evaluate the academic life of the universities in the light of the best contemporary opinion. However, the commissioners were unequivocally ordered by the act:

> To enquire and take tryall what hes being the cariage of the masters etc since the late happie revolutione as to ther coming to the croune and to enquire into ther dictats or papers emitted by them what are ther principles as to the constitutione of the government by King and Parliament.[31]

The results of such enquiries could be drastic. At St Andrews, where most of the university teachers had displayed rare loyalty and abysmal timing by joining with the Scottish bishops in issuing a laudatory *Address to the King* (i.e. James VII) just before he fell, there was almost a clean sweep. All three constituent colleges were purged of their staff so efficiently that the only survivor was one John Monro whose good fortune it had been to take up post so soon before the Revolution that he had not had time to compromise himself, let alone carry a class through a session.[32] Filling so many posts at short notice was not at all easy, so the commission had to resort to the extraordinary device of issuing a printed broadsheet, designed to be pinned on the doors of parish kirks and other public places, which invited applications for academic posts in the University of St Andrews from those who deemed themselves suitably qualified.[33] The situation became, if anything, odder when appointments were made. The pre-Revolution university had been dominated, like pre-reformed Oxford in the nineteenth century, by very young men, especially amongst the regents or tutors who led groups of students through the entire curriculum. Indeed one of the many recommendations later made by the commissioners, with respect to the academic activity of the university, was that nobody should be appointed to a professorship or regentship until he had achieved the age of twenty-one. On the other hand, extreme old age has its drawbacks too, and yet the only way in which the senior posts in the university could be quickly filled by politically reliable men involved recourse to very old men. This was because university-trained Presbyterians, by and large, had ceased to be produced after 1660. The inevitable result was that the first generation of post-Revolution academic appointments tended to be of short duration, for within half a dozen years several of the new incumbents were dead.

As is not infrequently the case, St Andrews pushed a common academic problem to rather eccentric extremes. No other Scottish university experienced so grave a trauma in 1690. In Aberdeen the committee of visitation was composed of local aristocrats such as the Earl Marischal, Viscount Arbuthnott, Lord Elphinstone, the Master of Forbes, and the Laird of Brodie. They more or less had to act against James Garden, the Professor of Divinity, who refused to recognize their jurisdiction or take the oath of loyalty to the new regime, but even he was allowed to conduct a lengthy delaying action before he was deposed in 1696. There were no other depositions.[34] In Edinburgh there was an unseemly public display of venom when the committee of visitation indicated that it was prepared to receive criticisms of the character and conduct of existing senior members of the university. The upshot was less draconian than had at one point seemed likely, though the Principal of the University was dismissed, as was the Professor of Divinity. In Glasgow the visiting committee, headed by Lord Carmichael and Sir John Maxwell of Pollock, was regarded as very moderate, but even so Principal James Fall, who had been appointed in 1684, was deposed along with the inevitable Professor of Divinity, James Wemyss, and a couple of the regents. Financial arrangements of a generous kind cushioned their fall, and the new tone of the University of Glasgow was set by Principal William Dunlop, who held office between 1690 and 1700. This masterful Presbyterian clergyman had refused to serve the Restoration ecclesiastical establishment. After tutoring in the Dundonald family he emigrated to Carolina in the early 1680s, where he made a name for himself as a preacher and soldier. When he returned to Scotland after the Restoration he had the great advantage of being both cousin and brother-in-law to William Carstares, William of Orange's principal adviser on Scottish affairs.[35]

Glasgow, with its mercantile and Protestant traditions, was a natural bastion of the Revolution. Its university rapidly assumed the outlook of the community around it. Academic grumbles were stilled by the success of the well-connected Dunlop in securing state aid in the shape of grants of revenues which had once belonged to the Archbishopric of Glasgow. Edinburgh University was taken very firmly in hand by the supporters of the Revolution. It was the creation of the Town Council of Edinburgh, and in 1703 that body elected William Carstares himself to the post of Principal. He held it until his death in 1715, by which time Edinburgh University had become, in the words of its modern historian 'pre-eminently the Whig University of Scotland'.[36]

North of the Forth, the atmosphere of St Andrews, and perhaps more significantly of the university communities in Old Aberdeen (King's College) and New Aberdeen (Marischal College), was much less favourable to the new regime. St Andrews was a town full of resentful men who had once served in university posts, or who had been connected with the archbishopric, and who had been driven out of their jobs. The purging of the Scottish universities in general, and of the University of St Andrews in particular, had been supervised by the Earl of Crawford, a Fife nobleman of unimpeachably Presbyterian and pro-Revolution views, but he was an exception in his county. The great bulk of the Fife nobility and gentry were unenthusiastic about the Revolution, when they were not positively hostile to it, and their sons made up a large proportion of the student body in St Andrews. Even the new establishment of academic teachers in St Andrews had little reason to be content with their position. They complained that their salaries were miserable, their classes huge, and that there was no money for development. The explanation was simple: despite studious boot-licking directed towards anyone who succeeded to an office of consequence in the Scottish government, the university could not secure adequate financial grants from the state.[37]

Eventually a rather miserable grant of a few hundred pounds from the revenues of the defunct archbishopric was wheedled out of King William, but it scarcely solved the problems of the St Andrews academics, who continued to moan about 'the desolate state' of their college. They were also on very bad terms with the town around them, to the point of having to draw up interim concordats designed to keep feuds between town and gown under control. The University of St Andrews seriously considered the possibility of moving, lock stock and barrel to Perth.[38] In the midst of all these misfortunes, in August 1697, the learned men realized that they had not had a Chancellor to represent them since the Revolution. They therefore elected John Earl of Tullibardine, Joint Secretary of State for Scotland, a future second Marquis and first (after 1703) Duke of Atholl, to this office. This conscientious and sensible nobleman did his best as Conservator of Privileges and Chancellor, but he presided over a University of St Andrews rife with discontent, and indeed at certain levels, Jacobitism.[39]

Aberdeen's universities faced not dissimilar problems after 1690. There was the same desperate shortage of funds, hardly alleviated by a miserable £300 annual donation from King William. Only in May 1713 did Queen Anne add £210 per annum to be divided between Marischal and King's Colleges. Furthermore the 1690 visitation, for all its moderation, left a heritage of strife in King's which exacerbated even the bad relations which normally exist between the members of academic bodies. Briefly the issue was whether the Act of Visitation of 27 September 1690 gave two professors holding chairs of comparatively recent creation equal rights in the governance of the institution with those professors on the ancient foundation. The Principal of King's bitterly resisted the aspirations of Thomas Bower and George Gordon, trying to exclude them from business meetings and threatening them with heavy damages if they dared to try to enforce their rights at law. In the last analysis this display of academic beastliness was bluff, for faced with defeat in the courts and an uncompromising threat of horning (or outlawry) if he did not grant Bower and Gordon their rights Principal Middleton backed down in March 1712, to the accompaniment of mutterings from his colleagues that he was doing precisely what he had often sworn he would not do.[40] Poverty and bitterness were the hallmarks of academic life in Aberdeen in this era and Middleton was in fact a Jacobite sympathizer.

In a much broader sense, poverty and bitterness went hand in hand in Scotland after 1690, creating very favourable conditions for the spread and flourishing of Jacobite sentiment. Long-term economic trends in late seventeenth-century Scotland were such that any government in power after 1690 was likely to be unpopular, because times were so hard. The Restoration regime after 1660 benefited from the steady recovery of the Scottish economy from the very low levels it had reached in the mid seventeenth century. This recovery, at least in Glasgow and the western Lowlands, may well have begun in the later 1650s during the Cromwellian occupation,[41] but it certainly accelerated in the 1670s when grain was cheap, overseas trade buoyant, and manufacturing industry prosperous. The 1680s were a decade when Scotland's economic fortunes were more chequered than in the 1670s, but there was no sustained relapse into depression. After 1690 a whole series of disasters shattered the general prosperity of Scotland in a way which any Jacobite worthy of the name unhesitatingly described as evidence of God's wrath against a sinful nation which had dared to repudiate its God-given sovereign.[42]

In the first place, the Revolution ushered in an era of wars with France which lasted from 1688 to 1697 and then from 1702 to 1712. These wars were not only longer but also infinitely more damaging to the Scottish economy than the Dutch wars of the Commonwealth and Restoration. Direct trade with France, a major trading partner of Scotland, became very difficult indeed, except after 1703, when political developments changed the situation. Demands for manpower for the Royal Navy led to forcible conscription of Scottish merchant seamen, on a sufficient scale to cause dislocation in the vital coastal trade, not to mention riots in coastal burghs. Finally French privateers were extremely active and destructive, finding in Scottish shipping a particularly attractive prey, for the English Admiralty did not accept overall responsibility for the Scottish merchant marine. Dragged into war, taxed to sustain it, and then denied protection, the Scots were naturally resentful.

The impact of war was pervasive and particularly destabilizing politically when it hit the pockets of the gentry, as it was bound to do. Most estates depended heavily on victual rents, which were gathered in great girnels or granaries and marketed to obtain the vital cash flows essential to the maintenance of an aristocratic style of living. To bring a large proportion of these grain surpluses to market coastal shipping was essential. In 1696 a cadet of Wemyss of Wemyss in Fife, Wemyss of Bogie, arranged a deal with the dowager Lady Seaforth, involving the movement of coal and salt from Fife north to the Cromarty Firth, in exchange for a return cargo of barley and oatmeal. It is symptomatic of the hazards of the time that the charter-party of the ship hired for the occasion, the *Elizabeth* of Findhorn, had to include provision for the size of the ransom payable in the event of capture by a French privateer.[43] Hostility to the second phase of the post-Revolution French Wars was all the sharper in Scotland because Scotland was virtually hi-jacked into war with France in 1702. In 1696 the Scots Parliament had passed legislation whereby it was to meet within twenty days of the death of a sovereign, solely to secure the succession to the throne, the defence of the realm, and the security of the Protestant religion. A parliament was in being but not in session when

William of Orange died in March 1702, so it should have been summoned within the statutory twenty days in terms of the Act of Security of 1696. It was not, for by a piece of legal chicanery which even the normally obsequious Scottish Privy Council had difficulty in swallowing, Queen Anne's English ministers first adjourned, then postponed the Scottish Parliament until ninety days had passed since the death of the late monarch. The explanation for this behaviour was only too obvious. It enabled the Scottish Privy Council to declare war on France in the meantime, without having to face the furious opposition which would have undoubtedly erupted had a parliament been sitting.[44]

Such behaviour on the part of the English ministry which ultimately controlled government policy in Scotland as well as England goes far to explain the angry mood of the Scots Parliament in the early years of the reign of Queen Anne. The 'Act anent peace and war' of 1703 removed from the sovereign the right to declare war without the consent of the Scottish legislature. The Wine Act of 1703, a government-sponsored device to secure tax revenue, reluctantly restored trade in wines and spirits with France, despite the existence of a state of war. The only qualifying sentence in the act was, typically, one reserving 'to the Peers and Barons of the Kingdom the same immunities and freedoms from customs for wines which they had by the two hundreth fifty first Act fifteenth Parliament King James the Sixth'. Even more drastic was the Act of Security, which eventually became law in 1704, and which laid down that on the death of Anne her successor was to be nominated by the Scottish Parliament, was to be Protestant and of the ancient royal stock of Scotland, but was not to be the person already designated to succeed to the crown of England, unless legal guarantees were given securing the religion, political independence, and trade of Scotland.

The single most important explanation of the Scots Act of Security was the fact that when in 1701 the English Parliament, by the Act of Settlement, conveyed the succession to the English throne to the Electress Sophia of Hanover and her heirs, it had taken no heed of Scotland. There was no malice in this behaviour, merely the usual high-handedness and underlying arrogance. Surprised by the violence of the Scottish response, English opinion was only too ready to ascribe the growing crisis in Anglo-Scottish relations to Jacobite intrigue. Most unfortunately such an attitude made leading English politicians, and their Scottish allies, excessively susceptible to the statements of a man so crooked as Simon Fraser, Lord Lovat, the shiftiest of the many rascals who prowled on the outskirts of the exiled Stewart court. From the start of his adult career Simon Fraser had been locked in bitter dispute with the Murrays of Atholl over the succession to the ancestral estates of the Lovat Frasers, chiefs of the clan. Simon, himself a Beaufort Fraser, probably was the rightful heir of Lovat, but a mind so naturally dishonest as his could turn even a good case into a scandal. His abduction of and forcible marriage to the Dowager Lady Lovat, a daughter of the Marquis of Atholl, so far from settling the matter, had raised his quarrel with the Murrays to new heights. Saluted by Madame de Maintenon, morganatic wife of Louis XIV, as 'un homme ravissant', Simon Fraser ingratiated himself with the exiled Stewarts (partly by a well-timed conversion to Catholicism) and returned to Scotland in 1703 with every intention of smearing Atholl as a Jacobite conspirator.[45]

The mechanics of the plot seem to have hinged on Simon Fraser's possession of certain unaddressed general letters furnished by the exiled court and doctored by Simon so as to implicate Atholl. The Duke of Queensberry, the principal Court 'manager' of Scottish politics, proved only too ready to believe Simon Fraser's convenient revelations which rapidly expanded so as to implicate the Duke of Hamilton, and Lords Home, Seafield, Cromartie, and Tweedale, all as it happened political opponents of Queensberry. There probably was a substratum of truth to Fraser's tale, but it was obviously exaggerated, the evidence was clumsily faked, and Atholl was warned in time to take defensive action by a double agent, Robert Ferguson, whose career proved that a Lowlander could be even more slippery than Lovat. Queensberry became the centrepiece of a major fiasco which temporarily destroyed his political credibility, while the English House of Lords did not endear itself to Scotsmen by setting up a committee to investigate the 'Scots' Plot' which was, significantly, known in Scotland as the 'Queensberry Plot'.

The conclusions of the openly partisan committee of the English House of Peers were that:

> there had been dangerous plots between some in Scotland, and the Court of France and St. Germains, and that the encouragement of this plotting came from the not settling the succession to the crown of Scotland in the House of Hanover.[46]

Scottish opinion was enraged that a committee of the English legislature should sit in judgement on Scots affairs, and if the conclusions reached seem self-evident, they displayed the violent bias which lurks behind most 'self-evident' truths. It would have been more to the point to recognize that the agony and humiliation of Scotland under a very bad, and ultimately an English-controlled, system of government went far to explain the mounting vitality of Jacobitism in the northern realm. An act of indemnity at the start of Anne's reign had encouraged exiled Scots Jacobites to return home. Undoubtedly the many crypto-Jacobites in the Scots Parliament had been very active in supporting the legislation which English opinion found most obnoxious, yet the Episcopal and Jacobite interest in the Scots Parliament would have been powerless had not Providence and the English politicians done so much to help them by creating a general sense of anger and despair in the Scottish ruling classes.

Providence certainly dealt unkindly with the Scots in the 1690s when the nation was burdened with a major crisis of subsistence, with all the horrors of famine, disease, and widespread social dislocation. Such crises were a recurring feature of most pre-industrial economies. Almost certainly the Scottish famine of 1623 was more severe in intensity than that of the 1690s, nor was Scotland alone in her sufferings in the late seventeenth century. Despite the blessings of indefeasible hereditary rule France was deep in famine in 1693–4, emerging just as Scotland plunged into a similar crisis in 1695. The famine lasted roughly four years with peaks of severity in 1696 and 1699 and a relative respite in 1697–8. Nevertheless, men reared on a providential view of history may be forgiven for taking this terrible experience as a sign of God's wrath. Modern scholars tend to explain the episode in terms of world-wide adverse weather cycles. Scottish Jacobites preferred the analogy with a Biblical Pharaoh, and stretched the chronology to fit a very successful propaganda phrase about 'King William's Seven Ill Years'. For contemporaries the 1690s were indeed apocalyptic.[47]

Even when it can be said that the Scots went far to pull a particular disaster down on their own heads, as was the case with the ill-fated Darien scheme, bad Anglo-Scottish relations can be shown to have been a major contributory factor. Darien is a site on the Isthmus of Panama. In the late seventeenth century it was in the heart of Spain's vast American empire, but was not effectively occupied by the Spaniards. The Company of Scotland Trading to Africa and the Indies, a body created and granted certain privileges by the Scottish Parliament in 1695, decided to establish a Scots colony at Darien, 'this door of the seas, and the key of the universe'. Despite the apparently splendid position of the proposed colony, and two major expeditions, the whole episode had culminated in total fiasco by 1700. Scots shareholders, led by the very highest nobility, but including a huge cross-section of large and small property owners, lost over £153,000 sterling in paid-up capital. This was a vast sum for a country notoriously short of circulating capital. The Scots were left to nurse their wrath with such comfort as they could derive from the memory of the gallantry with which Captain Alexander Campbell of Fonab and his Scottish and Indian forces had fought the Spaniards. Unfortunately the Scots also chose to vent their spleen by means of the wholly unjustified judicial murder of Captain Thomas Green of the English ship the *Worcester*, along with two of his crew, in 1705 at Leith sands on trumped-up charges.[48]

The irrationality of the Scots can be almost entirely explained by the transports of rage induced by successive demonstrations that the Union of the Crowns made in 1603 worked invariably to Scotland's disadvantage when Scottish and English interests clashed. The group of Edinburgh merchants who had given the plans for an overseas trading corporation their initial impetus were primarily interested in a modest and practical trade to Africa. More ambitious schemes for using the Company of Scotland to challenge the monopoly in eastern trade of the Honourable East India Company of England were the product of London merchants led by the erratic London Scot William Paterson. They were bound to create a storm of hostility, given the immense political influence of the East India Company. A successful challenge to that company's monopoly would no doubt have been of great advantage to many English consumers (in the eighteenth century the Swedish East India Company was dedicated to smuggling cheap tea into England[49]). However, the successful elimination by the English Parliament of English support for the Scottish company in 1695 and 1696 led the Scots to increase their own financial stake still further while succumbing to Paterson's fatal enthusiasm for Darien. There, in the rain-sodden jungle, a Scottish community split by many tensions, including ones generated by the participation of some colonists in the massacre of Glencoe, discovered the futility of trying to break through the vicious circle of poverty which gripped their country. They would have been wiser if they had, like the Swedes, stuck to honest smuggling.

From the point of view of the exiled Stewarts, the late seventeenth and very early eighteenth century was thus a good time. James VII and II was the sort of monarch whose attractiveness was much enhanced by exile. His determination to send his heir to France at the the time of the Revolution had been something which even his loyal adherents found difficult to stomach. It was, of course, another manifestation of that militant Roman Catholicism which could worry his co-religionists. Thus in 1670 Alexander Abercrombie, holder in wadsett (i.e. mortgage) of the Barony of Fetternear in Aberdeenshire, was sufficiently disturbed by the prospect of the eventual accession of James to the throne to take out insurance in the shape of a Papal Charter, dated 20 September 1670, from Pope Clement X, confirming the original grant which was composed of ecclesiastical land misappropriated about the time of the Reformation by a Catholic family.[50] Once safely ensconced on a permanent basis in the Chateau of Saint-Germain-en-Laye, which Louis XIV placed at his disposal, James became a convenient peg on which acutely disgruntled subjects of William III could hang their grievances.

Being so blatantly a pensioner of the French king did have its drawbacks for the exiled Stewart. It made him the tool of the great national enemy in the eyes of many Englishmen. Scotsmen were a good deal less sensitive on this issue, as they were often singularly unenthusiastic about the endless French wars. On the other hand, Louis XIV did give James solid support expressed in hard cash and rooted in conviction. The French king may not have possessed an original mind, but he thought hard about the profession of kingship, and the Christian principles on which kingship should stand. His belief in indefeasible hereditary right, and in royal absolutism, was therefore all the stronger because he could express it in a rational and articulate fashion. To Louis succession to thrones lay in the hands of God alone. God's divine will, Louis was sure, was expressed through the providential, if at times unpredictable, mechanism of strict hereditary succession. Louis was prepared to shout his convictions at the most inappropriate moments. In 1700 his grandson Philippe of Anjou, second son of the Dauphin, succeeded, surprisingly, to the throne of Spain as Philippe V, in accordance with the will of the last Spanish Hapsburg Charles II. All Europe knew that peace could only be preserved if the principle of rigorous separation of the succession to Bourbon France and Bourbon Spain was strictly upheld. Yet in December 1700 Louis drew up an official recognition of Philippe's place in the line of succession to the French throne. It was made public early in 1701, and contains a passionate statement of the view that it was unthinkable for mere men to tamper with that hereditary succession which is the will of God.[51] This was a major diplomatic blunder.

Louis could, of course, bend before events. Very reluctantly indeed in 1697 he had accepted the necessity to recognize William of Orange as King of England, and the need to promise that neither he nor his successors would aid the exiled Stewarts in their plots against the English throne. This was part of the price for the much-needed peace secured by the Treaty of Ryswick. Presumably Louis classed these clauses in the treaty among the things which, in his own words 'Kings are often obliged to do . . . against their natural inclinations and which wound their natural goodness'.[52] Certainly Louis was totally insincere in both diplomatic commitments: to him William was a usurper to the end, and ironically it was a dramatic gesture by Louis in favour of the exiled Stewarts which finally made it politically possible for William to bring a willing England into the War of the Spanish Succession. Louis genuinely regarded the Glorious Revolution as blasphemy and James VII and II as something of a martyr. In 1690–92 when the French Highways Department had been reduced to an annual budget of 100,000 livres, James and his intensely dull court at St Germain were allowed to eat up no less than 600,000 livres per annum, at a time when the French state was deep in economic and military crisis.[53] It is not therefore really surprising, though it was diplomatically extremely inept, that when the life of James VII and II finally ebbed away in September 1701, French heralds appeared at the gates of St Germain and proclaimed his thirteen-year-old son James King of England, Scotland and Ireland (the title of King of France which previous English kings had borne was discreetly waived).

War between England and France was already inevitable, but this grand gesture by Louis (opposed by his Chancellor and other ministers on grounds of prudence) was a great help to William of Orange. Nevertheless, the new Stewart claimant at St Germain, who became in course of time best known as the Old Pretender, grew to maturity under conditions not unfavourable to his political aspirations. The three kingdoms of the British Isles, under English leadership, were locked in a lengthy, expensive, and increasingly unpopular war. France provided the exiled dynasty with a secure base. French commitment to the Jacobite cause was inevitably tinged with expediency and affected by changing circumstances, but some foreign help was essential. Above all, a very substantial and apparently growing section of the Scottish ruling class was prepared to embrace Jacobite principles as an expression of a complex of resentments against their English masters. All that was required, from the point of view of St Germain, was more provocation of Scottish sentiment. When Queen Anne's ministers decided to make serious moves to effect a parliamentary union between Scotland and England they rendered the exiled dynasty no small service.

4 The Union, the '08 and Post-Union Disillusionment

The idea of an incorporating union between England and Scotland had a long history behind it even in the early eighteenth century. Three centuries of war between 1296 and 1560 had naturally conditioned the two peoples to mutual hostility, but after 1560 the predominance of, admittedly rather different, forms of Protestantism in both realms helped to foster a sense of common aims and a common destiny. The employment of English rather than Lowland Scots for the translations of the Bible used by the Scots Reformed Kirk hastened the displacement of the Scottish vernacular by English as the literary language of the northern realm. The Gaelic-speaking area of Scotland tended to diminish and by the seventeenth century it is clear that the vast majority of the important chiefs and magnates within that area were bilingual in English and Gaelic. When James VI succeeded to the English throne in 1603 even the name Great Britain, which he favoured for his newly-expanded dominions, had been current for over a century.[1] It must, however, not be forgotten that no such state existed between 1603 and 1707; that James did not succeed in his attempt to create formal union between England and Scotland; and that after the forced union with the Commonwealth government of England between 1652 and 1660 most Scots were delighted to resume their separate identity.

Thereafter the idea of an Anglo-Scottish union tended to be a gambit embraced by English politicians in response to crises which they could not solve. Charles II seems to have toyed with the idea of swamping his recalcitrant English Parliament with loyal Scottish peers and M.P.s, while William of Orange's deathbed enthusiasm for Anglo-Scottish union was very much a commentary on his abysmal record as King of Scots. His successor, Queen Anne, more or less from the moment of her accession in 1702 stoutly championed the unionist cause. She had no love for Scotland or Scotsmen. Indeed she regarded the Scots as 'strange' and 'unreasonable', in a way which clearly meant that she found them only a shade less unpalatable than the Irish. Union to Anne was necessary for the sake of the security of England. The royal sense of urgency on this matter was, however, not very widely shared in either of her British realms, and by early

1704 the union policy was simply part of the political debris which surrounded the downfall of Queensberry as the principal 'manager' of Scottish politics on behalf of English politicians. It seems to have been the crisis precipitated by the Crown's grudging acceptance of the Scots Act of Security in that same year which persuaded English ministers that only an incorporating union could eliminate the many difficult problems created by the visible bankruptcy of their Scottish policies.[2]

As it was common knowledge that few even among those Scots well-disposed towards Anglo-Scottish union were in favour of an incorporating union (there was much more support for some variety of federalism), the real aims of the English ministry were revealed only at the very last moment. The first objective was necessarily to deprive the Scots Parliament of any initiative in the matter, and this was achieved in three stages. First the English Parliament applied blackmail against the Scots nobles, the key group in the Scottish legislature because of their immense influence on the lairds and burgesses who made up the other two orders. The English Alien Act passed early in 1705 laid down that unless negotiation for Anglo-Scottish union was in train, or the Hanoverian succession accepted in Scotland by 25 December 1705, all Scots not already domiciled on English territory would be treated as aliens, and the three main Scottish exports to England – cattle, linen and coal – would be banned. It is clear that the main sufferers, if the Alien Act had ever become effective, would have been the Scots nobles.

Ever since 1603 there had been a slow but significant process of inter-marriage between the nobilities of the three kingdoms in the British Isles, as was only natural when they were subject to a single monarch. Few aristocrats exemplified this process as well as Sir George Fletcher Baronet of Hutton Hall in the English county of Cumberland. He succeeded to his estate in 1645 on the death of his father in action against Parliamentary forces during the English Civil War. After the Restoration he came into his own and was especially noted by the contemporary local historian Sir Daniel Fleming on the ground that he had contrived to wed first the eldest daughter of an Irish peer, and after her demise the eldest daughter of a Scots peer.[3] Exceptional events like the marriage in 1673 of the Scottish heiress Anne Countess of Buccleuch to James Duke of Monmouth, the favourite bastard son of Charles II, were paralleled in many less exalted aristocratic families. Inevitably, Scots nobles came to possess extensive estates in England. The Duke of Buccleuch was just an extreme case (Charles made Monmouth and his Countess Duke and Duchess of Buccleuch immediately after their marriage).

The fierce, old-fashioned, anti-union patriotism of that great Scots noblewoman Anne, Duchess of Hamilton (1656–1716), was rooted in a complex of landed property which was exclusively Scottish, and which had nearly been bankrupted by her father's expensive career as the leading 'court Scot' in the England of Charles I. By the end of her life Duchess Anne was something of an anachronism.[4] When in 1703 Sir George Mackenzie of Tarbat, recently created Earl of Cromartie and Viscount Tarbat, and Secretary of State for Scotland at the accession of Anne, came to assesss the political weight of various Scots magnates, he lamented that the Duke of Lennox was not as useful to the government as he might be. Lennox held an ancient dignity. He had very great heritable feudal superiorities and jurisdictions, and he had Admiralty and Chamberlainry prerogatives which gave him leverage in the Scottish burghs. Unfortunately he kept 'a very small estate in that kingdom, and, not residing in it, he is the less useful to the Crown there'.[5] By 1706 even the fourth Duke of Hamilton had a major seat at Aston Hall in Lancashire in the north of England, and it is clear that many Scots magnates and gentry had property holdings which would have made the collapse of the joint citizenship engineered by James VI for all Englishmen and Scotsmen born after his accession to the English throne very embarrassing.

It is equally clear that the main Scots exports to England were vital to the rent-rolls of the Scottish nobility. Coal mining was very much in the hands of the landowning class, for whose benefit Acts of the Scottish Parliament passed in 1606, 1641, 1661 and 1672 had fastened a system of hereditary serfdom on miners and indeed on workers in the associated salt industry (which used low-grade coal to fuel its salt pans). Reinforced by legal decisions and estate custom, this bondage endured to almost the end of the eighteenth century, until legislation of 1799 finally swept it away.[6] A great deal of rent in early eighteenth-century Scotland was still paid in victual, mainly grain, but the black cattle and the linen trades were, apart from coal, the principal sources of such cash payments as a landlord could hope to squeeze out of his estates. Black cattle, mainly originating in the Highlands and Islands and in Galloway, possessed the great virtue of being able to walk on the very long journey to the London market. As early as 1663, 18,574 Scottish beasts paid toll (8*d*. a head) at Carlisle on their way south. They were usually fattened up on East Anglian pastures before being driven to Smithfield market. Linen was another standard rent-payer. Its production could involve the labour of entire agricultural families, and did so usually during the lengthy periods in the agricultural year when farm work was slack.[7]

After waving such a formidable economic bludgeon in the direction of the Scots aristocracy, the English ministry set out to recapture the initiative within the Scots Parliament. This it achieved in 1705 when it sent the young Duke of Argyll north as Queen's Commissioner to the Estates of Scotland. Argyll was, at this stage in his life, more interested in his career in the British army than in politics. Hoping to trade political services for military promotion, he rallied a confused Court interest and gave it a brusquely aggressive tone. Above all, Argyll presided over the supreme double-cross of Scottish politics. The English ministry wanted union but not genuine negotiations on union proposals. That would give Scottish opinion too much influence and might produce terms which were unacceptable to Westminster. It was therefore crucial that the Scots Parliament be persuaded to allow Queen Anne (i.e. her English ministers) to nominate the Scots commissioners who it was proposed should discuss union with a similar body of English commissioners. Those members of the Estates who were not actually in the government's pocket were naturally passionately opposed to so transparent a device. An English observer of the key debate on this issue, Joseph Taylor, has left a very succinct summary of the views of the opposition, as expressed by Andrew Fletcher of Saltoun:

> Fletcher oppos'd the Queen, for says he, you had as good leave it to my Lord Godolphin, and we know that our Queen is in England, under the Influences of an English Ministry, and 'tis not to be expected that the Interest of Scotland should be so much considered by her, as the Inclinations of an English Parliament . . .

The reference to Queen Anne's leading English minister, Godolphin, was perfectly realistic, which makes the outcome of the debate all the more startling. For want of a better leader, the Scottish opposition had been compelled to rally round the fourth Duke of Hamilton, the unworthy son of Duchess Anne. On 1 September, after assuring his supporters that a vote on the composition of the commission was unlikely and thereby ensuring that many of those supporters went home, Hamilton rose in a thin house with 'his usuall haughty and bant'ring Ayr' and proposed that the nomination of commissioners be left to the queen. On a snap vote the motion was carried by four. The full story expired with Hamilton in 1712 as he died of a severed artery immediately after a duel with Lord Mohun in Hyde Park in London. However, his behaviour in the Parliament House in Edinburgh in 1705 only makes sense on the assumption that pressure had been brought on him by the English government, perhaps through his debts, perhaps through the Lancashire lands acquired by means of his marriage to an English wife, perhaps even by threat of legal action over his characteristically obscure and irresolute dealings with Jacobite agents. The correspondence in the years 1705–7 between George Baillie of Jerviswood and two other pro-Union Scots politicians of the so-called Squadrone Party, John Earl of Roxburgh and James Jonstone, contains a substantial body of evidence showing that Hamilton was secretly offering himself for sale to the English government as early as 1705, because of his financial needs.[8]

Thereafter there is no reason to doubt the allegations of George Lockhart of Carnwath, a Jacobite sympathizer who was made, probably by mistake, one of the Scottish commissioners for the union negotiations, that the Scots commissioners only pretended fleetingly to bargain for a federal settlement. What emerged in 1706 was a pre-arranged package containing, it was hoped, enough concessions to major Scottish vested interests for it to be possible to ram through the Scots Parliament the basic aim of English policy – an incorporating union. Not all the concessions were embedded in the Treaty of Union itself. Religion was excluded from the terms of reference of the commissioners, on the assumption that the two national ecclesiastical establishments would remain unaltered. Nevertheless, it was essential to give the Scottish Kirk a formal assurance of its privileged position, if only because the ministers could have raised a storm of protest over the proposed treaty if they had preached violently against it. There had for some time been sympathy in the very highest circles of Scottish Presbyterianism for the idea of an Anglo-Scottish union as a shield against 'the common enemy' – Jacobitism. In 1706 William Carstares, now Principal of the University of Edinburgh, wrote to the English politician Robert Harley that '. . . the desire I have to see our Church secured makes me in love with the Union as the most probable means to preserve it . . .'.[9] There were signs that Presbyterian opposition to the proposals was already fading in 1706, though when the Presbyterian nationalist minister of the Tron Kirk in Glasgow urged his flock to 'up and be valiant for the city of our God', they sallied out to start a cycle of anti-unionist riots lasting several weeks. However, an Act for securing the Protestant Religion and Presbyterian Church Government, passed by the Scots Parliament at the same time as the Treaty of Union, confirmed both Presbyterian support for and Episcopalian opposition to, the latter measure.

Article 21 of the Treaty of Union was designed to reassure another major interest – the Scottish burghs. It stated:

That the Rights and Privileges of the Royall Burroughs in Scotland as they now are, Do Remain entire after the Union, the notwithstanding thereof.

This did not stop a twentieth-century British Parliament from summarily abolishing the Scottish burghs, nor did it greatly affect the widespread opposition in the Scottish burghs to the Treaty of Union in 1707. That part of Article 4 of the Treaty which guaranteed the Scots access to 'the Dominions and Plantations' of the old English empire cut very little ice with Scots merchants. They had recovered from the insane obsession with the colonial trades which lay behind the disasters of the Darien Scheme, and they were aware that their shortage of capital and shipping would necessarily limit their participation in oceanic commerce.[10] In any case they knew full well that no early eighteenth-century government could effectively police its colonies so as to prevent them from trading with foreign merchants offering desirable goods at reasonable prices. Despite the technical illegality of the business, a customs official reported in 1695 that there were two dozen Scottish ships trading regularly with the American colonies. Even earlier, in the 1670s, Charles II had tried to penalize imports of tobacco into Scotland.[11] Besides, in terms of volume the Atlantic trade remained of little consequence compared with, say, the French trade which the first Earl of Seafield, who was nothing if not an obedient hack of the English ministry, described in 1705 as 'the foundation of our customes and the encouragement of our fishing and support of the government'.[12]

Above all, it was essential for the Treaty of Union to win over the nobility, and many of its provisions were designed with this in mind. Article 22 of the Treaty provided that the Peers of Scotland (almost as numerous as the total English peerage despite the much smaller population of Scotland) were to elect sixteen Representative Peers to sit in the House of Lords of the new United Kingdom, but the Scots nobility naturally assumed that any of their number who acquired British peerages after 1707 would automatically take their seats in the House of Lords. More immediately significant was Article 20 which laid down that 'all heritable Offices, Superiorities, heritable Jurisdictions, Offices for life, and Jurisdictions for life, be reserved to the Owners thereof, as Rights of Property as they are now'. One of the most striking features of the Scottish scene was precisely that many of the subjects of the Crown were not subject to the criminal jurisdiction of its courts either at central or at local level. In its most developed form this judicial autonomy was expressed in numerous regalities, which ranged in size from quite small units like Dunfermline and Haddington, to name two significant but not large Lowland towns, to very large territories like Atholl and Argyll. The latter was administered by the Earl, Marquis or Duke of Argyll, Paramount Chief of Clan Campbell, in his capacity as hereditary Justiciar of Argyll and the Isles. He had been confirmed in this position in 1628, in exchange for surrendering the office of 'hereditary justice-general of Scotland'.

To understand fully the implications of such a system it is essential to grasp that any indweller of a regality who came before a royal court for any crime other than high treason could be and regularly was 'repledged' into the regality jurisdiction, i.e. officials of the regality, on providing guarantees that justice would be done within a given time, simply took over the case. Holders of the bigger regalities were often possessed of those

Scottish earldoms, unique in Europe, which gave their holders the status of 'subreguli' (i.e. sub-kings) in Scots heraldic law. They were often referred to as 'the high and mighty prince' in their formal documents, and even so staunchly royalist a legal authority as Sir George Mackenzie of Rosehaugh, King's Advocate in the late seventeenth century, admitted that regalities were mini-kingdoms. Even at the level of baron courts, which were omnipresent in Scotland as the barony was the basic unit of land tenure and administration, there was a very large element of autonomy. The competence of the baron court was equivalent to that of the royal sheriff court in criminal and civil matters alike. The main qualification on this autonomy was that capital crimes could only be tried in a baron court when the sheriff or a sheriff-depute was present and that there was an appeal from the baron court to the sheriff court. In the bigger regalities, of course, an elaborate structure of courts culminated in the supreme court of the regality.

Not surprisingly, the Crown disliked this system and James VI complained in his *Basilikon Doron* that 'The great hindrance to the execution of our laws' was 'the great men in possession of heritable jurisdiction and regalities'. However, there was really no alternative to the system, as the Scottish Crown lacked the financial strength to impose or pay for a bureaucracy in the localities. Indeed, many royal officials were themselves hereditary holders of their posts. The sheriff was the principal representative of the Crown in the localities, but by the early eighteenth century the majority of Scottish sheriffdoms were the hereditary property of noble families. In key areas like the Borders virtually all sheriffdoms had become hereditary. Article 20 of the Treaty of Union was thus both a guarantee of local autonomy after 1707, and an essential concession to the Scots aristocracy.[13]

It was by no means the only such concession in the Treaty. Article 18 provided as broad a protection for the quite distinctive nature of Scots Law as circumstances would permit. Modern Scots Law is often, and misleadingly, described as a Romano-Dutch system. It certainly is different from, though not uninfluenced by, the Common Law of England, but in its modern form Scots Law was largely pulled together into an organic whole by the so-called Institutional Writers of the late seventeenth and eighteenth centuries, of whom the most important was the first, Lord Stair. Obviously it was essential that the laws governing public policy be rendered uniform in Britain after 1707. At the same time Article 18 laid down that 'no alteration be made in Laws which concern private Right, except for evident utility of the subjects within Scotland'.

Article 19 was much more detailed for it had several issues embedded in it. It guaranteed, for all time coming, the survival of the central Scottish Courts, the Court of Session and Court of Justiciary, while ensuring that only trained Scots lawyers were eligible for elevation to their benches. Accepting that all Admiralty Jurisdictions must go under the British Admiralty, Article 19 nevertheless guaranteed the survival of a Court of Admiralty in Scotland and that 'the Heritable Rights of Admiralty and Vice-Admiralties in Scotland be reserved to the respective Proprietors as Rights of Property'. Reasonable regulation of these arrangements by the British Parliament was naturally envisaged. In the same way Article 19 provided that a Scots Privy Council should be maintained 'for preserving of public Peace and Order, until the Parliament of Great Britain shall think fit to alter it or establish any other effectual method for that end'.

The biggest single bribe offered to the Scottish ruling class was undoubtedly the £232,884 5s. 0d. which the Treaty provided should be used in repayment, with 5 per cent interest, of capital lost by shareholders of the Company of Scotland when the Darien fiasco brought their enterprise to bankruptcy. Virtually every member of the Scottish ruling class, from the Duchess of Hamilton downwards, had been a shareholder and it was universally agreed that without this payment there would have been no hope for the Treaty of Union. This apart, the jobbery and pressures used to expedite the progress of the Treaty through the Scots Parliament would appear to have been little different from the behaviour which was standard government practice in the eighteenth century. It was perhaps neither less nor more reputable than the practices of government in late twentieth-century Britain, another patronage-ridden society. Certainly the representation of forty-five M.P.s and sixteen peers which the Treaty offered Scotland was a reasonable compromise by the standards of the time. It was less than could be justified by a population ratio of 5 to 1 in England's favour but much more than was suggested by the appalling disproportion of 38 to 1 in wealth, as measured by taxable capacity.

Over a third of the Scottish shires and some quarter of the royal burghs (besides a few presbyteries and parishes of the Established Kirk) petitioned against the Treaty of Union. Argyll was contemptuous to the point of saying these petitions were only fit to make kites with. On the other hand it was known that the full weight of governmental approval and patronage lay behind the Treaty, so the mere act of publicly expressing opposition required both courage and commitment of no mean order. Such petitions did not seriously affect the overall outcome of the struggle in the Scottish Parliament, even though the representatives of most of the petitioning bodies usually could be found in the opposition. Broadly speaking, the nobility supported the Treaty of Union by over two to one while the barons and burgesses, despite the leverage of the nobility over the other Estates, approved the Treaty by much smaller margins.[14] Opponents of the measure said it was desperately unpopular. Its supporters publicly denied this, but in fact privately agreed that it was extremely unpopular, for they were careful not to allow the Scottish constituencies to elect the first Scottish representatives to the new Union Parliament. The latter were chosen by the old and discredited Scottish Parliament. Actions always speak louder than words, and this provision speaks volumes. It would only have been inserted by men frightened of an anti-Union landslide in an early election. The Jacobites certainly regarded the Union as a major political gift to them, for it handed them the leadership of nationalist sentiment in Scotland. That old Presbyterian nationalism, so typical of the last persuasive defenders of the independence of the Scottish state, was a dead cause after 1707. Fletcher of Saltoun had no doubts in 1703 that the English and Dutch would have to assist the Scots 'against any party who set up in our country for the pretended King James VIII' but he added 'though if our own people be at liberty, there will be no need of foreign auxiliaries'.[15] After 1707 only force could reverse the decision that the English state should absorb Scotland, and only Jacobites were prepared to give a lead in resorting to force to break the Union. They had nothing to lose.

At the same time, it is clear that Jacobite opinion was over-sanguine in expecting to be able to cash in at once on the unpopularity of the Union. Here the best source is Colonel Nathaniel Hooke (1664–1738), a man educated at Dublin, Glasgow and Cambridge who had at one time been the principal London agent for the unsuccessful rebellion against James II and VII mounted by the Protestant Duke of Monmouth in south-west England. Turning right round in his allegiances, Hooke became a devoted servant of James. He served under Dundee in 1689 and then became a Jacobite secret agent in Ireland, Flanders and Scotland. In 1707 he was on his second mission to Scotland, observing at first hand the 'great discontent and hearty dislike of the nation' towards the Treaty of Union. However, anyone who reads the account of Hooke's dealings with the magnates of Scotland provided by Hooke himself, will do well to keep a straight face. Hooke had all the egregious optimism of the professional political agent. Very few of the great men of Scotland were prepared totally to cold-shoulder the exiled dynasty. The main line of the Stewarts had come back from exile before. It might again. On the other hand very few noblemen were prepared actually to deal directly with Hooke. His narrative is a slapstick comedy of dealings through third parties due to the real or imaginary illnesses of principals. The Duke of Gordon refused to sign a memorial to the King of France asking for substantial military backing for a Jacobite rising, on the touching ground that he could not bear the thought of exposing the person of his dear exiled sovereign to the hazards of war.[16] The great Marquis of Montrose had always found Clan Gordon irritatingly addicted to fence-sitting in a crisis. It was a Gordon tradition, and a very sensible one too. The Union was not threatened by its unpopularity in Scotland as long as the Scots nobles, who had foisted it on their country, expected ultimately to benefit by it. Political unions are often primarily arrangements between ruling élites with a view to mutual benefit, usually with a substantial cash element in the benefit envisaged. The Union of 1707 was no exception.

Equally cynical was the outlook of the servants of the Most Christian King of France, Louis XIV, towards the Scottish problem in 1708. They were, of course, attracted by the idea of slipping James Francis Stewart, the self-styled James VIII and III, into Scotland. There he could be guaranteed to cause some sort of upheaval which, even if totally unsuccessful, would divert British troops and resources from Flanders where the Duke of Marlborough had recently confirmed the military ascendancy he had first seized at the Battle of Blenheim. In May 1706 Marlborough had led his Allied army into the mighty combat of Ramillies and had inflicted on the French commander the Marshal de Villeroi 'the most shameful, humiliating and disastrous of defeats'. Thus it is not surprising that Louis XIV himself and his Minister of Marine, Pontchartrain, planned to sponsor an invasion of Scotland by 'James VIII' early in 1708. Thirty vessels carrying six thousand French troops eventually set off from Dunkirk, that haven of privateers, in March. James had the bad luck to catch measles just before he was due to embark, but he eventually went aboard with all the enthusiasm of a nineteen-year-old bent on fulfilling his destiny. Neither the naval nor the military commanders of the expedition shared his zeal. The army commander, the Comte de Gacé, had to be bribed with the offer of both an ambassadorship and a marshal's baton should he reach Scotland before he would do his duty. Admiral the Comte Claude de Forbin, the supreme commander of the expedition, was even less keen on the business. Descended from a fourteenth-century Scots mercenary, Peter Forbes, who had settled in Marseilles, de Forbin had an extroverted Provençal temperament which led him to tell Louis XIV that he thought the whole scheme mad. Sent packing by his sovereign, de Forbin was convinced he was in charge of a mere Forlorn Hope, likely to be obliterated if ever brought to action.

Severely battered by storms, as it ploughed across the icy grey waters of the North Sea in winter, de Forbin's armada eventually cast anchor at the mouth of the Firth of Forth, opposite the small Fife ports of Crail and Pittenweem. For the soldiers cramped below decks it had been an appalling voyage. James himself and all his attendants had been horribly sick, but the sight of the sandstone cliffs between Crail and Pittenweem was a tonic to the exiled Stewart. It was as King of Scots that he meant to make his appeal after he landed. The proclamation he carried was an appeal by James VIII to the loyal people of his ancient realm of Scotland to break the Union with England. All other political arrangements were to be left to a free Parliament in Edinburgh. It was a shrewd political programme and in Stirlingshire Jacobite lairds were already marching around with armed followers, drinking the health of the Pretender and trying to raise the countryside. However, there was no response to the signals made by de Forbin at the mouth of the Forth, so when the English Admiral Byng came in sight with a superior squadron the French commander fled north, ignoring the despairing pleas of James that he be set ashore, anywhere, with only a few followers. Though Byng did capture one enemy ship (the *Salisbury*, an English prize re-used by the French), de Forbin had the advantage that most of his vessels were clean, fast Dunkirk privateers. He soon left the English warships behind, toyed with the idea of a landing near Inverness, and then under stress of bad weather swung on a northerly course right round Scotland and Ireland to return to Dunkirk. If the outward voyage had been bad, the homeward one was ghastly, being completed only with significant loss in lives and ships.

Perhaps it is unreasonable to ask an admiral to sacrifice his squadron. Forbin never meant to. Nevertheless it is intriguing to speculate what would have happened if the French ships had moved up the Forth to disembark their 5,000 infantry. The state of the defences of Scotland was simply shameful. There was no money, few troops, little ammunition. The Commander-in-Chief in Scotland, David Earl of Leven and Melville, reckoned that if the French landed his only course was to retire to Berwick. That Leven's despair was perfectly rational is underlined by the fact that after the whole affair was over Lord Haversham publicly lambasted the government's record in the House of Lords. There was no possible reply. Nothing underlined so clearly the fundamental lack of interest in Scotland displayed by post-Union English politicians than their willingness to strip it of the bare minimum of a garrison needed to contain quite small insurrections or invasion by tiny regular forces. In 1715 and 1745 they paid heavily for their policies. In 1708 they were just lucky.[17]

On the other hand, no great magnate or peer moved to support the handful of Jacobite lairds posturing around the eastern part of Stirlingshire. The Jacobite fleet was only off the Fife coast for an afternoon before Sir George Byng arrived, but its reception, or lack of it, suggests that the natural leaders of Scottish society were not ready for a rising. That is not to say that there was not a great deal of passive sympathy for the abortive rising. In November 1708 five lairds, James Stirling of Keir, Archibald Seton of Touch, Archibald Stirling of Carden, Charles Stirling of Kippendavie, and Patrick Edmonstone of Newton were tried for high treason in Edinburgh for their blatant Jacobite activity, spread over several days, in the previous March. Considering their open treason, there were astonishingly few witnesses: David Fenton, tavern-keeper at Dunkeld; John Macleran 'change-keeper' at Bridge of Turk; and Daniel Morison and

Peter Wilson, servants to the laird of Keir. These lesser mortals developed acute amnesia on the witness stand, recalling nothing more than erratic journeyings on the part of the accused. 'Not Proven', that splendid Scots verdict which means 'we think the correct verdict is guilty, but we cannot prove it' was the inevitable result. Even the accused found the proceedings amusing.[18]

This conspiracy of silence was to reappear after the much more serious rebellion in 1715. Curiously enough, the last Jacobite attempt, the 1745, also echoed the abortive '08 in a vital respect – the reliance on French privateers to transport the original expedition through the British naval screen. Nevertheless, at the time, the '08 seemed such a fiasco that the British government was genuinely clement in its handling of the aftermath. Nobody was executed, not even the few Scottish and Irish Jacobites captured on the *Salisbury*. Lord Griffin, one of these prisoners, was condemned to a traitor's death as a returned outlaw, but Queen Anne pardoned him, to the disgust of hard-line Whigs. Griffin died in prison a few years later. Where the government did show anger was in its handling of the Scots nobility, for the Earl of Leven, after the Pretender's departure, was ordered to conduct a swift and singularly indiscriminate round-up of potentially dangerous notables. He was then told to send them up to London, a move which enraged Scottish opinion, understandably, because those arrested included such impeccable Whigs and Presbyterians as Lord Belhaven, who was clearly being victimized for opposing the Union.

Other prisoners, like the Duke of Hamilton, had little difficulty in negotiating their own release as part of a rather sordid political deal. After all, there was absolutely no hard evidence against any of them. Men like the Earl Marischal and Viscount Kilsyth had actually started to negotia-ate the bargain which released them before they left Scotland for London. It was all tied up with the struggle to control the election of Scottish Representative Peers at the forthcoming General Election. At one point the Earl of Glasgow urged the release of Lords Aberdeen, Bute and Balmerino, on the grounds that nobody believed they had had a hand in the rebellion, and they were likely to vote for the Court interest to which Glasgow adhered.[19] Twenty-one of the twenty-two peers of Scotland dragged to London were eventually to return home. Belhaven died in London, after an emphatic protest against his arrest. His death was symbolic, just as was the fate of Andrew Fletcher of Saltoun who was, absurdly enough, taken into protective custody as a suspected Jacobite, but not deemed important enough to go to London.[20]

However, if Fletcher and Belhaven were left behind by history, the nobility and gentry of Scotland were, like the poor, something English politicians always had with them. Nor was the temper of the top segment of Scottish society much improved by the way it was being handled. What happened in the aftermath of the '08 was just an extreme case. The pressures which Westminster was routinely prepared to apply to leading Scots to secure compliance with the policies of the English ministry may be demonstrated from the archives of the House of Atholl. In August 1703 the Marquis of Atholl was created Duke of Atholl, Marquis of Tullibardine, Earl of Strathtay and Strathardle, Viscount Glenalmond and Glenlyon, with a patent ante-dated 30 June. It was the last sign of royal favour for a long time. This staunch Presbyterian and supporter of the Revolution gave his support in the Scots Parliament to the Act of Security, thereby mortally offending the Duke of Queensberry and the government interest.[21] Forewarned about the scheme to use Simon Fraser to implicate him in Jacobite plotting, Atholl managed to survive this crisis, though Queen Anne had to intervene to stop Atholl's heir Lord Tullibardine challenging Lord Stair to a duel because of the allegations Stair made against Atholl in council.[22] A threat to erect the estates of Stewart of Grantully into a regality, thereby challenging the Duke of Atholl's powers within his Perthshire jurisdictions, was fought off in April 1704, when the impending political eclipse of Queensberry as the result of the failure of the allegations of a 'Scotch Plot' placed the government in a weak position,[23] but by July 1704 Lord Godolphin, Queen Anne's principal English minister, was writing menacing letters to Atholl to the effect that Anne was deeply angry at 'your carriage in this session of parlt'.[24]

The deeply patriotic Atholl was unapologetic. He replied with dignity that he saw nothing disloyal in his insistence that before Scotland accepted the Hanoverian succession, there should be a satisfactory Anglo-Scottish settlement enshrined in a treaty. Prophetically Atholl insisted of the Hanoverian succession that:

> For as I was always convinced it was impracticable without a treaty, so if it could be done, it would be neither safe nor lasting.[25]

Dismissed as Privy Seal for his pains, Atholl reminded the Earl of Seafield, Secretary of State for Scotland, that the government had yet to pay him a farthing of salary or expenses for the duties he had performed while holding it. The duke added that he was comforted by a sense of loyalty to his queen and country (by which he meant Scotland) and hoped that the government would deal as honestly with him as he did with his own servants.[26] It was a fond hope. The Duke of Atholl remained primarily concerned with his Perthshire estates, guarding his markets with the usual squad of armed retainers, and inspecting his fencible men at a great muster at Huntingtower in June 1706. There is not the slightest evidence of serious Jacobite intrigue on his part. Indeed the closest the Duke of Atholl himself ever came to direct dealing with a Jacobite in this period was probably when he commissioned Mr Alexander Edward, parson of Kemback, Fife, to design a monument to his parents, the Marquis and Marchioness of Atholl. The commission had, of course, no political overtones, for the episcopal and Jacobite Edward was acceptable as a designer to the Presbyterian Scottish Whig Atholl. About the same time the duke can be found challenging Sir John Stewart of Grantully to a duel which was averted only by a timely apology from Sir John.[27]

The ducal temper was undoubtedly strained by the pressure to push the Act of Union through the Scots Parliament, a procedure of which the duke wholly disapproved. He was, quite rightly, disgusted when the English ministry, working through the Earl of Dunmore and the Lord Clerk Register of Scotland, had the impudence to try to bribe him not to turn up to the crucial 1706 session of the Scottish Parliament by suggesting that if he stayed away they might pay the backlog of salary due to him. The duke replied with great dignity that the regime must rate him cheap indeed to think that it could bribe him with his own.[28]

The regime was not, however, finished with its harassing of Atholl, for in the spring of 1708, during the 'scare' which accompanied an attempted Jacobite invasion, Atholl was cited to appear before the Scots Privy Council in Edinburgh. Pursued by government troops and run to ground in his ancestral fortress of Blair Castle, Atholl produced the ritual collection of physicians and ministers of religion who could usually be relied upon to testify that a Highland magnate was unfit to travel into the clutches of the government. From his sick quarters the duke bombarded Queen Anne and her ministers with requests for release and the removal of royal troops from his castle. By June 1708 the Duke of Atholl was complaining that he was High Sheriff of Perthshire, had taken every conceivable oath of loyalty to the government, and was now the only prisoner in Scotland not released on bail. He was released in July, just after his eldest son had sent him an account of his part in the British victory at Oudenarde in the Netherlands. The duke's Edinburgh agent, Mr Scott, and his man of business in the Highlands, Leonard Robertson of Straloch, were both arrested that summer and dragged up to London on suspicion of treasonable practices. Altogether it was a fitting culmination to a lengthy demonstration that the average English minister of the Crown was not very good at distinguishing between conscientious opposition to the will of Westminster and high treason.[29]

Oudenarde was an encounter battle which Marlborough could fight because de Forbin had fled the coast of Scotland. The Allied army could never have risked a decisive engagement had not the ten battalions of English infantry despatched from Ostend to the Tyne at the news of the attempted invasion of Scotland returned to Flanders. The vicious infantry battle in the marshes of Oudenarde, with Marlborough as supreme commander and Argyll as the fighting general who led the British infantry in the thick of the contest, seemed to confirm the unity and might of the new state forged by the Union of 1707. In fact what was happening in the minds of the Scots nobility and gentry in 1708 was the start of a very serious threat to the unity of that state. Atholl, for all his good reasons to despise Westminster, never budged from his Whig and Presbyterian commitment. It was far different with other members of his immediate family, but it would be wrong to see their change of loyalties in too parochial a light. They were part of a general swing of significant Scottish opinion. Perhaps the best approach to an understanding of that swing is through one simple fact. The Scots Privy Council, which issued the legal documents enabling Leven to conduct his unfortunate preventative arrests, was itself already under sentence of extinction.

This was an extraordinary and very dangerous situation. The Treaty of Union had clearly envisaged the continuation of the Scots Privy Council, or its replacement by an even more effective body. It was the executive government of Scotland, the one body capable of responding reasonably quickly and efficiently to serious threats to law and order. Since the departure of the King of Scots to richer pastures in the south in 1603 its importance had been greater than ever before, and in the unstable political atmosphere obtaining in Scotland after 1707 it was very necessary in its primary function as the supreme guardian of public order. Technical arguments were advanced why the Scots Privy Council should go. It was alleged that it was redundant since the British Privy Council had jurisdiction in Scotland. This was specious reasoning since the British body was remote and did not have the executive capacity of the Scottish one. A few dogmatists like the Earl of Marchmont wanted to abolish any institution which was a reminder that Scotland had once been an independent kingdom. However, there is no doubt that the decision to abolish the Privy Council was in reality almost entirely due to the mechanics of the struggle for power at Westminster.

The government was led by Marlborough's ally Godolphin, with the Duke of Queensberry as principal manager of Scotland for the Court interest. Faced with vociferous English Tory opposition to an increasingly unpopular Continental war Godolphin was forced to rely on the support of the group formed around 'the Junto' of five Whig peers – Lord Somers and the Earls of Wharton, Halifax, Orford and Sunderland. Godolphin, characteristically, was doing his best to make as few concessions as possible to the Junto lords in exchange for their support. The upshot was to present a fortuitous opportunity to that handful of Scots M.P.s and peers still known as the Squadrone. Though in favour of the Union, the Squadrone was at odds with Queensberry and it was afraid that he would use the formidable influence of the Scots Privy Council against them at the next general election. As the Junto leadership was looking for an issue on which it could punish Godolphin for his meanness, the Squadrone was able to put together a quite cynical alliance of itself, the opposition Tories, and the Junto. The Scottish Privy Council died, despite the efforts of Godolphin and his colleagues such as the young Robert Walpole to save it.[30]

One of the Scottish law officers, the Lord Advocate, provided a partial and unsatisfactory substitute for some of the functions of the deceased Privy Council, but the bulk of the Scots aristocracy were angry with good reason and on a scale regarded as prejudicial to the stability of the Union. Quite apart from the practical difficulties created by the decision, it severed important links between the government and the Scots nobility, a considerable number of whom had traditionally always held Privy Councillorships. Merely as patronage these posts were not to be despised. More significant was the fact that because of them the old Privy Council had provided an arena for continuing vitally necessary dialogue between government and the leaders of the regional communities which were the basic building blocks of Scotland. Nor was it pleasing to the natural rulers of the Scottish regions that one of the offices which the government tried to build up in the aftermath of the abolition of the Privy Council was that of justice of the peace.

Within the framework of the traditional Scottish polity there was no place for an English-style Commission of the Peace working in the way it worked in England. There it was the most important single administrative institution in the English counties. Unpaid local gentlemen acting as justices of the peace after being nominated to the Commission by their sovereign were the real rulers of most of England and the essential mechanism whereby the will of the central government was made effective in the provinces. In Scotland there were just too many other jurisdictions, most of them hereditary, from the omnipresent baron courts to the mighty regalities. There was no space for a justice of the peace to spread his wings. James VI had introduced them to Scotland by an act of 1587 which is perhaps best seen as part of his policy of bringing Scottish society closer to the norms of the English society which he was so anxious eventually to rule. The provisions of the 1587 act seem never to have become generally effective. In 1609, six years after he had left Scotland for the south, James secured the passage through the Scots legislature of an act confirming and extending the provisions of the 1587 act. The text of the 1609 act establishing justices of the peace is a remarkable piece of vituperation. It raves about the brutal custom of deadly feuds and the general depravity of the lieges. Modestly it points out that no solution could be found until King James 'bending the excellent wisdome and rare graces of his royall mynd (wheirwith God hes indewit him mair abundantlie than any king that evir did regne in this iland)' had condescended to secure legislation against feuds and now further legislation reinforcing the office of justice of the peace, itself a sovereign remedy against continued disorder.[31]

The remarkable fact is that generations of historians have been willing to take this impudent royal propaganda more or less at its face value. Its very words are suspiciously similar to passages in the *Basilikon Doron* and other earlier products of the royal pen, and the text of the legislation would be finalized by the Lords of the Articles, a committee of royal nominees who virtually usurped the authority of the Scottish Parliament. In the Highlands and Islands much the most irresponsible, trouble-making, disruptive and generally bloody-minded influence was in fact the policies of James VI. In the Lowlands the royal record was mercifully better, but even there the act of 1609 was ineffective. From 1641 to 1655 justices of the peace found no place in Scottish administration, but in the latter year the English occupying regime, which had abolished heritable jurisdictions, re-established them, with real powers. They were particularly charged to curb moral offences such as cursing, swearing, mocking at piety, and so on, which may help to explain why their powers largely lapsed in 1660 at the Restoration. Thereafter they were minor figures, agents of the Scottish Privy Council. Simply to operate the post-1707 Customs and Excise system effectively, it was essential to give the justices more power, as they were an important part of its punitive side. However, the abolition of the Privy Council was rapidly followed by the granting to Scottish justices of the peace of exactly the same powers as were exercised by their historically much more significant fellow-justices in England. There is no doubt that the Commission of the Peace for a given county could be marked by political bias. That for Lanarkshire immediately after 1707, for example, was dominated by the Carmichael interest led by the Earl of Hyndford and his sons, James Lord Carmichael, William Carmichael, and Daniel Carmichael of Mauldsley. As first President elected by a session of the justices in Lanark Tolbooth, Hyndford was able to nominate two men of his name, James and John Carmichael, as Clerk of the Peace and Constable of the Shire respectively.[32]

The justices were expected to administer oaths of loyalty to persons suspected of Jacobite leanings, but they could also come into conflict with old-fashioned Whigs. The Earl of Selkirk (a younger son of the ducal house of Hamilton) was a staunch supporter of the Glorious Revolution, to the point of having crossed to Ireland with King William to fight at the Battle of the Boyne. He was also a fervent Scots patriot, having strenuously opposed the Union in the Scottish Parliament. He was, of course, out of favour under Queen Anne. His appointment as Lord Clerk Register was terminated and in 1709 the justices of the peace of Lanark were pursuing his chamberlain in the parish of Crawfordjohn, James Gray in Ballgray, for forcibly refusing to allow Robert Lang, minister of the parish, access to the manse. Here the justices were backing up the presbytery of Lanark, but even so strongly Presbyterian a clergyman as the Reverend Robert Wodrow, librarian of Glasgow University, regarded the growth in the significance of the justices of the peace as an index of the erosion of local liberty.[33] Like Fletcher of Saltoun, Belhaven, Atholl, or Selkirk, Wodrow spoke for a dying cause – Presbyterian nationalism. At the time of the decisive debate on the Union he had told one correspondent that

> this is the most dismall aspect ane incorporating union has to me, that it putts matters past help. Though many a time we have been over run and our civil and religious rights invaded, yet at the nixt turn we had them restored some way, as 1572, 1638, 1688. But nou, once lost, ever lost.[34]

His resignation at the prospect of the reduction of an ancient kingdom to a province was not shared by his Jacobite fellow-countrymen, least of all by the significant number of that persuasion who accepted nomination to Commissions of the Peace after 1707.

It was not at all unreasonable for holders of heritable jurisdictions to feel that there was a long-term conspiracy against their rights. There were too many signs of the underlying hostility of the British government to the whole system. For example, after the Union the High Court of Justiciary in Edinburgh just assumed the power of reviewing sentences in regality courts in causes criminal. There was no statutory authority for this development. Even more than the attempt to build up the role of justices of the peace, it was a straw in the wind.[35] It is difficult for our minds to grasp the significance of jurisdiction in an early modern society, yet when Hugh O'Neil Earl of Tyrone launched his great rebellion in Ulster against the Elizabethan government of Ireland, the immediate cause had been the determination of that government to impose English sheriffs on the Gaelic lordships of Ulster. The final act in that tragedy – the flight of the Northern earls in the early seventeenth century – seems to have been rooted in the conviction of the Ulster earls that no understanding with King James VI and I was possible if they were deprived of jurisdiction over their people.[36] The Scots nobles of the early eighteenth century, Protestant and English-speaking as they nearly all were, lived in a world not wholly different from that of Elizabeth's Earl of Tyrone.

The nobility and gentry of England rejoiced in two basic safeguards against the abuse of executive power within their relatively centralized legal and political system. Not only did they, as justices of the peace, provide the key local agents of government, but they had also established the landed interest as the preponderant partner within the central organs of government. However much individuals might be victimized, the class-interests of the landed ascendancy were ultimately safe until major economic change altered the balance of social power. It was therefore doubly unfortunate that just when the Scots nobility were becoming worried about the security of their local jurisdictions, they also experienced a major blow to their hopes of adequate participation in the British legislature. The natural objective for an ambitious Scots magnate after 1707 was a British peerage. The peerage of England, like that of Scotland, had been closed in 1707. Argyll had been granted the English earldom of Greenwich in 1705, but Queensberry had been rewarded in 1708 with a dukedom of Dover in the new British peerage, the sole source of future titles. As well as the sixteen representative peers, Scots nobles naturally assumed that they would be represented in the House of Lords by those of their number who secured British titles. It was therefore a serious matter when political circumstances threatened to close the latter avenue of advancement.

Queensberry had sat in the House of Lords by virtue of his British peerage and the only restriction placed on him by that chamber came in 1709, when it ruled that he was not entitled to vote in the election of the representative sixteen. Despite this, when the importunities of the Duke of Hamilton secured for himself a patent as Baron Dutton and Duke of Brandon in the British peerage in 1711, his right to take his seat in the Lords was challenged. In strictly legal terms the attempt to stop Hamilton from taking his seat was indefensible. What gave it edge was the political situation. Robert Harley, Earl of Oxford and head of a predominantly Tory government, was trying to secure parliamentary approval for the highly controversial settlement of a great Continental war which was finally enshrined in the Treaty of Utrecht in 1713. The opposition Whigs, though clamorous and bitter, knew that the government had a safe majority in the Commons. The position in the Lords was a different matter, and the way in which the government had in 1710 manipulated the election of the sixteen representative peers by securing the return of what was effectively an official list created grave suspicions in the House of Peers that any additional Scots would be government tools. Late in 1711 the upper chamber firmly excluded Scots peers who subsequently sought admission on the strength of British titles. This did not stop Queen Anne from creating a dozen new peers (including the heir to the Scots Earl of Kinnoull) to secure the peace preliminaries, but it left Scots peers with British titles in the absurd position that they could neither use their British title as a means of entry to the Lords, nor vote for the sixteen. Not until 1782 was the verdict of 1711 reversed.[37]

The crisis over Hamilton's British peerage was seen at the time as a threat to the Union. Though no doubt there was an element of bluster in the public expressions of anger by Scots peers, the brutal fact is that the Earl of Mar, perhaps the most articulate spokesman for the irate Scots nobility, did go on to lead the greatest of all Jacobite rebellions. The determination of the House of Lords to put parliamentary tactics before legality and common sense was deeply provocative. In July 1711 Mar had assured Oxford that though he personally was 'not yett wearie of the Union', an adverse decision on the peerage issue would be 'contrair to all sense, reason and fair dealing'. Mar continued 'and if our trade be no more encuradg'd than yett it has been, or indeed is like to be, how is it possible that flesh and blood can bear it? and what Scotsman will not be Wearie of the Union, and do all he can to get quit of it?'[38] The question was rhetorical, but shrewd, and it brought out the way in which political and economic discontents were intertwined in the minds of influential Scotsmen. It was no accident that it was on an economic issue that the Scots peers in the House of Lords chose to make their major demonstration against the way the Union was working out.

On the eve of the conclusion of the Treaty of Utrecht in 1713 the British government announced a plan to levy an equal duty on malt in Scotland and England. The Scots were enraged, for three excellent reasons. First, the Treaty of Union exempted Scotland from contributing to the costs of the war, but the new tax was expressly designed to meet those costs. Secondly, the Treaty specifically exempted the Scots from a tax on malt during the war, which was not at an end. Thirdly the Act of Union specified that future taxes be fairly apportioned, yet the annual value of the Scots barley crop was a mere fraction of the value of the English one, so an equal tax was unjust. Scots M.P.s and peers stood solid against the tax and agreed that a motion to dissolve the Union be moved in the House of Lords. Seafield (by this time Earl of Findlater), a major architect of the Union, now moved its dissolution, on the grounds that it was exacerbating Anglo-Scottish relations. The vote showed fifty-four peers present on either side and the deadlock was resolved only by a slender majority of proxies (17 to 14) against the motion.[39] Sophisticated men like the Scots peers knew perfectly well that such a proposal would never pass the Commons. The government carried its legislation for the malt tax, but secretly agreed not to apply the tax to Scotland. So far, the demonstration had been successful. What it failed to convey was the fact that the expressions of general discontent were not a mere tactical device.

The trading classes of Scotland were as bitterly discontented as many of the nobles. They had made a quick killing at the very start of the Union by exploiting the fact that though Union was certain by February 1707, it did not become operative until 1 May 1707. In between they imported large quantities of goods such as tobacco and French wines, exploiting the fact that Scottish tariffs were much lower than English ones to sell the same goods at a large profit behind the English tariff barriers, which applied to the whole of Britain from May onwards. Much resented as this behaviour was by the English legislature, it was unrepeatable, and very rapidly the boot was on the other foot. The imposition on Scotland of a Customs and Excise system on the English model came as an appalling shock for two reasons. First the Scots were simply not acquainted with such an authoritarian state bureaucracy at local level. Their own customs had been auctioned off to tacksmen always willing to wink for a consideration or a friend, and not exactly over-endowed with the physical means of law-enforcement. The Town Council of Dundee in the seventeenth century, for example, resolved never to lease a particular public warehouse to the tacksmen of the customs, on the ground that it would 'discourage' local merchants if the tacksmen gained so convenient a facility.[40] Secondly, it can be argued that the economic assumptions and objectives embedded in the English tariff structure were simply inappropriate for the Scottish situation in the early eighteenth century.

After the accession of William III to the English throne in 1688 there had been a spectacular increase in the level of protection in that country. The general level of duties on the import trade roughly quadrupled between 1690 and 1704. All other changes in tariff structure in the next eighty years were of minor importance compared with this rise. From the 1690s French goods were prohibited on the grounds that France and England were at war, but the system did include some rather extraordinary drawback arrangements (i.e. provision for the repayment of import duties if a commodity was re-exported) which could actually allow raw materials to be sold more cheaply abroad than at home. This nonsense, along with such anomalies as taxation of exports, was only dealt with in 1722 by Sir Robert Walpole, but at the same time he strengthened the overall pattern of protection.[41] French claret, the national drink of Scotland (much more so than whisky), was heavily taxed and discouraged in favour of the heavier sweeter port wine of England's Ancient Ally (and satellite), Portugal. However, it was not only the French trade of Scotland which suffered, but also her important Dutch trade. The English Acts of Navigation, which began under the republican regime of the Interregnum but which were re-enacted and extended by the Restoration governments after 1660, were specifically aimed at the Dutch carrying trade. Dutch ships frequented Scots harbours less frequently after 1707. Scots east-coast ports, especially those in south Fife, could continue to export coal to Holland, but importing Dutch paper, soap, machinery, or gin was much discouraged, and the use of cheap Dutch shipping was in many trades just forbidden.

The new fiscal system cut across long-standing trading patterns. In Dundee, the family of Wedderburn of Blackness was both landed and mercantile, and it had a long tradition of involvement in business dealings with the Netherlands. The Notarial Archives of Amsterdam contain the grant of a power of attorney, dated 26 December 1663, to Sir Alexander Wedderburn of Blackness, to enable him to collect debts in Dundee on behalf of a merchant then in Amsterdam. Sir Alexander (1610–75) was Town Clerk of Dundee when he died in 1675. His son became the first baronet of Blackness, while Sir Alexander, fourth baronet of Blackness (1675–1744) was Town Clerk of Dundee in 1715, being deposed as the result of his open sympathy for the Jacobite rebellion of that year. His career is a classical illustration of the close links between the Scots burghal patriciates and the landed gentry.[42]

Behind the protective system of England lay an assumption that it was possible thereby to accelerate the development of England's trade and manufactures to the point where they matched or surpassed those of the most sophisticated of European nations. Though pre-industrial, early eighteenth-century England was, compared with the rest of Europe, heavily urbanized, and possessed an exceptionally large commercial sector in its economy, not to mention significant enclaves of industrial activity. Scotland was quite different, and the vast scale of smuggling in Scotland after 1707 was in effect an assertion of the economic facts of life. When Scotsmen alleged that all the thieves in England had come north to man the new Customs and Excise services they maligned both the character and the composition of a service which included plenty of Scots, as well as the inevitable English experts. What Scots critics were really saying was that it was still probably the best option open to them to continue to exchange the products of their agricultural, fishing, and extractive industries for the luxuries and sophisticated manufactures of the Continent.

One illustration of this point was the Scottish wool trade. The export of raw wool had always been a valuable aspect of Scottish commerce providing foreign currency needed to buy vital imports. From the Restoration period attempts were made to encourage a fine woollen goods manufacture in Scotland, and the handful of companies set up for this purpose, all state-supported and heavily dependent on expensive foreign craftsmen, pressed for a ban on the export of wool and the import of cloth. The idea was to deny raw material to foreign rivals while preserving the domestic market in fine woollen goods for home firms. The large domestic market for coarse woollens was almost entirely in Scottish hands and remained so after 1707. By 1704 the landed interest in Scotland had fought back successfully to confirm its right to export wool, while the native fine wool manufacturers were consoled with a ban on the import of foreign cloth and a more realistic concession in the shape of the exemption of exported Scottish woollen cloth from duty. The Act of Union was bound to disturb this balance of power, for the English Parliament was adamant in enforcing a total prohibition on the export of wool in order to deprive foreign manufacturers of raw material. The woollen industry was England's traditional staple. It is hardly surprising that after the Union the Scottish fine woollen industry was largely destroyed by cheaper, better English imports.[43] Even allowing for the importance of coarse woollens, where Scots domestic manufacture seems to have fared well, the Scots were not as successful as the Irish, whose woollen industry virtually drove English imports off the Irish market in the early eighteenth century.[44] To add injury to insult, from the point of view of the Scots nobility, the ban on the export of wool in 1707 was followed by a sharp fall in Scottish wool prices.

Smuggling was the inevitable result. At a very early stage in the history of the new Customs service the Customs Board in Edinburgh was circulating the Collector and Controller at Dundee to the effect that he must be vigilant against the importation of foreign wool-working equipment.[45] About seven months later the same official received, in March 1709, a blistering circular from the Board to the effect that his slackness was depriving them of vital intelligence, and urging him to a more active zeal in Queen Anne's service.[46] He appears to have borne these thunders with commendable fortitude, but by June 1712 the Board was expressing its dissatisfaction at the scale of the clandestine export of sheepskins with wool attached. Not only was the revenue cheated but foreign rivals were also being supplied with vital raw material.[47] It was a very familiar tale, and the economic calculations behind it were not confined to wool.

On the import side there were manufactures which were virtually unobtainable in Scotland, were costly when brought in from England, and which could with advantage, if illegally, be procured elsewhere. In August 1708 the Edinburgh Board was waxing indignant that French paper was being smuggled in quantity into Scotland from the Netherlands despite the state of war which existed between Britain and France.[48] Yet this was to be expected. Even in 1712 there were only seven paper-making firms in Scotland as compared with 209 in England, Wales and Berwick-on-Tweed, and the Scots had a long tradition of importing paper from the more advanced industries of France, Holland, and Germany.[49] All along the eastern coast of Scotland an old economy based on the exchange of goods across the North Sea was thus struggling against the new British protectionism. In itself such smuggling was not necessarily a breeder of Jacobitism, but where it was combined with a burgh in which Episcopal sentiment was strong, and where the surrounding lairds tended to be disaffected to the House of Hanover, it was another element in a witches' brew bubbling towards the boiling point of rebellion.

Montrose was just such a burgh. Because the export of grain and salmon had always been an important part of its economy, the links between its merchant class and the lairds were unusually strong. Indeed its leading merchants partly to secure grain and fresh-water fishing rights had for generations been the lairds in the landward area. Episcopalianism flourished there. So did Jacobitism. The Board in Edinburgh was never very happy about the efficiency of the local Customs and Excise officers, but it knew that the immensely complex regulations which they had to administer bred endless bad blood, if only because of the opportunities which they offered for dishonesty.[50] In particular the fact that certain imported commodities earned refund of duty or subsidies on re-exportation was a permanent incitement to skulduggery. Foreign salt used to cure fish sent for export was the classic example. Article 18 of the Treaty of Union is mostly about salt. Salt was imported because the product of Scotland's own seaside, coal-fired salt pans was not of high enough quality for curing fish destined for export. Stored in bonded warehouses, the foreign salt was issued on the giving of security for the payment of a heavy duty within six months. However, a cargo of fish exclusively cured with such salt earned a drawback (or repayment of duty) when exported. Scottish salt also earned a drawback when it was exported. The officials of the Customs and Excise service knew very well that many cargoes were surreptitiously re-landed after nominal departure for foreign parts.[51] Other obvious devices included the refusal to pay full duty on such colonial products as tobacco, on the grounds that a high proportion of the cargo had been ruined during the long voyage across the Atlantic. Shortly afterwards drawback would be brazenly demanded as 'hopelessly damaged' tobacco was re-exported.[52] Allied to the positive boom in honest smuggling, such incidents bred not only bad feeling but also violence to the point where the Edinburgh Board in early 1714 was trying to persuade the Commander-in-Chief Scotland to move troops into the Montrose area. The Board had just been favoured with an account of how a mob had 'deforced' the local Customs officers by relieving them of a quantity of smuggled brandy which they had seized.[53]

Ironically, in the face of all this seething political and economic discontent in Scotland, the principal talent displayed by English politicians was a rare knack for upsetting and irritating those groups in 'North Britain' which might reasonably be considered loyal backers of the Union. The outstanding example here was the ministry of the established Church of Scotland. Presbyterian clergymen were clearly divided over the desirability of the Union, but the most influential among them were strongly for it, and after 1707 all clergy of that persuasion were effectively prisoners of the Union cause. A successful Jacobite-led rebellion against the Union was bound to involve the overthrow of the existing constitution of the Kirk, in favour of that Episcopalianism which was the creed of most Jacobites. It was highly significant that the declaration which the Pretender carried with him in '08 offered no guarantees to the existing ecclesiastical establishment in Scotland. That establishment assumed that the guarantees given to it in the Union settlement necessarily involved an acceptance of the concepts, enshrined in its Westminster Confession of Faith, that it had a right to legislate on matters ecclesiastic for the whole Scots nation and that the civil power was bound to help enforce that legislation. Hence the readiness of the General Assembly of the Kirk to legislate against liturgical innovation when the influence of the English Non-Jurors was leading Scots Episcopalians to adopt a 'higher' form of service (hitherto Episcopal and Presbyterian services had been broadly similar). Hence also the willingness of Edinburgh Town Council to detain the Reverend James Greenshields as a prisoner in the Tolbooth when he refused to obey an order of the Presbytery of Edinburgh that he desist from using the English Book of Common Prayer at his Episcopal services. The Court of Session concurred in the action of the magistrates.

Greenshields' successful appeal to the House of Lords not only established the principle that such appeals were allowable, but was also rapidly followed by the passing of an Act of Toleration in March 1712. Passed by a rampantly intolerant Anglican Tory majority at Westminster this legislation granted complete freedom of worship to any clergyman willing, like Greenshields, to forswear the Pretender, pray for Queen Anne, and take an oath of loyalty to the government. Presbyterians had great difficulty over the oath, because of its blatant Erastianism. It seemed to assume that, like everything else, religion was at the absolute disposal of Westminster. In the very next month of 1712 the point was underlined when legislation restored lay patronage in the Church of Scotland, despite protest from the General Assembly. Since 1690 appointments had been in the hands of elders and heritors, subject to congregational veto, and it is a fact that every single split and secession of consequence in the Church of Scotland up to 1843 can be traced back to the mischievous patronage legislation of 1712.

For once the Scots nobility were not offended. They regarded the Patronage Act as mildly useful. Yet the overall effect was to put out of countenance the Presbyterian interest, while encouraging Scots Episcopalians, many of whom were, of course, patrons of livings in the Kirk. Parliament, dominated in the latter years of Queen Anne by a High-Anglican Tory spirit, was simply incapable of appreciating the extent to which Scots Episcopalians were uncompromising Jacobites. Westminster, ever quick to blame a crisis in a peripheral region of the United Kingdom on anyone but itself, tended to see in Scotland fellow Anglicans persecuted and provoked by a boorish Presbyterian ascendancy. However, a man like William Smyth, the last Episcopal minister of Moneydie in Perthshire, was not just an admirer of the English liturgy which he was accused of reading, illegally, in 1709 at the funeral of Mr Patrick Strachan, late incumbent of Mains. Smyth was an ejected Jacobite Episcopalian, a son-in-law of a former Bishop of Galloway, and acted as chaplain to the family of Threipland of Fingask, to which he was related. The nature of Smyth's doctrine may be deduced from the record of those close to him. Sir David Threipland of Fingask was a Jacobite active in the 1715 rebellion. Smyth's own son James became a physician. Sir Stuart Threipland, heir to Sir David and christened by William Smyth, became President of the Royal College of Physicians of Edinburgh. James Smyth was a convinced Jacobite 'out' in both the '15 and the '45. He joined the latter along with a clergyman called Robert Lyon, sometime pastor to an Episcopal meeting house managed by Smyth. Lyon became chaplain to Lord Ogilvie's Regiment and was executed for treason at Penrith in 1746. Smyth died in his bed in 1765, probably unrepentant.[54]

Individual conviction was obviously the ultimate determinant of a man's adhesion or non-adhesion to the Jacobite cause, but it is intriguing to notice how far conviction tended to correspond with the particular circumstances a man had to face. A good example is the Arbuthnot family of Kincardineshire which split between Unionists and Jacobites. Alexander Arbuthnot, minister of Arbuthnot in Kincardineshire from 1662 to 1689, was deposed for Jacobitism. The second of his eight sons, Robert, fought for King James at Killiecrankie before retiring to Rouen where he became a merchant active in Franco–Scottish trade, a bitter foe of the Union, and an active supporter of the 1715 rebellion, to which he sent such supplies as a rich French merchant could. He was a banker and later was the Pretender's recognized Paris agent. The family was distantly related to the Earls Marischal, so it had all the flavour of a classic Jacobite household. Yet Robert's older brother John, a physician who qualified in Aberdeen and St Andrews, was a well-known London literary figure, the cherished friend of Pope, Swift and Gay, and indeed the man whose writings fixed the character of that symbol of all things British – John Bull. One wonders if the good doctor would have developed so differently from his Jacobite brothers but for a happy accident at Epsom when he was called in to prescribe for Prince George of Denmark, the uninspiring but fertile spouse of Queen Anne. By 1705 he was physician to Anne and his professional fortune was made.[55]

Doctor John actually preached a sermon at the Mercat Cross of Edinburgh in December 1706, in defence of the Union. His text was Ecclesiastes x.27: 'Better is he that laboureth and aboundeth in all things, than he that boasteth himself and wanteth bread.' London politicians, their Scots associates, and their propagandists like Defoe and Arbuthnot laboured to create a conviction that the Union would bring instant and substantial economic benefits to Scotland. The concept was even written into Article 15 of the Treaty of Union which refers to 'the Increase of Trade and People (which shall be the happy consequence of the Union)'. In that sense the Union debate closely resembled the debate about the British Common Market entry in the 1960s and was followed by the same sort of anti-climax. For the politicians what mattered was securing the irreversible political decision they wanted, and economic disappointment, though vexing, was not ultimately important. Hence the casual way in which Queen Anne's ministers threw away opportunities to conciliate Scots opinion after 1707. That part of the Equivalent needed mainly to pay off the stockholders of the Company of Scotland Trading to Africa and the Indies and to compensate those who lost by the substitution of English currency for Scottish was paid over so late that it was greeted in Edinburgh by indignant stone-throwing mobs. Moneys set aside for the promotion of industry in Scotland by the Treaty of Union and other legislation was simply not made available for this purpose before 1727. Behind all this lay not so much malice as financial stringency and political insensitivity.

The very form of the Treaty of Union, with its emphasis on terms and perpetual guarantees, shows that Scotsmen did not understand in 1707 that they were about to be absorbed into a political system rooted in a concept of uncontrollable legislative absolutism. Legal niceties, in the last analysis, meant nothing to Westminster compared with its own will-to-power. This was abundantly clear with respect to Anglo-Irish relations in the early eighteenth century. William Molyneux, the Irish Whig, philosopher and publicist, and a close friend of John Locke, the great English Whig political philosopher, had pointed out as early as 1698 that there was no legal basis for the way the English legislature had usurped the power wielded by the King-in-Council over Ireland before 1690. Threats of impeachment against Molyneux and retrospective legislative assertion of their power over Ireland in 1719 were the predictable responses of the men at Westminster. By 1715 many members of the Scottish ruling class were convinced that their position was not dissimilar from one they had long dreaded – that of the Protestant gentry of Ireland.[56]

In the archives of the Dukes of Atholl there is a contemporary copy or draft with corrections of an address or petition presented by the leading men of Perthshire, through the Duke of Atholl, to King George I in 1715. The address was presented by Atholl in his capacity as Sheriff Principal of the county, and it was penned for men who professed to rejoice in the guarantee of a Protestant succession secured by the happy accession of their new Hanoverian sovereign. It is a petition for the dissolution of the Union on the ground that the advantages expected from it have turned out to be imaginary while the disadvantages threaten to ruin Scotland. The document lists the difficulties facing Scots woollens, the discrimination against Scots linen, and the increase in taxation burdens, all the more irritating when the moneys due to Scotland under the Rising Equivalent were being withheld. It complains about the loss of ultimate judicial autonomy with the establishment of appeals to the House of Lords, while stating that 'There is scarce the face of a Government left amongst us' due to the abolition of such institutions as the Scots Privy Council. The petition thunders against the political emasculation of the Scots peerage by the judgement of the House of Lords in the Brandon case. It states that the great bulk of Scots were hostile to Union even in 1707, admits that there may have been a threat to the Protestant Succession in 1713 when the last bid to repeal the Union occurred, but insists that there is now none and asks George I to restore the Scottish state. Some exaggeration of language apart, the petition is a recital of fact.[57] It was no doubt regarded as a bad joke by the London political establishment of the day, but those who find that the force of their argument is ignored are liable to resort to the argument of force. Most alarming of all was the fact that in parts of England, as well as in Scotland, men were moving towards the idea that the most effective kind of petition, when dealing with Westminster, was an armed demonstration.

5 Roots of Rebellion I—the 1715 in England

In all ages successful rebels cease to be rebels in the eyes of the law. They become patriots, heroic revolutionaries or counter-revolutionaries. So far from fearing the law, they may choose to use it against supporters of the overthrown establishment. However, nobody other than a born fool could feel absolutely confident of success when embarking on rebellion against an early eighteenth-century British government. The fortunes of war are notoriously fluctuating. The Royal Navy was a formidable obstruction to aid from abroad, and British governments usually maintained large military forces, albeit much of their strength was liable to be deployed on the continent of Europe. After the Treaty of Ryswick of 1697, which put an end to one great cycle of conflict, the English military establishment had been hastily run down to a 'guards and garrison' strength of a mere 7,000 men. However Louis XIV, when he quixotically recognized in September 1701 the son of the recently dead James II as 'James III' of Great Britain, virtually declared war on William III and enabled that monarch to initiate a rapid build-up of the army which continued under his successor Queen Anne. The War of the Spanish Succession lasted from 1702 to 1713. It saw British forces peak in 1711 at no less than 75,000 men, though by 1713, with peace imminent, the total with the colours had fallen to 23,000. At the accession of George I in August 1714 the British establishment maintained only 8,000 effective troops. Ireland maintained another 12,000 on a separate establishment, and by July 1715, with political tension mounting, orders were issued in Britain for the raising of thirteen regiments of dragoons and eight infantry regiments. Five dragoon and eight foot regiments were moved from Ireland to Britain, while the Irish government used its power to raise similar units to replace the draft. All this does not mean that the British military establishment in late 1715 was adequate to meet any likely challenge. It was not. The point is that the British government, like most contemporary European governments, was much concerned about and expert in military matters.[1]

Failure was therefore always the likeliest destiny of a rebellion, and failure implied for those involved the hazards of the statutory pains and penalties for treason. Before 1708 the Scots laws of treason were relatively clear and comparatively humane. Treason was an assault on the majesty of the state (*crimen majestatis*), either directly by, say, intending the death of the sovereign, or indirectly by attacking his judges. Certain offences, though not in their nature treasonable, were regarded as so heinous that statute declared they should be punished as if they were treason. Major economic crimes like setting fire to coal heughs (*anglice* pits) or standing crops (with the very real danger of local dearth resulting) came into this latter category. Treason was punished by death, and by forfeiture to the Crown of the traitor's estate, both real and personal. However, such forfeiture did not cut off the right of creditors, tacksmen (leaseholders), feudal superiors, vassals, heirs of entail, or widows of the forfeiting individuals. After the abortive '08 rising and the débâcle in the Scottish courts when the attempt to prosecute the Stirlingshire lairds broke down, the British legislature set out to replace the treason laws of Scotland by those currently in force in England.

In 1709 this was done by the significantly named 'Act for improving the Union of the Two Kingdoms', commonly known as 'the Treason Act' (7 Anne c. 21). As a result, the non-treasonable acts deemed statutory treason by the former law were declared simply capital crimes, while treason proper was subject to the forms of trial and penalties of English law. The latter were uniquely beastly even by the standards of a casually brutal age. Traitors were drawn on a hurdle to the place of execution. They were hung for a few minutes only before being cut down, alive but choking, to be castrated and disembowelled. Ideally they were to see their entrails burned before their eyes before being hacked into the several pieces which were subsequently displayed publicly for the terror of others. A 'gracious' sovereign might remit parts of the sentence, but the whole penalty was always available and not infrequently enforced. That contemporaries looked on it as revolting and unworthy of a civilized government is proved by the violence of Scottish resistance to the proposal that it be introduced into Scotland. Equally disturbing to an age which thought in dynastic terms, and equally barbarous, was the further concept of 'corruption of blood' which visited upon the family of the traitor penalties which a humane jurisprudence reserved for the criminal alone and which called in question the succession to landed estates.[2] It is not surprising that Scots M.P.s and Representative Peers unanimously opposed the Treason Act. Dropped by the Commons the bill was pressed by the House of Lords and finally rammed through, as the Earl of Mar ruefully remarked to his brother the Lord Justice Clerk of Scotland a couple of years later, 'against the Scots members of both Houses'.[3]

With such horrendous penalties awaiting a convicted traitor and his family, it was likely that rebellion on any scale would reflect fairly deep-seated and widespread social malaise, at least amongst a section of the ruling classes. Naturally enough, the bulk of Jacobite sympathizers would very much have preferred to rise in arms after the arrival in the British Isles of a substantial foreign professional army bent on furthering the Pretender's cause. As an insurance policy, such a force had no match. The snag was that from early in 1712 the elaborate negotiations needed to conclude the War of the Spanish Succession were in progress. France, the only power before 1715 likely to lend a substantial body of troops to the Jacobite cause, was desperate for peace, though not for peace on any terms, and well aware that the Tory government in power in England since 1710 was far more anxious for peace than the other major partners in the anti-French coalition. In a sense, the negotiations in the period 1712–14, which produced a bundle of treaties conveniently described as the Peace of Utrecht, already showed a tacit Anglo-French understanding at work. Louis XIV was probably never more sincere than when he ordered *Te Deums* in all the cathedrals of France for the end of his greatest war. For an old man the Sun King of France remained astonishingly vigorous, but he was in no position to sponsor Jacobite adventures. Indeed it was a provision of the Treaty of Utrecht proper (signed in April 1713) that the Pretender should leave the realm of France, which he did by taking up residence in Bar-le-Duc in the hospitable and independent Duchy of Lorraine. August 1714, which saw the demise of Queen Anne at the start of the month, also saw the final illness of Louis XIV, and with his death even the vague hope that France might act on behalf of the Pretender vanished. As hopes go, it had not been very robust since January 1712, while the history of the '08 shows clearly that even earlier the French military and naval establishment did not believe that Louis intended to make a serious strategic commitment to the Jacobite cause.

Afer the 1715 rebellion had failed, the British political establishment had to produce its own explanation of why there had been Jacobite risings, not just in Scotland but also in the north-east of England. The official line was embedded in the preamble to the articles of impeachment of the rebel lords tried in 1716 and expounded in memorable words by Nicholas Lechmere in January 1716 when he opened the case against the Jacobite peers. Lechmere was a hard-line Whig political manager and the personal lawyer to Thomas fifth Baron Wharton, a rampantly anti-Jacobite member of that crucially important clique of Whig peers known as the Junto. Lechmere was emphatic that the rebellion of which the prisoners had been guilty was the fruit of sustained plotting:

> he thought it plain that it was the effect of many years' labour, of the joint and united labour of great numbers, both Protestants and Papists, the plain and necessary consequence of the measures which had been carrying on for some years past.[4]

It is a view which tends to be popular amongst those who feel themselves part of a threatened establishment and can be paralleled from the obsession with the machinations of Antichrist so common in seventeenth-century England to the articles on 'Britain's Enemies Within' which send a frisson down the spine of the average reader of the late twentieth-century British edition of the *Reader's Digest*. Whether there is any substance to such phobias is always a difficult question.

By and large historians have, until recently, been inclined to accept the view that there was an elaborate web of Jacobite intrigue in England in the years before 1715; that it reached into the very highest offices in the state; and that the restoration of the Pretender by peaceful means was a very real possibility foiled only by the sudden death of Queen Anne. From this point of view it was easy to reach Lechmere's conclusions, which had the great virtue of explaining why there was a small but significant Jacobite rising in north-east England as well as a large rising in Scotland north of the Tay and a much smaller rising in the south-west Borders of Scotland. All of these upheavals could be seen as reflections of a widespread plot, successfully curbed in southern England by the vigorous action of a nearby government. Yet the basic assumptions behind such an interpretation are of debatable validity.

Recent scholarship has established beyond serious doubt that the turbulent politics of early eighteenth-century England were dominated by a savage struggle between two great organized parties – the Whigs and the Tories. It was a conflict over attitudes, policies, and principles. The age of oligarchy, patronage, and non-ideological politics dominated by a struggle between 'ins' and 'outs' for political office only came later in the eighteenth century and its midwife was probably Sir Robert Walpole. Certainly, by the time that Sir Robert's long period of personal ascendancy came to an end in 1742 the 'rage of party' such as had existed in the first two decades of the eighteenth century was a phenomenon of the past.[5] In the heyday of party conflict, divisions within parties could be as important as the divisions between them, but crudely the Whigs were identified with 'Revolution Principles', virulent Francophobia and a war policy in Europe. They were closely linked to the unpopular Dissenting interest in religion, and to the even more unpopular Moneyed Interest in the City of London. The Tories were the party of the Church of England, and of the Landed Interest. They were identified with staunch support for the Crown and with opposition to excessive commitment to European wars.

Two points quite fundamental to an understanding of Jacobite history are that the Tories were the natural majority party in the legislature before 1715, and they undoubtedly had an out-and-out Jacobite wing. In the very frequent elections which followed the passing of the Triennial Act of 1694 (which made it illegal for any English monarch to prolong the life of a Parliament beyond three years), the Tories were only liable to lose heavily, as in 1708, when there was doubt about their soundness on the question of the Protestant Succession. The fact that the 1708 election was held in the aftermath of an unsuccessful Franco-Jacobite invasion attempt helped to return, in the words of Lord Sunderland 'the most Whig Parliament [there] has been since the Revolution'. However, as the popularity of what was seen as a Whig war waned, the Tories steadily recovered. The disastrous miscalculation made by the Whig leaders when they impeached an irresponsible and incendiary High Anglican preacher, Dr Henry Sacheverell, before the House of Lords early in 1710 merely hastened this process. The trial rapidly assumed the form of a political debate on the validity of the Glorious Revolution of 1688. Participants were as much looking forward to the Hanoverian succession as back to the question of resistance to constituted authority in 1688. The trial ended with nominal punishment and real triumph for Sacheverell. A nearly hysterical response to this debate in Tory circles undoubtedly stimulated Jacobite elements in the party. The election of 1710 saw more Jacobites returned to the House of Commons than had been present there since 1702. In theory a statutory Abjuration Oath whereby they had to forswear the Pretender should have kept these men out of the Commons. In practice intelligent Jacobites like John Lade, future M.P. for Southwark, were reported as saying, roughly at the time of the passage of the legislation imposing this oath, 'that his friends, meaning the Jacks, were milksops for kicking at oaths, asserting they should never be able to do anything if they, his friends, did not take all the oaths that could be imposed'.[6]

In the years after 1710 Lord Scarsdale, a prominent Tory peer, openly entertained known Jacobites and Papists at his Derbyshire seat. A notoriously militant Jacobite, Charles Aldworth, was returned, improbably enough, as M.P. for the royal burgh of Windsor. In 1711 the M.P. for Bridgnorth, Richard Cresswell, publicly toasted the Pretender and said that most of his fellow Tory M.P.s needed little encouragement to do the same. When Anne's last Parliament opened in 1714 the Whig spokesmen in the debate on the royal Address devoted their time to allegations that the Tory benches were crawling with uncompromising Jacobites.[7] Certainly the Tory administration led by Lord Oxford quarrelled bitterly with the House of Hanover in the winter of 1711–12 over the question of peace negotiations with France. The Elector of Hanover was heart and soul with the war policy of the Whigs, so it was natural for people to believe that Henry St John, Viscount Bolingbroke, Oxford's increasingly restive and extreme Tory colleague, was plotting to avert the Hanoverian succession by bringing in the Pretender, with the tacit support of the dying Queen Anne, a Stewart and a sentimental Jacobite. The Pretender himself reinforced this interpretation in two manifestoes which he issued in 1714 after being informed of the death of Queen Anne, and that the French government meant to do nothing for him. Both documents stated that Queen Anne had undoubtedly intended to restore her exiled half-brother to the thrones which he claimed, but that this plan had been foiled by her sudden death and the machinations of a vile faction.

The tale loses nothing in the telling from a Whig point of view, with the fate of three kingdoms poised on the last appointment made by a dying Queen, which appointment just tipped the balance for Hanover. It is probably all nonsense. Jacobites and Whigs tended to agree in their interpretation of the Tory party. Neither were ever reliable witnesses to the overall position within that complex coalition. In a letter written to the French foreign secretary, the Marquis de Torcy, a month before Anne's death, the Pretender admitted that he had never had any correspondence with, or reliable channel of communication to, Queen Anne. Anne appears never to have had any compunction about supplanting James Edward Stewart on the throne. Though she started the absurd story that James was not her father's child, Anne was unshaken by the general Whig admission after 1710 that James was legitimate. She did not want to have the Hanoverian heir in England, complicating its politics, but she was firm for the Protestant Succession. It may be doubted whether she would have tried to repeal the Act of Succession and restore James, even if he had converted from Catholicism, which she realistically did not expect him to do.[8] Oxford and Bolingbroke bored and irritated her by accusing one another of Jacobitism in the closing stages of the reign, when they were locked in a bitter conflict for control of government policy. Both men had the usual ambiguous feelers out towards the Jacobite court as a form of political insurance, but there appears to have been no thought in either of their heads that James could be restored to the throne of his ancestors after March 1714, when James made it clear that he was not prepared to change his religion. Even Bolingbroke knew that after that the Grand Turk was probably a marginally more acceptable candidate for the British throne.[9] Despite the ravings of committed Jacobite M.P.s, James was not acceptable to a large proportion of the Tory party.

Jacobites tended to be absurdly optimistic about the degree of committed support for their cause in Britain. A good example of this is Charles Leslie (1650–1722), a famous Non-Juror and relentless controversialist who was the sixth son of John Leslie, Bishop of Clogher and the only Anglican bishop who remained at his post in Ireland during the Interregnum in the seventeenth century. Charles Leslie was both an aggressive Tory propagandist and an uncompromising Jacobite. His political theory, expressed with great violence in the periodical called *The Rehearsal* which he started to publish in 1704, was old-fashioned patriarchalism as a justification for the divine right of kings. In April 1711 Leslie was forced to flee the country, repairing to St Germain where he presented the Pretender with a memorial on the state of the parties in England, representing the position as very favourable to the Jacobite cause. In August 1713 he went to Bar-le-Duc in Lorraine by invitation of the Pretender, for whom he penned pamphlets seeking to calm the fears of Anglicans at the prospect of a popish Pretender, but when in 1722 he was buried in Glaslough church-yard in his native Ireland it may be doubted whether his political activities had ever had much relationship to reality, let alone any chance of changing it.[10]

The dramatic story that only the arrival of the Whig Dukes of Argyll and Somerset at the last Privy Council of Anne's reign foiled Bolingbroke's plan to bring in the Pretender rests on no evidence. It was Bolingbroke's close ally Lord Harcourt who suggested to Anne that the Duke of Shrews-bury be given the White Staff signifying appointment as Lord High Treasurer, and this, the last decision of Anne's political life, placed a known champion of the Protestant Succession in a key position. The Tory government alerted the armed forces to secure the smooth accession to power of George I. The whole mischievous mythology of a pervasive Jacobite plot was given shape and vitality by the unscrupulous pen of Daniel Defoe, literary genius and political hack. In October 1714 Defoe published *The Secret History of the White Staff*, which was propaganda disguised as and indeed mixed up with recent history derived from Defoe's patron, the Earl of Oxford. The latter nourished bitter hostility towards his late colleagues, Bolingbroke and Harcourt, as well as misplaced confidence in his own political future. Defoe depicted Bolingbroke and Harcourt as mere dupes of the real master plotter – the High-Church Tory Francis Atterbury, Bishop of Rochester. It was all very persuasive and completely worthless.[11] Defoe, after all, was the 'expert' who had assured the Scots that their trade with England would double immediately after the Union. He was the 'authority' whose *History of the Union* contained passages designed to reassure the Scots 'That the Parliament of Britain being the Creature of the Union, formed by express Stipulations between the two separate Parliaments of England and Scotland cannot but be unalterably bound by the conditions so stipulated, and upon which it received its Beeing [*sic*], Name and Authority'.[12] Defoe was a dishonest but persuasive writer of political and economic tracts, as well as a worthless guide to constitutional realities. His peculiar flair for convincing fiction served his employers well.

In reality the Jacobite rising in England in 1715 can be explained by two main factors. The more immediate one was the sudden collapse of the Tory party as an effective political force. There were two main reasons for this débâcle. The first was the long stubborn rearguard action by Robert Harley Earl of Oxford against pressure from most of his own Tory sup-porters, but above all from Bolingbroke, for an out-and-out Tory policy.

This would have involved not only Tory measures but also Tory men in every post at the disposal of government from Westminster down to the humblest magistracy in the counties. Historians have been far too ready to label this policy 'extreme' and 'impractical'. It was because it was practical that Harley fought it so hard. It was also the only way in which the Tory party could ensure its own survival after the arrival of a Hanoverian dynasty hostile to the authors of the Peace of Utrecht. Even a well-entrenched Tory party was likely to take a severe battering with the influence of the Crown ranged, at least at first, against it. Harley did not believe that there was any case at all for restoring the Pretender. As a strong Tory leader he could easily have rallied the bulk of his party behind the Protestant Succession. In fact he gave no lead.

One historian has tried to explain Harley's views in terms of the strong Puritan religious influences in his background,[13] yet a purely secular explanation surely fits the case better. Like almost all other leading British politicians since 1690 Harley was utterly determined to confine the power of taking key decisions to a small inner circle at Westminster. Once they had raised him to power, his Tory supporters were, from his point of view, a nuisance, especially after their overwhelming triumph at the polls in 1710. Party government implied party power. Weary, stressed to breaking, fuddled with drink even in front of Queen Anne, Harley clung with mulish obstinacy to the principle that key decisions should not, if possible, be taken under pressure from 'popular' forces outwith the magic circle of government. In this he stood for a central, if seldom acknowledged, principle of British government and one which was to be upheld just as stubbornly by Gladstone and Salisbury in the late nineteenth century, and indeed by the leading politicians of late twentieth-century Britain. Harley's optimism about his own political future proved misplaced. He was impeached, went to the Tower, and was only released in 1717. These events were small consolation to the party he had steered to disaster. In particular the way in which the Crown and the Whigs together were able to inflict a crushing defeat on the Tories at the polls in 1715 came as a terrible shock to a Tory party which had gone into the election with some confidence in its 'natural majority' in the electorate.[14] Like other 'moderates' clinging limpet-like to the levers of power in British politics, Harley had helped to produce very extreme political developments. The 1715 election was the prelude to the growth of something like one-party government.

Such dramatic developments at the centre of politics could not be divorced from the other main explanation of Jacobite rebellion in England – deep-seated regional discontent. Though the ruling class revelled in the exercise of power at local level, its life-rhythm included 'the season' in London, where people who mattered met one another. Thus the Bloomsbury Square house of the wealthy and fashionable physician Dr John

Radcliffe, whose name is commemorated in the Radcliffe Camera, the Radcliffe Infirmary, and the Radcliffe Observatory at Oxford, was both a meeting place for the political and literary élite of London, and a cross-roads where the paths of provincial nobles and gentry could converge. Radcliffe was a High Tory M.P., a friend of Dr Sacheverell and of the suffering Scots Episcopal clergy. He was an acquaintance of Swift and of Dr John Arbuthnot of 'John Bull' fame. Radcliffe's 'Jacobitism' seems to have been of the most tepid kind, for he attended both King William and Queen Anne, and it was never put to the test, as he died in 1714. He bought land in Northamptonshire and Yorkshire, partly for status no doubt, but also partly for security. He is known to have lost £5,000 in 1692 when the French captured a ship in which he had a stake.[15] Radcliffe was extremely anxious to establish a relationship with the Roman Catholic and Jacobite family of the Radcliffe Earls of Derwentwater. His blood relation-ship to these Northumberland noblemen was very dubious but the good doctor proved persistent and unsnubbable, so his hospitality by 1709 embraced both James Radcliffe, third Earl of Derwentwater, and William, fourth Lord Widdrington, a neighbour and relative of Derwentwater. Both Derwentwater and Widdrington were to be attainted of high treason after the '15.[16]

There had been a great deal of sporadic rioting by Jacobite and Tory mobs all over England earlier in 1714 and 1715. Riots occurred on King George's coronation day in October 1714 in Bedford, Birmingham, Chip-penham, Norwich and Reading. Oxford, the citadel of High-Anglican clerical Toryism, was in perpetual uproar. During the general election there were riots at the polls in Brentford, Bristol, Cambridge, Hertford, Leicester and Taunton. The upshot was the passing in 1715 of a stiff Riot Act which enabled the courts to convict of a capital offence anyone who, being in a crowd of twelve or more, failed to disperse within an hour of being commanded to do so by a duly constituted authority.[17] The Riot Act was part of a general Whig offensive designed to destroy the Tory Party before the Hanoverian dynasty grasped its full potential as a counter-balance to Whiggery. The offensive ranged from the really outrageous persecution of Tory leaders like Lords Bolingbroke, Ormonde, and Oxford, to precisely the sort of systematic purge of government posts, deputy-lieutenancies in counties, and justices of the peace, which Oxford had refused to allow shortly before. Whig threats to his life broke Bolingbroke's nerve. In April 1715 he fled to France and, inevitably, the court of the Pretender. Publicly outraged, the Whigs were privately even more gleeful when Ormonde joined him there. Obsessed with total victory at West-minster, Whig leaders spared no thought at all to the north-eastern part of England where frustrated and embittered Toryism marched hand-in-hand with profound economic and social discontent.

As early as the autumn of 1714 the limited number of committed Whigs in Northumberland and Durham were extremely nervous about the tense political atmosphere surrounding them. They were, of course, aware of the Jacobite disturbances elsewhere in England. 'Black William' Cotesworth, the principal local agent of the Whig government on Tyneside between 1715 and 1719, had a nephew at Cambridge who regaled his uncle with tales of Jacobite antics in that city on the Pretender's birthday in July 1715. Basically these consisted of inebriated university gentlemen drinking the health of 'James the Third' and then emerging from a tavern to pay the inevitable crowd of curious loafers to career through the streets doing the same.[18] 'Black William' was probably annoyed rather than seriously worried by the tale, but by October 1715 his close friend and fellow Whig Henry Liddell was warning him that social tensions on the Tyne were a serious threat to the stability of the new Hanoverian regime. Both men were heavily involved in the Tyne coal trade. London drew the great bulk of its vital fuel supply from the Tyne and Wear, and the coastal shipping which was needed to transport these bulk cargoes made up a very significant part of the English mercantile marine. The trade was a nursery of prime seamen, of whom the most famous was to be the explorer of Australasia, Captain James Cook. However, none of these facts were a guarantee of continuous prosperity and in fact in the autumn of 1714 demand for coal was so low that prices were depressed. This exacerbated the tensions between the many rival interests in the trade, breeding a serious industrial dispute. Henry Liddell, like his friend William Cotesworth, was a hard man who believed in playing to win. An offensive Jacobite pamphlet was to Liddell just another lever to be used to persuade George I that all Tories were Jacobites.[19] Yet in the autumn of 1714 Liddell was preaching appeasement. He argued that any industrial struggle should, if possible, be settled on compromise terms, because the general political situation was so fraught with danger.[20]

Nobody could begin to pretend that the interests of the various groups involved in the coal trade were identical. The landed gentlemen who engaged in mining ventures, often with financial assistance from lawyers and goldsmiths, had to deal with a whole hierarchy of other groups, and when one group did well it was often quite inevitable that another group or groups fared ill. Between the London merchant and the north-eastern mines stood a complex of shipping interests including the London lightermen, the masters of the colliers proper, and the sturdy keelmen who did the arduous and dangerous job of rowing coal barges on the Tyne. The powerful and privileged Hostmen's Company of Newcastle exercised certain monopoly rights over the Tyne trade, but it could not control that of the Wear, and its own membership was increasingly divided between a small group of mineowner oligarchs and a larger group of simple 'fitters' ultimately dependent on the men who owned the mines. Strikes were frequent, especially after 1707, culminating in the famous 'mutiny' of 1710 when both keelmen and shipmasters organized themselves to fight for what they saw as their rights, and troops had to be called in to contain the situation.

What made such industrial unrest politically significant, as the local Whigs well knew, was that it occurred in a countryside where Jacobite views were widespread amongst the gentry and the clergy. Non-Jurors and Roman Catholics were extremely numerous. A very sharp edge was given to political disputes by the fact that they often overlapped with purely economic ones. The coal trade in the early eighteenth century was in a state of crisis. Shipments of coal from the Tyne had reached a peak before the Glorious Revolution, but thereafter decline set in. The comparatively shallow seams in the manors of Whickham and Gateshead, where the Elizabethan coal industry had experienced dramatic expansion, were virtually worked out and two options faced the industry. One was to dig very much deeper. This was tried, but the drainage problems of the deeper levels usually proved too much for the horse gins, windmills, pumps and other devices of the day. Such failures could be terribly costly. The other option was to fan out and mine more distant seams, but this was also a difficult and expensive process due partly to the cost of timber-railed horse-drawn wagonways needed to take the coals to navigable water, and partly to the vexed question of the vital wayleaves for wagonways. With fine indifference the gentlemen proprietors fought one another with indictments and gangs of cudgel-swinging ruffians.[21]

The rent-rolls of many a north-eastern gentleman had once been greatly increased by the results of various kinds of mining. After 1693 the depression in the coal trade coincided with the imposition of a new land tax, basically to pay for the huge cost of the wars of King William and Queen Anne. In the period from 1689 to 1702 no less than £58 millions were raised in taxation, mostly on land. Clergymen of the Church of England could be very hard hit for most of them lived off their tithes and the glebe they cultivated or rented, so the bulk of their income derived from land. Tithes were assessed for support of the poor rate and poll taxes levied in the 1690s taxed clergymen at a high rate. By 1697 it was argued that beneficed clergymen were often paying between a quarter and a third of their income in taxes. Clerical Toryism therefore had economic as well as theological roots. It was nourished by that dislike of taxation which burned in the bosom of many Tory squires. Just how heavy the burden of the land tax was on the landed interest is not something one can safely generalize about. In the late seventeenth century it rose to the level of four shillings in the pound. However, this 20 per cent levy, extremely severe by contemporary standards, was to some extent theoretical. The counties near

London, where alone it appears to have been levied at its full rate, saw its impact lessen over time, for the assessments atrophied and did not reflect increases in land values. The farther an estate lay from the capital, the less the levy seems generally to have paid. It was said that in Westmoreland the gentry were paying 'not ninepence in the pound' in the 1690s.[22]

Be that as it may, it is clear that many northern gentry, a very large proportion of whom were Roman Catholics, were in desperate financial straits by 1715. This fact can be meticulously documented from two independent sources. Legislation of 1715 required Roman Catholics to register their estates, and these returns can very often be checked by the papers of the Commissioners for Forfeited Estates, a body set up after the failure of the rebellion. Both tend to tell the same story. Lesser gentry were often mortgaged to the hilt, both in the shape of personal bonds and in the shape of trust deeds for marriage settlements or for portions for younger children. Of course, all eighteenth-century landed estates carried debt burdens, but smaller estates were always much more vulnerable than large ones, and on quite a few properties forfeited in 1716 the Commissioners for Forfeited Estates discovered that the creditors had already foreclosed and were in possession. One way in which many a landed family could hope to increase its financial resources was by the securing of salaried posts in the civil, military, or naval service of the state for its male members. Roman Catholic gentry could not hope to do this, except in the service of foreign princes. In Britain they were subject to penal laws which, if seldom enforced in every detail, did effectively exclude them from civil or military office under the Crown.

Not all the families who participated in the '15 in Northumberland were in financial trouble. A Roman Catholic landlord with a good estate, a sound head for business, and the sense to keep a low profile in political matters could do well for himself in the decades before the rebellion. The Radcliffes of Dilston Hall, whose head was the Earl of Derwentwater, had steadily accumulated wealth over several generations. For them, the rigours of the penal laws were softened by the simple kindness of Protestant neighbours. Many a squire who thundered against the menace of Popery in the House of Commons refused to admit that Roman Catholics were a danger, when they were old neighbours of good family. Other Northumberland families involved in the rebellion such as the Thorntons of Netherwitton, the Collingwoods of Eslington, the Shaftoes of Little Bavington, the Widdringtons of Cheeseburn and the Swinburnes of Capheaton were free of serious money problems. Lord Derwentwater became entangled in the rebellion through a mixture of bad luck and bad judgement. His bad luck was hereditary, for as the descendant of an affair between Charles II and the actress Moll Davis he was regarded as peculiarly close to the exiled Stewarts by blood. Though his mother was a Protestant she was estranged from her much older Roman Catholic husband who in 1702 made the extremely dangerous decision to send his heir, along with his second son, to be companions at St Germain to their cousin, the Pretender, or as the Radcliffes styled him, 'James III'. There is no doubt at all that the young Earl of Derwentwater, for all his Jacobite convictions, was settling down happily under the Hanoverian regime when in September 1715 he was frightened into leaving his young wife and family to join a rebellion by a clumsy attempt of the London government to take him into preventive arrest. The real tragedy of Derwentwater was that nobody persuaded him to submit to the indignity of arrest. He would have emerged, in due course, unscathed.[23]

Nor is it fair to say that the English rising was entirely a Roman Catholic affair. Roman Catholics were usually Jacobite in sympathy but not necessarily actively so. It was common sense for a Protestant regime to try to deprive such a minority of military potential and political influence but Popery was just too handy as the bogey which justified the Whig ascendancy. Like Spain in the sixteenth century or the Russian menace in the twentieth, a Popish Pretender was useful to the British political establishment of the eighteenth century as a threat which could be used to make British society unite behind it. Rampant Whigs like William Cotesworth, in the aftermath of the failure of the '15, were liable to blame all the trouble on 'the Papists' and to demand that that minority be made to pay for the cost of suppressing the rebellion.[24] It was, however, commonly accepted within Cotesworth's private circle that the town of Newcastle would have been only too willing to succumb to a Jacobite coup. Cotesworth's own reputation in government circles rested on the assumption that he had saved the day in Newcastle by bringing in Hanoverian troops early enough to contain the situation. Certainly Cotesworth's nephew, writing to him in 1716, referred to the fact that 'Newcastle tho' not delivered as perhaps was agreed into the hands of the Rebells' was 'still labouring under the too epidemical distemper state ruining discontent'.[25] Roman Catholics were disproportionately prominent among those who actually rebelled, but they were feared by local Whigs less for their own inherent capacity for mischief than for the way in which they might be the flame which ignited the powder-keg of discontent on which the regime sat.

Fortunately for the Illustrious House of Hanover the rising in Northumberland bore from start to finish the signs of an unplanned and ill-executed enterprise. It was precipitated by the response of the British government to the news that the Earl of Mar had, early in September 1715, formally raised the standard of rebellion in Scotland. Regular troops rapidly moved into key towns in the south and west of England. James was actually proclaimed king by disaffected elements in St Columb in Cornwall, and indeed by night in Oxford, but with Oxford, Bristol and Bath all policed by regular regiments, there was no chance of a successful rising in the south. Secretary Stanhope and Lord Chancellor Cowper embarked on a policy of systematically arresting suspected Jacobite activists. Cowper was particularly well-informed of the politics of Northumberland and Durham through his marriage to a Clavering of Chopwell. On 21 September Stanhope secured the agreement of the House of Commons to the arrest of six of its members including Thomas Forster, the High Anglican Tory M.P. for Northumberland. Forster chose to flee northwards. There had already been some talk in London in Jacobite circles about the possibility of a rising in Northumberland. Such talk seems to have derived from the excitement caused by the news of Mar's rebellion. One of the London plotters, Captain Robert Talbot, an Irishman who had been in the French service, certainly sailed from London to Newcastle early in September carrying letters which were duly distributed around the Tory and Jacobite gentry of Northumberland and possibly Lancashire. The couriers included a Protestant clergyman from Derbyshire called Buxton, Nicholas and Charles Wogan (Irish gentlemen of whom the latter became a valued correspondent of Swift), Colonel Henry Oxburgh, Mr Beaumont, and Mr Clifton (brother to Sir Gervase Clifton).

Forster was a cousin of Derwentwater. He was also in dire financial difficulties, so he had little to lose. Politically and financially he was a ruined man. After a series of agonized private discussions Derwentwater threw in his lot with Forster and on 6 October at a place called Green-riggs south-west of the market town of Hexham the Jacobite gentry met in arms. Because Roman Catholics were so prominent in the small band of rebels, Forster became the inevitable leader, on account of his Protestantism. Nobody forgot that the drama was being played before a predominantly Protestant audience, and it must be remembered that similar calculations helped Charles Parnell to the leadership of the Irish Home Rule Party in the nineteenth century. Parnell was a man with the drive of a charismatic dictator. 'Tom' Forster was quite remarkably useless at everything except saving his own skin. It was believed at the time, on good authority, that during the brisk action which was to form the climacteric of his rising Forster lay in bed steadying his nerves with a hot spiced milk and wine drink.[26]

With such leadership even a well-organized rising would rapidly have been in difficulty, but the Northumberland rising consisted originally of little more than sixty miserably-armed men, divided between gentlemen and their servants. They were nearly all mounted but hunting saddles and dress swords gave them an unimpressive appearance to the professional eye. So short were they of weapons that, though they grew in numbers, they had to turn away many who offered to serve as infantry. Their only hope was a lightning strike at Newcastle, in whose streets they should indeed have made their first publicized appearance. Instead they delayed until Hotham's regiment had secured Newcastle for Hanover, and then wandered off somewhat disconsolately across the bleak rain-swept northern moors, a body of some 200 horse divided between the Anglican Tories who had taken the key initiatives in launching the rebellion, and the Roman Catholics who had rallied to them. Justice John Hall of Otterburn and 'General' Forster, both bankrupt and both incompetent, were not unfair representatives of the Protestant element, while a significant proportion of the Roman Catholic gentry present had their own financial worries. These were the warriors who, hearing that a small Scottish Jacobite force from the Borders had crossed into England, linked up with it at Rothbury, and then retreated into Scotland to meet another Jacobite force under Brigadier Mackintosh of Borlum at Kelso.

After a great deal of argument and manoeuvring the united force finally marched south again in hopes of raising the Jacobite Roman Catholic and High Anglican gentry of Lancashire and the north-western counties of England. Given the close social and family ties between the Northumberland gentry and those of Lancashire in particular, such hopes were not surprising. They may even have survived the extremely depressing experience of the march through Cumberland and Westmorland. As they crossed from Scotland into Cumberland the Jacobite force undoubtedly entered a county where the machinery of government was very firmly in the hands of friends of the House of Hanover. The first loyal address published in the *London Gazette* in 1714 after the accession of George I had come from the sheriff, grand jury, clergy and gentlemen of Cumberland assembled in Carlisle for the county assizes. Brigadier Thomas Stanwix, mayor of Carlisle, M.P. for the city since the succession of Anne, and later governor of Carlisle, was a very reliable government man. He had served in Spain, where Stanhope had made his name as a dashing general officer. Carlisle was garrisoned, albeit not heavily, and unattractively to Jacobites who had spiked their few light cannon and left them behind at Langholm at the very start of this their last march.

The Earl of Carlisle, the absentee Lord-Lieutenant of Cumberland and Westmoreland, was a staunch Whig. On 25 October 1715 he wrote to his Deputy-Lieutenants for Cumberland and Westmoreland congratulating them on the grounds that:

You have perform'd what the Government expected from you in Securing all Roman Catholicks, Nonjurors and other Disaffected People whom you had reason to Suspect would be Aiding to the Pretender upon this Occasion. The Direction's you have likewise given in Relation to the Militia are very proper and what I intirely approve. – Hitherto Your care and Vigilance have done all that I should have thought necessary or would have done If I had been present.[27]

Certainly potentially seditious Papists in Cumberland were vigorously pursued in the weeks before the Jacobite invasion. Their horses and arms were seized. They were harassed with an oath of allegiance and other devices supplied by an ingenious and frightened legislature. A good many Roman Catholic gentlemen like Howard of Corby, Curwen of Workington, and Warwick of Warwick Hall had been arrested and clapped in Carlisle Castle. The most important fact about this persecution was that it worked. An aggressively Whig secular government backed by a strongly Whig Bishop of Carlisle so cowed the Roman Catholics of Cumberland and Westmoreland that they offered virtually no support to the Jacobite army. As the Jacobites squelched through the streets of Kendal in drenching rain, with six sodden bagpipes wailing at their head, they must have prayed that Lancashire would show more enthusiasm for the cause.

In only two ways could events in Cumberland and Westmoreland be deemed encouraging for the rebels. The Earl of Carlisle's satisfaction over the steps taken to prepare the county militia for active service proved fatuously misplaced. This ill-armed and virtually undisciplined force was nominally commanded by the Lord-Lieutenant, but in fact it was one of his deputies, Viscount Lonsdale, who mustered certainly the Cumberland militia and possibly some Westmoreland militia at Penrith Fell with a view to blocking the path of the Jacobite advance just before it reached Westmoreland. Lonsdale's militia were supported, if that be the word, by an even more motley crew in the shape of the *posse comitatus* summoned by the sheriff. This last body was primarily meant to assist the suppression of riots. It technically comprised 'the power of the county' in the shape of all men over fifteen years of age. Both bodies were swept aside by a Jacobite force which they probably heavily outnumbered. To describe the episode as a fight would be to flatter it.

Apart from the rout on Penrith Fell, the second aspect of the Jacobites' march through the north-western counties which was moderately impressive was the ease with which they uplifted the excise and other public moneys in towns along their route, such as Brampton, Penrith, Appleby and Kendal. After the rebellion certificates were rapidly forthcoming to the effect that these payments had been 'extorted' and not willingly paid, but the significant point is simply that they were paid. A flow of cash like this made it vastly easier to maintain discipline and cohesion in the invading force, whose needs could to some extent be financed from the surrounding country without the need to resort to systematic plundering, a process both politically counter-productive and subversive of military discipline. However, there is no doubt that the Reverend Robert Patten, that former curate of Penrith, who marched with the rebels as Forster's chaplain and who turned King's Evidence at the end to save his neck, summed up the prevailing emotion of the rebel army when he said in the account he later wrote of these events that they were deeply affected by the fact that in traversing two populous counties they had acquired precisely two additional gentlemen volunteers.[28]

The two and a half thousand or so men who marched into Lancashire under the Pretender's banner were therefore quite desperate for signs of support. Nor was it at all unreasonable for them to expect to find it in Lancashire. The county had a long tradition of particularism rooted in antipathy to the central government. It had never fitted very happily into the Elizabethan system of administration, partly because few of its gentry were willing to act as justices of the peace. It had suffered greatly during the civil wars of the seventeenth century and had settled into a pattern of extremism in politico-religious loyalties, a pattern which was still very marked in 1715. There was a large Roman Catholic population in the county as well as many High Anglican Tories, nor was the temper of either of these groups improved by the rival presence of a substantial Whiggish Dissenter minority, with a particularly obnoxious Presbyterian element in it. The Roman Catholic gentry of Lancashire in particular were closely connected by marriage with one another to the point where the Tildesleys, Molyneuxes, Standishes and other houses moved almost like a clan. Immediately after the Glorious Revolution many refused to take the oaths to the new regime, while others left the country, or their principal seat for a more retired one, in order to avoid open acknowledgement of William of Orange. Their Jacobitism was common knowledge and had drawn on their heads much persecution. Several Roman Catholic gentlemen, for example, were tried at Manchester in 1694 on what seem to have been trumped-up charges of being involved in an elaborate conspiracy which included the assassination of William, a Lancashire rising, and a French invasion. To the eternal credit of the court which tried them, they were acquitted. In dismissing the accused, Mr Justice Eyre referred in a matter-of-fact way to the circumstance that 'Most of you if not all have been brought up in France'.[29] However bogus the allegations of 1694, most Lancashire Roman Catholic gentry clearly were Jacobite in sympathy.

Nor were Jacobite sympathies confined to strongly Roman Catholic areas in the north of the county. Manchester, already a rapidly-growing urban community, had attracted to it a fair number of the younger sons of the Lancashire gentry, who tried to make their way in business there. These men, along with other immigrants from the countryside, naturally carried their High Anglican, Roman Catholic, Tory and Jacobite convictions with them. When George I announced that he was resolved to uphold the Toleration Act, which secured a very large measure of toleration for

Protestant Dissenters, the result in Manchester was a quite terrifying outburst of High Anglican and Roman Catholic mob violence. From about the tenth of June (the Pretender's birthday) noisy crowds of demonstrators began to gather in the streets of Manchester. Very soon they started to wreck all the Presbyterian meeting-houses in the town. The mob was to some extent organized under a 'Colonel' and a 'Captain' whose name is known, for he was 'Siddal the blacksmith'. Dissenters were as unpopular a minority as their Whig patrons but the Manchester rioting was soon seen to be out of hand, especially when columns of rioters began to sally forth in the direction of Yorkshire, smashing any Presbyterian meeting-house on their route. On 20 July a proclamation was issued that any riotous or tumultuous person who attacked a place of worship after the last day of July 1715 would be regarded as guilty of felony (i.e. a crime punishable by death) and that the death sentence would be enforced without benefit of clergy. Militia forces were mobilized to support two troops of Lord Cobham's regiment under Major Wyvil which, along with detachments of Lord Stair's regiment, proved enough to crush the disturbances. The Mob-Colonel and Mob-Captain ended up in the pillory after conviction, though it is significant of the prevailing mood in Manchester that nobody dared throw anything at them.[30]

Here was a rich vein of potential support which the Jacobites hoped to mine. Nor were they totally unsuccessful in doing so. The government sent two hangmen on a circuit through the principal towns of Lancashire in January and February 1716 in order to execute successive batches of Jacobite prisoners condemned to death at the Liverpool assizes held in the first few weeks of the year. At Manchester five men suffered. Three were labourers, one seems to have been a simple countryman, and one was Thomas Siddal, blacksmith and former 'Captain' of the Manchester mob. His head was subsequently fixed on the market cross. However, it is clear that the general response of the High Anglican Tories to the Jacobite rising was so apathetic as to constitute a decisive blow to the prospects of the rebels. Recruits did start coming in to join the invading army in fair numbers after it reached and occupied the town of Lancaster. Only two of the townspeople themselves, a barber and a joiner, both Roman Catholics, are said to have enlisted but gentlemen such as Hodgson of Leighton Hall, Dalton of Thurnham Hall, Butler of Racliffe, and Tyldesly of the Lodge rallied to the Jacobite colours, in each case with an accompanying group of servants. What acutely depressed the men they joined, and especially the Scots, was that almost without exception these gentlemen were Roman Catholics. Politically Anglicans were essential. Roman Catholics were tolerable as a stiffening for a Protestant force. By themselves they were, and everyone knew this, the kiss of death.

After Lancaster Forster led his men to Preston, whence he intended to march on Manchester. The local Whigs had been thrown into some dis-array by the switch of the Jacobite forces from Newcastle to Lancashire and it was only along the River Ribble south of Preston that Sir Henry Houghton, the M.P. for Preston and an arch-Hanoverian, was able to organize some sort of defence. Significantly, Houghton considered that the loyalties of the bulk of the local people were so dubious that he preferred to reinforce his militia force with armed Presbyterians led by such militant men of God as 'General' the Reverend James Woods. Even so, it was only the arrival of General Wills, a brisk but unimaginative soldier who had served under Stanhope in Spain, with regular troops that enabled the Hanoverians to cross the Ribble and contain the Jacobites in Preston.[31]

On its way south the rebel army had been shadowed by a Hanoverian force from Newcastle under General Carpenter. It was inferior in numbers to the Jacobites and composed of raw troops, so it is difficult to avoid the conclusion that Forster should have listened to the aggressive spirit of Mackintosh of Borlum who was all for bringing Carpenter to an action and destroying him. The fact that the Jacobites were now making a stand in the town of Preston was ominous. It is true that Borlum was able to fortify the place in such a way that when General Wills sent his infantry blundering into it they were decimated by a vicious crossfire from well concealed Jacobite troops. However, such a successful tactical defence only made strategic sense if followed by a devastating sally. The Highlanders were all for sallying out sword in hand, but Forster first allowed General Carpenter to link up with Wills, thereby sealing the encirclement of Preston, and then negotiated an abject unconditional surrender.

Unlike Lancaster, the town of Preston seems to have shown a good deal of positive enthusiasm for the rebels, at least if one judges by those who saw fit to make themselves scarce after the surrender. Of the twelve carriage-keeping gentlemen of Preston, six simply disappeared, while it was remarked that the Roman Catholics of the place, usually very numerous, were hard to find after Forster threw in his hand.[32] Indeed the detailed study of the English rising in 1715 brings out how very much more formidable it was in potential than in reality. It was rooted both in regional discontent and in the despair and frustration of a great national party. What it needed to pull out the High Tories in significant numbers was success. Without success only the highly-motivated and counter-productive Roman Catholic element was moved to commit itself on any scale. 'Tom' Forster's antics alone go far to explain why, long before Preston, his standards lacked the sweet savour of success, but it is essential to turn northwards to the Earl of Mar and his rebellion fully to appreciate why the Jacobite banners in Lancashire, even before the end, were surrounded by the rank and musty odour of defeat.

6 Roots of Rebellion II—the 1715 in Scotland

In one sense the 1715 rebellion in Scotland was the result of a private decision taken by one man because of his personal circumstances. The man was John Erskine Earl of Mar, and the circumstances were simply the complete collapse of his political career. Mar had been a very active champion of the Act of Union. After raising the standard of rebellion he had to try to talk this episode away but it was in fact typical, for Mar was a government man through and through. He loved office, revelled in the deference which a minister of the King could extract from his contemporaries, and appreciated the salary. Political principles were never Mar's strong suit. He was a Tory, but a staunch supporter of Oxford in the latter's power-struggle with Bolingbroke. Mar was appointed a Third Secretary of State in 1714, with special responsibility for Scotland. He acted with great propriety in securing the smooth accession of George I, and although he had enough sense to see that he could not hope to retain his Secretaryship of State, he seems, like Oxford, to have cherished pathetic delusions about the ability of the Tories to hang together and remain a viable political alternative after the accession of the Hanoverian dynasty. He wrote suitably grovelling assurances of his undying loyalty to the new king and even beat up a gelatinous address of a similar kind signed by various chiefs from the Highlands, including several who joined him in the rebellion. Mar's reputation had in fact been destroyed in the eyes of George I by Whig slanders about his secret Jacobite sympathies. With characteristic rudeness George I literally turned his back on the erstwhile Secretary of State when he appeared at Court and thereby turned a depressed man into a desperate one.

What Mar then did is highly revealing. He did not set about consulting with the Pretender. The exiled court was of course always engaged in endless and futile intrigues which came to nothing, but it is a measure of its real influence that it was taken by surprise by the news of Mar's rebellion. Mar did not even have a commission from the Pretender when he raised the Jacobite standard and was reduced to using what some historians, with a tact worthy of a public relations officer, have called an 'anticipatory draft'. Mar's rebellion was really on behalf of the man Mar cared for most in this world – himself. On the other hand, Mar knew that the only cause for which men were going to be willing to fight against the House of Hanover was that of the exiled House of Stewart. In a sense, once he had decided to rebel, he had no strategic political options left, only tactical ones. Physically, his movements mirrored some of the tactical options which must have seethed in his mind.

First, Mar embarked at Gravesend in a collier bound for Newcastle. We know for certain that he was accompanied by a military adviser, General George Hamilton, and a couple of personal servants. He seems to have transhipped at Newcastle into 'John Spence of Leith his boat' meaning to land in Scotland near St Andrews but being forced by bad weather to land at Elie on the southern shore of the peninsula of Fife. Now both Mar and Hamilton were well-connected in the area. Hamilton went from Elie to Kilrenny, to the house of his son-in-law Colonel Balfour. Mar went to the house of Thomas, sixth Earl of Kinnoull, the father of his first wife (who had died in 1707). Kinnoull's third son, Colonel John Hay of Cromlix, joined Mar's rebellion in which he rose to be a Brigadier-General and Master of the Horse. The county of Fife was full of disgruntled gentry with Episcopal and Jacobite leanings. Amongst the Fife lairds who consulted with Mar on the very eve of his rising was Alexander Erskine of Cambo, the Lord Lyon. Erskine of Cambo was the son of Lord Lyon Sir Charles Erskine, the family having, as we have seen, been granted the office by letters patent for two lives. Lyon King Alexander Erskine was a very typical example of the entrenched conservative nobility of Restoration Scotland. Yet along with Sir Patrick Murray of Auchtertyre he was one of the only two men among those summoned by proclamation by the Hanoverian government who actually surrendered themselves at the start of the rebellion. The Earl of Kinnoull and many others had to be seized before they could be put under preventive arrest. By the time this happened Mar had moved north on horses thoughtfully provided by Kinnoull. He made no attempt to reach his main estates, which lay in the small county of Alloa adjacent to Fife on the west. On the contrary he rode for his much less valuable properties in the north-east Highlands, where he embarked on a series of meetings with Highland and Lowland notables. Some specious cover to part of these proceedings was provided by describing them as a great deer hunt, for the encirclement of large numbers of deer, known as the *timchioll* in Gaelic, normally began several days beforehand and involved hundreds of beaters whose job was eventually to drive the deer past the gentry waiting for the kill. It was on the Braes of Mar on 6 September 1715 that the Jacobite standard finally streamed to the breeze.[1]

From this sequence of events alone it is natural to leap to the assumption that there was a peculiar relationship between the Highlands and the

Jacobite cause. Such an assumption leads on to the conclusion that this relationship must have been rooted in the distinctive culture of the Gaelic-speaking Highlands and more particularly in those aspects of its intellectual and social heritage which marked it off from the apparently much less Jacobite-inclined Lowlands. The case for this viewpoint, implicit in most writings on the '15, has been given depth and great intellectual distinction by two outstanding historians of Scottish Jacobitism. The first of these in point of time was Audrey Cunningham who published an important work on *The Loyal Clans* in 1932. Her book was a study of the Jacobite clans, and it elicited from Sir James Fergusson of Kilkerran, that staunch hereditary Whig and Keeper of the Records of Scotland, the snorting comment that *The Disloyal Clans* would have been a more appropriate title. Be that as it may, Audrey Cunningham argued at length a relatively simple thesis to the effect that there was a deep underlying sympathy between the Stewart dynasty's patriarchal view of the function of kingship and the social and intellectual world of the Gaelic Highlands. To put it crudely: the Stewarts saw themselves as the authoritarian fathers of their peoples and in the Highlands men still lived in clans which were a sort of authoritarian extended family. Of course, the argument was much more complex than this and involved the contention that late Stewart kingship had in fact displayed a fatherly concern for the Highland people, partly because of their exemplary record of loyalty in the mid seventeenth-century civil wars. In particular, Audrey Cunningham saw James VII as the best friend of the Gael who ever sat on the throne of Scotland.[2]

The argument of *The Loyal Clans* was carried much further in a book published by George Pratt Insh in 1952. Insh was best known as the meticulous historian of the Darien Scheme, but his last book, *The Scottish Jacobite Movement: A Study in Economic and Social Forces*, is in many ways the most intellectually stimulating piece he ever wrote. As with Cunningham's book, a summary is bound to be distorting, but Insh saw the Jacobite risings as a clash between 'the spiritual strength of the old Celtic civilization of the Highlands of Scotland reinforced by the old scholarly civilization of the Episcopal North-East' and 'the commercial and industrial civilization of the South' with 'its materialistic ambitions'. To Insh the Lowlands had become an extension of the advanced commercial and manufacturing complexes which dominated England and only behind the Highland Line did an older world of patriarchal authority and devoted loyalty shelter 'an older Scotland, the Scotland of the poets and the scholars'. To him therefore the Jacobite rebellions were almost a cosmic drama in which an ancient civilization, with many spiritual virtues, hurled itself unsuccessfully against the inexorable advance of the hard-faced politicians, businessmen and merchants who within the framework of the Hanoverian state were building the foundations of an industrial Britain.[3]

It is interesting that Insh had to qualify the simplicity of a clash between Celtic and Anglo-Saxon civilization by finding a place on the side of the angels for the north-east, by which he meant primarily the counties of Aberdeen and Banff. He owed his knowledge of the strength of Jacobitism in this region primarily to the devoted labours of a remarkable brother and sister, Alistair and Henrietta Tayler, descendants through their mother of the Earls of Fife. The Taylers started publishing significant genealogical work before the First World War, but only turned to specifically Jacobite history in 1928 with their *Jacobites of Aberdeenshire and Banffshire in the '45*. Thereafter they produced many volumes on Jacobitism including *Jacobites of Aberdeenshire and Banffshire in the '15*, an edition of the Jacobite cess-roll for Aberdeenshire in 1715, a biography of the Old Pretender, an account of the 1715 rising, and other works whose flow was hardly interrupted by Alistair's sudden death in 1937. For some years Henrietta Tayler published books based on material on which they had worked together, and then she turned in the closing years of a very long life (she died at eighty-two) to a series of precise and scholarly editions of original Jacobite sources, including material from the Royal Archives at Windsor. Needless to say, no Scottish university recognized Henrietta Tayler's massive contribution to Scottish and indeed British history with an honorary degree, but the Taylers between them profoundly influenced the modern interpretation of Jacobitism. No Jacobite cranks themselves, they gracefully bore the importunities of cranks as well as scholars from all over the world. Devoted children of the north-east Episcopalian tradition and related to scholars who had preceded them in the Jacobite field (they were cousins of Walter Biggar Blaikie, the great authority on the '45), they were at all times extremely careful to draw no conclusions other than those they could document from their sources. After their researches it was impossible to ignore the fact that the north-east made a very significant contribution to the major Jacobite risings, despite the fact that the greatest part of the region clearly belonged to the Lowlands physically and culturally.

Insh was able to accommodate this fact within the framework of his general hypothesis by arguing that what most distinguished the pattern of life in the north-east was its intense conservatism. Indeed the concept of 'the Conservative north-east' is one which historians have found useful in the sixteenth and seventeenth, as well as the eighteenth centuries.[4] Insh was greatly helped in weaving the fabric of his argument by another historian, perhaps the most percipient ecclesiastical historian produced by twentieth-century Scotland, G. D. Henderson, Regius Professor of Church History in the University of Aberdeen. Henderson drew on papers in the Charter Room at Cullen House, Banffshire, the home of the Earls of

Seafield, to recreate the extraordinary currents of religious mysticism which were so potent in Episcopalian and Jacobite circles in the north-east in the first half of the eighteenth century. Three men who occupied the position of Professor of Divinity at King's College Aberdeen in the seventeenth century, John Forbes of Corse, Henry Scougall, and James Garden, all made very influential contributions to the literature of mystical religion. King's College was in the seventeenth century a stronghold of conservative Episcopalian views, but with such Professors of Divinity it was also a nursery of mystical spirituality. The north-east was an extreme example of the difficulty of inserting Presbyterian ministers into Scottish parishes after the Glorious Revolution. The General Assembly in Edinburgh in 1690 was attended by only two representatives of the whole Synod of Aberdeen, and in 1692 there was only one representative of that Synod present. There was no Presbyterian communion service in Aberdeen from 1690 to 1704. Attempts to induct a Presbyterian minister could lead to fierce rioting as in the town of Fraserburgh in 1707 when the members of the Presbytery of Deer were chased away by 'a rabble of people who threw stones and dub or mire upon them'. There was no Presbyterian clergyman in the parishes of Gamrie or Forglen until 1717, at Fyvie or Alvah before 1718, or in the parish of Monquhitter before the end of 1727. Thus Episcopalianism was a vital spiritual tradition, and indeed an ascendant one in the north-east in 1715.

Despite the fact that most Episcopal clergymen had qualified themselves for toleration by taking the Oath of Abjuration of the Pretender in 1712, the Episcopal community in the region was violently Jacobite. The classic illustration of this fact is Dr George Garden, a key figure in those circles interested in mysticism. He was an authority on Forbes of Corse whose *Spiritual Exercises* he translated into Latin and whose collected works he had published by the Wetstein Press in Amsterdam in 1702–3. He was intimate friend of Henry Scougall, whose funeral sermon he preached in 1678, and he was the brother of Professor James Garden. He was deeply influenced by two remarkable French ladies, Madame Guyon and Madame Bourignon. Both these pious laywomen were exponents of a tradition of mysticism within Western Christendom which went back to at least such striking late medieval writers as Thomas à Kempis, and which had produced within the context of Counter-Reformation Spain extraordinary souls such as St Teresa and St John of the Cross. All mystics tend to be suspect to the conventionally orthodox. Madame Guyon was no exception. She was at one stage patronized by Madame de Maintenon, the dominant figure at the French Court in the later years of Louis XIV, and by the immensely distinguished François de Salignac de la Mothe-Fénelon, Archbishop, Duke of Cambrai. Unfortunately the orthodoxy of Madame Guyon became an issue between Fénelon and the equally charismatic, and temperamentally incompatible, Bishop Bossuet of Meaux, and in the resulting struggle Fénelon was worsted. However, Madame Guyon's influence continued to spread, mainly due to the efforts of a remarkable propagandist, the Frenchman Pierre Poiret. It was he who did more than anyone else to establish the reputation of Antoinette Bourignon, whose life he wrote, and whose works of mystical divinity he edited.[5]

Through Poiret the mysticism or Quietism of this tradition deeply influenced north-east Episcopalians such as the Garden brothers, Lord Deskford, and the saintly Alexander, fourth Lord Forbes of Pitsligo. In theory Quietism should have bred indifference to worldly politics. Dr James Keith, M.D., an Aberdeen doctor practising in London and an enthusiast for mystical religion wrote in just this vein to Lord Deskford in August 1715, saying that:

> In a time of general perplexity and distress the sober, the pious and the good one way or the other must suffer also. Their principle is to submit to all Powers and Governments, as Christ and his disciples did, and to disturb none.[6]

Despite these moving words, the bulk of the leading Quietists of the north-east were strongly Jacobite in sentiment and many of them were active in the '15 rebellion. The clearest comment on the situation, graceless and jaundiced of course but substantially accurate, was made by the Presbyterian authors of a pamphlet entitled *An Apology for the Aberdeen Evictions* which was published in 1718 or 1719 as an answer to an Episcopal pamphlet complaining about the deprivation of Episcopal clergymen in the aftermath of the rising. It prints the Oath of Abjuration and then, quite devastatingly, 'The address of the Episcopal Clergy in the diocese of Aberdeen to the Pretender'. This document was presented by, among others, James and George Garden, at Feterresso on 29 December 1715. The representatives of the Episcopal clergy were introduced to 'James VIII' by his host, the Earl Marischal, and his Commander-in-Chief, the Duke (in the Jacobite peerage) of Mar. The address is fulsome, to put it mildly, and places the Pretender in the same school of princes as Moses, Joseph and David. The last-named was, incidentally, one to whom His Late Sacred Majesty James VI was much given to comparing himself. The *Apology* then went on to say that the Episcopal clergy were being persecuted not so much for their enthusiasm for the liturgy of the Church of England (as they were alleging in order to curry favour in London), as for their demonstrated zeal for a Popish Pretender in the field.[7]

Given a socially conservative part of the Lowlands tucked away, like the north-east, behind the main line of the Highland Boundary Fault which separates the bulk of the Lowlands from the Highlands, it seems reasonable to argue that it is likely to have more in common with the Highlands than with the rest of the Lowlands. When to geographical apartness is added a conservative Episcopal religious tradition, shot through with unusual Quietist influence from the Continent, the case for taking the north-east as a special case seems overwhelming. It certainly included out-of-the-way places, as can be easily demonstrated from the history of the Roman Catholic community in Scotland. After the Reformation there were comparatively few Roman Catholics in the country. They tended to exist in isolated and scattered pockets, one of which was the Enzie, the area between the town of Keith and the Moray Firth, where the protection of the ducal house of Gordon ensured the safety of the numerous Roman Catholics. The altar vessels of the Chapel Royal at Holyroodhouse, threatened by the rioters who wrecked the chapel as a symbol of the regime of James VII in December 1688, were saved by one of the resident chaplains, David Burnet. In his own phrase, he 'horsed for the north country', taking refuge in the Enzie. There the precious and flamboyant vessels designed to express the splendour of a proud dynasty were hidden. Later they were gifted by the Queen Dowager, Mary of Modena, to the Scottish Catholic Mission and used in very humble kirks in Banffshire in the Enzie until the nineteenth or twentieth century.[8] Relations between Roman Catholics and Episcopalians, usually bad when the latter were in power, undoubtedly improved when both were being persecuted by the Presbyterians, so it is possible to see the north-east in the early eighteenth century as an unreconstructed wedge of the Restoration Lowlands stubbornly resisting the spirit of the new century.

Sophisticated men educated in the polite learning of Restoration Scotland were undoubtedly capable of co-existing with the immeasurably ancient attitudes and prejudices which can be found just under the surface of clan society in the eighteenth-century Highlands. Alexander Nisbet, author of a *System of Heraldry* and by common consent the greatest scientific authority on matters heraldic ever produced by Scotland, was a gentleman who died in 1725 and whose known Jacobite views prevented him being appointed either herald or poursuivant in his lifetime. Himself the landless son of a bankrupt Berwickshire laird,[9] he gave a ruling on the chieftainship of the Stewarts of Balquhidder, awarding the dignity to the then Mac Mhic Bhaltair on the interesting grounds that he was custodian of the Clach Dearg (the Red Stone in English), the Charm of Ardvorlich. This was a crystal ball mounted in silver. Owners of sick cattle from forty miles around would bring kegs of spring water to the custodian's wife who dangled the stone by its chain in the water, swirling it round three times whilst reciting a Gaelic charm. Provided the owner took his keg home without entering a house, the water was then deemed a sure cure for the cattle.[10] There was nothing unusual about the cult of the magic stone of

Ardvorlich. The Robertsons of Struan in Perthshire, a clan which was 'out' in every Jacobite rebellion it was physically possible for them to join, had their own magic stone, the Clach na Brataich which not only cured cattle but was also regularly used as a talisman in war when its changing colour could tell the chief whether the outcome would be victory or defeat. Another Perthshire magic stone was the Clach Bhuaidh (Stone of Virtue) of Glenlyon, of which it was said that it had the property of bringing men safely back from battle. Glenlyon men drank water in which it had been dipped before venturing out to war.[11]

Altogether, Insh's model of the Jacobite risings as an epic clash of cultures is deeply seductive. It pulls together a great deal of scattered but relevant evidence in a way which confirms rather than challenges the romantic aura which has always surrounded the Jacobite story. At the same time it deepens the significance of the lost cause of the exiled dynasty. It gives to the last Jacobite charge at Culloden something of the significance Bruce Catton gives to the charge of General George Pickett's Virginians 'moving out of shadow into eternal legend' at the Battle of Gettysburg in the supreme climacteric of the American Civil War.[12] Like the men of the Old South who died under the Federal guns on Cemetery Ridge in the summer of 1863, the Jacobites can be seen as the doomed champions of an ancient, aristocratic rural civilization fated to crumble before an uglier but more dynamic way of life riding the wave of the future. There is only one snag to this otherwise satisfying interpretation. It does not adequately fit the known historical facts.

No sensible unprejudiced person will of course try to deny either that the north-east has always been an area steeped in the cultivation of ancient virtues, or that it has as a result invariably produced a steady stream of superior men and women singularly fit to take charge of the affairs of their frailer fellow humans. However, neither the social texture nor the political record of the region in 1715–16 differed in any significant way from other Lowland regions. Quietism is perhaps the one unique attribute of the north-east, but it must not be over-stressed, for it was a minority tradition even amongst Episcopalians in Aberdeenshire and Banffshire and was deeply distrusted by the conventional majority, which is why George Garden could not, even in 1720, be seriously considered by the Scottish Episcopalians for a bishopric. The taint of 'Bourignonism' clung too close to him.[13] All the way down to the Tay the eastern Lowlands of Scotland, from the Howe of the Mearns in Kincardineshire to the eastern part of Perthshire, exhibited much the same Jacobite loyalty as the north-east, for roughly the same reasons. Contemporaries were well aware of this. The best example is the Duke of Argyll, the Hanoverian Commander-in-Chief in Scotland during the critical period of the rebellion. Sent north a week after Mar raised the Jacobite standard, Argyll was worried from the start about the extreme weakness of the government garrison in Scotland. Indeed he was convinced that if the Jacobites acted at once with the vigour which common sense suggested to men in their circumstances they could probably beat the Hanoverian forces out of Scotland before they could be reinforced. A long series of letters by Argyll to Lord Townshend included remarks about the appalling consequences likely to follow if the Scots rebels were to break through the government lines and link up with the northern English rebellion. On 24 September a worried Argyll wrote to Townshend that the government forces were still inadequate and that 'beyond the Forth, the rebells have a hundred to one at least in their Interest'. The suggestion that these letters display a yellow streak in Argyll has been made. It is as unworthy as it is silly. 'Red John of the Battles' was a title Argyll had more than earned several times over before 1715 by displays of outstanding physical courage in combat. His personality combined two qualities rarely found together in lesser mortals – fathomless arrogance and a fund of solid common sense. His statements to Townshend no doubt made unpleasant reading, but they were shrewd and correct. Benorth Forth, and not just in the Highlands, support for the rebellion was overwhelming.[14]

A glance at the Lowland parts of the county of Angus confirms the widespread support for Jacobitism amongst the ruling classes. At the apex of county society stood the great landed magnates such as the Earls of Southesk. The third Earl was a devoted Episcopalian, a choleric and authoritarian character, and a pillar of the Restoration regime. The fourth Earl reluctantly accepted the Glorious Revolution long before he died in 1699 but his widow lived on at Leuchars Castle full of Jacobite sentiment which she imparted to her son the fifth Earl. Urged on by his mother, Southesk was one of the noblemen who met with Mar at Aboyne on Deeside on 3 September 1715, and the Earl returned from that fateful tryst to Angus to proclaim the Pretender at Montrose. He subsequently raised 30 horsemen and 150 foot, with which he joined the rebels at Perth. He commanded the Angus horse at the battle of Sheriffmuir, and after the battle entertained the Pretender at his residence at Kinnaird. This dashing young noble is the hero of the song 'The Piper of Dundee'.[15] In every other respect his role in the rebellion was typical of that played by other great men of his county. His friend James Maule, fourth Earl of Panmure, though an older man, followed a very similar course. The firmness of his Jacobite convictions was well known, but he had always led such a quiet life that the Hanoverian Lord Justice Clerk of Scotland was surprised when he left Edinburgh to join the rising. In the eyes of the Justice Clerk, Panmure's action in sailing north from the Forth and landing 'in a small fisher creek near his own house of Panmure' was an indication that the Jacobites deemed the game as good as won. It was Panmure who proclaimed the Pretender in Brechin, a town which was much under his influence. Thereafter he marched to join the Jacobite army at Perth with a force half composed of Highlanders and half of Lowlanders, a living reminder that Angus is a county with a large Highland area in it. Altogether Panmure led some 500 men into the Jacobite army and like Southesk he contributed funds to finance the raising of more troops. After Sheriffmuir the great gates of Kinnaird Castle were closed, and have remained closed from that day to this.

Close family ties, some the result of intermarriage, help to explain the social and political cohesion of the Angus nobility. Panmure's sister Mary was the mother of 'Bobbing John' Earl of Mar, so Panmure came as Mar's uncle when he led his men into Perth. On the battlefield at Sheriffmuir Lord Panmure was severely wounded and captured by the Hanoverians but he was rescued by his gallant and enterprising brother Harry Maule of Kellie, who was by profession Depute Lord Lyon. As such it had been he who proclaimed King George in Edinburgh. His adhesion to the rebels seems to have been the product of family pressure and fear of arrest by the Hanoverian authorities. Harry Maule was nevertheless representative of a major strand in the Jacobite heritage – the conservative preoccupation with birth, status, and succession.[16] Since this preoccupation led a scholarly man towards the detailed study of medieval charters, it could and did stimulate much that was of permanent value in the historical writing of the period. The great French Benedictine scholar Jean Mabillon had published his technical study of medieval documents *De Re Diplomatica* in 1681 and his techniques for authenticating documents were publicly applied in 1694 at a meeting in the Scots College in Paris to validate a medieval charter confirming the legitimacy, which had been doubted, of the main line of the royal House of Stewart. To the exiled Jacobites present this was a vital issue of contemporary politics. In his long years of exile after 1716 (he died in 1734) Harry Maule worked steadily at the history of his own family, from its Norman origins to the year 1733, and produced the remarkable two volumes of the *Registrum de Panmure* which is in many ways of more enduring value than some of the meretricious works of those enlightened 'Scotch historians' who in the second half of the century won fame and fortune by their facile prose.[17]

Two closely-linked Angus families with a consistent tradition of opposition to the Act of Union were the Houses of Airlie and Strathmore. James, Lord Ogilvy, heir to the Earl of Airlie, was a young man born in 1698 but he was early in the field for the Jacobite cause in 1715 along with his youthful cousin the Earl of Strathmore and their uncle Patrick Lyon of Auchterhouse. Because of the peculiar topography of Angus, with its long glens running from Lowland Strathmore into the Highlands, it was normal for the Angus magnates to be able to recruit both Highland and Lowland supporters. Panmure, who had a general commission to organize the men of Angus, had in August 1715, probably with a view to increasing his political power, purchased the extensive Highland properties of the gifted but bankrupt Lindsays of Edzell. The last head of the elder branch of the Lindsays ended his days as an ostler in Orkney. Edzell, Glenesk, and Lethnot all passed into the hands of Panmure for a payment of £192,502 Scots equivalent of £16,042 sterling. All these areas provided a living rent of swordsmen for the Pretender in 1715. On the whole Angus did not show the sort of pattern discernible amongst the gentlemen Jacobites of Northumberland, where there seems to have been a much higher chance of a squire joining the rebellion if he was already financially embarrassed. In Angus the rebellion was very much a revolt of the rich and the powerful. Those who were in financial difficulty either faded out of history like the last of the 'lichtsome Lindsays' or sat on the fence like David, fourth Earl of Northesk. He had been made Sheriff Principal of Forfarshire (the contemporary name for Angus) by Queen Anne and had voted for the Union in the Scots Parliament, but he had taken very little part in politics after Anne's death and had failed to attend the coronation of George I, though he was invited. There seems to be little doubt that he sympathized with the '15, though he did not join his brother the Earl of Southesk or his friend the Earl of Panmure under the Jacobite flag, thereby avoiding the forfeiture of his estates for treason. Even so, his creditors forced him in 1723 to sell off part of his estates, including the barony of Lunan and the Redcastle.[18]

To keep the lands within the family they were purchased by Northesk's kinsman, Carnegie of Boysack, an event which can serve as a reminder that the concept of 'the name', the Lowland equivalent of the Highland word 'clan', was far from dead in the second decade of the eighteenth century. Many lairds were linked to local magnates by blood as well as interest. The Lyons and Carnegies who supported Strathmore and Southesk had counterparts elsewhere in Lowland Scotland, just as 'Bobbing John's' relatives could be found elsewhere than Angus. The Honourable James Forbes was the second son of William, thirteenth Lord Forbes, who supported the Union and who was appointed the Hanoverian Lord-Lieutenant of Aberdeenshire and Banffshire in August 1715. However, James Forbes broke with the family tradition in politics by joining the Jacobite rising. It may be coincidence, but his wife Mary was a first cousin to the Earl of Mar, not to mention the sister of Alexander, fourth Lord Forbes of Pitsligo, who was out in both the '15 and the '45.[19] Probably one should not exaggerate the importance of family links amongst the Jacobite gentry in 1715. They were real and important, but the main Jacobite recruiting agent was clearly widespread discontent. Disgruntled lairds were not at all a scarce commodity in Lowland Scotland in the autumn of 1715. Some were more committed Jacobites than others but passionate Jacobitism can be found far south of Aberdeenshire. In Perth-shire, in the parish of Kilspindie a few miles outside Perth itself, lay the castle of Fingask, overlooking the Carse of Gowrie. Sir David Threipland of Fingask was the son of Patrick Threipland, Provost of Perth and an ardent supporter of the Restoration regime, who was knighted for his diligence in suppressing Presbyterian conventicles. Sir David with his sons and retainers was one of the first to join Mar and though he paid the usual price of forfeiture, the family was as forward in the '45 as the '15.[20]

Enough has been said to demonstrate that the north-east was no exception in 1715 as far as the nobility and lairds were concerned. The region merely reflected a general malaise amongst the landed classes of much of Lowland Scotland. The same is true of the towns. Common sense ensured that few towns kept a detailed account of what went on in them during a rebellion, but it is clear that there was plenty of support for the Jacobites in Lowland burghs. On 20 September the young Earl Marischal, the twenty-two-year-old head of the Keith family, rode into Aberdeen with his nineteen-year-old brother James, the Earl of Errol, and other landed gentry and proclaimed 'James VIII' at the market cross. Next day the Earl Marischal was wined and dined by the strongly Jacobite Incorporated Trades of Aberdeen, and on the way home to his castle of Inverugie outside Peterhead that same afternoon he proclaimed the Pretender in Old Aberdeen, the distinct former Episcopal burgh on the Don. An election to the Town Council was due, so on 29 September the Jacobites announced that any burgess could come and vote in the New or East Kirk of St Nicholas. What transpired there we know not, but it is highly significant that the Jacobites were prepared to envisage an 'open' election (however pressurized), as distinct from the normal hole-in-corner affair where the retiring Council simply nominated the new one. There was no difficulty in finding a suitably Jacobite council with Patrick Bannerman, fourth son of the laird of Elsick, as Provost.[21] Elsewhere in the north-east the smaller burghs were usually burghs of barony whose allegiance was determined by that of their feudal Superior. It is therefore scarcely surprising to find Thomas Arbuthnot proclaiming King James at the market cross of Peter-head in 1715, for his own sincere Jacobite convictions were reinforced by those of the Earl Marischal, Superior of the burgh, whose factor Arbuthnot was, as well as Provost and Baron Bailie. On the other hand, Lord Saltoun, Superior of the neighbouring port of Fraserburgh, was opposed to the Jacobites, and when King James was proclaimed in Fraserburgh the ceremony was conducted by an armed band from Peterhead which had just outfaced an indignant Lord Saltoun.[22]

Further south there was, if anything, less opposition to the Jacobites in the coastal burghs. The magistracy of Arbroath, for example, had a tradition of opposition to the Union and seem to have regarded payments made to the Jacobite army during the rebellion as legitimate charges on the revenue of the town after that rebellion collapsed.[23] Such a convenient degree of continuity was not possible in Dundee. The local Jacobites were much more flamboyant and hopelessly compromised themselves at an early stage. William Graham of Duntrune, a local laird who was the heir-male to Viscount Claverhouse, promptly assumed the title of the dead Jacobite paladin and proclaimed King James in Dundee. The Pretender made a formal entry to the town on 6 January 1716, with the Earl of Mar on his right, the Earl Marischal on his left, and a train of some three hundred gentlemen. He was given a most enthusiastic welcome by the town authorities. As a result, when the Jacobite forces withdrew and the Hanoverians under Argyll occupied Dundee early in February, the entire magistracy deemed discretion the better part of valour and vanished, forcing Argyll to nominate five local worthies to take charge in the following terms:

> Whereas there are no Magistrates at present in this city, who can act or take care of the affairs of the city, whereby his Majesty's service as well as the city may suffer, you are therefore hereby required and authorized to take upon you the care of this city, and the affairs thereof, till such time as the proper Magistrates can be appointed by lawful authority.[24]

Even in Perth, a city which the Jacobites seized by means of a swift cavalry raid aided by a fifth column in or rather consisting of the Hanoverian garrison, it proved feasible for the Jacobite Governor to organize an election of complaisant magistrates. North of the Forth there was widespread urban sympathy for the rising.

Nor does the pattern of events in the Highlands give much comfort to exponents of a simplistic model of the Jacobite rebellion as an elemental clash between Gael and Anglo-Saxon. The situation in the Highlands was in truth one of labyrinthine complexity, and even the basic social unit of the Gaelic Highlands – the clan – was not nearly so straightforward a phenomenon as many historians assume. The concept of a clan system is so pervasive in Jacobite historiography that it is essential to clear the ground on this issue before further progress can be made. The Gaelic term *clann*, meaning children, is as much a hindrance as a help when it comes to analysing the historical reality of the Highland clans, for though the concept of kinship which it implies was important as a cement within clan society, it was never adequate as a binding agent in its own right, and in the early modern period it can be shown, in most cases, to be based mainly on make-believe rather than rooted in genealogical fact. In the case of northern clans such as the Grants, Chisholms and Frasers, whose chiefs were probably all of Norman origin, there cannot possibly have been any blood-tie between the first chief and his people. The surnames which are the hallmark of modern clans were not in general use in the Highlands before the seventeenth century. Instead most people were identified by nicknames or by a system of patronymics which, as in modern Iceland, changed with each generation and thus gave no indication at all of the clan of the bearer. The earliest rental of a Highland estate dates from 1505 and gives us the names of many tenants in Kintyre. Most of these are patronymics starting with 'Mac' but though these people all belonged to the following of the great Clan Donald, not one is called Macdonald.[25] By the eighteenth century it was very common for clansmen to bear their chief's surname and it seems clear that this was the result of a progressive tendency on the part of the peasantry on Highland estates to adopt the name of their landlord. In no other way could the Gordons, for example, have become the most powerful clan in the north-eastern Highlands, for their chiefs were Normans who settled in Scotland first in Berwickshire on the Borders, and who reached Strathbogie in Aberdeenshire only in the fourteenth century.[26]

None of this should be regarded as dismissing the kinship element in the clan. It was important, though in most clans it was at its most genuine and effective in relations between the paramount chief and the tacksmen or lairds to whom he leased large tracts of his territory at a low rate. These tacksmen were the gentry of the clan. They were usually cadets of the chief's line and they were essential instruments of control in both peace and war. Humbler clansmen were undoubtedly inclined to think of themselves as part of one great patriarchal unit, but it is worth emphasizing that in the eighteenth century it was quite common for men to change their clan surname for another one, either temporarily or permanently, when they changed their allegiance or place of abode or both. The aristocracy were the hard core of most clans and the world of the Highland aristocracy was by no means a closed one. Just as clans had existed until the seventeenth century in the Borders, so the feudal ideas and pattern of landholding characteristic of the Lowlands since the medieval period had steadily infiltrated across the Highland Line. Indeed in the heyday of Scottish feudalism it has been argued that there was no meaningful division between the Highland and Lowland aristocracy.[27] Be that as it may, by 1700 it is clear that most effective clan units were formed of a combination of feudal and ancient celtic elements, and that of these two the feudal element was the more important.

The basic method of landownership in the Highlands was by feudal charter from the Crown, and the fundamental unit of estate administration in the Highlands, as in the Lowlands, was the barony, a title, dignity, and legal entity normally erected by grant under the Great Seal of Scotland.

There were, of course, other jurisdictional units in the Highlands, some closely linked with a particular clan, others less so. It is instructive to compare and contrast two examples of the very highest level of hereditary jurisdiction in Scotland – the regality. Regalities, as royal lawyers were prepared to admit, were little kingdoms in which the King's writ in theory ran only in cases of high treason. Any regality could reclaim or re-pledge one of its indwellers who had by accident been brought before a royal court. Some of the old Scottish earldoms of celtic origin wielded regalian rights primarily as heirs of ancient sub-kingdoms whose origins are lost in the mists of time. Two of these earldoms were Argyll and Atholl. In exchange for surrendering the office of 'hereditary justice-general of Scotland' in 1628 the Earl of Argyll, Chief of Clan Campbell, was confirmed in his regalian powers over Argyll and the islands of the Campbell empire. His central court was the justiciary court of Argyll, and though its records differ very little from those of contemporary royal central courts,[28] there is no doubt that the authority of the justiciary court at Inverary was also a symbol of the majesty of the greatest of eighteenth-century clans. Quite different was the Regality of Atholl, despite its equal antiquity. The Earls, Marquises, and Dukes of Atholl held an ancient dignity, though one which passed through the hands of many different families. By the eighteenth century the ducal family name was Murray, and in Highland fashion a good many people in northern Perthshire had adopted that name, but Atholl was a palimpsest of surnames belonging to previous local dynasts, and the 'Clan Murray' was a non-event, really quite unnecessary in a region which was still recognizably a local kingdom.[29]

Nobody thought of the Duke of Atholl primarily as Chief of the Murrays. Yet when Daniel Defoe wrote about him in his *Tour through the Whole Island of Great Britain,* first published in 1724, he recognized that Atholl was potentially the most powerful man in Scotland, let alone the Highlands, for he was reputed to be able to put 6,000 men in the field if he really tried. Defoe sensed the regal nature of Atholl's dignity, saying:

> The pomp and state in which this noble person lives, is not to be imitated in Great Britain; for he is served like a prince, and maintains a greater equipage and retinue than five times his estate would support in another country.[30]

Defoe even recognized the ultimate source of this power – feudal superiorities. At the opposite end of the scale to the variegated human structure of the larger Highland political units such as Atholl, or the Campbell or Mackenzie empires lay a small homogeneous group inhabiting a compact block of territory like Clan Cameron in Lochaber. Clan Cameron was, however, an exception which proves the rule. Locked in interminable dispute, mostly with the Mackintosh of Mackintosh, as to the validity of conflicting charter rights over their territory, the Cameron leaders deliberately stripped down their territorial ambitions and tried to uphold them with a solidly loyal Cameron tenantry whose stout hearts and sharp swords had to compensate for a lack of an unambiguous title to jurisdiction.[31] For every Highland clan the hereditary right or power to do justice was the indispensable key to discipline, cohesion and effectiveness.

By definition so complex and potentially fluid a society was unlikely to have a history of stability. Passionate loyalties there were within clan society but over the centuries Highland history was marked by a continual flux in which clans rose, fell, merged, split and indeed disappeared. It can even be argued that, like most political structures with a strong kinship element in them, Highland clans had a built-in tendency to fission once they expanded beyond a certain size and it became difficult to maintain the immediacy of the relationship between the chiefly house and the all-important cadet branches. This can be seen in the case of Clan Campbell in 1715. There really were two Campbell territorial empires, one presided over by the Duke of Argyll, that peremptory Hanoverian loyalist whose Gaelic title was Mac Chailein Mor (the Great Son of Colin), and the other ruled by the Glenorchy branch of the clan whose chief was the Earl of Breadalbane. Breadalbane's Gaelic title was Mac Chailein mhic Dhonnachaidh (the Son of Colin Duncan's-Son) and he was a very much more complex and ambiguous character than the great Argyll with whom he endlessly jockeyed for the moral and political leadership of the Clan Diarmaid as the Campbells called themselves, on the ground that they were descended from Diarmaid, one of the heroes of ancient Fenian legend.

Broadly speaking, the dynamic element in sixteenth and seventeenth-century Highland history had been provided by the expansion of three great imperialist clans. In the south-west of the Highlands the Campbells had inexorably expanded mainly at the expense of the smaller clan units into which the Lordship of the Isles, once wielded by Clan Donald, had disintegrated after the forfeiture of the Lordship by the Crown. As the Campbells expanded into the islands of the Inner Hebrides they engaged in bitter and ultimately successful struggles with groups such as the Macleans, while the Glenorchy Campbells at one stage waged ruthless warfare against Clan MacGregor which had the misfortune to lie in the way of the westward expansion of that branch of the Clan Diarmaid. In the same way, the Earls of Huntly and their Gordons had long made a prey of Clan Chattan. This was a confederation of clans in Lochaber, Strathnairn and Badenoch which for the purposes of self defence rallied Macphersons, Cattanachs, MacGillivrays, Macleans, McBains, and many others behind the leadership of the Mackintosh of Mackintosh. In the northern parts of the Highlands Clan Mackenzie, a race of warrior herdsmen *par excellence*, rose to greatness, like the Campbells, on the ruins of the Lordship of the Isles, and then embarked on a career of conquest which saw them cross the waters of the Minch and overthrow, by a mixture of legal chicanery and brutal violence, the rule of the Siol Torquil, one of the branches of Clan Mac-Leod, in the island of Lewis.[32]

The relevance of such historic feuds to the events of 1715 can be greatly exaggerated. The Gordon drive against Clan Chattan had lost most of its impetus by that date. In 1715 the Duke of Gordon was in feeble health (he died in 1716), so political decision lay with his heir Alexander, Marquis of Huntly, who displayed all the characteristics of a worried, sated power. Personally, he was in a difficult position, torn between a furiously Jacobite mother who was a sister of Lord Strathmore, and a stoutly Whig wife, Lady Henrietta Mordaunt, daughter of the Earl of Peterborough. Huntly attended the meetings which Mar convened before raising the standard of rebellion, and he urged Mar and his supporters to behave circumspectly at least until the Pretender arrived in Scotland with the much-promised significant French reinforcement. Overborne by hotter heads, Huntly was a somewhat disillusioned ally of Mar as far as the battle of Sheriffmuir, after which he left Mar's camp, ostensibly to protect his estates from attack, but in reality to reach a truce with local Whigs and to work his passage with the victorious Hanoverians. This Huntly effected so successfully that he was not penalized and was allowed to succeed peacefully as second Duke of Gordon in 1716. On his part, it was a sensible performance under difficult conditions.[33]

The Mackintoshes had on the whole a Whiggish tradition. It is interesting that in a commission of fire and sword (a traditional means of using one Highland clan to discipline another) issued by the Crown to Mackintosh of Mackintosh against the Macdonalds of Keppoch in 1698 William Mackintosh of Borlum is named, for this man effectively dictated the Mackintosh policy in 1715. Borlum proved to be the best soldier in the Pretender's service during the rebellion. He began it by persuading the heir to the chieftainship to join him in a swift occupation of Inverness where they proclaimed 'King James'. The opposition of the magistrates was entirely nominal. Thereafter Brigadier Mackintosh of Borlum went on to glory and defeat in a rebellion which was joined by the Macdonalds of Keppoch. Not that anyone was surprised to see Keppoch fight King George. Safe in his impenetrable homeland, Keppoch had sallied out to fight King James, King William and Queen Anne, so the tough and intelligent little bandit, for such he was, was merely displaying his consistent eye for the main chance.

Several of the small clans into which the once-mighty Clan Donald had split can be found under Mar's banners. However, the presence of the Macdonalds of Glengarry and Macdonalds of Clanranald should not be interpreted as part of an anti-Campbell crusade vaguely aimed at recreating the vanished glories of the Lordship of the Isles. Both clans were led by men who happened to be devoted Jacobites. Alexander Macdonnell of Glengarry had carried the standard of King James VII at Killiecrankie, and Clanranald marched behind their Captain (or war-leader) Alan Macdonald, who had been in exile in France for some years after fighting on the same field. No doubt it was a matter of added satisfaction to the men of Clanranald and Glengarry that the MacChailean Mor was on the other side, but of course there were plenty of Campbells in the Jacobite camp in 1715. Sir John Campbell, eleventh of Glenorchy and Earl of Breadalbane, was nearing the end of a long life in 1715 (he had been born in 1635). 'Cunning as a fox, wise as a serpent', Breadalbane was known in the Highlands as Iain Glas (Grey John). With characteristic slipperiness the aged Breadalbane half joined the rising whilst brandishing in the direction of the government testimonials from his physician and the Minister of Kenmore, of which parish he was patron, to the effect that he was disabled by a remarkable list of ailments. He probably was suffering from most of them but the will of Iain Glas was quite strong enough to ignore all of them had he wanted. His men joined Mar under Campbell of Glenlyon.

It is true that when Glenlyon, operating in the west, met a war party of Hanoverian Campbells under the veteran warrior Campbell of Fonab, he struck a bargain with Fonab to the effect that Campbell should not fight Campbell just because Stewart and Hanover were grappling for a throne.[34] Nevertheless, two battalions of Breadalbane men fought with spirit at Sheriffmuir. Thus Campbells stood in the Jacobite ranks with such clans as the Camerons whose anti-Campbell tendencies have been much exaggerated. Their aged chief Ewan, seventeenth of Lochiel, who had at the age of sixty led barefoot the victorious Jacobite charge at Killiecrankie, had been born of a Campbell mother in a Campbell castle. His elder son John, who led the clan out in 1715, also married a Campbell. The Lochiel chiefs differed from Argyll in politics, but the mortal enemies of the Camerons were Huntly and the Mackintosh. Even the MacGregors were far from motivated by singleminded hatred of the Campbells. The struggle for the fair land of Glenlyon was ancient history and individual MacGregors were by 1715 welcome as tenants of the Breadalbane Campbells. The MacGregors had migrated westwards. Many lived among other clans on the Moor of Rannoch while only a small section of the MacGregor people, the Clan Dougal Ciar, maintained a distinct identity in three remote glens to the east of Loch Lomond. Even there the chieftainship was in dispute and the best-known MacGregor leader in 1715, Rob Roy, uncle to Gregor Glun Dubh (Black Knee) of Glengyle, was certainly not the paramount chief. He was a former speculator in livestock who had failed in business and had turned to selling a rough and ready sort of insurance known as blackmail. Since the Duke of Montrose had lost capital lent to Rob Roy, and had then seen his Menteith tenants blackmailed by this enterprising but unscrupulous man, relations between Rob and Montrose were poor. Rob Roy had an excellent relationship with Argyll, who, probably to annoy Montrose, actually patronized him. Rob often used the name Campbell. He sat out Sheriffmuir at the head of a group of Mac-Gregors and Macphersons, showing a detachment worthy of the homespun philosopher he was, and then when the rebellion collapsed 'surrendered' to Campbell of Fonab on terms so easy as to free him at once for further mischief.

The Highland support for the '15 came mainly from the Grampian Highlands. The Mackenzies under Seaforth were the most northerly Jacobite group of any significance. Their leader, like Huntly, rather went off the cause after Sheriffmuir, but botched his settlement with Hanover. Apart from the Macleans, who simply resumed where they had left off in 1692, there was comparatively little active support in the Hebrides for the Pretender. The islands were just too remote from events. In Skye the Macleod of Macleod was a mere babe in arms and his Tutor or guardian John Macleod, second of Bernera, known as Contullich, certainly had Jacobite sympathies. His son Donald, known as the Old Trojan, was out in both the '15 and the '45. Despite this Contullich refused to allow the Skye Macleods, the Siol Tormod, to be drawn into the maelstrom of rebellion, and apart from a few isolated individuals they did indeed stand aside.[35]

Modern historians tend to be slightly embarrassed by the famous letter written by Mar to 'Black Jock' Forbes of Skellater, one of his principal Highland tenants and supporters, telling him to burn out Mar's vassals in Kildrummy if there was no other way of making them join the Jacobite army, but this was in fact a classic example of the tacksman and his strong-arm gang of immediate supporters mobilizing the human rent on a Highland estate. The '15 was so widely supported in the Grampian Highlands because the aristocracy and gentry of that area shared the general discontent of the Scottish aristocracy and gentry, of which they were a part. It follows that there were likely to be dissenters amongst the gentry from the majority Jacobite views of their class. No sooner had Mackintosh of Borlum marched south than Inverness came under threat from local Whig forces which captured it under the leadership of John Forbes of Culloden and his brother Duncan, along with their relative Hugh Rose of Kilravock and his brother Arthur who returned from a long captivity in Turkey to die in the assault on Inverness.

John Forbes had travelled north from London to raise the Jacobite siege at Culloden House, which was being defended by Duncan Forbes and the tenants of the Laird of Culloden. His travelling companion, who shared the hazards of the boat trip necessary to outflank Jacobite-held territory north of the Forth, was the rascally Simon Fraser than whom no man better epitomizes the dependence of the events of the '15 at regional level on the often erratic will of local aristocrats. In the end, he cooperated with the Culloden and Kilravock families, and with the Earl of Sutherland in the recapture of Inverness, and typically wrote a pamphlet claiming most of the credit for the operation, but he could just as easily have joined the other side. Compared with Simon Fraser a corkscrew was a straightforward instrument.[36]

Simon had one consistent objective in early life – to have himself recognized as Chief of Clan Fraser. The clan lands lay just to the south of Inverness and Simon, who was Fraser of Beaufort, probably had a reasonable claim to the succession to Fraser of Lovat, which succession carried with it recognition of chieftainship. However, Simon Fraser's naturally dishonest mind had enormously complicated his career by leading him to try to secure the Lovat inheritance by kidnapping and forcibly marrying the widowed Lady Lovat, a daughter of the House of Atholl. Pipe music drowned the bride's shrieks while the bridegroom's faithful gillies passed the time of the service in thoughtfully slitting Lady Lovat's stays with their dirks. The wrath of the House of Atholl was great, and exacerbated by the almost unbelievable effrontery of the principal villain.[37] Such was his magnetism that there was difficulty in bringing him to heel because of the amount of local sympathy for him around Inverness.[38] Nevertheless, this episode, eighteen years in the past by 1715, had been the start of a long period of wandering for Simon, a period which included substantial spells at the exiled Jacobite court, and which saw him perfect the arts of betrayal, doublecross, and mendacious propaganda. This was the man who argued in print that he rather than the Roses, or Forbes brothers, let alone the Earl of Sutherland marching in from his remote northern castle of Dunrobin, had conquered Inverness for Hanover. He clearly had many of the talents necessary for success in Whig politics, so the '15 proved the decisive episode in the protracted transition whereby Fraser of Beaufort emerged as Simon Fraser, Lord Lovat, Chief of Clan Fraser. The inner man changed not at all.

Such lack of principle as lay at the heart of the tortured career of Simon Fraser does not seem to have been at all common during the '15. Even the Earl of Breadalbane, whose views were often as elusive and shifting as the grey mists which coiled around his remote lair of Finlarig Castle, seems to have acted out a long-standing movement within his own mind towards the streak of Jacobitism latent in his character. Basically the split in the Highlands, as in the Lowlands, was between two sections of the gentry and was on a party basis. Andrew Fletcher of Saltoun lay on his deathbed in

Paris during the later stages of the rebellion. He died with a Christian stoicism and a Roman patriotism worthy of his adamantine character. To him the '15 in Scotland was a clash between Whigs on the one hand and Tories and Jacobites on the other, and the tragedy of Scotland lay in the fact that there was so little to be said for either side.[39] Whatever may be thought of the old patriot's pessimism, his analysis of the crisis deserves respect. Conviction rather than cynicism is the key to patterns of loyalty in the early stages of the '15. At the time of Killiecrankie the Atholl family undoubtedly hedged their bets. It looks as if they did the same in 1715, for the Duke of Atholl remained firmly Whig and Hanoverian while his heir William, Marquis of Tullibardine, came out for the Jacobites. Tullibardine was an officer in the Royal Navy who had become Marquis of Tullibardine in 1709 after his elder brother John, Colonel of a Scots-Dutch regiment, had been killed fighting under Marlborough at the Battle of Malplaquet in 1709. Two other sons of the House of Atholl, Lords George and Charles Murray, both officers in the British army, joined Tullibardine. The 1,400 or so Atholl men whom Tullibardine managed to raise for the cause were formed into four regiments officered by the three brothers and their uncle Lord Nairne that 'mighty stickler against the Union'.

The split in the Atholl family was based on deep conviction. Tullibardine, Charles and George had simply had enough of the post-1707 British establishment and its ways. Charles and George were younger sons but Tullibardine lost a great inheritance as the result of his behaviour, becoming the shadowy exiled 'Duke William' of the Jacobite peerage, as distinct from Duke James, his Hanoverian younger brother who became the legal successor. There was nothing bogus about the anguish of the old Duke of Atholl at the behaviour of his three Jacobite sons, the more so as their rebellion against the prevailing system started with a withdrawal from the public worship of the Presbyterian Kirk, and a turning to Episcopalianism. Above all the sincerity of the Jacobite brothers is proved by the way their father moved heaven and earth to try to mitigate the consequence of their actions after the failure of their venture. His behaviour contrasts strikingly with that of Duke James after the '45 and underlines the way in which conscientious opponents of the '15 like Atholl and Argyll could see that the Hanoverian regime, on top of the last years of Anne, constituted a very grave temptation to a patriotic Scottish gentleman to seek redress of grievance by the sword.[40]

So far from being rooted in the immemorial culture of an anachronistic Celtic past, the Highland aristocracy which came out for the Pretender in 1715 was conspicuously anglicized and indeed rather cosmopolitan. Tullibardine came north from London to rebel. He moved to join Mar in company with his brother Lord George, who had soldiered in Flanders and whose regiment was currently stationed in Ireland. Along with them on the last stage of their journey went the man Tullibardine called 'the good Elector of Rannoch', Alexander Robertson of Struan, poet and Jacobite. Educated at St Salvator's College in the University of St Andrews, Struan had lived abroad in exile between 1690 and 1703. At one time he had lived in considerable penury in Rotterdam, after which he is believed to have entered the service of the King of France. His experience of life was therefore already wide, and international. His private culture was, however, unmistakably that of the Augustan England of Pope, Swift, and Addison.[41]

Here the primary evidence must be his own verse which was collected in a single octavo volume published probably within a couple of years of his death in 1749. Despite the enthusiasm of one late eighteenth-century admirer, who was convinced that in future ages the lustre of Struan's literary reputation would far outshine that of Homer, the truth is that these are rather bad poems, clothing the platitudes of Augustan thought in measured Augustan clichés shaped into formal and pompous verse. 'A Short Meditation on the Nature of Man', for example, takes precisely forty-one lines to survey, in a truly unmemorable fashion, some central problems of human existence and religious faith. Struan's 'Epitaph on the Earl of Mar' is, like most formal epitaphs, remarkable neither for virtuosity nor veracity. Sadly, even his erotic verse lacks the fire of inspiration. Instead it oscillates uneasily between the ludicrously stilted and the rampantly phallic. What is valuable in these poems is the evidence of a Scots patriot with an Augustan personal culture. Both traits are summed up in his 'Epitaph upon the Captain of CLANRANNALD, who was killed at *Sheriffmuir* 1715', where he wrote of Allan, Captain of this Macdonald clan:

> He fell supporting his true Prince's Cause,
> To raise his Country and restore her Laws.[42]

Although Struan was clearly an outstanding personality, he was by no means in the select group of great Highland magnates. Those potentates and their families fitted very naturally into an aristocratic culture which embraced, however strong their local patriotism, the ruling élites of the three kingdoms subject to the British Crown, and which was itself recognizably a local variant on a Western European aristocratic tradition heavily dominated by the values and achievements of Bourbon France. It is more to the point to ask how deeply this polite culture penetrated the ruling class of the Grampian Highlands from whence, with marginal exceptions like the Macleans, the Mackenzies, and the Macdonalds of Sleat in Skye, the bulk of Highland support for the '15 came. Robertson of Struan is evidence that tells us of a class of chiefs below the level of the regional magnates, but even at the level of the lairds or tacksmen it must be recognized that we are dealing with a class of men with many contacts outwith the Highlands. Apart from anything else, they had a strong tradition of military service in the armies of foreign powers. This tradition had existed long before the seventeenth century, but it was in that century and more particularly during the period of the Thirty Years War (1618–48) that Scots in general, and Highlanders in particular, became famous as a major element in the great European pool of mercenary military labour. Highland gentlemen can be found holding commissions on all sides of the European power struggles of the seventeenth and eighteenth centuries. Clan Mackay, from the northern Highlands, confirmed its Protestant and its later Whiggish inclinations by service as a military unit in Protestant armies in seventeenth-century Germany. Roman Catholic Highlanders held commissions from the Hapsburg Holy Roman Emperors. Those who served the Tsar of All the Russias tended to return to Scotland with a confirmed taste for absolutist methods of government. The very many Highland gentlemen who helped to officer the Scots Brigade in the service of the United Netherlands until the end of the eighteenth century naturally tended to reflect the Protestant and constitutionalist flavour of their Dutch employers.[43]

Nor is there any reason to think that the clergy – arguably the lowest rung of the Highland élite – were notably different from, say, the contemporary clergy of Lowland Scotland. They were much thinner on the ground than their opposite numbers in the Lowlands, and they had to come to terms with the Gaelic culture of their flocks, which many of them shared, but their conscious mental world tended to be formed by the institutions which educated them for their profession. A single Jacobite clergyman of the Church of Scotland will suffice to make the point. Alexander Robertson, Struan's namesake, was Minister of Fortingall. Educated at St Leonard's College in the University of St Andrews (a college with a remarkable flair for breeding stormy petrels), he was presented by John Bishop of Dunkeld in 1687, and deposed from his charge in October 1716 for 'reading traitrous papers issued by the rebels'. As it happens, one of his college notebooks survives, full of fair copy of notes on ethics and physics from the dictates of his old regent at St Leonard's. The language used is, of course, the Latin which was the common speech of the European academic community in the 1680s. Much later, as Minister of Fortingall, Robertson used blank pages in this notebook to jot down lists of books belonging to him and lent by him, not to mention the odd Latin poem on themes which included the death of Martin Duke of Luxemburg. His books are very typical of what one would expect to find on the shelves of any cultivated Scottish clergyman of the Kirk by Law Established. Divinity dominates the collection, with a fair representation of leading

English theologians, and the usual strong dash of anti-Roman Catholic polemic.[44]

It will therefore not do to claim that it was an urge to defend a unique, archaic culture which propelled a disproportionately large section of the ruling class of the Grampian Highlands into active support for the 1715 rebellion. The reverse is the case. These men adhered to the Jacobite side because they shared the mental world of their social counterparts in the Lowlands. A minority of Highland gentry families were permeated by militant Jacobite ideology. Most were susceptible to it, but usually they managed to contain their latest Jacobite sympathies until, as patriotic Scots and disgruntled Britons, they decided that force was the only way out of the political dilemmas they faced. What was different about the Highlands was the much greater ease with which a landlord could mobilize human rent in the shape of armed men from his estates. Even in this respect in 1715 the difference between the Highlands and the Lowlands is one of degree rather than kind, but the degree of difference was already extremely marked, as men like Mar well knew.

On his Lowland estates Mar was a conspicuously progressive landlord full of ideas and initiatives and with a particular interest in industrial development ranging from his extensive coalworkings, to which he tried to harness water-powered machinery on the grand scale, to the glass industry which he helped to stimulate from exile after the '15.[45] In this he was far from unique amongst the Jacobite leadership. The redoubtable Mackintosh of Borlum was already noted for his zest for improvement on his properties before 1715, having a particular interest in reafforestation. It is well known that during the long imprisonment in Edinburgh Castle which was his later fate, he produced two works strongly urging agricultural improvement on the Scots nobility and gentry. Published in 1729 and 1732 respectively, the books commended long leases, systematic enclosure, fallowing, new root and grass crops, and of course afforestation.[46] In the Highlands, however, opportunities for a more commercially-orientated agriculture were limited, and for industrial growth virtually nil. The chains of dependence reaching down through a land-based social hierarchy were inescapable. Men who in early eighteenth-century Clackmannan might have tried to make their fortune by working a coal pit, or by overseas trade, or by distilling whisky for export to London, could in the Highlands aspire only to a tack or a pulpit.[47]

In the last analysis there were two parties virtually everywhere in Scotland in 1715, though the balance between them varied markedly from region to region. The aristocracy and gentry, including the burgh town councils, were the only significant actors on the political stage, being linked so intimately and commandingly with the other members of Scottish society that they carried their dependants and inferiors with them. Among the ruling class there were some, like Fletcher of Saltoun, who called a plague on both political houses, but they were few, and Fletcher himself undoubtedly regarded Hanover as the lesser of two evils. A simple regional model of the rebellion shows Jacobitism overwhelmingly ascendant in the Grampian Highlands, in the north-east, and every part of the Lowlands north of the Tay. Most east coast burghs north of the Tay showed strong support for the rebellion. The Jacobitism of Clan Mackenzie in the north-west of the Highlands was balanced by the strongly Whig position of the Argyll Campbells in the south-west. The northern and western isles of Scotland were, with a few exceptions, too remote to be actively involved in the struggle.

Against this threatening and extensive Jacobite territory was set the southern part of Scotland, which the Hanoverian government managed more or less to control. Edinburgh and the Lothians throughout history tended to be amenable to control by pro-English regimes. There are two obvious reasons for this. One was the accessibility of the region to English power. The other was the extent to which the city of Edinburgh had developed an instinctive deference to government on account of its dependence upon government expenditure and jobs. There were plenty of Jacobites in Edinburgh, most of them attenders of its numerous Episcopal chapels. The Faculty of Advocates had quite seriously considered accepting a Jacobite medallion offered to it by the Duchess of Gordon in 1711. A furious Whig response secured the rejection of the proposal, but the Faculty was not the only upper-class Edinburgh association riddled with Jacobite sympathizers, for the Royal Company of Archers – the King's Bodyguard in Scotland – was deemed very unsound from a Hanoverian point of view.[48] Indeed, an impudent attempt to seize Edinburgh Castle for the Pretender in 1715 was ruined only by a botched execution of perfectly feasible plans. Nevertheless, Sir George Warrender of Lochend, the zealous Whig merchant who was Lord Provost of Edinburgh in 1715 and also the M.P. for the city, was able to keep the situation under control, though by an uncomfortably slender margin. His good friend and fellow Whig the Duke of Montrose, who was the Secretary of State responsible for Scotland, in 1715 had urged him to return to Edinburgh on the ground that he was more valuable to the regime there than at Westminster. After the failure of the Jacobite attempt on the castle in September 1715, Warrender wrote to Secretary Stanhope and Lord Townshend appealing desperately for the assistance of more regular troops, on the ground that:

> . . . hade not I given detatchments of our city guaird on that immediat exigence and service the Conspirators hade been masters of the Castle and we hade then been reduced to the extreemest danger, and by this the

Government of the city taken out of our hands and lodged in the hands of our enemies . . .[49]

Warrender had a very good idea of the parlous nature of the Whig position in the northern parts of Britain in September 1715 for he was in correspondence, through the Whig Mayor of Berwick, with William Cotesworth of Gateshead.[50] In October Warrender was the alarmed witness of a rapid Jacobite coup in Fife. That county was an exception to the general rule that in any Scottish region a broadly similar consensus tended to unite the strongest sections of both the landed interest and the ruling élites in the burghs. Nobody was clearer than Lord Provost Warrender that such unity of purpose was essential for any effective political action. In the period of mounting tension which had preceded the outbreak of the '15 Warrender had urged the magistracy of Edinburgh to avoid quarrels with the surrounding landed gentry. As he said:

> I wish a good understanding betwixt the Gentlemen of the Shyre and you Especially at this Juncture for Differences at this time are Dreadfully ominous.[51]

Fife was a county where most of the burghs were studded along the south coast and had a strongly Whig and Presbyterian tradition. In the landward areas, still relatively unimproved and dominated by heath and bog, a numerous class of lairds harboured a deal of resentful Jacobitism.

The Jacobite thrust into Fife was precipitated by the news which reached their camp in Perth early in the morning of 2 October 1715 that an English ship carrying a large quantity of arms and ammunition destined for the Whig Earl of Sutherland had put into Burntisland harbour on the north shore of the Forth. Oddly enough the Duke of Montrose had, late in 1714, worked himself into a state of excitement over the seizure of a cargo of arms in a Fife ship, the *Margaret* of Leven, though it proved impossible to trace those behind the shipment.[52] It was certainly not part of any systematic plan, for Mar's army was at one stage very short of weapons. To remedy this, the Master of Sinclair swooped on Burntisland with a party of horse, commandeered boats for a boarding party, and seized both ship and arms. An official enquiry conducted by the Hanoverian Lord Advocate immediately after this episode tells us some significant details. For example, Sinclair's troopers had a simple test of political allegiance for anyone who fell into their hands. They asked if their prisoner went to the Meeting House (i.e. Episcopal) or the Church (i.e. Presbyterian), and they treated anyone who said he went to the latter as a nonsympathizer. Faced by the Jacobite force the town guard of Burntisland had sensibly but unheroically thrown down its arms and run away.[53]

Without a stiffening of 'men of honour' trained in the military ethos of the aristocracy, burghal forces were always likely to take this option which had the great virtue of sparing their own lives and those of their fellow-citizens who might have been killed in a massacre after the attackers had taken losses cutting their way into the town. Shortly afterwards Jacobite detachments occupied all the Fife burghs and proceeded to levy the cess and other taxes. The Earl of Rothes, the local Whig magnate, prudently withdrew, so Fife was not only an interesting case of political division, but also an illustration that superior force plus the usual Jacobite fifth column made it very easy for Mar to take over territory. Edinburgh and Lothian would have been no different.

Only in the south-western part of Scotland does the Whig interest seem to have enjoyed overwhelming support. Counties like Ayr and Galloway had very old traditions of radical Protestantism which made them highly resistant to Jacobitism, while the regional capital, Glasgow, though anti-Union was Whig and Presbyterian to the core. It sent several hundred citizens as a formed regiment into Argyll's camp at Stirling where they served under a former Glasgow Provost, John Aird. The small aristocratic rising which occurred in the south-west Borders of Scotland was notably out of sympathy with the general feeling of the area and is best explained by the survival of strong Jacobite views in a limited number of sometimes related noble households. Lord Nithsdale, for example, seems to have been personally a rather colourless fellow, but he was a Roman Catholic, he was financially near to bankruptcy, and he was related to that convinced Jacobite, the Earl of Traquair.[54] Lord Carnwath was a Protestant but brought up, like his sister who married the Earl of Kenmure, in staunch Jacobite principles. Lady Carnwath's fiery adherence to the cause of the exiled Stewarts is said to have helped to decide her husband's divided mind, but it does seem that the decisive factor for Kenmure, Carnwath and Nithsdale was the appearance of their names in the warrant attached to the Act for Encouraging Loyalty in Scotland of 30 August 1715. This euphemistically named legislation was of course an attempt to sweep all significant figures of dubious loyalty to Hanover into preventive custody. As with Derwentwater in England, such tactics were equally capable of precipitating a frightened man into premature rebellion. Poorly armed, and devoid of strategic direction, the Border Jacobites wandered aimlessly around. They were capable of effecting a rendezvous with the eccentric Earl of Wintoun, a very odd man indeed who had estates outside Edinburgh, and whose Jacobitism was typical of his perversely original approach to life, but they were quite incapable of seizing any significant town in the face of local Whig opposition. Eventually they linked up with Mackintosh of Borlum and Forster in that pilgrimage of futility which culminated at Preston.

All in all, however, it cannot be gainsaid that Mar faced an almost unbelievably favourable position in Scotland in the autumn of 1715. His appeal was heavily based on a firm promise to repeal the Union, a measure deeply discredited in Scottish eyes, and in the more general desperation of a Tory interest faced with virtual annihilation by the Whigs. Though General Whetham, Argyll's predecessor in command of the government forces in Scotland, rapidly concentrated such troops as he had at the key point of Stirling, the sheer weight of Jacobite manpower massed for the attack on that bog-made bottleneck was for weeks totally overwhelming. Argyll was quite right to be appalled by the prospect. His opponent outnumbered him by many thousands. There was no need for tactical skill on Mar's part. All he had to do was attack and keep on attacking. Two days fighting would have finished off Argyll even as late as Sheriffmuir, because Argyll just could not replace casualties on any scale. It is ironic that in minor operations Jacobite commanders in both Scotland and England showed spirit and initiative. The Burntisland raid captured the imagination of friend and foe. Lindisfarne Castle on Holy Island not far from Berwick was captured and held briefly for the Pretender by a bold Newcastle skipper Lancelot Errington. Mackintosh of Borlum's crossing of the Forth with over a thousand men was a remarkable feat. Yet with 'Old Borlum' literally snapping at Argyll's heels, Mar did nothing when the situation cried out for an immediate offensive.

Once Argyll had been brushed aside, the prospects facing the Jacobite army would have been spectacular. There was more than enough sympathy and support in southern Scotland to enable local Jacobite regimes to take over and secure a broad passage to England where the rebellion in the north-eastern area was more than matched in potential by latent Jacobite sympathies in Lancashire. To turn latent into active sympathy in this, as in all other rebellions, military victory was essential. Forty-eight hours of conflict around Stirling should have seen Mar through to Derby with over 20,000 men behind him and a disreputable and deservedly discredited regime before him. Foreign aid was quite unnecessary. On the other hand delay was fatal. Not only could the Hanoverian regime build up concentrations of its own troops, but it could also count on reinforcements from its allies. The Dutch Republic was a committed supporter of the Protestant Succession in Britain. In accordance with the Treaty of Barrier and Succession it eventually sent 8,000 troops to Great Britain.[55] Mar was not very different from his Hanoverian counterparts like the Earl of Islay, Argyll's brother, whose defence of Inveraray against a not very vigorous Jacobite siege was marked mainly by such offensive arrogance on Islay's part that many a Campbell laird muttered that Islay was behaving more like a British Cabinet Minister than a leader of Clan Campbell. Both Mar and Islay were good administrators. They shuffled paper well, but were better at imperiously demanding obedience than at that achievement of practical results which alone justifies a man of action. Both were essentially manipulators of patronage. Mar was the Jacobite leader because he had been deprived of access to patronage. The British political system in 1715 was so corrupt and so obnoxious that it was ripe for a fall, but it was saved by the fact that the challenge to it was led by one of its own. The many gallant gentlemen who rallied to Mar's standard rallied, in the last analysis, to a self-centred, monstrously incompetent poltroon. He deserves all the contempt history has traditionally showered on him.

7 The Aftermath of the '15

The battle of Sheriffmuir was fought on Sunday 13 November 1715. It was a confused clumsy affair, but at the end of the day before light failed Argyll, with a mere 1,000 or so men, was left making a stand behind some turf walls, in the expectation that Mar and the roughly 4,000 men still under his effective command would launch a final, irresistible attack which would obliterate the remnant of the Hanoverian army. Mar withdrew. The tide of events was already, unknown to him, running strongly against him. At almost exactly the same time the southern Jacobite army was surrendering in the streets of Preston, and Inverness was being stormed by the northern Whigs. The belated arrival of James Francis Edward, the Pretender, late in December, with no serious French assistance in men or supplies, did precious little to inspire the army fighting for his cause. When a reinforced Argyll moved forward at the end of January, the Jacobite army began its retreat in bitter winter weather. In a cruel but futile attempt to slow Argyll's advance, Jacobite troops burned the small settlements of Auchterarder, Blackford, Muthill, Dunning and Crieff which lay between Perth and the Hanoverian army. The Pretender's conscience was much disturbed by a measure which could only alienate Scottish hearts, but the way in which he, Mar, the Earl of Melfort, Lord Drummond and a few others simply abandoned their army by slipping away in a small ship by night from Montrose was, if anything, more damaging to his credit. This was not the stuff of which heroic legend is made.

The rebellion had at one stage constituted a desperately serious threat to the Whigs, whose own behaviour had done a great deal to bring it about. Once it had failed, miserably and with little dignity, it became an absolute godsend to them. It gave irresistible impetus to their basic propaganda line, which tried to exploit anti-Roman Catholic and anti-French prejudices by depicting the Whigs as the only possible alternative to foreign absolutism and rampant Popery. The Whigs had faced, long before the rebellion, sustained popular protest against their rule even at its very heart in London. The City of London in particular contained elements bitterly hostile to the oligarchic and anti-libertarian tendencies so clearly established in the behaviour of the government before Mar raised the standard of rebellion. London artisans and petty tradesmen found the rhetoric of the Protestant succession empty when allied to a greedy, corrupt and exclusive regime all the more obnoxious because it was tactically allied to a Nonconformist interest already bent on imposing its puritanical morals on a recalcitrant populace. The natural result of all this was riot, and it was equally natural for rioters to shout Jacobite slogans, whether they believed them or not. These slogans were known to infuriate Whigs. It was to curb such riots, and the leniency of popular juries towards rioters, that the Whigs had passed the Riot Act. By October 1715 it was possible for the government to stage horrific spectacles in London like the hanging, drawing, and quartering of three soldiers in the First Regiment of Foot Guards, for treasonably enlisting with the Pretender. Political processions brandishing the crudest of anti-Stewart and anti-Papal symbols were still being organized in London and massively funded by Whig magnates like the Duke of Newcastle in 1717–18. It was all part of a barrage of manipulative propaganda essential to cover the actions of the government.[1]

In 1694 a Triennial Act had made a general election obligatory every three years, unless the sovereign chose to dissolve the legislature earlier. At a time of feverish party strife frequent elections were a severe, though probably a salutary, strain on any government. Ministers of state, then as now, instinctively believed that important political decisions should be taken only by men as informed and percipient as themselves, and they viewed the electorate with the usual mixture of contempt and fear. Besides, no Whig politician could in his heart fail to sense the basic unpopularity of the regime. The trials of captured Jacobite gentlemen from Lancashire were treated as part of the immense propaganda campaign centred on London and designed to whip up support for the government, yet even here results were often unsatisfactory. In Lancashire itself there had been a great many executions. The first notable Lancashire prisoner to be arraigned at Westminster was the Roman Catholic Colonel Oxburgh who was found guilty, butchered at Tyburn, and had his head set up on Temple Bar. The upshot was a very real revulsion in London at the thought that the hangings, drawings and beheadings which had taken place in Lancashire might be repeated in the metropolis. The day after Oxburgh's passion two other hereditary Jacobites from Lancashire, Richard Townley and Edward Tildesley of the Lodge, came up for trial before the Court of Admiralty in the Marshalsea. In the face of crushing evidence that both men had raised and commanded a troop of cavalry for the Jacobite army, the jury accepted the palpably fatuous contention of the accused that they had been forced into the rebellion, and returned a verdict of not guilty, to the fury of the judge, Mr Baron Montague. Thereafter convictions were obtained against twenty-four accused but public opinion was such that it was thought expedient to reprieve twenty-two of them. Sacrificed at

Tyburn as an example to others were the crazy Northumberland Justice of the Peace, Jack Hall of Otterburn, and the Anglican priest William Paul.[2]

It is in this context that a startling constitutional innovation, the Septennial Act, must be seen. This received the royal assent in May 1716 and had the effect of prolonging the legal life of the existing, and every subsequent, Parliament for a maximum of seven years. The specious excuse advanced for this legislation was the danger of a revival of Jacobite agitation at the election due in 1718. Fundamentally, the Whigs were much more frightened by the idea that with the rebellion out of the way legitimate opposition might revive on a scale which would make the next Parliament difficult to handle. In theory earlier dissolution was still possible, but in practice eight of the eleven British Parliaments between 1716 and 1783 lasted for between six and seven years.[3] There is no need to mince words about the Septennial Act. It was designed to reduce the already very limited influence of the highly restricted contemporary electorate to virtually nil. In so far as anything worth the name of a principle survived from the Glorious Revolution in 1688, the Septennial Act marked its final and total betrayal. The sort of propaganda churned out by publicists like Defoe which depicted the British as 'the Freest People on Earth' became even more of a humbug than it had been. They now had little or no control over their government. The main constraint on government, and of course it was a very serious one, was the class interest of between 600 and 700 M.P.s and peers.

As if the Septennial Act was not sufficient, by 1719 the government, now dominated by Stanhope and Sunderland, was talking of further major constitutional change. Stanhope and Sunderland even toyed with the idea of repealing the Septennial Act, without of course proposing any alternative, so as to produce the executive's dream – the potentially perpetual Parliament. The idea was so extreme as to be impractical but they might have succeeded in their attempt to turn the House of Lords into a 'closed' preserve. The Peerage Bill of 1719 proposed that the number of English peers be not enlarged beyond six above the existing number, though on failure of male issue to a given title the Crown was to be allowed to keep up the total number by a fresh creation. The sixteen elective peers of Scotland were to be replaced by twenty-five hereditary peers whose number, on failure of heirs male, was to be made up by other Scots peers. The whole scheme was designed to perpetuate the grip of Sunderland and Stanhope on the House of Lords. The six new creations would give them a majority while Scots peers like Montrose, Annandale, Islay and Argyll assumed that they would be among the chosen twenty-five and so supported the plan. By 'closing' the upper chamber the existing regime would deprive any future monarch of power to alter the balance of power there by such creations as had secured the passage of the Peace of Utrecht in 1713. Given the foul relations between sovereign and heir-apparent normal in the Illustrious House of Hanover, it is not surprising that George I was very happy to deprive the Prince of Wales of this future power.[4]

The scheme foundered on the misgivings of the House of Commons, misgivings brilliantly exploited and expressed by Robert Walpole. That remarkable man was in opposition because of a great rift in the Whig ranks in 1717 which had placed him and his brother-in-law Viscount Townshend outside the charmed circle of government. Nobody had advocated a harder line against the important Jacobite prisoners after the '15 than Walpole. From the influential place of Chancellor of the Exchequer he had been absolute for death. He was also a rabid supporter of the Septennial Act, and harshly vindictive about the long drawn-out impeachment of Bolingbroke's old colleague and foe, Lord Oxford.[5] However, the need to obstruct ministerial plans to the point where he would be bought off with office mellowed Walpole's Whig views marvellously, the more so as he could not successfully obstruct without Tory help. Walpole even attacked the Septennial Act. He helped to wind up the quite unjust pursuit of Oxford, and his success against the Peerage Bill made it clear that the post-rebellion era when a cohesive Whig clique could ram outrageous measures through in an atmosphere of carefully-cultivated hysteria was over.

Nothing had done more to sustain that hysteria after the last guttering flame of rebellion had been snuffed out in the north than the protracted process of trying and punishing the more important rebels captured by the government. Of the rebel rank and file significant numbers were captured only at the encirclement of Preston. After the flight of the Pretender what was left of the northern Jacobite army eventually escaped into the Highlands, and at Ruthven in Badenoch in mid February simply broke up as men marched home. The process was unimpeded by Hanoverian troops, partly because of very bad weather. In thick snow the Grampian peaks, whipped by vicious chilling winds, were a death-trap for the inexperienced or unwary, as well as a scene of stark and barren beauty. Nor was the London government particularly interested in rounding up humble men who had probably acted throughout under the orders of their social superiors. Legislation of 1617 empowered the Crown to hand over prisoners to contractors for deportation to the American colonies as marketable slave labourers on seven or fourteen year contracts. To avoid trial for treason it was quite normal for a prisoner of relatively unimportant status to petition for banishment and this was the way in which the bulk of the Preston prisoners were handled. They virtually all petitioned successfully to be shipped to America. They were kept under noisome and pestiferous conditions in Liverpool before embarkation, and those who could afford liquor kept themselves dead drunk. It helped, when reality consisted of a stinking cellar, broken hopes, and the fever-spotted corpse of a Highland comrade lying uncovered because his plaid had been sold to buy a rough coffin.[6]

Although the Jacobite army in Scotland never surrendered, there were inevitably quite a few Jacobite prisoners in government hands at the end of the campaign, mostly in custody in Edinburgh or Stirling. Furthermore as Argyll's army moved slowly north one of its jobs was to pick up known Jacobites and send them under escort to Edinburgh for trial. The escort was often provided by Swiss or Dutch troops and was not over gentle in its handling of the prisoners, but the widespread sympathy and active kindness displayed towards the prisoners in the areas through which they were marched was the first sign that Scottish opinion simply would not tolerate the scale of executions which had occurred in Lancashire. In any case, the government was not at all confident that Scottish juries would be prepared to convict Jacobite prisoners. Habeas corpus, that much-prized protection against indefinite detention without trial, had been suspended by Parliament during the tense period before the outbreak of rebellion. Less defensibly, the suspension was maintained after the rebellion came to an end, but in June 1716 Habeas corpus became effective again. A good many prisoners who had submitted to the government well before the end of the fighting, or who were deemed men of no consequence, were released.

That still left a significant number of prisoners in Edinburgh Castle. Both the government and General William Cadogan, who had succeeded Argyll as Commander-in-Chief Scotland, were insistent that they be tried, so in batches they were marched south over the English border to Carlisle to be tried under a commission of oyer and terminer (Norman French for hear and determine). As peers, Lords Strathallan, Rollo, and Stormont were left in the Castle at Edinburgh, and the Marquis of Huntly, heir to the Duke of Gordon, who was started on the march on the grounds that he was a commoner with a mere courtesy title, was almost immediately recalled and subsequently released in exchange for a pledge that he would use his influence to reconcile the north-east to the House of Hanover. Politically, the Carlisle trials proved an egregious blunder. By sending men furth of Scotland for trial the government had blatantly violated the guarantees for the Scottish legal system which were central to the Act of Union. A surge of patriotic indignation united all Scottish classes and parties, from the Jacobite sympathizer to Fletcher of Saltoun. In the event thirty-four out of seventy-four prisoners had to be released without trial. Another thirty-two were tried. One was acquitted on the grounds that he was an old man who had plainly been compelled to join the rebels by force. No sentence was ever passed on the majority who were found guilty. All were released in due course under an Act of Grace of 1717. The single execution in either Edinburgh or Carlisle was that of Sergeant Ainslie who had tried to betray Edinburgh Castle to the Jacobites and who was hanged over its walls.[7]

Given the contemporary attitude to imprisonment, which was that prisoners could pay for their keep and ward, or starve, the men released in 1717 by no means escaped without a penalty. They paid a lot of money, as well as a fair amount of time, for their involvement with Jacobitism. A good number of prisoners just escaped from Scottish jails, including Edinburgh Castle, though very few Lancashire Jacobites seem to have managed to make a break for freedom. Much more significant than the escapades of these small fry were escapes amongst the important prisoners brought to London for show trials. At first sight it is astonishing that so many of these men managed to break out, the more so as the insufferable and useless 'General' Thomas Forster M.P. was of their number, but a closer examination of custodial arrangements does much to explain events.

Forster escaped from Newgate on 11 April 1716 a week before he was due to be tried. He fuddled the Governor of Newgate, Mr Pitt, with drink, and then used duplicate keys to lock up prison staff and to reach the streets of London, whence he was whisked off to Paris. On 4 May 'Old Borlum' characteristically led a determined rush by over a dozen prisoners in the exercise yard, whereby they bowled over the turnkeys and burst out of Newgate. Most were recaptured, but not Borlum, whose subsequent incarceration in Edinburgh Castle was the result of a rash decision to return from the Continent to Scotland. Later still Lord Derwentwater's brother, Charles Radcliffe, walked out of Newgate disguised as a visitor, while another Jacobite, James Swinburne, who had thoughtfully developed symptoms of lunacy about the time of his trial made a sufficient recovery to give the Hanoverian authorities the slip. Newgate was not in fact difficult to escape from. Its sinister reputation derived partly from the high percentage of people condemned to death amongst its inmates, but mainly from the noisome stench which rose from its inadequate, squalid and unhealthy buildings, a stench so bad in summer as to compel nearby shopkeepers occasionally to close their businesses. Chronically overcrowded, Newgate was always rife with 'gaol fever', a particularly virulent form of typhus, and those committed to it were, of course, expected to pay for the privilege. Everyone in authority there was out to make money from his job including the chaplain, the Ordinary of Newgate, who made a lot of money by publishing an *Account* of the confessions and last moments of those hung at Tyburn. Newgate was therefore run rather like a stinking and restrictive hotel. Alcohol was available in terrifying quantities for those who could afford it. The facilities of a good brothel were also available since the prison housed both men and women, and most women prisoners were anxious to be got pregnant so that they could 'plead their bellies' at trial and thereby escape the noose. An enterprising Governor ran a brisk business in receiving stolen goods, and all the staff made money out of the many visitors. Boozing, fornication, corruption, and an endless flux of tourists provided an excellent setting for escape by a determined man who kept his health.[8]

Jacobite prisoners of rank even managed to escape from the Tower of London. The Earl of Nithsdale's escape, on the eve of his execution, was achieved by the almost hoary device of bringing in a woman with a hooded cloak who then changed places with the prisoner who escaped in her clothes. The Earl of Wintoun is said to have drawn on expertise acquired during several years as a blacksmith in France to cut through the bars of his Tower cell with a watch spring. Ultimately, on 24 February 1716 only two peers were beheaded for High Treason (a privilege of their rank: commoners were hung, drawn and quartered). They were the Earls of Derwentwater and Kenmure. Both were, in a sense, desperately unlucky. Kenmure remarked on the scaffold that he had been so confident of reprieve that he had failed to obtain a suit of mourning. Given the scale on which the nobility had participated in the rising, two or three executions was the bare minimum the government, or indeed any conceivable government, was likely to settle for. Lady Nithsdale believed that her husband had been marked down for death as one of the few Roman Catholics and Jacobites in largely Whiggish south-west Scotland.[9] The Protestant, but similarly isolated, Kenmure and the Roman Catholic Derwentwater were eminent enough to serve as examples and not well enough connected with people who mattered to leave dangerous resentments.

Even so, the beheading of a young man like Derwentwater caused considerable revulsion in Tory London, and probably as a result of public opinion there were only four more executions in the capital in May and July 1716, when the full grisly procedure of a traitor's death was visited on Henry Oxburgh, Richard Gascoigne, Jack Hall, and the Reverend William Paul. The punishment which no attainted rebel could hope to avoid was forfeiture of chattels and lands, and this was clearly the principal penalty which many Hanoverian Whigs counted on imposing on those sections of the propertied classes who had supported the '15. Forfeiture had the great virtue of destroying the economic and social basis for a future rising. On 22 June 1716 therefore a bill from the Commons entitled 'An Act for appointing Commissioners to enquire of the estates of certain traitors etc.' was finally passed by the House of Lords by forty-four votes to nineteen and became an act (1 Geo. I c. 50). By it the estates and property of attainted persons (or of anyone attainted before 24 June 1718) convicted of acts of high treason perpetrated before 1 June 1716 were forfeit to and vested in the Crown. The Commissioners were to ascertain the names of those attainted and convicted of high treason. They were to establish the nature of all real estates, interests and revenues vesting in the Crown by virtue of this legislation and they were to discover by what tenure this property was held and to what incumbrances it was liable. In theory the Commission was to be financed out of the moneys deriving from the forfeited estates. Although this was a very normal arrangement, it did not always prove practical. However, that problem lay in the future and when the Commissioners first met in the Exchequer Chamber, Westminster, on 27 June 1716, the outstanding problem seemed to be the unwieldy nature of both the Commission and its task. Eventually it was reckoned that thirty-eight estates were forfeit, with a total valued annual rental of £29,771. At a series of meetings in the Speaker's Chambers at Westminster the Commissioners agreed to divide into two bodies, one for Scotland and one for England and Ireland. The former body moved to Edinburgh for September 1716.[10]

The subsequent history of the 'Commissioners Appointed to Enquire of the Estates of certain Traitors in that Part of Great Britain called Scotland' was not a very happy one. They met in Edinburgh on 1 September 1716 and ordered lists of persons attainted by Parliament to be made out and supplemented by lists of others convicted and attainted either by the courts, or by their failure to turn up to their trials and the subsequent automatic outlawry. Thereafter the Commissioners no doubt looked forward to a businesslike process of forfeiture. They were rapidly disillusioned. The first shot across their bows came from the Barons of the Exchequer in Edinburgh, the judges who were primarily responsible for legal disputes of a financial nature between the Crown and its Scottish subjects. As it happened, almost everyone of any consequence in Scotland forfeited after the '15 had previously been guilty of the very much less serious offence of failing to turn up in Edinburgh when summoned under the act commonly known as the Clan Act. Its real title was an interminable piece of eighteenth-century long-windedness which started 'An Act for Encouraging all Superiors, Vassals, Landlords, and Tenants in Scotland', and which included, several lines later, words about the need to stop any cunning legal settlements designed to avoid the effect of forfeiture. Ironically, this act was itself used to obstruct forfeiture, for the Barons issued writs to the Scottish sheriffs ordering them to secure 'the single and Life-Rent Escheats of the most considerable of the Convicted and Attainted Persons, (that is) all the Moveable Goods and Chattels they were Possessed of, and the Rents and Profits of the Real Estates formerley belonging to them during their Lives; and to Levy from their Estates, Goods, and Chattels, the several sums of £500 by them respectively Forfeited.'[11]

The last-named sum was the monetary penalty for not appearing in Edinburgh. Altogether, the Barons' gambit was a fine one. They insisted that their own writs must exclude any interference by the Commissioners, thereby paralysing that body in a large number of relevant cases. Despairingly, the Commissioners complained publicly to Secretary of State Townshend that to cap it all:

> The Commissioners also have ground to believe, that Personal Estates of considerable Value have been Carried off and Imbezzled in Scotland, which they might probably have come to a Discovery of, if their Powers in that Matter were not questioned by the Barons of Exchequer.[12]

However, the Barons were only part of the legal cross which the unhappy Commissioners had to bear. The august Court of Session, the highest court in matters civil in Scotland, was even more obstructive of the process of forfeiture. In the words of the Commissioners:

> The Lords of Session, or Judges of Scotland, have, at the Petition of some Persons pretending to be Creditors on the Forfeited Estates (and instigated, as your Lordships Commissioners have reason to believe, by the forfeiting Persons, or their friends, to petition) Sequestered all the most considerable Forfeited Estates, (that is) have Seized and Secured the Possession of them, and appointed Factors (or Stewards and Receivers) with Power to Distrain Tenants for Non-payment of Rents, for the behoof of those pretending Creditors.

The Commissioners were clearly not mincing words about the Lords of Session, but then they had been exposed to extreme provocation for when they summoned these factors to demand that they either pay the rents collected into the Exchequer, or give surety that they would do so, they received an emphatic refusal. In the eyes of the Commissioners this was adding insult to injury, for they had good reason to believe 'that many of the Tenants and Possessors of the said Forfeited Estates, continued to pay their Rents to the Forfeiting Persons, or their Agents for their Behoof'.[13]

There ensued a lengthy legal battle before the Court of Session with the Commissioners striving to have the sequestrations for behoof of creditors recalled, while the creditors naturally fought tooth and nail to prevent any such outcome. From the start the Commissioners received less help from the Scottish legal establishment than they thought their due. They went so far as to publish a letter which was a clearly implied rebuke to the Lord Advocate for his failure to turn up to defend the public interest before the Court of Session in the face of the original demands for sequestration by real or bogus creditors. With it they had to print his freezingly offhand reply.[14] His attitude becomes vastly easier to understand if his family connections are examined, for Lord Advocate Sir David Dalrymple of Hailes was the fifth son of James, first Viscount Stair, author of a famous work, *Institutions of the Law of Scotland*, and at his death in 1695 Lord President of the Court of Session. The great institutionalist's eldest son, the future first Earl of Stair, has gone down in infamy in the historical record, deservedly, as the evil Master of Stair who organized the Massacre of Glencoe. However, as a good government man he survived the uproar over that episode; became an earl; was a very active supporter of the Act of Union; and died of apoplexy after a strenuous defence of its twenty-second clause in the Scots Parliament. His father's third son, Sir Hew (or Hugh) Dalrymple, succeeded his parent after a three-year gap as Lord President in 1698, so it was the Lord Advocate's brother who presided over the Session in its battle with the Commissioners.[15] Their Lordships did agree to delay any further sequestrations, but they refused to recall those they had granted.

The fury of the Commissioners found expression in various ways, none more interesting than a document they published entitled 'Observations on Several Factories granted by the Lords of Session'. As the name suggests, this is a catalogue of infamous factors including ones appointed on some of the most valuable of the estates forfeited. Sir John Carnegie of Pittarow, appointed factor on the estates of James Carnegie Earl of Southesk on 20 July 1716 was, in the words of the Commissioners, 'the late Earls next Heir; and therefore most likely to preserve the Rents of the Estate for his Use'. A clutch of indignant clerical letters from the Moderator of the Presbytery of Brechin and the Ministers of Carmylie and Montrose were cited to the effect that Pittarow was an open Jacobite. When the Synod of Angus and Mearns in 1712 issued an act supporting the Hanoverian succession and calling on loyal subjects to pray and fast about the obvious disaffection of the bulk of the gentry of Angus towards that succession, Pittarow as Preses (or Chairman) of Quarter Sessions had summoned the Ministers concerned to face aggressively hostile questioning by himself and his fellow Justices of the Peace. Finally, he publicly burned the offending act. Yet by July 1716 he was factor for an estate worth £3,200 a year sequestered for totally unspecified debts at the petition of a group which included two Lords of Session.

Equally unspecified were the debts for which the Court of Session sequestered the estate of James Stirling of Keir, worth £900 per annum. The debtors, allegedly deeply 'apprehensive that the Rents of the Estate may perish', were suspiciously humble people – 'Three poor Tradesmen', a tenant of the estate, and an Edinburgh merchant. The factor appointed by the Session on 4 July 1716 was Mr Walter Stirling, whom the Commissioners denounced as not only the trusted agent and trustee of the attainted but 'also remarkable for his Disaffection to the Government; and was imprisoned during the late Rebellion, for keeping Correspondence with the Rebels'. To cap it all Walter Stirling was a writer (or attorney) and in appointing him the Court of Session was violating one of its own acts of November 1710 whereby all writers and attorneys and other dependents of the Court of Session were debarred from acting as factors on sequestered estates, even with the consent of creditors. Such was the cavalier approach of the Session to its own rules that it had also appointed writers as factors on the Earl of Wintoun's estate (worth £3,390 per annum); on that of James Home of Ayton (£320); the estate of the Viscount Kilsyth (£860), the Earl of Nithsdale's (£800); and the lands of William Greer the younger of Lag (£420).

Nor were these appointments the most outrageous made by the Lords of Session. On the estate of the Earl of Carnwath (worth about £1,000 a year) they very considerately appointed Dame Henrietta Murray factor. She just happened to be 'the Mother of the said late Earl of Carnwath the Forfeiting Person'. Sir David Threipland's father-in-law, a known Jacobite, performed the same office for his son-in-law, while George Drummond of Callender, factor on the forfeited lands of Lord Drummond, was not only disaffected and an intimate of the forfeited man, but the father of a son captured at Preston and hanged. Again and again the Session cheerfully appointed the agent of the forfeited landlord to the factorship and on the estates of the Earl of Mar and the Earl Marischal the Commissioners angrily alleged that these agents or stewards had actually been 'out' in the rebellion with their masters.[16]

Before becoming too sympathetic towards the Commissioners, who undoubtedly met with sustained and impudent obstruction at every turn, it is just as well to recall that their job had its consolations, mainly financial. There were thirteen commissioners originally, all warm partisans of the Whig government. They divided into seven for England and six for Scotland, all paid at the then lavish rate of £1,000 per annum. To have some idea of how well-off the six commissioners who sat in Edinburgh were, it is only necessary to point out that an ordinary Lord of Session had a salary of £500 per annum. Only the Lord President of the Court of Session scaled the dizzy heights of £1,000 a year, and he had been raised to that level after the Act of Union. The Commissioners must therefore be considered to rank amongst those who, while striving to achieve great things for their country, have contrived to do not at all badly for themselves.[17]

Under them, the six Commissioners had a small bureaucracy amongst whom the most important figures were the Surveyor General, Patrick (later Sir Patrick) Strachan of Glenkindy, and his assistants. Surveyors moved into counties where the real estate of attainted rebels lay. Before the Sheriff, Sheriffs-Depute, or Justices of the Peace they held judicial enquiry into the rental of estates and the location and value of movable property belonging to forfeited persons. It was the duty of the county magistrates to administer the oath to tenants and others summoned to testify.[18] Surveyors normally liked to move with a small military escort. Glenkindy, for example, reported to his superiors in November 1716 that he intended to cross the hills from Fettercairn to Deeside to survey Mar's Highland estates because he happened to have a lieutenant's command from Clayton's Regiment available to accompany him.[19] In practice these procedures seldom worked smoothly. Hugh Baillie, one of Glenkindy's assistants, reported despairingly to Edinburgh in February 1717 that in Inverness-shire the Sheriff and Depute Sheriffs had dragged their feet over the business of securing the movable property of attainted rebels with the result that most of this property had been either discreetly concealed or actually shipped abroad for the comfort and sustenance of those outlawed for treason. Simon Fraser was still locked in elaborate legal battles over the honours and estates of Lovat, battles which were only concluded in his favour as late as 1733. Nevertheless, he was by March 1716 the proud possessor of a complete pardon for his past peccadilloes in the Jacobite interest. He celebrated this Hanoverian vote of confidence by becoming in 1717 perhaps the most conspicuous amongst those engaged in removing Jacobite property before it could be legally sequestrated. Baillie even reported 'that the rents due are pay'd to the Rebells, however unwarrant-able'.[20]

There was usually a wide gap between the bark of an eighteenth-century British government and its administrative bite. Baillie just happened to be caught in a situation which was an extreme example of the point. Commissioners drew up comically exact rules for the valuation of forfeited property. Statues, for example, were to be valued at a basic 50 shillings sterling a foot. There was some reference to the fact that fashionable work might rate higher but when faced with group statuary the conscientious valuer was expected to apply his foot rule to each figure and then tot up the footage represented by Venus and Cupid or whatever. As far as pictures were concerned, artistic sensitivity suddenly blossomed in the midst of the rules which laid down that two and a half foot square quarter-length pictures might be worth £3 to £4 'if not very bad'. By similar criteria half lengths made £8 and full lengths £16 to £20.[21] The 'Scotch Commission' would have been better employed if it had expended more energy on the basic problem of identifying rebels and seizing their landed property. In May 1717 Patrick Strachan of Glenkindy reported to the Honourable Commissioners that he had not surveyed the estates of four persons. With reference to William Ferguson, late of Carnaby, and Alexander Stewart, late of Loguerate, he stated plaintively that 'I can't find upon the strictest Enquiry that there were ever such men in Scotland'. Glenkindy also reported that as far as he could ascertain 'John Killoch physician' was not 'ever possessed or in Fee of any real Estate'. His fourth case was of greater general interest for it involved that acid-tongued Jacobite the Master of Sinclair. John, Master of Sinclair, was the eldest son and heir of Henry St Clair of Herdmanston, tenth Lord Sinclair. The father was the head of a family which had been conspicuously loyal to the Stewarts in the civil war of the seventeenth century and was himself the only peer who publicly protested against the accession of William of Orange to the throne of the ancient dynasty of Scotland. His eldest son had been elected M.P. for the Dysart group of burghs in Scotland in 1708 only to be promptly declared ineligible as the eldest son of a peer. It was an inauspicious and vexing entry on the public stage.

Nevertheless, the Master of Sinclair entered the British army as a 'captain-lieutenant' in Preston's Regiment in 1708. His military career under the Duke of Marlborough in the Low Countries was brief and lurid. Ensign Hugh Schaw of the same regiment made aspersions on his courage at the battle of Wynendale, whereupon Sinclair mortally wounded him in a bout of swordplay during a casual encounter. Shortly afterwards Sinclair shot Captain Alexander Schaw of the Royals, brother to the deceased, stone dead at the head of the regiment after high words about Sinclair's conduct in the earlier duel. Condemned to death by a court martial, but with a recommendation to mercy on grounds of provocation, Sinclair seemed in acute danger of execution due to the influence of Sir John Schaw of Greenock, brother to the deceased, who naturally made all the interest he could in favour of the supreme penalty. In practice judicial execution of a gentleman under these circumstances was unthinkable, so Marlborough virtually arranged for Sinclair to escape and enter the Prussian service. Despite the efforts of Sir John Schaw, Sinclair was granted a royal pardon when the Tory administration came to power in 1712. The Master appears until the start of the 1715 rebellion to have resided at the family seat near Dysart in Fife. In the peculiarly venomous memoirs of the rising which he composed later the Master of Sinclair did not hesitate to depict Mar as not only an incompetent but also a liar who lured men to ruin by persuading them to enlist under him on the strength of specious promises of substantial aid from France. Henry Lord Sinclair died in March 1723. The title lapsed due to the attainder, for though the Master secured a pardon in 1726, it granted him only his life.

From the point of view of the family the main objective was to preserve the estates for the second son, James, who was a regular soldier in the British army. He rose to be a full general, represented several places as an M.P., and was eventually also a distinguished diplomat. His long and loyal service in so many capacities goes some way to explain and justify the sort of chicanery which met Patrick Strachan when he went to Dysart to wait upon Lord Sinclair. His lordship being sick, Strachan was received by his chamberlain or steward Mr George Fortoune who smoothly explained that the Surveyor General was wasting his time. He explained 'that the Master of Sinclair had indeed been infeft, but the infeftment was redeemed in the year 1712 and consequently James Sinclair my Lords second son was infeft in the said Estate'. Mr Fortoune stressed that he was more than willing to produce before Glenkindy's superiors 'the said Instrument of Redemption and other Writings', so the Surveyor General retired baffled.[22] It must be said that early eighteenth-century Scots lawyers were notorious for their cavalier approach to the business of dating documents.

As he faced the stolidly hostile landed society of Scotland Glenkindy could not even seek comfort in the thought that he was being consistently supported by all the agents of the government he served. It was not so much that the right hand of Hanoverian government did not know what the left hand did. Rather was it the case that the right hand was often reluctant to acknowledge the existence of the other. When he was contemplating a trip to Skye and Lewis in May 1717 in order to survey the estates of rebels, Patrick Strachan quite reasonably asked for an escort of fifty infantrymen to ensure that he returned from his labours in those remote and unfriendly parts. He sent his request to Lieutenant-General George Carpenter, the victor of Preston, who was by this time Commander-in-Chief, Scotland. Now as well as being a brave and competent officer Carpenter was an outstanding military administrator. As Quartermaster-General in Spain under the Earl of Peterborough during the War of the Spanish Succession he was deemed to have no equal. This experienced man, on receipt of the Surveyor General's request, at once wrote to London asking for confirmation that the government would pay the bill for the expenses of fifty foot. No confirmation was forthcoming. Carpenter promptly wrote to Colonel Murray, the Officer Commanding, Inverness, that unless he received orders from the government or Carpenter himself 'you give him no Party for those Isles'. The letter sounds outrageous to modern ears and the Commissioners for the Forfeited Estates obviously regarded it as outrageous. In fact it was plain horse sense. Any officer who despatched fifty soldiers on a lengthy mission for a civilian agency without written orders from the War Office would almost certainly have been asked to meet the bills for the operation himself.[23]

Even when a surveyor gained access and surveyed a forfeited estate, the battle for effective sequestration was often only beginning. The thickets and tangles of Scots Law provided ample cover for a sustained and potentially crippling guerrilla warfare fought with the utmost ingenuity by patriotic dacoits who advanced to the attack under the black and ambiguous banner of Debt. These struggles occurred on so many estates and were in the last analysis so broadly similar from one to another that they may be adequately illustrated from a single example – that of the forfeited estate of Alexander Mackenzie of Applecross in the north-western Highlands. Basic to the ensuing legal battle were the two standard preliminary processes of ascertaining the rental and then inviting, investigating, and confirming claims by legitimate debtors who were owed money by the estate at time of forfeiture. The Surveyor General Sir Patrick Strachan of Glenkindy had by the autumn of 1718 penetrated the most remote townships on the estate and was in the presence of David Bethune of Culnaskea, Sheriff Substitute of Ross, securing statements from tenants of whom Donald McLellan of Tarradale is not untypical, for he:

> Makes Oath that he hes no written tack of his possession, but possesses a part of the said Lands by a verbal order from the said Alexander Mckenzie Late of Applecross, for which he pays yearly Eight bolls of victuall,* One Mutton, One Lamb, and Eighteen poultry and two Merks of money and no more.[24]

It was all delightfully artless and bucolic. However, the second stage of the game – the registration of claims on the Mackenzie of Applecross estate – saw the first appearance of trouble. There were a goodly number of claimants. Several were influential people. For example, there appeared before the impeccably Whig Hugh Rose of Kilravock, Sheriff of Ross, the equally sound Alexander Mackenzie Chamberlain (i.e. factor) of Ferrintosh, with a claim against the Applecross estate. As Ferrintosh was the most important property belonging to the staunchly Whig Forbes of Culloden family, which was related to the Roses of Kilravock, Mackenzie was an important man. To compensate for their sufferings from Jacobite troops during Dundee's rising, the Forbes of Culloden family had been granted exemption from customs and excise on the estate of Ferrintosh where whisky distilleries afterwards sprang up like mushrooms and from whence the Culloden family later derived a large part of its income as well as an hereditary tendency among the males to alcoholism. Drunk or sober, the Chamberlain of Ferrintosh was unlikely to have his suit rejected. Other debts which were acknowledged by the Commissioners included, as might be expected in an estate on the western seaboard, ones due to Rory Mackenzie, merchant in Stornoway, and Kenneth Mackenzie, merchant in Inverness. Another successful claimant was John Macleod alias Macneill Vic Conchy in Glen of Raasay (an island which lies between Skye and the mainland). He had the wit to secure the services of an Edinburgh lawyer to press his case, which was complex as it involved debts due originally to his father-in-law Murdo Macleod Tutor of Raasay (i.e. guardian of

* A boll was a Scots measure of meal latterly generally equated with a weight of 140 lb. avoirdupois.

Macleod of Raasay), and transferred by inheritance to John Macleod's children.[25]

Most of the claimants came very well prepared to establish their rights, armed usually with at least one piece of parchment which showed that the alleged debt had been registered in due form with a court of record. The Commissioners had little choice but to accept most of the claims, even when the claimant was John Mackenzie, the brother of the forfeited person. He claimed on the strength of a marriage settlement made on him by the estate and duly registered in the Burgh Court of Dingwall. Most of the claims made against forfeited estates may well have been genuine. Highland lairds seem to have acted, effectively, as quasi-banks or at least as credit-creating institutions. They supplemented their small cash rents by marketing what they did not eat of their victual rents, but every now and again when they needed large sums of money quickly they would borrow in various forms such as wadsets (common in the Highlands) or heritable bonds (more popular in the Lowlands). Bonds secured against an estate could be used by the creditor as a form of negotiable security. It was a device for increasing the money supply in an economy notoriously short of metallic currency. In theory an estate was not supposed to be mortgaged beyond its own real value, but there was no way of preventing a landlord from accumulating other kinds of debt, beyond the total real value of his property. Thus after the estate of the attainted George Earl Marischal was sold, the heritable debts proper were treated as the first charge on the sum realized and were paid in full, along with interest due. The many personal creditors could not be paid in full. They had to accept a proportion, albeit a very substantial one, of the sums owing to them.[26]

All these complexities made ruthless confiscatory action quite impractical. Unless creditors were treated with extreme care, the government was liable to end up creating many more enemies than it started with – a process which was inherently self-defeating. However, respect for legal niceties enabled some very odd situations to arise. To return to Applecross: it was, of course, possible to treat an accredited claim on a forfeited estate as a negotiable security, just as if it was a wadset or bond. The commissioners therefore had to honour claims even if they passed into other hands by purchase. The process was referred to as translation and assignation of claim, and on Applecross virtually all the claims were promptly translated, for unspecified sums, to one man, Roderick Mackenzie of Kinchulladrum. He simply had to produce forms signed by the certified claimants, saying they had assigned their claims to him. There was no need to say more, and one does wonder whether by this stage the Commissioners could tell what was really going on. It may have been legitimate. It may have been a mere device.[27]

It must have been scant comfort to those who had to wrestle with the problems of forfeiting estates in Scotland that their English counterparts were facing very similar difficulties, but such was indeed the case. The procedure followed in England with respect to the identification and valuation of the attainted rebels' estates was exactly the same as in Scotland. In the County Palatine of Lancaster the High Sheriff, Thomas Crisp Esquire, 'in obedience to a Precept under the hands and seales of six of the Commissioners Appointed to inquire of the Estates of certain Traitors and others' made diligent search after the personal estate of such as were convicted of high treason or rebellion. This property could take a myriad of forms. One of the more unusual was the timber ready-cut to make a ship which was discovered near the River Wyre and which was confiscated, valued by a shipwright, and sold as the property of Joseph Wadsworth, executed for high treason.[28] Francis Anderton of Lostock, convicted of treason and rebellion, owned a very varied estate whose hard core was the demesne land at Lostock worth about £100 per annum, but which also embraced the tithes of the parishes of Dean and Eccles, as well as a coalmine let to James Haworth for £20 per annum, and a slate quarry.[29] Many of the estates forfeited in this southern part of Lancashire were small properties valued between £50 and £200 per annum, but even on small estates the usual problems could arise. Men convicted of high treason might quite reasonably be found not to be owners of land they farmed. They might, for example, have leased land belonging to others. However, arguments about ownership could threaten the effectiveness of forfeiture when widows or mothers of executed traitors insisted that they owned all or part of the family estates in their own right as the result of prior legal settlement.[30] Inevitably there was also an element of outright rascality, especially in an atmosphere poisoned by the use of informers to identify property liable to forfeiture. The estate of Richard Shuttleworth of Preston, gentleman, executed for high treason, was recorded as taken and embezzled by Penny, 'an informer'.[31]

As in Scotland, it is very difficult to believe, after a detailed examination of the records of the forfeitures, that the Jacobite gentry were less commercially minded than their Whig contemporaries. They appear to be very like any other cross-section of the contemporary ruling class in their approach to managing their estates. The English equivalent of Strachan of Glenkindy was Chambers Slaughter and his letter to the English Commissioners written at Newcastle on 9 December 1716 shows how bafflingly complex were the arrangements surrounding a colliery and salt-works at Blyth, the property of the attainted Lord Widdrington, or so Slaughter believed. According to Slaughter, Widdrington had loaned large sums to a local businessman called Bowman who had made over the salt and colliery complex to his noble backer by way of security in the form of a forty-year lease. His lordship entered into possession and operated the works through agents in his own name. However, when it became clear that Widdrington was going to be forfeited, Bowman reappeared on the scene brandishing a highly dubious document which he claimed entitled him to repossess the works. No opposition was offered by the locals when he next carried off the valuable accumulated stocks – 300 tons of salt and 200 chaldrons* of coal – and sold them. This procedure laid the onus on the state to recover the sum realized, if it could prove that the stocks rightly belonged to the Crown, but the state had great difficulty in challenging Bowman at all because documentary evidence that Widdrington held a forty-year lease just mysteriously vanished.

Chambers Slaughter knew full well that the attitude of the local communities among which the forfeited estates lay was a major determinant of the success or otherwise of the process of forfeiture. Already in early December 1716 it was known that the prisoners in Carlisle were unlikely to be treated with the sort of severity visited upon those unfortunates who were executed in the Lancashire towns immediately after the collapse of the rebellion. A Mr Clavering, an English gentleman 'of very good Estate', had been the beneficiary of a decision not to prosecute him for his Jacobite activities. It was generally expected that several captive English gentlemen who had joined the Jacobite army, but dropped out of it before it reached Preston, would be released without further penalty. Slaughter was afraid that 'softness', as he saw it, would make his own task even more difficult, for it would offer a prospect of the return of known Jacobites to positions of influence in the localities.[32]

As it was, Chambers Slaughter was making heavy weather of the various mining enterprises which it was his duty to survey and value. He was at the mercy of the various managers who might or might not produce adequate and honest accounts for Slaughter to work on. One enterprising man of this kind produced what Slaughter called an 'Artful Account' clearly designed to mislead and bamboozle rather than to assist. His victim was convinced that he was being shown totally bogus books concocted for the occasion, while the real books were kept strictly out of sight. The only shaft of silvery sunshine on a grey and bleak horizon was an offer from the inevitable Mr Cotesworth to place his own vast experience of the coal and allied trades at the disposal of the forfeiting authorities. Even where only landed property was at stake the help of the few committed and influential local Whigs proved indispensable. Leases of land with a substantial term to run were valuable pieces of property easily concealed by a conspiracy of silence if the leaseholder happened to be a convicted Jacobite. Informers were unpopular because, from the government's point of view, they were essential.[33]

* A chaldron was originally a dry measure; latterly a Newcastle Chaldron held 53 cwts. of coal.

Nowhere were informers more important than in the tracking down of estates 'given to superstitious uses', or in plain English to the support of the institutions and clergy of the Roman Catholic Church. It was standard Whig propaganda that if most Tories were Jacobites, every Papist was a rabid Jacobite. Neither statement was defensible, but both gained weight by endless repetition, and certainly the Roman Catholic gentry of the north of England seem to have been a relatively greater security risk in 1715 than their Protestant neighbours. It was therefore gratifying when Chambers Slaughter managed by means of an informer to identify a trust fund of no less than £1,000 pounds given over to the support of the English College at Douai from which many missionary priests had sallied across the Channel generation after generation to minister to their co-religionists at home.[34] Such incidents helped to sustain bureaucratic morale in the usual morass of obfuscation. There were endless claims that attainted rebels had been mere life tenants whose property holdings vanished with their death on the scaffold. Mulishly obstinate wives or mothers of Jacobites, on these or other grounds, seized control of estates and forbade tenants to pay rent to anyone but themselves.[35] One bold fellow, who was only outlawed, not only held his estate by force but also made it a haven for several Jacobite prisoners who had escaped from Lancaster jail. The Hanoverian authorities dared not use troops to arrest him for fear that he could contrive to be tried for resisting arrest. Given the feeling of the area, they were sure that any local jury would acquit him, regardless of evidence or argument.[36] Local feeling was often very hostile indeed to the forfeitures. In Manchester Chambers Slaughter found it quite impossible to sell forfeited goods belonging to a man whom the locals, to the rage of their Whig masters, persisted in calling 'honest James Garsides'. The goods had to be shipped to Liverpool where a bargain lot was not likely to be shunned.[37]

There had always been a desire for obliterating, violent action against the Tory interest in Whig circles in the north of England. It surfaces in intimate correspondence in revealing phrases. Thus in March 1715, immediately after the Hanoverian accession and Whig takeover at Westminster Henry Liddell wrote to William Cotesworth about the impeachment of Oxford and the other Tory ministers for high treason, saying that he knew that this news would make Cotesworth feel an inch or two taller, for 'It is what your heart hath long lusted after.'[38] The snag was always that the Whigs were such a tiny minority. Cotesworth was, from September 1715, virtually a government spy, on the nomination of Liddell, but the arrangements made for transmitting and receiving his news were exactly what one would expect of an agent operating in hostile territory, which is what he was.[39] He was a vitally important agent, as his superiors told him,[40] though like many spies he ended up resentful that not enough appreciation was shown for the services he had rendered.[41] Nevertheless, what really sustained him through the crisis was the hope and assurance 'that the Government seemed resolved when this hurly burly was a little over to make a large Reform in that Part and elsewhere'.[42] By this there is no doubt that Cotesworth and his friends meant a sustained attack on the Jacobite-inclined section of the ruling class. Though they distrusted the lower orders, and thought it the vilest of all insults to suggest that a political opponent was 'a man capable of insinuating himself with the meaner sort',[43] their concept of active politics stopped below the level of the gentry and merchant oligarchs. Ironically, even the correspondence of this hard-line inner group, as early as December 1715, shows that they were arguing with one another about the precise legal implications of forfeiture proceedings.[44]

It is clear that there were good reasons why any large-scale forfeiture of landed property should generate complex legal and financial problems. Obstruction apart, and there was plenty of that, innocent third parties were bound to be involved. People regularly bought annuities by paying lump sums to landlords like Widdrington. The annuity was effectively an annual interest charge and both it and the capital were secured against the estate.[45] In any case, few legal systems in eighteenth-century Europe could easily be used to impose draconian penalties on people with whom a large percentage of the local ruling class either actively or passively sympathized. The Lancashire justices seem to have decided to take the required action to identify Roman Catholics who had been involved in the rebellion but to go easy on the less 'visible' Protestants. The Whig authorities, far from blinded by their own propaganda, demanded severity all round.[46] It was never on. What buried the Jacobitism of much of the north of England was not a swift political purge but relentless, irreversible social and economic change.

Rebellion losses accelerated the ruin of many already declining Tory, High Anglican and Roman Catholic squires. The future lay with a new élite which seized the opportunities offered by the mounting embarrassment of older stock, often in stages. Sir William Chaytor, Bt, was finally arrested in his ancient manor house of Croft near Darlington and conveyed to the Fleet prison in London for debt in 1700, but part of his estate had been possessed by creditors as early as 1690. In April 1716 Chaytor was joined in the Fleet by Lady Clavering of Axwell Park, whose arrest was engineered by William Cotesworth, acting on behalf of his brother-in-law, Alderman William Ramsay, a goldsmith and merchant of Newcastle whose loans were the silken snares which gradually entrapped many an old-fashioned landed family. In the north-eastern parts of England the future lay with the new men, the Cotesworths, Ramsays, and Liddells, with their Whig politics and their ruthless efficiency as landowners and businessmen. Jacobitism just faded away in those parts after 1718. By 1727 the Lord-

Lieutenant, magistrates, clergy and freeholders of Durham were presenting a loyal address to King George condemning the impudent attempt of a foreign power to stir up another Jacobite rebellion among them.[47] So much for the hopes of Spain and Austria who had been toying with the idea of playing the Jacobite card in the course of a confrontation with Britain and France. In the north-west of England there had been very little active Jacobitism, and in any case the years after 1716 saw the rise of such landed and coal-working dynasties of impeccable Whig loyalty as the Lowthers. Sir James Lowther (1736–1802), later Earl of Lonsdale, as M.P. for Cumberland had so strong a sense of local identity and ascendancy that he at times spoke of his county as if it were a separate state.[48] Most Lancashire Roman Catholics after 1716 drew the sensible conclusion that they were too exposed and disliked a minority in England to risk playing the game of high politics.

In Scotland the pattern of events was quite different. The failure of the rising was a sickening blow to Jacobite morale, but the social structures which had provided such a fertile forcing ground for the seeds of sedition survived to a surprising extent. Indeed, in some respects they were strengthened. To understand how this could be so, it is instructive to read a memorial presented to the British government in 1749 by the learned Principals of the two universities of Aberdeen, King's College in Old Aberdeen, and Marischal College in New Aberdeen. They alleged that the Earl Marischal, as hereditary patron of the college founded by and named after his ancestor, had filled it full of Jacobite professors all of whom had joined the rebellion in 1715, with the exception of the Professor of Divinity Thomas Blackwell ('The Elder'). After the rising patronage was forfeit to the Crown; Blackwell became in 1717 Principal of Marischal College; and the rest of the professoriate was dismissed. Blackwell, incidentally, was no scion of the north-east. He was a Glasgow alumnus.[49] However, the expelled academics promptly took to opening schools all over the country-side from Aberdeen to Inverness whereby they disseminated their own Episcopal brand of Jacobitism. According to the memorialists of 1749:

> They poisoned the greatest part of the Young Gentry of those Parts with Principles that have since thoroughly appeared – For as the young Gentlemen came to their Estates, Nonjuring meeting houses were instantly erected on their Lands; and they were themselves almost to a man the officers in the Rebell army in 1745.

Now it has to be said that this analysis is part of an attempt by two Presbyterian academics to put the wind up the government with a view to extracting money from it. They wanted to amalgamate their two institutions and to secure handsome endowments, partly by selling surplus academic buildings to the British army for use as a barracks.[50] Nevertheless, anyone acquainted with the subsequent history of Jacobitism in Banffshire and Aberdeenshire will vouch for the realities which underly their rhetoric.

An area in which one might expect to find severe upheaval in the wake of the '15 is the membership of the commissions of the peace. There are in fact technical problems in establishing with complete certainty who were Justices of the Peace at any given period in Scotland, due to the nature of the surviving record, but enough evidence survives for generalization to be possible. After 1707 nominations to the commissions for the various Scottish counties were ultimately the responsibility of the Lord Chancellor of Great Britain. This great political lawyer naturally took advice from appropriate sources about local situations with which he could not be expected to be familiar. Patronage was one element in the decision to nominate, but by no means the only one as a comparison of appointments by the Whig Lord Cowper and the Tory Lord Harcourt before and after 1710 easily shows. After 1710 there does not appear to have been any systematic purge of Whigs, as the more extreme Tories had hoped. The reasons for this are not far to seek. Justices of the Peace were in Scotland a comparatively new and uncertain factor to whom the logic of the English commissions applied with double force: the commissions had to reflect roughly the existing landed social élite in any county if they were to be treated with respect. Even in the crisis of the 1715 election there was no partisan remodelling of the Scottish commissions.

The impact of the rebellion could not be ignored. Lord Cowper was still Chancellor and when he remodelled the commissions of notoriously Jacobite counties such as Aberdeenshire and Banffshire late in 1715 there was indeed a purge of up to a third of the existing Justices. However, these counties do appear to have been exceptional, apart from the case of Kincardineshire in 1716 when a general review of county commissions in the light of reports from the Hanoverian Lord-Lieutenants produced something like a clean sweep of existing Justices. Elsewhere, though notable rebels were removed, the astonishing aspect of the period 1715–17 is how many members of Jacobite families, such as the Oliphants of Gask in Perthshire to name a very extreme example, survived as Justices of the Peace. In the remoter Highland areas, and in some parts of the Lowlands, the ruling class was so permeated with disaffection that a reliably Hanoverian bench was unobtainable. In any case it could be argued that if the government's basic policy was to conciliate the Scottish aristocracy and draw it back into the orbit of the existing political ascendancy, the last thing it wanted to do was to purge it ruthlessly from an institution of local government whose status it was anxious to enhance.

By and large this policy was adhered to despite the provocations of the Glasgow Malt Tax Riots of 1725 and the 1736 Porteous Riots in Edinburgh. Especially in the Highlands, the government tended to insert more and more military men on the commissions, with a view to securing a more effective administration of the 1716 and 1725 Disarming Acts. In this respect, the new appointments were not wildly effective, and the same mixture of mild jobbery and underlying non-partisan respect for social realities continued to govern the nomination of Scottish Justices of the Peace until after the Jacobite era was over. Even when the last Jacobite rebellion in 1745 stimulated a serious backlash on the party of the Hanoverian authorities, there was no attempt to drive everyone suspected of disaffection out of local positions of power. No new commissions of the peace were issued for any Scottish county between July 1744 and May 1750. Eventually under the great Lord Chancellor Hardwicke, in the early 1750s the last identifiable Jacobites were squeezed off the commissions, sometimes in groups constituting small pockets of disaffection as in Inverness-shire in 1754–6.[51]

It is very probable that the government would have found it impossible to stop representatives of the forfeited families from buying back their own lands after 1716, at low prices because of lack of competition, had not the stock-jobbing craze in England given birth to a company designed specifically to speculate in the purchase of rebel estates. A company promoter called Case Billingsley took over the Company of Undertakers for raising the Thames water in York Buildings for the sake of its parliamentary charter, common seal, perpetual succession, and power to buy and alienate lands and buildings. By early 1720 a fund of over a million and a quarter pounds had been raised by subscription to enable the York Buildings Company to purchase rebel estates. The company even survived the bursting of the South Sea Bubble, though it was driven to dark and devious courses to do so. One of the 'Scotch Commissioners' was Patrick or Peter Haldane. He was one of the two Scots among the six Commissioners; came from the distinguished stock of the Haldanes of Gleneagles; and had held a chair in the University of St Andrews. He was also one of the best-detested Scots lawyers of his day, so unpopular that his nomination as a Lord of Session had to be withdrawn in the face of a storm of protest. As an M.P. Haldane managed, no doubt in exchange for and with the assistance of heavy bribery, to insert in a routine piece of legislation an unrelated clause allowing the York Buildings Company to sell annuities by way of a lottery.

Meanwhile the Commissioners had finally reached the point of being able to offer the bulk of the forfeited estates for sale. The York Buildings Company won a vital victory in October 1719 when it purchased the Panmure estates, the most valuable of them all. The Countess of Panmure first tried to block the sale, with the active and open support of two Lords of Session. Next she did her best to buy them, acting through an agent, Mr

James Maule. His defeat at the auction cleared the way for the company to buy the bulk of the Scottish estates as well as those of Lord Widdrington in the north of England. Despite a willingness to speculate not only in leases of land, but also in timber, coal, glass and iron working, the company's absentee ownership did not thrive. By the late 1730s it was virtually bankrupt and only the fact that Scots Law hardly envisaged liquidation protracted its demise.

The York Buildings Company had always been notably soft towards the family of the forfeited Earl of Linlithgow, allowing his daughter Ann, who married the Earl of Kilmarnock, to acquire a disguised but advantageous lease in 1721. By 1742 this had been converted into virtual ownership by the Earl and Countess of Kilmarnock. About this time the company, under heavy pressure from such influential people as Lord Advocate Craigie, negotiated a lease on the Fingask property in the interest of its former proprietor Sir David Thriepland who was living in the neighbourhood lightly disguised under the name of Mr Hume. By the early 1760s the York Buildings Company was anxious to liquidate its assets as part of the process of repaying its most pressing debts, so when the leases on certain properties leased to Sir Archibald Grant and Mr Garden of Troup ran out, they were put up for sale. Grant and Troup had already made over the properties either to the forfeited families or to their representatives, so the sale was highly predictable when it came up in 1764. The Earl Marischal, the Earl of Panmure, and Sir James Carnegie of Pitarrow, heir male of the Southesk family, all appeared in person to buy at a very modest upset price the estates formerly belonging to their respective families. Care had been taken to ensure that there would be no other bids. Even the small estate of Pitcairn was bought in the same way for behoof (i.e. on behalf) of the heirs of the celebrated Jacobite physician Dr Archibald Pitcairn.[52]

Some estates came back into the hands of forfeiting families a great deal faster than others. Mar's estates, for example, were unsold in October 1720, but thereafter were rapidly disposed of to his brother James Erskine of Grange, a Lord of Session, for £36,000. The Earl of Seaforth's estates can hardly be said to have been effectively forfeited. A devoted factor held them by main force and the Commissioners could make nothing of them, so the government was just recognizing reality when it restored them to the Mackenzie chief as part of a deal in the 1720s. Bizarre though many of these events may seem to modern eyes, it is worth emphasizing that there was a consistent and logical strand of thought underlying policies which left the rebel families and the Episcopal Church deeply entrenched in parts of Scotland. Basic to that thought was the assumption that there would be no social change in Scotland comparable to the process which created a new Whig ascendancy in the north of England. The Hanoverian government would have to live with much the same Scottish nobility and gentry as had dominated the country before 1715. A memorandum written and privately printed in 1716 by an unknown Scots M.P., with a view to swaying the policy of Westminster, spelt it all out. It started with the usual plea for clemency for prisoners who were swept into the rebellion by threats of violence, or who were under-age when they joined the rebels, or who followed the lead of a father or master. Thereafter it came down to brass tacks and pointed out that the 300 or 400 men of birth and breeding chased to the hills after the rising were a potential threat to the regime if they escaped into European exile with no hope of regaining their estates. As refugees in a Roman Catholic power it was likely that they would add cultural to political estrangement by converting to the prevailing religion. Given their family contacts and influence in Scotland they would then constitute as dangerous a potential fifth column as exiled Irish noblemen. Finally the memorialist, with great shrewdness, argued that the process of forfeiture might well prove interminable and self-defeating, if the example of the Douglas family was any guide. Granted the forfeiture of Viscount Dundee in 1692, they had made virtually nothing of it, despite strenuous efforts and heavy expenses.[53] For all its exaggeration, the memorial was right in its basic premiss: the optimal solution to the problem of the influential Scots Jacobites was reintegration into and reconciliation with the existing Whig Establishment in Church and State. By the 1720s the British government had accepted this.

8 A Decade of Disasters—Jacobitism 1717–27

After the fiasco of the '15 it was inevitable that the exiled Stewarts would resume fishing in the troubled waters of European diplomacy. There was nothing else for them to do. The immediate problem from their point of view was that the decade or so which followed the signature of the Peace of Utrecht in 1713 was a most unusual one in the history of Anglo-French relations in the eighteenth century. That peace had represented a direct deal between France and the Tory government of Britain. It was bitterly resented by Britain's allies in the War of the Spanish Succession and it was followed, even under the new Hanoverian dynasty in Britain, by a sustained and genuine effort by both countries to solve their clashes of interest by diplomatic means while trying to maintain on major issues the united front which enabled them to give the law to most of Europe. Contemporaries reckoned that, judged by the criterion of capacity to fight a major war without depending decisively on the help of others, there were only two Great Powers in western Europe – Britain and France. All the other countries were either hopelessly outclassed, like those former Great Powers the Netherlands or Sweden, or hopelessly dependent on massive financial transfusions from wealthy allies if they were to keep fighting for any length of time, like Austria.

Normally France and Britain were natural enemies. They fought or indirectly supported armed opposition to one another for so much of the period 1688–1815 that the relatively short periods of genuine peace may not unreasonably be regarded as truces. Underneath all the clashes of dynastic, political and economic interests lay a deep-rooted cultural antipathy which the historian ignores at his peril. It was never a particularly rational phenomenon, for both countries misrepresented themselves, as well as the other, in their passionate assertions of what was at stake in the long duel. Nevertheless the mutual hatred of articulate French and English society was such that it is a minor miracle that an 'Entente Cordiale' emerged by 1716 and lasted as long as it did. The Whigs used their parliamentary power to smash the proposals for closer Anglo-French economic relations which had been an integral part of the original Utrecht settlement. Despite the fact that a perfectly good case could be made for co-operation with Britain, the great bulk of the political, social and military leadership of France regarded that policy as a betrayal of the national interest for the sake of the selfish ambitions of the Regent, Philip of Orleans, who stood to succeed to the throne of France if the sickly child Louis XV died, provided he could with British help resist any bid from the grandson of Louis XIV who sat on the Spanish throne.[1]

Obviously it had been a formidable psychological handicap to the exiled Stewarts that they had since 1688 been pensioners of France. Equally obviously, only France had the military and naval muscle to mount the sort of invasion of England which might put the exiled dynasty back on its thrones. The teasing question is whether France ever really wanted to do this. There is no doubt that England went to war with France in 1702 to protect the Protestant Succession against the open challenge offered to it by Louis XIV's public recognition of the Pretender as King of England, Ireland, and Scotland, but even at this stage, there was another side to the story. The French foreign minister Jean-Baptiste Colbert, Marquis de Torcy, and one of his leading propagandists, the Abbé Jean-Baptiste Dubois, both repeatedly denied that the recognition of the Pretender violated the obligations of Louis XIV under the Treaty of Ryswick. These obligations were not to trouble William III in the possession of his states, nor to give military backing to any claimant to his thrones. Torcy pointed to the ultimate absurdity of the traditional claim by English monarchs to be Kings of France. France did not treat this empty formula as a cause of war. Dubois insisted that all 'James III' would receive at the hands of his French patron would be 'ceremonial treatment'. Of course Dubois would have written in this vein regardless of the truth, since it was a French interest to separate England from the Grand Alliance against Louis. Yet Dubois was a close friend of the English political philosopher John Locke, and his arguments were often consciously close to those of the contemporary English political economist Charles Davenant.[2]

In the sphere of the great crisis over the succession to the Spanish Empire there is a case for the view that Louis XIV accepted the throne of Spain for his grandson under pressure of circumstances and in the sincere belief that this was the option most likely to be compatible with peace. Such is the irony and complexity of human affairs that it is just conceivable that an urbane hack like Dubois was telling, roughly, the truth about the attitude of his sovereign to the Pretender. Certainly we have seen that the '08 was rendered abortive mainly by the firm conviction of the French naval and military commanders that their expedition did not represent a serious commitment by Louis XIV to restore the unfortunate James. Now it is true that in 1709 after the Battle of Malplaquet, the last and costliest of the Duke of Marlborough's victories over a French army, the Marquis de Torcy turned his attention to a possible diversionary expedition to

Scotland. The idea was strongly supported by Marshal Villars, the French commander at Malplaquet. Torcy visited the exiled court at St Germain where he conferred with James himself, with the Jacobite Queen Mother, Beatrice Eleanor d'Este, and with the Jacobite Secretary of State, Lord Middleton. Louis XIV even appointed a commander for the expedition, the Marshal d'Estrées, but it must be stressed that Louis never believed in the project. It was a throw which attracted Torcy at a time when the dice seemed to be turning against France. Louis was never prepared to allocate adequate numbers of troops to the scheme. Torcy eventually concluded that the sheer ineptitude of the leadership offered by the Jacobite court was enough to damn the plan. James was well-meaning, but weak. Despite the fact that they were both Scotsmen and that two of their children had married one another, Lord Middleton and the titular Duke of Perth were the heads of rival factions whose feuds split the court.[3] There was no sound military talent available. The Marshal Duke of Berwick, a bastard son of James II and VII by a sister of the Duke of Marlborough, had shown himself a good commander of French armies, but in connection with the Scottish expedition he vacillated between having cold feet and indulging in unrealistic over-confidence.[4]

Certainly by 1717 France had publicly abandoned the Jacobite cause, which did not mean that she would never take it up again in her usual cynical and half-hearted fashion. After the Treaty of Utrecht the Pretender was banned from French soil and the Regent Orleans needed British backing so badly by 1717 that the terms of the formal Anglo-French alliance concluded in that year were remarkably favourable to Britain. The crushing of the '15 strengthened the hand of George I so much that he was able to some extent to impose his will upon Orleans and to insist that the terms of the alliance include a specific underlining of the French commitment to shun the exiled dynasty. Such Franco-British amity could not possibly last indefinitely but it meant that the Jacobite court had to look elsewhere than Versailles for political backing. Even in a situation of virtually permanent hostility between Britain and France, it may be doubted whether any rational French government after 1714 could clearly prefer to see the Stewarts on the British throne rather than the House of Hanover. In the days of their regal glory the Stewarts had never been particularly reliable allies of France. James II and VII is a classic example of this, for he was incorrigibly insular and aggressively British. By comparison the Hanoverians were extremely convenient because their Continental dominions were vulnerable to French military power. France could thus use Hanover as a bargaining counter at peace conferences, usually with a view to recovering overseas territories and trading rights lost to the superior might of the Royal Navy.

Contemporaries were perfectly cognisant of these facts of life. They eventually became a platitude amongst British politicians and were most succinctly expressed by a great master of elegant platitudes, Philip Dormer Stanhope, fourth Earl of Chesterfield, who in 1742 wrote that 'Hanover robs us of the Benefit of being an Island, and is actually a Pledge for our good Behaviour on the Continent'.[5] It was ironic that it was the foreign policy of Hanover which provided the first opening eagerly, indeed too eagerly, seized by the Jacobites as a means of recovering from their loss of face after the failure of the '15. George I, King of Great Britain and Elector of the Holy Roman Empire of the German Nation, remained at heart pure German and obsessed with the consolidation and expansion of the hereditary lands of the House of Brunswick-Luneberg (better known as Hanover). In particular he was anxious to incorporate the formerly Swedish territories of Bremen and Verden into his electoral lands, the more so as they gave Hanover a strategically invaluable grip on the estuaries of the Rivers Weser and Elbe. The once formidable Swedish Baltic empire was after 1709 clearly breaking up under the strains and stresses of the Great Northern War. Attacked by a coalition led and inspired by Tsar Peter the Great of Russia, Charles XII of Sweden had marched on Moscow in the spring of 1708 in an attempt to use his own transcendent military talents in a decisive stroke against the very heart of the superior forces threatening to overwhelm Sweden. The upshot of the campaign was the crushing Swedish defeat at Poltava in 1709, and a protracted exile for Charles XII on Turkish territory.

Britain had vital trading interests in the Baltic. It was from this area that she drew the naval stores, without which the Royal Navy could not maintain its fighting efficiency for any length of time. These stores comprised such commodities as the long mast timbers required in an age when battleships were growing both in absolute size and in their spread of sail, as well as tar which was the basic naval preservative, and the hemp and flax essential for cordage and sailcloth. Sweden herself did not hold a crucial position in the supply of naval stores to Britain, but Charles XII tried to impose an embargo on neutral trade with former Swedish territories on the southern shore of the Baltic which had been overrun by Russia and which were important sources of naval stores. Where Sweden was essential to the British economy was in the supply of bar iron for the ever-increasing needs of English iron-masters. When the grave state of Anglo-Swedish relations caused a serious interruption in the flow of Swedish iron to Britain in 1717, there was widespread agitation amongst British merchants and manufacturers about the need to find alternative sources of supply. Russia was one possible source, and an Anglo-Russian treaty of 1734 helped to deflect trade from Sweden, but it was not until the 1750s that Britain was in a position to take direct retaliatory action against Sweden in the economic sphere.[6] What George I meant to do after 1714, despite the fact that it ran clean counter to both the letter and spirit of the Act of Settlement of 1701 to which he owed his throne, was to use the powerful Baltic Squadron maintained by the Royal Navy for the purposes of commerce protection as an instrument of Hanoverian foreign policy.

The Hanoverian confrontation with Sweden was sub-belligerent, but armed, and it assumed new urgency with the return of Charles XII from exile in 1714 to assume the leadership of the desperate and ultimately unsuccessful defence of Stralsund, one of the last Swedish toe-holds on German soil. By 1715 Swedish privateers had become a menace to British shipping in northern waters. Bailie John Steuart of Inverness, who usually insured his ships at Rotterdam, had to accept that insurance charges for ships sailing to the Baltic in the autumn of 1715 were much higher than for, say, a ship sailing to France, 'there being no hazard of Swede privateers that way'.[7] Since a privateer was no pirate, but a privately-owned vessel licensed by the Swedish government to take retaliatory action against the shipping of states deemed hostile to Sweden, the political basis of the problem is clear. By April 1716 Bailie Steuart had had his first ship plundered by Swedish privateers in the Kattegat, the narrow waters between Denmark and southern Sweden.[8] Of course, the Bailie, like any prudent shipowner, joined his vessels to an escorted convoy when he could, but in September 1716 he was taking it for granted that if there was no negotiated political settlement of Anglo-Swedish differences, costs from insurance premiums to payments to skippers would remain higher than normal.[9]

Bailie Steuart is an interesting example of the impact of this crisis on the Scottish merchant community, because he was a confirmed, if very canny, Jacobite. A haunter of Episcopal chapels, and a subscriber to funds for the relief of Jacobite prisoners in Edinburgh and Carlisle in 1716, the Bailie was a cousin of Colonel John Roy Steuart (Ian Ruadh – red-haired John, in the Gaelic), a notable Jacobite whose 'Psalm' composed in his period as a hunted fugitive after Culloden in 1746 starts:

> The Lord's my targe, I will be stout
>   with dirk and trusty blade,
> Though Campbells come in flocks about
> I will not be afraid.

The Bailie was on good terms with his militant cousin and kept his own Jacobite convictions right through to the '45 when he was a man of seventy odd years, but he did not display the same joyous intransigence as John Roy. On the contrary, he was more than happy to deal with local Whigs such as 'Bumper John', Laird of Culloden and elder brother of the great lawyer Duncan Forbes, not to mention a whole succession of Hanoverian military gentlemen from General Wightman downwards, all of whom shared something of Culloden's fearsome thirst, and helped slake it with the Bailie's wines. A merchant with interests ranging from Danzig to Venice could not afford to let political sentiment stand in the way of business. His losses from Swedish privateers were irritating rather than crippling. If a ship missed a convoy it might be virtually immobilized, and Steuart had then to consider such options as alternative, preferably neutral, freight. On the other hand, even when one of his ships which was on its way from Inverness to Cork with a cargo of herring late in 1717 was captured by a Swedish privateer off the North Foreland, the worst that was likely to happen to its master Thomas Greig was that he be sent to Gothenburg, in which Swedish port he would literally 'buy back said ship'.[10] This was standard privateering practice among all nations. The financial penalty could be insured against and could not be so heavy as to paralyse trade without wrecking that symbiosis between prey and predator by which privateers lived. In fact Greig and his crew overcame the Swedish prize-crew, escaped into a Norwegian port, and finally even escaped the clutches of a Danish prize court to sell their herring not in Ireland, but in the Baltic.[11]

Bailie Steuart's reaction to the whole business was phrased with characteristic caution but was clear to those who knew him – it was a wish that the country be soon rid of George I, without whom there would have been no Anglo-Swedish crisis. Other British Jacobites were a good deal cruder in their emotional response to the conflict. They clutched at 'the valiant Swede' with the despairing enthusiasm of a drowning man clutching a passing plank. That extensive conversations did take place between Swedish officials and Jacobite spokesmen is clear. Any competent Swedish diplomat could see that it was his duty to explore, however tentatively, ways and means of hitting back at George I in the main seat of his power – Great Britain. By 1716 the British Baltic Squadron under Admiral Norris was quite openly cooperating with the Russian and Danish navies in an attempt to smother Swedish naval power in the Baltic. There were more subtle incentives to cooperation. For part of 1716 it seemed likely that a Dano-Russian force would invade southern Sweden. Tsar Peter the Great had massed troops for this purpose within the Duchy of Mecklenburg, a German principality adjacent to Hanover. George I was in fact very unhappy to have the Russian bear in such close proximity, but the demonstration of Russian might reinforced that party in the Swedish government which argued that if total disaster was to be avoided, conversations with Russia with a view to a separate peace were essential. Oddly enough, the Jacobites had a discreet line of communication to the Russian court, through Sir John Erskine of Alva, a cousin of the Earl of Mar who had been outlawed for his role as a Jacobite arms-purchaser on the Continent during the '15. He was brother to Sir Robert Erskine, private physician to Peter the Great. Because Sir John was reputed to hold the secret to valuable mining developments in his native Ochil Hills in central Scotland, the British government had just dispatched his nephew Sir Henry Stirling (at heart another Jacobite) to the Continent with a pardon for his uncle. Thus Sir Robert Erskine, who held plenipotentiary powers to negotiate on behalf of the exiled dynasty, lived at the centre of a tenuous but real web stretching from the Court of St James in England to that of the royal house of Muscovy.

On the Swedish side three men seem to have dominated the process of consultation with the Jacobites. One was Baron Eric Sparre, Swedish minister to France. He held a key embassy, for Sweden which had a long history of diplomatic and financial dependence on France was beginning to doubt whether the pro-Hanoverian swing in the foreign policy of the Abbé Dubois, principal man of business to the Regent Orleans, would allow France to apply friendly pressure to Hanover to take some of its pressure off Charles XII. A second important figure was predictably the Swedish minister in London Count Karl Gyllenborg, and the third was the leading Swedish Secretary of State, the German nobleman Baron Georg Heinrich von Görtz von Schlitz. Given the enormous distances involved, extensive correspondence proved unavoidable and this, plus the number of individuals concerned, ensured that security left much to be desired. The London government had always specialized in opening the mails while its minister in Paris, the crafty Scots Earl of Stair, spent a great deal of money on an excellent intelligence service. The major diplomatic moves of the period very rapidly became part of the political vocabulary of partisans at local level, be they Whig or Jacobite. To Henry Liddell and William Cotesworth it was intoxicating news that 'His Majesty has made a glorious alliance with the Regent', for they grasped at once how significant a blow to Jacobite hopes was the loss of French support.[12] On the other side, the Jacobites of the north-eastern parts of England remained surprisingly visible and vocal until the early 1720s, sustaining their party spirits with 'mighty talk that ye Sueed will make a descent into Scotland'. Local Whigs were sceptical, but worried.[13]

The reality of the so-called Swedo-Jacobite Plot was unutterably sordid. It is best described as a double confidence trick. The first con was abortive but very unsavoury. It seems to be quite clear that Charles XII of Sweden in no way committed himself to even discussing how he could help the Pretender. The Jacobites, gulled partly by their own eternal over-optimism, did not fully appreciate that they were dealing with individual Swedish politicians and civil servants rather than with agents of the King of Sweden. That country was literally fighting for its life. Those who believed, with Charles XII, that only military success would enable

Sweden to secure a tolerable peace settlement were logically committed to trying to drum up funds to sustain the war effort. That Swedish faction which considered that the monarch might come to terms with reality faster if he was starved of funds may safely be ignored here. Görtz in particular, despairing of raising the wind in Sweden, arrived in Holland in July 1716 after a hazardous journey during which he had escaped capture by a Danish frigate by a hair's breadth, and then embarked on the heroic task of trying to raise 1,000,000 riksdalers, or rather the silver equivalent of that amount of Swedish coin, for the war chest of Charles XII. As befitted the quixotic nature of his enterprise, Görtz was only too ready to tilt at a series of windmills, ranging from British Jacobites to Madagascar pirates, on the off-chance that they might be jerked into grinding out precious metal. The pirates were, not surprisingly, unreliable in financial as in other matters, but there were wealthy British Jacobites who might well have been tricked out of a lot of money by this shady nobleman, who had no intentions of taking on fresh military commitments, had not the British government decided to put an end to the whole charade.

Its motives for so doing were as muddy as its methods were disreputable. Lord Stanhope, the dominant figure in the ministry, waited until the very end of January 1717 before he proposed to the Council of State in London that Count Karl Gyllenborg be arrested and his papers seized. Both steps were outrageous violations of diplomatic immunity and international law. General George Wade, best remembered as a man who built military roads in the Highlands of Scotland after the '15, was the chosen agent of Stanhope in the business of violating the Swedish embassy. He always did dirty jobs of this nature with an air of solidity and moderation which made them look almost respectable. It was the basis of a career which was essentially that of an internal security specialist rather than of a good roadbuilder and indifferent army commander. Stanhope leaned heavily on the Dutch government to arrest Gortz and seize his papers. To its credit, the Estates General of the United Netherlands moved with reluctance, but eventually it complied with Stanhope's demands. Meanwhile the British government unleashed a lavishly-financed propaganda offensive which used material from Gyllenborg's papers to whip British opinion into an anti-Swedish fury. All the ingenuity of teams of writers headed by Jean Robethon, George I's private secretary, could not establish a connection between the Jacobites and Charles XII himself, but the point could easily be glossed over. It was a splendid and early demonstration of non-open government in Westminster using its control of the initiative and of the most significant contemporary media (pamphlets and the press mainly) to manipulate a largely unsuspecting British public. There was a price to be paid for this success. Tensions within the ministry between Stanhope and Sunderland on the one hand and Walpole and Townshend on the other became unendurable and culminated in a split which drove Walpole and Townshend into bitter and factious opposition. However, in the short run George I and Stanhope had their way for it proved possible to secure in the heated atmosphere of the time, the military and naval grants needed to finance British support for Hanover's foreign policy. In 1718 Charles XII was killed in action. By 1719 Sweden had signed a preliminary agreement with George I ceding the long-coveted provinces of Bremen and Verden.[14]

Nothing better illustrates the mixture of desperation, dishonesty, and confusion which characterized Swedo-Jacobite dealings than the fact that those exotic creatures, the Madagascar pirates, were still dealing with both Sweden and St Germain at the time of the death of Charles XII. The great island of Madagascar set in the Sea of Zanj off the south-eastern tip of Africa had attracted European pirates since the early sixteenth century. It was a place remote from legal authority and yet athwart the important trade route between Europe and Asia which ran round the Cape of Good Hope. Just off the north-east coast of Madagascar the innocently-titled and very lovely St Mary's Isle, blessed by Providence with fertility and a glorious, easily guarded lagoon harbour, developed into a major pirate stronghold. The enterprising gentlemen who operated out of this haven were increasingly harassed by European naval activity in the early eighteenth century, so the deal they tried to offer a notoriously hard-up Sweden was cash for the Swedish war chest in exchange for the use of the Swedish flag as a flag of convenience capable of turning a pirate, who was hangable when captured, into a privateer, who was not.[15] The Jacobite dimension seems to have derived from the fact that one of the pirate captains who came to Europe to negotiate with the Swedish authorities was a former officer of the Royal Navy of Jacobite sympathies.

This man was called Jasper Morgan. He is repeatedly mentioned in an account of these negotiations purporting to be written by a Swedish official involved in the Madagascar projects, Johan Osthoff. His narrative is confusing and bears signs of having been penned with a view to securing Hanoverian patronage after Osthoff had found it expedient to flee from Sweden. Its underlying message is that Jacobites like Morgan were in continuous touch with leading figures from the entourage of the Pretender like the Duke of Ormonde, and probably meant to divert any Swedish expedition to Madagascar into the vortex of Jacobite plans to invade England.[16] Johan Friedrich Osthoff is not mentioned in Swedish sources, but it is clear that the Swedish government retained an interest in Madagascar after the death of Charles XII and that several of the pirates they were dealing with were known Jacobites. For precisely that reason, Count Eric Sparre in February 1720 urged the Swedish government to drop the project as incompatible with current Swedish policy of a rapprochement with George I with a view to securing British help against Russia. The whole Madagascar enterprise fizzled out, though it may have contributed to the interest in oriental trade which in 1731 led to the formation of the Swedish East India Company. That the tangled skeins of Jacobite plotting stretched from the grey waters of the Skagerrak to the azure blue lagoon of St Mary's Isle, with its myriads of darting silver tropical fish, is no doubt romantic, but also a measure of the sheer impracticality of the whole business. From it the House of Stewart derived no profit and less credit.[17]

One of the best of the many apocryphal and misleading phrases which litter the field of Jacobite history is the comment of the first minister of Spain, Cardinal Alberoni, when he heard of the death of Charles XII from an enemy bullet[18] in the trenches outside a fortress in Norway which he was besieging – 'Sembra regnare una constellazione maligna'. The implication of the words is that only the malign influence of the stars had spoiled the perfection of a web of intrigue which Alberoni, spider-like, was patiently weaving around George I. Certainly Jacobite hopes and negotiations centred as much on Spain as on Sweden in the bitter and frustrated years after 1716, but whether the fact that the two negotiations overlapped in time also implies that they were intimately interdependent is quite another question. Unlike Sweden, Spain was at daggers drawn with George I as King of Britain, rather than as Elector of Hanover. The main issue between the two powers was the refusal of Spain to accept the verdict of the War of the Spanish Succession, which had ended with a settlement excluding Spanish influence from Italy. The new Bourbon sovereign of Spain, Philip V, had many personal weaknesses, but he did preside over quite extensive fiscal reform and the Spanish state emerged from the succession conflict very much more centralized than it had ever been before. The new sense of power which these changes bred in Madrid was given specifically Italian objectives by the marriage of Philip V to his second wife Elizabeth Farnese, an Italian princess and niece to the Duke of Parma. Guilio Alberoni, an Italian clergyman who as agent for the Duke of Parma helped arrange the marriage, began a dizzy ascent to the heights of power and influence within the Spanish government. In 1717 and 1718 Spain launched an Italian offensive, rapidly seizing the islands of Sardinia and Sicily, and preparing her forces for the invasion of the southern Italian mainland. All this constituted an open challenge to the Austrian Hapsburgs, who had secured Spain's Italian lands as part of the 1713 peace settlement, and indeed to Britain, a major guarantor of that settlement. The Royal Navy struck at the sea routes which were the Achilles heel of Spain's nascent Mediterranean empire. Off Cape Passaro, near Messina, Admiral Byng shattered the Spanish fleet. Aware of Britain's Baltic difficulties, Alberoni immediately declared war on her.[19]

If no European government was willing to make the restoration of the Stewarts a major policy objective, they were all willing to play the

Jacobite card once circumstances had placed them in a state of belligerence with Britain. Spain was no exception. Alberoni promptly invited the Duke of Ormonde, the Jacobite leader who was deemed to enjoy the highest degree of popularity in England, to Madrid. Official Spanish denials that the Madrid government was in any way involved with Jacobitism were treated with well-deserved contempt by other governments, for Alberoni was clearly bent on a diversionary attack on England. Whether he ever intended to back such an attack on a scale sufficient to give it a good chance of success may be doubted. His conversations with Ormonde were marked by a great deal of evasive waffle on his part about the precise nature of Spanish links with Charles XII and about the difficulty of releasing Spanish troops from the Mediterranean theatre of war (arguably the only one Alberoni was really interested in). Where Ormonde does seem to have had serious talk with Alberoni was in the technical field of the strategy to be employed in attacking Britain. Alberoni was primarily interested in an invasion of England led by Ormonde, but the latter persuaded him that there was a strong case for a simultaneous diversionary attack on Scotland. Ormonde even nominated the exiled Earl Marischal as a suitable commander for this enterprise.

For the main expedition, Spain made available some twenty-nine ships carrying 5,000 soldiers and arms for another 30,000. This armada sailed from Cadiz early in March 1719. Ormonde was meantime lurking in Corunna in the north of Spain, where he was to be picked up by the fleet. In Britain he was to act as Captain-General of the King of Spain. Suspiciously, he was authorized to assure all land and sea officers of the British service who joined him after he landed that in the event of failure, they would be employed by His Catholic Majesty of Spain in their existing ranks. By the time the fleet sailed Ormonde had already lost heart due to the infuriating delays in mounting the expedition. He could see the futility of invading England with 5,000 men after the Hanoverian regime had been warned of the impending blow and had had time to mount naval and military precautions, as indeed it had. Ormonde need not have worried, for a fearful storm quite shattered the Spanish fleet before it could put into Corunna. The Pretender had meantime embarked on a characteristically hazardous and unlucky voyage across the Mediterranean. Battered by storms, ravaged by fever, and pursued by British cruisers, he landed eventually in Catalonia in north-east Spain and then posted across country to Corunna. He arrived in time to share Ormonde's gloom at the sight of the handful of storm-tossed ships which were all that reached Corunna from a now quite useless invasion fleet. At the end of April the Earl of Stair, the beneficiary not only of his own intelligence network, but also of that of France, was cheerfully writing from Paris that the risk of a Spanish invasion of Britain that year seemed totally to have evaporated.

The rogues and charlatans attracted to the Jacobite cause when it seemed that Madrid was willing to back it on a significant scale began to fade away. Among them was a Westphalian nobleman, Theodore Baron von Neuhoff, who had been hanging around in Ormonde's entourage at Corunna. This penniless adventurer had dabbled in the machinations of Baron Görtz; had ingratiated himself with Alberoni; and clearly felt at one point that it might be profitable to insinuate himself with 'James III and VIII'. After the dispersal of the invasion fleet he returned to Madrid where he resumed his usual career of impudent confidence trickery. His last contact with the Pretender was indirect. He married an Irish Jacobite wife for her money and then abandoned her in a pregnant state, after stealing her jewels. Leaving Spain hastily von Neuhoff embarked on a spectacular rake's progress which culminated in his death in London in 1756 in the direst poverty, but which at its apogee saw him actually crowned as King Theodore of Corsica in 1736. With such friends Jacobitism hardly needed enemies.[20] It was all the more remarkable that 1719 did indeed see a Jacobite invasion of Britain.

It never had any prospect of success, even in the eyes of those who organized it. The prime objective was always England. Alberoni had to consider the possibility that Ormonde and the main expedition might have to be diverted so as to land in Scotland, but he was emphatic that Scotland was to be regarded as the last resource and even then, only in desperate circumstances.[21] As it was, the main expedition was literally blown to pieces and it was only a tiny diversionary force of some 307 Spanish infantrymen which sailed with the Earl Marischal and managed to reach Scotland. Ormonde made no bones about the expected role of this stage army. He told Alberoni that the sight of their white uniforms with yellow facings in the Highlands would at once set rumours flying. In a society where the art of conversation has always been held in high regard, their numbers were expected to increase tenfold before they reached the length of being translated from Gaelic into English for the benefit of the Hanoverian authorities.[22] The only aim of this force was to tie up as many regular Hanoverian troops as possible for as long as possible. This was very desirable because the London government was well prepared to receive any attack. Apart from a powerful naval screen on all likely approaches, it had brought over four regiments from Ireland and had secured from the Dutch the reinforcements which they were committed to offering in the event of a threat to the Protestant Succession. The French government was supplying the British government with remarkably accurate information as to Ormonde's likely target area, so the West Country of England was thick with Hanoverian military very much on the alert. On the other hand, French dislike of the heretical and obnoxious English was as pervasive as ever, so even the Regent Orleans and his man of business, the Abbé Dubois, managed to inject a subtle note of ambiguity into their intimacies with His Britannic Majesty's ministers. Mr Secretary Craggs, writing to the Earl of Stair on 16 March 1719 complained indignantly that if the French government was as friendly as it said it was, it was odd that it allowed notorious Jacobites freedom to move, consort, and indeed to take ship from French ports with a view to invading Britain.[28] There were indeed plenty of Scots aristocrats living in exile in France and raring for a chance to participate in a Jacobite rising, if only because they were mostly desperately hard up. Orleans was not keen on paying the pensions which Louis XIV had generously distributed to Jacobite exiles.

The Earl Marischal's two Spanish frigates were therefore reinforced, if that be the word, by a small group of Jacobite exiles from France, organized by James Keith, the younger brother of the Earl Marischal and a future Field Marshal in the armies of Frederick the Great of Prussia. Of these men the most significant were the Marquis of Seaforth, the Marquis of Tullibardine (heir to Atholl) with his younger brother Lord George Murray, and Campbell of Glendaruel. Sailing in a twenty-five ton cockleshell from Le Havre they swung out into the Atlantic to round Ireland, but even so were nearly caught by the Royal Navy. Incredibly, given the distances and hazards involved, they managed to meet up with the two Spanish ships in the harbour of Stornoway in the Isle of Lewis. At this point the smaller vessel began to make its predictable contribution in the shape of divided counsels, quarrels over seniority in command, and that general air of mistrust and damaged pride which seems to be typical of bands of political brothers. To be fair to the Jacobite leaders, it must be recognized that they were the victims of quite unrealistic planning. In an age when all communication was at the mercy of the weather, and dependent on wind or muscle power even at the best of times, the attempt to coordinate two separate attacks on Britain over thousands of miles of storm-swept ocean was mad. Tullibardine and Glendaruel were for staying in Lewis until they heard, say, of the fate of Ormonde's force. The Earl Marischal insisted on landing on the mainland in Mackenzie country where Seaforth could be expected to attract support from his own clansmen, and making a dash for Inverness, which was known to be weakly garrisoned. The others fell in with his wishes, but Tullibardine then produced a commission which enabled him to supersede Marischal as commander of the land forces.

Catastrophically, the Earl Marischal surrendered his authority on land, but kept his command of the Spanish frigates, thus ensuring a lack of coordination between naval and military plans in what was essentially an amphibious operation. Jacobite headquarters were established at the old Mackenzie fortress of Eilean Donan Castle, a gem among Scottish tower houses situated on a small island at the head of Loch Alsh, a long sea loch opposite the Isle of Skye. Here the gloomy tidings of the collapse of Ormonde's venture reached the little army. Tullibardine, logical and cautious, wanted to return to Spain. Strategically his own force now made no sense. The Keith brothers, the Earl Marischal and James, were made of fiercer stuff and the Earl used his authority to destroy Tullibardine's line of retreat, by sending the frigates home. Shortly afterwards the Royal Navy sent a powerful squadron under Captain Boyle into Loch Alsh. The main Jacobite magazine in Eilean Donan was defended by forty-five Spaniards who were overwhelmed by a bombardment and a storming party. All the powder, shot, and weapons were captured; stores were burned; and the castle itself was blown up. Its fate was an exact repetition of that of the island magazine used by the Earl of Argyll during his ill-starred rising against James VII and II in 1685. There was a smaller Jacobite magazine at the head of Loch Duich, which branches off Loch Alsh, but when the long arm of the Royal Navy reached out towards that, its Spanish guard blew it up. With no retreat, few provisions in a desolate countryside, and an acute shortage of arms and ammunition, the position of the Jacobite army was desperate. From Glenshiel at the head of Loch Duich there is a route via Glenmoriston to the Great Glen which is the approach to Inverness. This was no doubt how the Earl Marischal would have tried to bear down on Inverness but in practice it was the Hanoverian Major-General Wightman, a veteran of Sheriffmuir, who took the route in reverse and bore down on the Jacobites with the heavily-reinforced garrison of Inverness.

Support from the clans for this mini-invasion was muted. News of Ormonde's misfortune acted as a dissuader throughout the Highlands. Lord George Murray brought in some men from Perthshire while the irrepressible Rob Roy Macgregor appeared with a handful from the north of Argyll and Stirlingshire. Seaforth mustered 500 or so Mackenzies. Ormonde had given Marischal a letter to Donald, third Maclean of Brolas, asking him to assist the Earl, presumably by raising the Macleans of Mull, but James Campbell, Sheriff-depute of Argyll, seriously warned Brolas of the sheer folly of such a course, and his sensible advice was heeded.[24] The two armies which converged in the heart of Glenshiel were therefore evenly balanced at a little over a thousand men each. The scene of the fight was extraordinary, for on both sides great mountains soar in steep rock-strewn heathery slopes from the narrow track along the River Shiel, and much of the action took place on these slopes. Wightman came upon the Jacobites after they had had a chance to throw up some rudi-mentary entrenchments, but despite these and the inherent strength of their position he seized the initiative, softening them up with a barrage from his battery of Cohorn mortars,* and trying to turn their flanks with brisk infantry attacks. In the end it was a rout. Jacobite morale was low and casualties were minimized because the Jacobite line of battle progressively disintegrated in flight. Any climber walking the glorious ridge of the Five Sisters of Kintail, which forms the northern wall of the glen, passes high up a corrie or ice-cut hollow called Bealach-na-Spainnteach, in English the Spaniard's Pass. The unhappy Spanish infantry were literally chased up and out of sight. On the bitter morrow, the Scots Jacobites could dissolve into the harsh but familiar Highland landscape. The Spaniards had no choice but surrender. As they said, they needed bread.

The Marquis of Tullibardine, whose gloom had proved wholly justified, wrote to the Earl of Mar, now the Jacobite Secretary of State, a lengthy and lucid account of the action, ending on a characteristically depressed note that the débâcle bid fair to 'ruin the King's Interest and faithful subjects in these parts; seeing we came with hardly any thing that was really necessary for such an undertaking'.[25] It was a shrewd remark. The whole episode verged on the farcical. Indeed it ended in sheer farce because of the standard eighteenth-century British refusal to pay for the expenses of prisoners. The Spaniards had no money. To feed them Brigadier Preston of the British army actually succumbed to the temptation to use his own credit. Such humanitarian folly invariably led to trouble. London was reluctant to reimburse the gallant Preston. Local tradesmen threatened to sue him, and Wightman, who deserved well of his government if ever a man did, had to appeal to his superiors to take pity on Preston.[26] In any case Wightman had similar problems, for London instructed him to extract from the Spaniards a signed I.O.U. for the cost of transporting them back to Spain. Presumably this document was to be used to dun the Madrid government. However, the Spaniards refused to oblige and in the end their commander was retained as a hostage for their debts.[27] Never serious, the Spanish invasion of Scotland fades from history on a positively Gilbertian note.

Lord Carpenter, the Commander-in-Chief Scotland, displayed rare common sense about the practical consequences of the '19. They were nil. The government suffered from the illusion that after such a victory the military could easily usher in a millennium in the Highlands by suppressing robbers, seizing rebels, and disarming the natives. Carpenter firmly pointed out that none of this was practical. He himself and Brigadier Preston had conferred with the Lord Justice Clerk, Robert Dundas of Arniston, and the King's Solicitor, to see what could be made of the new situation and they had concluded that nothing could be made

---

* A light bronze mortar suitable for field service named after its inventor the Dutch Baron van Cohorn.

of it. Regular troops had not the faintest chance of catching up with rebel fugitives. As for disarmament, it was the obvious story: if only the loyal disarmed the disloyal would be left even more dangerous. Carpenter dealt in brutal realities in a way which must have irritated his political masters, but which cut ruthlessly through all sorts of humbug. He was clear that the only effective way of disciplining Highland tenants was to persuade their landlords to burn their houses and seize their cattle, in winter. That would persuade recalcitrants to surrender hidden arms, but the landlords were not willing, and the idea of regular infantry tramping around in the summer trying to impound people and cattle was comic. Transhumance was practised in the Highlands, so the young people and the cattle would be in the high pastures as the sweating, red-coated representatives of their Hanoverian sovereign blundered about in an alien society and environment. If they ever reached the temporary shelters or shielings in the high corries they would certainly find them empty.[28] There was little need for action. The situation was very much altered in favour of the Hanoverian regime by 1720, but primarily by the effect which events had had on the minds of its subjects. Since 1715 Jacobitism had lacerated itself with a succession of self-inflicted wounds, starting with the appalling handling of the '15 but thereafter continuing through the sordid shambles of the Swedish intrigue, to the mixture of tragedy and comedy which was the '19. No sensible man, whatever his private views, could entertain much hope for an exiled dynasty which had become the dupe rather than the tool of foreign powers.

In the eighteenth century a Forlorn Hope was an assault party sent ahead of the main attack to draw fire. Exiled Jacobites had by 1720 become little more than a potential reservoir of Forlorn Hopes for European statesmen toying with the idea of distracting British attention from a real crisis. Domestic Jacobitism, though far from extinct, was at a low ebb, with its morale so shaken that another spontaneous rising like the '15 was unthinkable. Even the chances of a repetition of the '19 were remote. France finally intervened in the war against Spain and a French offensive across the northern frontier of Spain cut Alberoni's schemes down to size. By 1720 Spain acknowledged defeat, Alberoni was dismissed, Sardinia and Sicily were finally evacuated, and by 1721 Philip V had followed the adage about joining those we cannot beat to the point of entering into alliance with France and Britain. In the north of Europe Sweden had to acknowledge her decisive defeat at the hands of Russia in the Treaty of Nystad of 1721. British naval assistance in the last stages of the war had proved disappointingly ineffective from the Swedish point of view, so Sweden tended to swing back towards her traditional policy of dependence on France. However, France, here as elsewhere in the early

1720s, had a vested interest in conciliating any disputes which sprang up between Britain and her other allies.

Despite this deeply unpromising international scene, there was a major Jacobite scare in Britain in the years 1722–3, associated with the name of Francis Atterbury, the high-flying Anglican and Tory Bishop of Rochester. The government of Sir Robert Walpole did all it could to magnify the seriousness of 'the Atterbury Plot' and went on trying to sustain a general atmosphere of panic about possible Jacobite invasions and pervasive Jacobite plotting well into the 1730s. The problem facing the modern historian, as so often in Jacobite history, is to sift out the realities of a situation from a mass of emotionally-charged contemporary propaganda and wishful thinking. What is clear is that during the '19 both the British and French governments were well aware that the Bishop of Rochester, despite his known Jacobite contacts, was not in any way involved in the planning and control of the invasion attempts. He had been deliberately excluded by the exiled court on the ground that he was too independent-minded and opinionated.[29] What propelled Atterbury back into the centre of Jacobite plotting was that wholly unforeseen, bizarre and spectacular concatenation of events known as the bursting of the South Sea Bubble.

Early in 1720 the then First Lord of the Treasury, the Earl of Sunderland, had responded favourably to a proposal from the South Sea Company, a joint-stock company originally set up in 1711 during the War of the Spanish Succession. From the start this body was primarily concerned with funding existing government debt (to the tune of £9,000,000). It was promised a monopoly of British trade to the South Sea or Pacific Ocean. In practice its main objective was trade with the Spanish Empire in Latin America, a trade which after 1713 quite failed to come up to the unreasonable expectations of a few years before. Thrown back on its purely financial functions the South Sea Company, with Sunderland's backing, persuaded Parliament to let it incorporate in its own capital some £30,000,000 of the National Debt. For this privilege it was willing to pay an additional £7,000,000. Obviously, the higher the company could puff the value of its shares on the stock exchange, the more lucrative the whole transaction was likely to be to its managers. Government officials at the very highest levels were party to the creation and manipulation of a positive orgy of speculation which crashed to its inevitable doom late in August 1721. As the excitement over South Sea stock had triggered off a huge range of other speculative ventures, many of them of a dubious nature, the short-term shock to the economy was severe.

Apart from Sir Robert Walpole, who more by good luck than by good management succeeded in distancing himself from his colleagues at the critical moment, virtually every significant member of the government was deeply tainted with bribery and corruption. It was a disgusting business and even the staunchest of Whigs was prepared to admit, in private, that the rage and resentment of the public against the regime was such that its survival was in jeopardy. Arthur Onslow, a future Speaker of the House of Commons, said that with George I abroad 'could the Pretender then have landed at the Tower, he might have rode to St James's with very few hands held up against him'. Nor did the handling of the crisis by the government do anything to strengthen its reputation for honesty and fair-dealing. It was impossible to completely protect the guilty men from a parliamentary enquiry. John Aislabie, the Chancellor of the Exchequer, and the Directors of the South Sea Company were all censured and had most of their property confiscated to help partially reimburse deceived investors. Three ministers died. Stanhope was felled by a fit of apoplexy induced by stress whilst speaking in the House of Lords. James Craggs junior, a Secretary of State, died of smallpox while his father, one of the Postmasters General, seems to have committed suicide. However, the government was determined to stifle any further serious investigation. Exerting every ounce of influence at its disposal, it saved Sunderland by securing an acquittal for him in the House of Commons. The episode was a blatant travesty of justice, and Sir Robert Walpole spent a great deal of the parliamentary sessions of 1721 in sustained and impudent stonewalling in the House of Commons, protecting, in so far as he could, guilty men and their property from well-earned retribution. Contemporary abuse hailed him as 'the Skreen-Master General'. This was no more than the truth. So far from cleaning up the mess left by the South Sea Bubble, Walpole earned the respect and gratitude of the Hanoverian ruling clique, from the monarch downwards, by his devoted and successful efforts to ensure that justice was thwarted. It was a sordid and disreputable start to a long and disreputable, if shrewd, tenure of power.

For obvious reasons, the Jacobites both at home and abroad were taken by surprise by the sudden bursting of the South Sea Bubble. Everyone was. Yet they above all others might hope to gain from the subsequent scandals and their leading parliamentary representative 'Honest' William Shippen, a Tory M.P. so incorruptible that even Whigs treated him with respect, was the principal scourge of the administration in the House of Commons. After the failure of the '15 every Jacobite leader of standing drew the conclusion that its lesson was the absolute necessity of massive foreign assistance if a future rising was to have any hope of success. Now, the obvious unpopularity of the British government acted like adrenalin in Jacobite veins. Lord Orrery, a leading Jacobite figure in the House of Lords, was one of many who suggested to the Pretender that even a small-scale invasion would be enough to restore him to the thrones of his ancestors. James, eating the bread of political affliction in Rome after the

complete collapse of his hopes in 1719, was transported with joy. General
Arthur Dillon, who had served as the Pretender's agent in Paris, promptly
produced a plan for an expedition without foreign aid, and Bishop
Atterbury was selected as the principal coordinator of a great Jacobite
rising.

Atterbury, despite the accusations of the Whig propaganda machine
after his fall, had never been a Jacobite before 1716. He did not accept the
increasingly messianic indefeasible hereditary right ideology of the exiled
court. For its predominant Roman Catholic religion and politics he had a
profound distaste. For Atterbury James was the only remaining device
capable of breaking the Whig one-party regime in Britain, based as it was
on total corruption at Westminster, and buttressed by an expensive standing army. Atterbury's Tory soul was compatible with a detached attitude
to the wilder Jacobite schemes. When the Pretender's emissary, a non-
juring Irish parson called George Kelly, made contact with him in October
1720, he was told that delay was essential because the English Jacobites
had neither organization nor funds. Dillon's plans Atterbury dismissed as
crazily unrealistic. He was all for postponing action, a bias which was
massively reinforced by a protracted wooing of the Tory interest by the
Earl of Sunderland. Initially it seems clear that desperation was Sunderland's main motive. He was terrified that his peccadilloes in connection
with the Bubble would lead to impeachment by the House of Commons.
To avert that well-deserved fate, he was prepared to look for allies anywhere. Once the heat was off, Sunderland had another motive which led
him to sustain his dalliance even with Jacobite Tories. This was his power-
struggle with Walpole and Townshend, where again Sunderland was not
squeamish about potential allies.

Atterbury had always believed that what slender hopes the Pretender
had of success hinged much more on arrangements with British politicians
in office, than on rebellion or invasion. By the time the prelate realized
that Sunderland was leading him on, and had no intention of offering a
serious deal to the Jacobites, it was late in 1721, and the exiled court
produced just at that moment the most ambitious of plans for an expedition led by the Duke of Ormonde which was to strike at England during
the General Election due to be held in the spring of 1722. Needless to say,
there were to be elaborately synchronized Jacobite risings in the provinces
as Ormonde sailed up the Thames. Reluctantly, Atterbury agreed to the
scheme. Any other response would have cost him his leadership of English
Jacobitism, but he grew more and more unhappy as the gap between the
complicated and expensive plans of the exiles and the facts of life in
England yawned wider and wider. The exiled court had taken to using as
one of its main channels of communication with the English Jacobites a
man who only served to reinforce Atterbury's disquiet. This was

Christopher Layer, the barrister son of a Norfolk squire. He was young, stupid, conceited and meddlesome, being driven on by passionate sentimental Jacobitism and a sense of his own importance which gave him the gall to start drawing up his own master-plan for the rebellion. Orrery was by this stage convinced that any invasion plan verged on lunacy, so the attentions of the indiscreet and patently unbalanced Layer were not welcome. Atterbury knew that Ormonde was pressing on with the organization of a tiny invasion flotilla in Spanish harbours, despite the fact that even this minuscule effort was really beyond the pathetic financial resources at the disposal of the plotters. In March, just before the General Election, Atterbury seems to have decided to wash his hands of the whole business. His wife was dying. His morale was at rock bottom. He wrote in unmistakable terms to the Jacobite caucus which was supposed to be managing the whole enterprise from Paris, describing the enterprise as 'wild and impracticable' and emphasizing that there was not enough committed support in England to justify invasion.

Had not Sunderland suddenly caught pleurisy and died on 19 April 1722, the whole Jacobite plan would probably have collapsed in discreet ignominy. It had never had the remotest chance of success. Apart from anything else, Jacobite security was abysmal. George Kelly, despite warnings from Atterbury, commonly used the normal cross-Channel postal services for conspiratorial correspondence, regardless of the well-known fact that the British government regularly and systematically opened and examined such mail. The Jacobites did take the precaution of using ciphers and cant names for the principal conspirators, but the British ministers maintained not only a Secret Office for opening foreign correspondence but also within it a Deciphering Branch under the very able leadership of the Reverend Edward Willes. Westminster also had at its disposal an elaborate spy network whose ramifications reached into the very heart of the Jacobite camp. One of the more depressing facts about the plot had been the way in which the Continental end progressively came under the management of the exiled Mar. Although early promoted to a dukedom in the phantom Jacobite nobility, Mar was very much a man whose reputation pursued him up the steps of that peerage. He had succeeded Bolingbroke as the principal Jacobite Secretary of State in 1716, but had been making efforts to effect some sort of rapprochement with the London government from a very early stage. He negotiated with the Earl of Stair, that government's representative in Paris, and by the end of 1719 had made arrangements to receive a credit of £1,000 from Stair to clear his debts as well as a promise of a future pension. Mar's royal master in Rome, the Pretender, was aware of this pension for the simple reason that Mar asked and received his permission to accept it. Mar insisted that the pension implied no disloyalty to 'James III and VIII'. The latter had his doubts. That someone like Mar managed to emerge as the presiding genius of the new plan, is a measure of its soundness and confidentiality. Not in vain had the British government applied diplomatic pressure to the Spanish and French regimes. Both were committed to stopping any Jacobite attempt to sail against England. Just in case their actions, as so often, did not match their words, massive counter-measures had been taken. The invasion was predestined to disappear, as it did in June 1722, under a horde of importunate Spanish creditors, all dunning Ormonde. Sunderland, who knew all this, could not have taken legal action against English Jacobites because of his own secret negotiations with them. His laughter would have been Homeric, but private.

But Sunderland was dead. In his place stood the menacing hulk of Sir Robert Walpole, conscious that although he was the inevitable successor to Sunderland as the royal man of business, he was far from having secured the crucially important affections of George I. Nothing was better calculated to fix him in the heart of that stupid but complicated and demanding sovereign than the 'discovery' of a good-going Jacobite plot and the salutary, indeed preferably sanguinary, punishment of the plotters. The whole question of Walpole's sincerity in his obsessive pursuit of Atterbury in particular and Jacobites in general is therefore less than straightforward. Already in 1722 he had a record of equivocation in this field having swung from the hardest of hard anti-Jacobite lines to a distinctly soft one, after his breach with the ruling ministry in 1717. The modern scholar best-acquainted with his papers has argued that throughout his life Sir Robert Walpole regarded the Jacobites as a serious threat to the stability of the Hanoverian regime, and he cites as revealing the fact that in his letters to his diplomat brother Horatio, where there was no need to keep up any public mask, Sir Robert showed a real fear of Jacobitism. By 1722 the century had seen the abortive invasion of 1708, the large-scale 1715 rebellion, a small invasion in 1719, and unmistakable signs that another invasion was being planned, though the British government knew full well that these plans were unlikely to come to anything. In the heightened political tension which followed the South Sea Bubble it was natural for Whig politicians to exaggerate the Jacobite menace.

It was also very profitable. When Sir Robert pounced on the conspirators his aim was not so much the foiling of their already still-born plans as the securing of spectacular public convictions for treason. Colonel Charles Churchill, a hard-drinking bastard nephew of Marlborough who was also a crony and ally of Walpole, was despatched to Paris with orders to apply pressure to Mar on whatever scale was necessary to secure evidence incriminating the Bishop of Rochester in Jacobite plotting. Mar duly obliged, writing a letter to Atterbury by the common post which was not only compromising but also, despite a transparent show of security,

designed to identify the intended recipient by a careful massing of circum-
stantial detail. By the end of September Atterbury was under arrest in the
Tower of London, along with two Jacobite peers, Lord Orrery and
William, sixth Lord Grey and North, and several of the lesser figures in the
conspiracy. Of the latter the most significant for the future of the prosecution on which Walpole had by now staked his political life was
Christopher Layer, who was rapidly reduced to a cringing, whimpering
state by the prospect of a traitor's death. Induced to give information by
a half-promise of mercy, he was eventually arraigned of treason and
executed in May 1723. Walpole's idea of mercy was not to dismember
him until he was dead. Nevertheless, the prosecution of the important
prisoners proved very difficult because the evidence available simply did
not add up to legal proof. Even Layer, when he realized that he had been
tricked and was doomed, had pulled himself together and refused to
divulge any more.

Walpole could and did indulge in spectacular military and political
theatricals. Troops, thousands of them, tramped through the streets of
London to set up camp in Hyde Park. It was a classic example of the use
of the armed forces not to defend but to manipulate a society. Their job
was to create an atmosphere of tension and panic. Nothing like this was
seen in British politics again until the twentieth century when the Royal
Navy was used to mount a very expensive charade of a 'blockade' of oil
imports into the rebellious colony of Rhodesia, when British governments
knew perfectly well that oil was getting through in bulk by other routes.
That episode was at least designed to calm down British and foreign
opinion, whereas Walpole was out to excite it. It was with this end in view
that he rammed through a reluctant Parliament two quite unnecessary and
provocative pieces of legislation. One was the suspension of the Habeas
Corpus Act. The other was the imposition of a fine of £100,000 upon the
Roman Catholics in order to cover the expense in which the plot had
involved the government. The sheer crudity of the smear tactics and
unfairness involved in the latter measure turned the stomachs of many
honest Whig M.P.s. Characteristically Walpole had the names of any who
voted against it ostentatiously noted, with the implied threat that their
access to patronage would be cut off.[30]

Yet, for all his ruthless manoeuvring, Walpole could not make a charge
of high treason stick on Atterbury in a court of law. Instead he was
compelled to resort to a bill of pains and penalties which deprived
Atterbury of his ecclesiastical offices and doomed him to perpetual banishment. The proceedings in Parliament were dramatic, culminating in a
great face-to-face duel between the bitter-tongued prelate and a formidably
collected and cogent Walpole. Beneath the surface, neither man had much
to be proud of. Atterbury was substantially guilty. Walpole was not really

concerned to punish a bishop for dealings which, in a milder form, had been very common in political circles. He was bent on self-aggrandisement and he was successful. When Atterbury sailed into exile on 18 June 1723 he left behind him a Britain over which Walpole towered like a political colossus.

Walpole never ceased to maintain a vast counter-espionage network aimed at the Jacobites. It was to its own post office that the Whig government owed the early information which had enabled it to take advantage of the Pretender's dealings with the Swedes and with Atterbury. However, the government knew perfectly well that another serious Jacobite assault could probably only be mounted with significant foreign assistance, so it spread its intelligence network throughout western Europe. By spending a great deal of money and employing talented and seasoned spies like John Macky, who had been apprenticed to his trade under William III, Sir Robert Walpole managed at one time or another to exercise control over the post offices of Danzig, Brussels, Louvain, Leyden, Antwerp, Calais, and Hamburg. He even managed to plant an agent at the dining table of the exiled Atterbury in the shape of the butler, John Semphill or Sample.[31] Atterbury himself soon discovered just how riddled with double agents and double dealing the world of the exiled Jacobites was.

As the exiled prelate landed at Calais no less a person than Bolingbroke was feigning illness in a hotel in the town, in order to avoid having to meet Atterbury. Bolingbroke was waiting for a passage home to England, having made his peace with the government by means of elaborate and, be it said, sincere protestations of his contempt for and total break with the Jacobite cause. There had been talk of his pardon as early as 1717. Walpole was unenthusiastic but for once he was out of sympathy with the vital court influence, so in 1724 Bolingbroke recovered his estates and money, if not his seat in the House of Lords. Meanwhile Atterbury had been received into the Pretender's service and charged with the depressing task of investigating the conduct of Mar as the principal Jacobite agent in Paris.

As late as May 1722 James had been sending Mar, from Rome, written authority to call a Parliament or Convention of Estates 'Upon your going to Scotland and seeing an appearance of success in the endeavours for our restoration'. From the same source Mar also received a 'warrand for an Order of New Military Knights', to be known as the Restoration order, 'when you are in Scotland'.[32] For his part, Mar was always ready to bombard the Pretender with presumptuous letters many of them demanding the dismissal of his own brother-in-law John Hay of Cromlix, second son of Lord Kinnoull, and afterwards Lord Inverness in the Jacobite peerage. This level-headed and devoted man had been, along with his wife, close to James at the time of the only Jacobite success of 1719 – the marriage of James to the wealthy young Polish heiress, the Princess

Clementina Maria Sobieski, a grandchild of that King John Sobieski who had once driven the Turks back from the walls of Vienna. Despite Clementina's adventurous journey to Italy and a romantic midnight wedding, there was little sentiment in the making of the match. James married her for her 25 million franc marriage portion (not to mention the fabulous Sobieski jewels) and in order to beget heirs. Early wedded bliss faded fast, being replaced by endless quarrels, and having grown even more neurotic after the birth of her children Clementina began to wage a hysterical campaign against the Protestants in her husband's entourage, including the Hays. James, whose religion was as enlightened and tolerant as it was sincere, was distressed. Mar, though himself a Protestant, jumped on to Clementina's anti-Hay bandwagon, assuring James unctuously that the retiral of Hay from the Jacobite court:

> was the more necessary then that the ill agreement there, upon his account, being wrote by the most part of the foreigne Ministers at Rome to their respective Courts, was become the publicke talk over Europe, which did much mischife to yr Cause in Britain and everywhere else.[33]

In the early summer of 1724 Atterbury worked his way through the business papers of Mar. He was investigating the man who had betrayed him but his conclusions were so solidly based on written evidence that even James was compelled to accept them. Mar was a double agent. In August 1724 he was formally dismissed. Inevitably, Mar issued oceans of self-justificatory drivel. His last gelatinous letter to the Pretender was apparently written in May 1727, but his day was long done. Atterbury replaced him as the principal Jacobite agent in Paris, while in Rome the faithful Hay as Secretary of State and Earl of Inverness worked hand in glove with him. Together these intelligent and able men piloted the Jacobite cause into the last and perhaps the most thorough humiliation of a decade of disaster.

It was a recurring Jacobite dream that the diplomatic alliances of Europe, that curious kaleidoscope of power subject to rearrangement by sudden shakings, would suddenly re-form in such a way as to menace the House of Hanover with a mighty hostile coalition. Suddenly, in 1725 it looked as if the pipe-dream was becoming a reality. The French court, anxious to have a queen capable of bearing children soon, sent back home to Madrid the seven-year-old Spanish Infanta Maria Anna Victoria who was affianced to the fifteen-year-old Louis XV. An enraged Spain allied herself with her recent foe, Austria, and seemed to be squaring up for combat with France and her ally, Britain. Both sides began a search for allies. Austria even tried to breath life into a rather tenuous relationship with Russia. Ever eager, the Jacobites started to negotiate with Madrid,

Vienna, and even St Petersburg. There was, of course, a plan for a rising in the Scottish Highlands and Atterbury was closeted with Seaforth, Clanranald, Sir Hector Maclean and Cameron of Lochiel, the most notable men among the Scottish exiles.

Reality broke in like a thunderclap. At a conference in July 1725 with Seaforth and Sir Hector Maclean, Atterbury was blandly told that Seaforth had cancelled all his plans and ordered his clansmen to surrender their weapons. It was an elegant double cross. Atterbury's secret conferences had all been betrayed to the British embassy and Seaforth had exchanged the Jacobite plans for a pardon and the restoration of his estates. He was shrewd, for there was no serious chance of war. The major powers were so frightened of the implications of a conflict that their diplomats were working hard at ways of evacuating advanced positions with dignity almost before they had been occupied. By 1727 the necessary sacrifices had been made and by 1728 the war which had obstinately refused to boil was finally laid to rest.[34] Atterbury knew that the Jacobite cause was finished. To him it had always been a means, not an end. To James Francis Stewart, the Cause was what gave life meaning, but even he knew it was by now hopelessly discredited. In 1730 James, the Old Chevalier, was a man of thirty with more than half his life before him, yet he never again did anything significant, and most of his British supporters were happy that this should be so.

9 Failure and Survival—Scottish Jacobitism 1725–39

The cocky insistence that they were spoiling for another round soon, an insistence common to both English and Scottish Jacobites in 1717, was a thing of the past by 1725. English Jacobitism was set on a course of rapid and irreversible decline as a serious force and all the efforts of Sir Robert Walpole failed to flog a very dead horse on to its feet again. In England the Jacobite cause became essentially a verbal exercise. Its slogans could be used to demonstrate hostility towards the Whig ascendancy, but the mere use of Jacobite slogans was no guide to the views of the user. They could be used by arch-conservative Tories like William King (1685–1763), Principal of St Mary's Hall Oxford and for long the leader of the so-called Jacobite party in that notably obscurantist university. In April 1749, on the occasion of the opening of the Radcliffe Library, King delivered a Latin oration in the Sheldonian Theatre in the course of which he raised his academic audience to frenzies of enthusiasm by archly inserting into his peroration no less than six times the emphasized word *'redeat'* (may he return). It was primarily a protest against the degraded state of the Church of England, ground under a crushingly Erastian supremacy in the hands of not infrequently godless politicians. Jacobitism as a political option had been killed stone dead on the battlefield of Culloden several years before. King met Prince Charles, the Jacobite heir, in 1750, when that prince secretly visited England. Charles quite failed to establish a stable personal relationship with King, who continued to dabble in totally unrealistic Jacobite schemings for only a few more years before he experienced a violent revulsion from the Stewart cause.[1] On the other hand the smugglers of Romney Marsh were reported as given to drinking the health of the Pretender in 1744 during their roisterings. In the absence of any serious radical opposition it was a way of expressing their contempt for King George and his minions.[2] William King would perhaps have drunk the smugglers' brandy. He would not have wished to associate with their scruffy and disreputable persons.

Even in Scotland, where committed Jacobites undoubtedly survived in significant numbers after 1725, it is remarkable how little positive advantage the Jacobite movement managed to derive from the trials and tribulations which came thick and fast upon the Hanoverian regime. Perhaps the simplest way of demonstrating this is by an examination of two traumatic episodes – the Glasgow Malt Tax Riots of 1725 and the Porteous Riot in Edinburgh in 1736. As it happens, a leading role in the immediate government response to both episodes was played by Duncan Forbes, a lawyer promoted in March 1716 at the age of thirty to the important post of Depute Lord Advocate of Scotland. The appointment was partly due to his influential political connections as a protégé of the Duke of Argyll, who appointed Forbes to the stewardship of his vast estates. However, the appointment of so young a man to a job which made him the principal working state prosecutor in the Scottish courts was mainly a tribute to his impeccable Hanoverian loyalty and Whig views, both underlined by his resolute behaviour during the '15 when he had not only helped to defend the family home of Culloden House near Inverness, but had also participated in the successful Whig assault on that burgh. Forbes was elected M.P. for the Inverness District of Burghs (Inverness, Fortrose, Nairn and Forres) in 1722. He was a strong Argyll man or Argathelian and in 1725, when the Squadrone Party Lord Advocate Robert Dundas was dismissed by Walpole during a power struggle within the ministry, it was logical that he should be replaced by Duncan Forbes, already Depute and an adherent of the other leading Scottish political faction.[3]

Barely had Forbes entered into his new dignity than he was confronted with a major crisis in connection with the Malt Tax. The Malt Tax Act had been passed in 1714 but was greeted with such a storm of protests that it never became operative in Scotland. Now Sir Robert Walpole proposed to apply the tax to Scotland at half the English rate of sixpence a bushel, and it was hoped to raise £20,000 per annum by means of this measure. Resentment against the proposal in Scotland was every bit as lively as it had been against the 1714 legislation, which was regarded as a breach of the Act of Union. To work the act, it was essential for excisemen to survey existing stocks of malt, but when the appointed day (23 June) for this exercise came, an indignant Duncan Forbes reported to Westminster that in Glasgow 'a parcell of Loose Disorderly people infested the streets', making it unsafe for the officers to perform their duties.[4] As was very often the case with riots in eighteenth-century Britain, the immediate prelude to really serious mischief was the appearance of 'ane assembly of women and children' expressing their scabrous hostility to Daniel Campbell of Shaw-field, the M.P. for the Glasgow District of Burghs. Charles Erskine, Solicitor General for Scotland, was convinced that vile machinations lay behind the thoughtless violence of 'the giddy multitude',[5] and this was a common theme in the reports which reached London from Glasgow. One Fairfax, reporting that the excise officers were hopelessly intimidated by the mob and that it was proving difficult to stop the English element in the service on Clydeside from making a bolt for the border, added that:

> Those who are Enemys to the Government and some who perhaps may be exasperated by what they call ill usage have I fear laid hold on the present uneasiness of the People which has been some time a fomenting, to inflame them against the English.[6]

Certainly Daniel Campbell of Shawfield was not a man likely to enjoy any popularity in Jacobite circles. He was almost a parody of a hard-faced, grasping Hanoverian Whig merchant oligarch. He was also an enterprising and imaginative businessman whose interests by the 1690s spanned most of the North Atlantic world. He was himself the second son of Walter Campbell of Skipness, and he managed to operate to a surprising extent within a family or kinship context. Thus a letter he wrote in 1695 refers to his brother Mathew, a partner in many of his ventures, as just having sailed for Cadiz in Spain as skipper of a well-fitted ship carrying twenty-two guns. The same letter bids his correspondent, a cousin called Duncan Campbell, to convey Daniel's greetings to his North American friends and especially the mercantile Puritans of Salem in Massachusetts.[7] Daniel Campbell is a good example of the way in which Glasgow capitalists were actively trading with the English colonies in America long before the Union of 1707. There is evidence in his surviving papers that using small ships bought in New England, Campbell was trading with tobacco colonies like Maryland and Virginia in the early 1690s, instructing his skippers to tell the authorities that they were bound for an English port on their home journey.[8]

Withall, Daniel Campbell was a very staunch adherent of the Argyll interest. How staunch may be judged by the fact that it was as Commissioner for Inveraray, the Campbell capital, that he had signed the Articles of Union. He was also a Commissioner for the Equivalent, and his surviving manuscripts make it clear that he did indeed organize and pay for the funeral of the First Duke of Argyll, who died in September 1703.[9] The reason why MacCailein Mor's man of business had to perform this final service was that the Duchess was estranged and incensed that her spouse had breathed his last in the arms of his devoted mistress Peggy Alison. To this deep loyalty to his chief Daniel Campbell added a not very scrupulous eye for the main chance, which was no less characteristic of the sons of the mighty Clan Diarmaid, a people named after a mythic hero sired by Fergus Cerr-bel, or crooked mouth. In the years before 1707 Daniel Campbell became Collector of Her Majesty's Customs at Port Glasgow, a vital centre for Glasgow's seaborne trade before the Clyde was improved. So profitably did he and his associates exercise their authority over customs and excise that they were still struggling with the Lord Advocate in the court of the Barons of the Exchequer in 1708, offering that august law officer of the Crown a substantial down payment by way of composition if he would agree to abandon a weary struggle.[10]

After 1708 Daniel Campbell continued to flourish, dealing extensively in Swedish iron and timber;[11] dispatching colonial tobacco from Glasgow to Hamburg and the markets of central Europe;[12] and expressing his good fortune as a merchant in the most traditional of ways – by buying land. By 1702 he was laird of Clochfin in Kintyre. He added other estates such as Woodhall near Bothwell, and he built for himself at Shawfield near Glasgow the first of the great mansions built by eighteenth-century Glasgow merchants. Ironically, his impoverished late nineteenth-century successor was John Francis Campbell of Islay, folklorist and author of a great collection of Gaelic stories, *Popular Tales of the West Highlands*. Daniel Campbell was not a gentle, retired scholar. He was prominent in business and politics to the point where the rival Squadrone Party, notorious for its unscrupulous opportunism, saw fit to spread rumours that he had not only supported the Malt Tax Act, which he undoubtedly had, but had also been its author. It was against Campbell, as the supposed originator of the detested measure, that the fury of the Glasgow mob turned on the second day of their rampage. More particularly, they marched to sack his grand new house.[13]

The authorities in Edinburgh had anticipated serious trouble in Glasgow and had moved into the city two companies of Lord Deloraine's regiment of foot under Captain Bushell. The soldiers were specifically told that their duty was to 'assist the magistrates and obey their orders in suppressing any tumults or riots'. What these orders did not envisage was the possibility that the magistrates of Glasgow might not be falling over themselves with enthusiasm to use brute force to intimidate their fellow citizens into acquiescing in a government measure of which they almost certainly did not themselves approve. When the tired soldiers marched into town at 7 p.m. they were allotted billets, and the guard room in Candlerigg Street was prepared for them to mount a watch. The crowd promptly seized the guard room keys, locked the doors, and made off. The Provost refused to smash down the doors, as suggested by Captain Bushell, on the grounds that this might provoke retaliation from the citizenry. Instead the Provost insisted that the troops disperse to their billets, and announced that the Town Guard would assemble between 10 p.m. and 11 p.m. That anti-quated force was reasonably effective when burghal opinion, defined as the views of substantial heads of households, was behind it, but it could do nothing to stop the crowds which sallied out, broke into Shawfield House, and wrecked and plundered both it and its policies.

It could scarcely have happened to a better man. Campbell could well afford it. He had never been unduly concerned with legal niceties in the course of amassing his fortune, and the riot served the salutary and desirable function of drawing to his attention the fact that though elected he was not in the least representative of his constituents. In that sense, the citizens of Glasgow were making a crude but not uncalled-for attempt to grapple with the central issue of modern British politics. Daniel Campbell naturally had his own interpretation of events which he conveyed to Lord Townshend in July 1725, in a letter starting with a bitter denunciation of the barbarous treatment he had received at the hands of the populace. Campbell then alleged that the key to his misfortunes lay in the fact that he and his allies had lost control of the Town Council at the last Michaelmas elections, and the hostile group which had taken over had tried to ensure that he made no come-back by slandering him with false tales of his authorship of the Malt Tax. Campbell's version merely moves the struggle back to Michaelmas and confirms the central point that what was happening in Glasgow was an explosion of wrath against the Walpole regime. Writing to Townshend, Walpole's brother-in-law, Campbell naturally argued that the dishonest merchants of Glasgow, deep in complex frauds in connection with the tobacco trade, were lashing out at honest Sir Robert and his loyal supporter Daniel Campbell, because both men stood for an end to corruption in the customs administration on the Clyde. Campbell had scarcely been a shining example of honesty in his pre-1707 days as a tacksman of customs and excise on the Clyde, but he scored a palpable hit at his tormentors when he said at the end of his letter that:

> The common cry at Glasgow nowadays is down with Walpole, down with Mr Campbell, down with the Malt Tax and up with Seaforth, a strange alteration in that place.[14]

The point of the reference to Seaforth was that he was still, just, a Jacobite hero, as the leader of the last rebellion, yet Glasgow had always been a Whig town. However, by the time Campbell penned his tale of woe to Townshend, there was blood between Glasgow and the Whig government. The morning after the sacking of Shawfield House the Provost had actually arrested a few inebriated souls still wandering in the streets after drinking too much in Campbell's cellars. These unfortunates were promptly rescued by a reassembled mob which then assailed Bushell's troops to the point where they had to fire into the crowd, killing several people, as the price of being able to beat an orderly retreat. The Provost very sensibly urged the military to leave Glasgow so that he could have some chance of restoring peace. Pursued by an angry crowd for six miles they did so, wheeling about from time to time to reply to the brickbats with volleys, and no doubt they felt very relieved when they finally reached the shelter of Dumbarton Castle.

What was really at stake was not law and order on the streets of Glasgow. The Westminster government was not particularly successful in maintaining order on the streets of London, and its concern for Glasgow as such was minimal. Yet it knew that the eyes of all Scotland were on Glasgow; that Hamilton, Paisley, and Ayr, as well as other places, had already forcibly debarred the excise officers from performing their duties; and that if a majority of the Scottish burghs united in firm opposition to the government, there was very little could be done about the problem. The issue was the capacity of the metropolitan regime to impose its will on a province. The attack on Shawfield House and the battle between Bushell's men and the crowd provided an ideal excuse for a massive show of force aimed at daunting Glasgow. At hand to manage it were the government's leading internal security specialist, General Wade, and its principal legal hatchet man, Duncan Forbes. No more than Campbell of Shawfield can either of them originally have supposed that there was any serious Jacobite content to the crisis.

General George Wade had authorized the despatch of the two original companies into Glasgow. He was busy supervising a much larger movement of troops towards Inverness, where he was anxious to concentrate an impressive force. This had nothing to do with the Malt Tax. It was part of a campaign to disarm the Highlands. In 1716 a Disarming Act had been passed whereby Highlanders were forbidden under penalties to carry weapons in public. Now Westminster had passed a tighter piece of legislation which demanded that all weapons be surrendered to the government. Wade reminded the Duke of Newcastle that his concentrations would not be complete until into July, a date which left only a short span before the weather broke and it became virtually impossible for regular troops to move in the Highlands. The general was concerned to move towards Inverness himself, as rapidly as possible, on the probably misguided grounds that 'they (I mean the Clans) seem to be intimidated by the preparations they see are making'. In the event the new Disarming Act turned into counter-productive comedy, for only the Hanoverian clans made any attempt to obey it, while their Jacobite fellow-Highlanders either evaded it entirely, or surrendered rusty, broken relics, some reputedly imported for the purpose after being bought abroad as scrap. The stout and serviceable blade or the well-greased long gun were retained, even if they had to be hidden in the thatch. Wade was afraid that delays might enable 'Enemys to the King and Government' to persuade Highlanders not to cooperate with the disarming exercise.[15] Most of them probably required little persuasion.

Oddly enough, the troops which Wade eventually had to divert into

Glasgow proved vastly more successful at intimidating the Lowland lieges than they were later to be in their attempt to do the same to the Highlanders. The way was prepared by Duncan Forbes. He first sent two spies to Glasgow to secure information. Next he betook himself unto the Convention of Royal Burghs, the ancient representative body of Scotland's most important self-governing towns, and applied all the pressure and persuasion of which he was capable to it, in order to extract a general denunciation of defiance of the Malt Tax. Two of Wade's dragoon regiments were poised outside Edinburgh to add point to the Lord Advocate's pleas. The Convention dutifully denounced those evil-minded persons who had spread the rumour that the Convention had resolved to oppose the levying of the Malt Tax. It hinted darkly that opposition to that measure would bring dire consequences on the head of any offending burgh, and clinched the point by ruling that a copy of the Riot Act, as well as a copy of the resolution, be sent to each and every Royal Burgh. Purring with satisfaction, Chief Baron Scrope forwarded the resolution to London after it had been humbly submitted to the Lords Commissioners of His Majesty's Treasury. It was promptly printed in the official *Daily Courant* of 13 July 1725.[16]

Meantime Wade had veered round to the view that the Jacobite slogans, and especially references to the warlike Mackenzies, indicated that the Glasgow riots were part of a premeditated Jacobite plot and probably heralded the outbreak of a new rebellion. All governments are always convinced that mass opposition to their policies is the result of fiendish machinations by 'extremist' agitators, but Wade's fit of jitters was silly even on the evidence of his own letters. Once the incubus of a party of soldiers trying to enforce an unpopular measure at the point of the bayonet was removed, Glasgow relapsed into tranquillity. Wade raged that the Provost had capped his record of dereliction of duty by retiring into the country, but even Wade had to admit, in private, that the town was guarded and policed by a force of a mere sixty to eighty men.[17] Thus the military juggernaut which bore down on Glasgow on Friday, 9 July 1725, did not come to rescue the citizens from the horrors of arson, rape, pillage and murder, but to win a crucial battle in what was essentially a game of psychological warfare. The column was headed by Wade and Forbes and comprised Lord Deloraine's regiment of foot, seven troops of dragoons, a company of Highland irregulars, and a battery of artillery. Simultaneously Captain Bushell and his two battered companies of infantry emerged from purdah in Dumbarton Castle to re-enter Glasgow.

As Lord Advocate, Forbes promptly organized a preliminary enquiry or 'precognition', which was a standard part of Scottish criminal procedure. It lasted for five days, from 10 July, and was not so much an attempt to probe the identity and actions of the rioters as a systematic grilling of the

Provost and Town Council by an openly hostile and angry Forbes and Wade. The latter clearly started with the passionate conviction that the magistrates of Glasgow ought to be punished for allowing the riots to occur. Wade sent an angry letter to the Duke of Newcastle on 17 July 1725 reporting that on the previous day the Glasgow magistrates had been arrested, and that they were now in process of transfer to Edinburgh Castle under guard. The tone of Wade's letter was very much of the 'hanging is too good for them' variety, for it insisted that those who objected to this unprecedented, and incidentally scandalous, proceeding were sympathizers with the rioters. Wade snarled at the failure of the magistrates either to act firmly in the crisis or to remember events and identities when asked to do so in order to assist the subsequent enquiry. His underlying motives emerge clearly enough from the nervous last paragraph of his missive which records a tumult in Dundee. The one local maltster there who was willing to admit excisemen had been disciplined by a mob in Shawfield style.[18] The warrants authorizing the arrest were signed by Duncan Forbes as Lord Advocate and as one of the Justices of the Peace for the Shire of Lanark. This is often represented as one of the Grand Gestures on behalf of legality which punctuated the life of Forbes. It was nothing of the sort. It was an outrageously improper and probably illegal step. There was no evidence whatever of illegal behaviour by the magistrates. The Provost had at all times acted within his powers and had defended his choices by rational arguments. He had, for example, the right to order Bushell to withdraw his men, a right conveyed on him by Bushell's military superiors, and the Provost's view that violent measures would prove counter-productive was reasonable. He may have decided to leave Glasgow temporarily, but he left a pacified city behind him. Furthermore, Forbes almost certainly was not entitled to arrest a group of fellow Justices of the Peace on charges which were not so much nebulous as non-existent.

Certainly by 20 July Wade, writing from Edinburgh, had to warn Newcastle 'that some Gentlemen of the Long Robe, and even the Justiciary have given countenance to the seditious', by trying 'to have the Magistrates of Glasgow set at Liberty before their arrival in this Town'. Wade was incensed to hear that the officer of the guard set over the magistrates was being threatened with legal action 'for having done his duty'.[19] The Commander-in-Chief, Scotland, had already convicted certain persons of sedition by trial in his own mind, but no legal system was likely to accept this as an adequate process of law. The Glasgow magistrates secured first-class legal aid and argued convincingly that no fellow Justice of the Peace had the power to arrest them, while the powers of commitment of the Lord Advocate had almost certainly lapsed with the abolition of the Scottish Privy Council in 1708. Released on bail almost immediately, the magistrates were never brought to trial. As one indignant Glasgow pamphleteer remarked, it was a fine business when Glasgow, which had raised several hundred men for the Hanoverian cause during the '15 and had sent them into the camp of the Duke of Argyll at Stirling under the command of a Provost of Glasgow, was itself treated as if it was a camp of rebels.[20]

At one level the government slunk away from legal confrontation. It hardly mattered. At a far more significant level, the government's triumph was total, for the Glasgow maltsters' resistance crumbled and with it crumbled the common front of the Scottish burghs against the Malt Tax. That front had never had anything to do with Jacobitism, despite a tendency on the part of the government to see Jacobites everywhere at the height of the crisis. Of this, the most diverting illustration is the minor panic which set in in government circles from early July, when the commander of the garrison at Fort William, Major Wansborough, forwarded to General Wade a remarkable dispatch from the Officer Commanding at Glenelg. The latter reported that he had just been informed by 'persons of undoubted candour and Loyalty' that three foreign men-of-war had just taken refuge in a bay 'two leagues south of Stornoway in Lewis'. The squadron was Russian and ostensibly bound for Spain, but what alarmed the Hanoverian authorities about the fact that this foreign force was lying off the Outer Hebrides, about six miles south of Stornoway, was the Jacobite flavour which seemed to surround its senior officers.

The Commodore, presumably Russian, said that his ship had sprung a leak, a statement which was just not true. The commanders of the two smaller ships were apparently an Irishman and a Frenchman but both spoke broad Scots rather than standard English, a fact which instantly suggested that they came from a Jacobite background. The conversation and toasts of the forty or so persons of distinction aboard seemed to reek of Jacobitism, while the news that they said they were bound for Spain, and the information that the ships seemed to be carrying weapons and naval stores was bound to be alarming only six years after the '19.[21] Wade, harassed by his task in Glasgow and by news of anti-Malt Tax tumults as far apart as Irvine in Ayrshire and Elgin in the north-east, had to send a sloop northwards from the Clyde to keep an eye on the Russian force, though by 12 July even Wade was sure that if the squadron had any hostile intent it would already have shown its hand, and he himself would have heard of it.[22] Two days later he was writing reassuringly to Newcastle saying that the Russian vessels were sailing away from Lewis and that the whole business was undoubtedly an unnecessary scare. The soldiers aboard were not an invasion force but detachments of marines such as were standard on Russian naval vessels. Wade added that 'their Jacobite conversation is not much to be wondered at since most of our sea officers of those principles entered into the Service of the Czar'.[23]

It was not inappropriate that these exiled adherents of a lost cause should slip out of the historical record as their weather-beaten Russian ships ploughed once more through the dark waters of the Minch, that storm-tossed seaway between the Outer and Inner Hebrides. Jacobitism was at a very low ebb indeed. It derived no benefit of a positive kind from the Malt Tax crisis in Scotland, though that crisis did undoubtedly underline the extreme lack of enthusiasm, even in Lowland Scotland, for the Westminster government and its policies. To be deemed irrelevant was the ultimate humiliation for the exiled dynasty, and it was a humiliation which the Old Pretender savoured to the full at the time of the death of George I and the accession of George II in 1727, just two years after the Glasgow riots.

George I, that mean-minded and unlovable but shrewd and honest monarch, died in his carriage in north Germany, on his way to Hanover, early in June 1727. For years he had cherished a profound dislike of his eldest son and heir George Augustus. This was a normal Hanoverian trait. George Augustus and his buxom wife Caroline regarded their own eldest son Frederick (known as 'Poor Fred') with pathological detestation. George II was a dapper little man who, on the strength of a gallant performance with the Hanoverian cavalry at the Battle of Oudenarde in 1708, had developed into a middle-aged military martinet and bore of the first water. His naturally unengaging temper was not improved by the fact that he had become a martyr to piles. That he never lost his youthful courage he was to prove by his dauntless conduct at the Battle of Dettingen in 1743 when he led his British infantry in person to victory over the French. In 1727, however, he was better known in upper-class circles in England for a compulsive parsimony which made even his father appear not altogether ungenerous.

The Old Pretender wholly miscalculated the implications of the death of George I. As soon as he heard of it he set off on a year of frenzied travel and intrigue aimed at generating another Jacobite rising. His home by now was the Palazzo Muti in Rome but he was soon writing excitedly from Nancy in Lorraine to the veteran Scottish Jacobite George Lockhart of Carnwath, saying that he felt it his duty 'to put myself in a condition of profiting of what might be the consequence of so great ane event, which I was sensible I could never do at so great a distance as Italy'. Lockhart himself seems to have suffered from no such illusions, for he knew that in Scotland the accession of George II had been greeted 'with the favour of the populace', though he added acidly that he could not tell whether this was primarily because people were so relieved to be quit of George I or because they ran half-witted after any novelty anyway. The peregrinations of James rapidly turned into a series of humiliations. He knew he was banned from France by treaty but the independent Duchy of Lorraine seemed a safe perch. From it he was promptly knocked down by an obvious diplomatic stroke. The British government applied pressure to the French government to apply pressure to Lorraine, which was totally exposed to French power, to expel the unfortunate James. The deed was done. James went to Avignon, a papal enclave in France, but the British government had no difficulty in applying effective pressure to Pope Benedict XIII. The pontiff was reminded of the extremely vulnerable position of Roman Catholics in Britain. He was also assured that if he continued to offer refuge to the Pretender in Avignon he ran the risk of seeing the British Mediterranean Fleet bombard the papal port of Civita Vecchia. It was all a very straightforward game of elementary power politics. Benedict XIII had no choice.

By January 1728 James was back in Italy, a sadder but surely a wiser man. His devoted supporter, Lockhart of Carnwath, lost all heart for the struggle. He blamed the removal of Mar from the direction of the affairs of the exiled court for the obvious incompetence with which those affairs were being handled. Knowing what we do of Mar's two-faced behaviour, it is difficult to agree with the laird of Carnwath. Lockhart died in 1731, but before then he had given up writing the account of events known to us as the Lockhart Papers. He laid down his pen in a state of deep dejection, convinced that no effective steps were being taken to further the Jacobite cause, and that the generation which had been willing to fight and suffer for the exiled James was dying out, to be replaced by one which regarded his master with at best cool indifference. Jacobitism 'consequently must daylie languish and in process of time be tottally forgot. In which melancholy situation of the King's affairs, I leave them in the year 1728.'[24] Lockhart exaggerated, but his testimony as to the apparent hopelessness of the cause he held so dear is of value and is confirmed by equally well-informed opinion from the opposite side of politics. When George II came to the throne he pressed for no additional military precautions against rebellion. The establishment was kept at about 30,000 men, scattered over three kingdoms and two hemispheres. George II, though a neurotic tyrant about trifles, was remarkably percipient about the major facts of political life. His attitude confirms Lord Orrery's report to the Pretender in the autumn of 1727 that 'There do not appear to be many discontented people.'[25]

The precise meaning of such a statement does, however, bear further investigation. It cannot be taken as meaning that almost everyone in Britain was satisfied with the political and legal framework within which the state demanded they live their lives. This was manifestly not true. Rather must the gloom of Lockhart and Orrery be seen as reflecting the complete failure of James to become the focus of any significant volume of discontent or disturbance. Disturbance was in fact continuous, over a range of issues, but perhaps over nothing so much as the customs laws. Smuggling was endemic in most places. In Scotland it was almost elevated to the level of a patriotic virtue and it provided the context of the next major clash between Scottish opinion and the London government.

A glance at any major Scottish port's customs' records in the 1720s and 1730s shows that the sheer elaboration of the law invited frauds. These could and did range from plain smuggling, such as concealing fine goods in the heart of bundles of tow or scrap iron, to ingenious and elaborate frauds designed to take advantage of the appallingly complex system of bonds and rebates used to impose differential levels of taxation on home and foreign trade. In between came such collusive devices as the listing of imported French wines as Portuguese, a trick which of course secured a much lower rate of duty.[26] It was all good clean fun, though beneath it there was still a very serious clash of economic principle. In 1728 the British government was beside itself with anxiety to try to strangle the nascent Swedish manufacture of woollens on a commercial scale by depriving the Swedes of British wool, in accordance with a very basic assumption of the English Acts of Trade and Navigation. The Scots, as sure that they could profitably export wool to Sweden as they were dubious of their capacity ever to sell wool clothes there, were less enthusiastic about this aspect of the law.[27]

Where the humour in the eternal battle between the smuggler and the government began to wear a little thin was at the point where violence became predominant. Montrose was, as usual, a good example of this, though according to the Collector there in 1728 Montrose was a haven of peace and friendliness compared with Arbroath which lay within the Montrose district but which the Montrose officers were terrified of visiting because of the ferocious hostility of the natives. One would have thought that a customs man trained in Montrose could cope with almost anything, for the action in that burgh could be very lively. Seizures did occur, as in April 1728, when customs officers, after watching several vessels hovering suspiciously off the coast for a few days, noticed a sudden concentration of carts by the shore. Reinforced by a party of the military they swooped and triumphantly captured a large quantity of brandy.[28] Almost at once difficulties arose. The country carts involved were confiscated and put up for sale, but nobody would bid, so they became the property of the officers who had seized them who, having to live with their neighbours, disposed of them for next to nothing, doubtless to the original owners and much to the rage and fury of their superiors in Edinburgh.[29]

The Edinburgh authorities should have saved their breath. Much worse was to follow. That particular seizure of brandy was hastily shipped out of Montrose on a sloop, for fear of repossession by those who had tried to run it. Comically, precautions had to be taken to ensure that it was not stolen by the thirsty matelots of the Royal Navy.[30] Nobody could be trusted. When the over-zealous Montrose officers made another substantial seizure of brandy in the autumn the locals decided that enough was enough. On the morning of 11 October 1728 a group of men armed with clubs and other weapons beat the two soldiers guarding the King's Warehouse sense-less, burst the doors, and liberated the contents. The Collector and Surveyor promptly went to the Provost to ask for a warrant for a general search of the town. It was refused. Acting as a Justice of the Peace the Collector issued a warrant to his staff to search for the missing goods. The Provost sent town officials to obstruct the search, a task which was eventually taken over by a large and violent crowd. As the Collector told Edinburgh, since virtually everyone in the town was hostile to the search, it had no chance of success.[31] Suspicion at one point centred on the house of Bailie Murison, and the usual deadlock between customs officers on the one side and town officers reinforced by a mob on the other was resolved by placing troops on guard outside pending appeal to a court composed of local justices. The Collector, with the support of a local laird, James Scott of Logie, obviously assumed he could override the recalcitrant Provost but that wily man summoned his fellow justices, the Provosts of the equally disaffected burghs of Brechin, Forfar and Arbroath. Together they made a clear majority to refuse a search warrant. The Collector protested. He also gave up.[32]

It might seem that the way to override local autonomy was to employ military force. However, there were grave difficulties involved in resorting to such a method. For a start, except under such unusual circumstances as the Glasgow Malt Tax Riots of 1725, there was just not enough military power available, nor any sign of the will to pay for more. In January 1731 the Collector at Montrose complained that nothing encouraged the local smugglers more than the fact that the soldiers who were stationed in the town were known not to mount a guard at night, the prime time for running smuggled goods. The reason for this position was simply that the officer in command of the troops refused to allow his men to mount a guard during winter nights unless some arrangement was made to provide them with coals to stop them from freezing and to supply them with candles to provide some light.[33] As it was, the guardhouse in Montrose was far from the King's Warehouse and it was only in 1732 that the Collector had a small lodge for a guard built outside the vital warehouse. Even then, the quarrel about coal and candles was still in full swing. A despairing Collector begged his superiors to agree to the expense, on the ground that the King's Warehouse was full of valuable, vulnerable goods.[34]

Even when reinforced by soldiers, the Montrose customs officers were liable to be overwhelmed. In May 1733 customs and excise men, along with a sergeant's guard of soldiers, seized smuggled brandy at Maiden

Cove near Montrose. Shortly afterwards a large crowd beat up the officers and soldiers, and deforced them of the briefly captured brandy. It proved impossible to secure witnesses to sustain a prosecution against the rioters, many of whose names were well known. A bitter note from the Collector pointed out that:

> The boatmen and Country people along the coast favour and assist the smugglers so much in carrying on their smuggling trade that it is almost impracticable for an officer to get intelligence or learn anything from them.[35]

Not much wonder that the Collector reckoned his officers could only hope to make seizures when they had a military escort. The trouble was that the soldiery was detested in the town, as a riot between soldiers and local seamen in 1735 illustrates. The seamen were rapidly reinforced by a rock-hurling mob which severely injured one of the soldiers. Lieutenant Williams asked the Provost to authorize the troops to fire in self-defence. The Provost wisely refused, thereby probably averting a major convulsion. Williams angrily withdrew his men. Two town and two customs officers stood guard over the King's Warehouse that night. There was no trouble and the Collector was obviously astonished to have to conclude that there had been no intention of looting the warehouse.[36]

So even in Montrose where Episcopalian Jacobites were probably the dominant element in the population, there was a distinction to be drawn between specific bones of contention between the inhabitants and Hanoverian officialdom, and the much broader general issue of the maintenance of traditional local autonomy over against the high-handed authoritarianism of Westminster, of which the supreme symbol was the 'base bloody and licentious' soldiery. Such a distinction goes far to explain the true significance of the Porteous Riot which in September 1736 quite suddenly created a major confrontation between the central government and Scotland's capital city, Edinburgh.

The events which led up to this crisis were simple, if moving and dramatic. For some time the legal authorities and especially Lord Advocate Duncan Forbes had been becoming increasingly worked up about the almost universal contempt for the customs regulations in Scotland, so when two notorious smugglers, Wilson and Robertson, were arrested and convicted of breaking into the Customs House at Pittenweem in Fife and stealing £200, it was not surprising that they were condemned to death. Confined in Edinburgh tolbooth prior to their hanging, the two men would have escaped had not Wilson, a very big man, insisted on trying to squeeze through a narrow window first. He stuck fast. Overcome with remorse at hazarding his companion's life, Wilson made amends at the service in St

Giles Kirk to which malefactors were traditionally taken on the Sunday before their execution. Himself an exceptionally powerful man, he seized his friend 'by the head band of his breeks', and threw him out of the pew. He then held a soldier fast in each hand and a third he pinioned with his teeth. Robertson scrambled over the pews, pushed aside elder and plate at the door, and, in the words of a letter written by the poet Allan Ramsay, he then 'got out of the Poteraw Port before it was shut, the mob making way and assisting him, got friends, money and a swift horse and fairly got off, nae mair to be heard of or seen.'[37]

Naturally, when Wilson was finally brought to the scaffold on 14 April, the sympathy of the very large crowd was with the sufferer, so it was not surprising that the city guard under its thoroughly unpopular commander Captain John Porteous was on edge about maintaining order in the Grass Market, the traditional site of executions. The precise details of the sequence of events which followed the uninterrupted hanging of Andrew Wilson was later the subject of furious controversy, but it does seem that Porteous, in response to a shower of stones, ordered his men to fire into the crowd and that as the guard retreated up the West Bow they turned and fired again. Six people were killed and about twenty wounded. Public indignation was very great.

It proved impossible to shield Porteous from trial. Indeed his indictment was drawn up by the Lord Advocate Duncan Forbes and he was convicted of murder. The execution date was set for 8 September. However, it was predictable that influence would be exerted from the highest quarters to save him. Andrew Wilson had been one of the most notorious of Fife smugglers and his raid on the Customs House at Pittenweem was, like the sacking of the King's Warehouse at Montrose, an attempt to recoup losses due to seizures. Besides, the whole question of crowd control by the military was so difficult in law that the precedent of the execution of Porteous was bound to be unacceptable to someone like General Wade, with his responsibilities for internal security. Wade it was who intervened first and it was as the result of considerable pressure, in the form of a petition from very influential people, that Queen Caroline gave Porteous a six-week stay of execution. A nod being as good as a wink, it was then fairly certain that Porteous would never swing, legally. What followed has been immortalized by Sir Walter Scott in his novel *The Heart of Midlothian*. On the evening of Tuesday, 7 September, a drum was beaten in the Grass Market by some boys who had earlier misappropriated it. The city fathers alerted the city guard, but at about 10 p.m. it was overpowered by a large and well-disciplined crowd which secured the gates of the city before it tore Porteous from prison and hung him on a dyer's pole in the Grass Market shortly before midnight.

The London government was beside itself with rage at this flagrant flouting of both its dignity and its authority. The Lord Advocate, the Solicitor-General and General Wade were all ordered to Edinburgh. They were instructed to identify, prosecute, and punish the perpetrators of the crime. It was easier said than done. They ran into the usual wall of silence and ended up with a few very minor fish in their nets, none of whom could be accused of more than a very subordinate role in the escapade. What is clear is that the magistrates of the city were in no way implicated and indeed gave every possible assistance to the enquiry, as even the widow of Porteous was willing to testify. It was therefore all the more inappropriate that the government should in its fury bring in a Bill of Pains and Penalties which proposed to imprison the Provost and other magistrates, to disable them from holding office again, and to demolish the Netherbow Port of Edinburgh, partly as a symbol of the crushing of local autonomy and partly as a practical measure to make it easier to rush troops and guns into the city.[38]

This vindictive and totally inequitable legislation, itself a classic demonstration that there is in the British political system absolutely no ultimate safeguard for basic human rights against the will of an unrepresentative Parliament, was stoutly opposed by the Duke of Argyll when it was first introduced into the House of Lords. From the Lords the bill progressed successfully to the Commons where it was vociferously opposed by the Scottish members, amongst whom Duncan Forbes was prominent. His argument was the simple one that the proposed legislation would punish the closed oligarchy which ruled Edinburgh and which was well-disposed to the regime, while leaving untouched and rejoicing the scum, or vast majority of the population, who had actually done the deed. With the Lord Presidency of the Court of Session standing vacant, and himself an obvious candidate to fill it, Forbes undoubtedly behaved with courage, though two facts must be borne in mind. One is that he knew that his patron the Duke of Argyll, a man too arrogant to rein in his feelings on a topic which genuinely moved him, was already totally hostile to the bill. Not for nothing did Lord President Forbes write to the Duke of Argyll in 1738 that:

> The possession of your Grace's good will upon principles that I think honest has been the chief pleasure – nay, indeed, the pride of my life.[39]

The other is that although Forbes spoke against the preponderant opinion in what may fairly be called the Whig Establishment of his day, he did so, as General Wade said to the House of Commons, from a point of view which left no serious doubt about his absolute loyalty to that Establishment. From the point of view of the Establishment Forbes was indulging in a permissible perversity, for he in no way challenged the bases of the existing political system.

The bill was finally passed in an amended form on 21 June 1737. In the course of forcing it through the Commons the government had been compelled to drop several of its more obnoxious features. Even so, Provost Alexander Wilson of Edinburgh, an entirely innocent man as far as the evidence is a guide, was banned from ever again holding office as a magistrate. A £2,000 fine, to be handed over to the widow of Porteous, was imposed on the city of Edinburgh, and further vigorous attempts to bring the killers to justice were promised. It was an inept performance rendered all the more counter-productive by the method adopted to honour the ill-advised pledge to intensify the futile search for the offenders. A measure was passed which ordered the clergy of the Church of Scotland to preach on the first Sunday of every month for a whole year a sermon summoning those who had contrived the death of Porteous to surrender themselves. The Earl of Islay, Argyll's extremely intelligent brother and manager, warned Sir Robert Walpole that this was asking for trouble. The legislation reeked of the basest English Whig view of the church – a very subordinate department of state whose activities, if of debatable value on a philosophic plane, were useful to its masters in connection with the moral policing of the lower orders. The long reign of the so-called Moderates not having yet set in in the Kirk by Law Established, there were enough old-fashioned clergymen with the spirit, or smeddum as the Scots put it, to bid defiance to the state on a scale which brooked no further response.[40]

Superficially, the Westminster government seemed to be making decisive progress in its long struggle to impose the authority of the English Crown on that sullen and restless province which since 1707 had been officially referred to as North Britain. The long arm of the Crown seemed to be penetrating even that bastion of Jacobitism and particularism, the High-lands. After the '15 it was to be expected that some initiative would be taken to establish an effective Hanoverian military presence in the High-lands. Irregular companies of Highlanders had in fact been raised from time to time by royal commission since the 1660s. Their function was that of a gendarmerie in their native countryside, and there were never enough of them. The Crown had also, on occasion, established garrisons within the Highland area, as had the Cromwellian regime in Scotland with its citadel at Inverness and its garrison at Inverlochy (later Fort William). By 1717 there were four permanent garrisons in the Highlands: Inverlochy, Killi-chiumen (later Fort Augustus), Bernera in Glenelg, and Ruthven near Kingussie. Each held a group of thirty Highlanders commanded by local officers and intended to act as scouts and guides for regular troops moving into the Highlands. It was, however, General Wade who pulled these two devices of local levies and strategic strongpoints together into something like a coherent system. Taking up office as Commander-in-Chief, Scotland, in 1725 (with primary responsibility for enforcing the Disarming Act) he managed, despite the distractions of crises elsewhere, to strengthen or extend the forts and to raise more Highland companies. The first three were commanded by Grant of Ballindalloch, Simon Fraser of Lovat, and Campbell of Lochnell. A company was a useful piece of patronage. One of the last duties Wade performed in Scotland was to review six of these companies in August and September 1738, when they had a total effective rank and file strength, exclusive of commissioned officers, of 402 men.

This was no military steamroller, but the significance of the companies must be seen in the context of their relationship to regular forces and, above all, to Wade's military road system. It is as a road builder that Wade is now primarily remembered, and however misleading this is as a way of looking at his career, it encapsulates an important fact about Highland history. Wade was the first man to set out quite deliberately to break down the traditional physical isolation of the Highlands by means of solidly-constructed roads. Two points must be made about the 'Wade roads'. The first is that they were military roads in the fullest sense of the word, being constructed by work parties of soldiers, and being designed first and foremost for the rapid transit of troops. Neither their routes nor their gradients were necessarily the most suitable ones for commercial traffic. Secondly Wade himself only supervised a part, albeit an important part, of the construction programme which continued many years after he had left Scotland under the care of men like Governor Caulfield and Lieutenant-Colonel Skene. William Caulfield, Wade's righthand man for roads, was another Georgian Irish gentleman, a grandson of the first Viscount Charlemont and a formidable toper as well as a competent engineer. He was Quartermaster to General Sir John Cope in 1745, rising from that grave of reputation to be Deputy Governor of Inverness Castle in 1747, a post from which his usual title of Governor derives. He settled near Inverness after Wade left Scotland in a house called Cradlehall, not because of its owner's excesses in bed, but because of his addiction to the bottle which led him to install a mechanical device for transporting sozzled guests to their rooms after an evening's serious drinking.

In the eleven years between 1726 and 1737 some 260 miles of military road were constructed, to a definite strategic plan pivoting on a road along the Great Glen linking Inverness with the western seaboard at Fort William through Fort Augustus. Further to secure this crucial string of garrisons, Wade built and launched a galley of thirty tons on Loch Ness. It was armed with eight cannon called patteroes.* Here in the Great Glen was the backbone of Hanoverian military power in the Highlands, with the

---

* Patteroe, and patteraro(e), are variants of pedrero meaning a small gun.

irregular companies which were later to develop into the Black Watch playing a vital role in reconnaissance. They were the eyes and ears of the regular forces, and should have enabled them to pounce on any incipient Jacobite rising as effectively and promptly as General Wightman had when he crushed the '19. To enable regular reinforcements to reach the Great Glen garrisons from the Lowlands by forced marches another great road ran north from Dunkeld, that gateway to the Grampian Highlands, to reach Inverness. Access to this north-south route from the Lowlands was further secured by a supplementary road from Crieff through Glenalmond which joined the main road at Dalnacardoch, while an obviously desirable facility for the rapid reinforcement of the centre or west of the Great Glen line was provided by a road which branched off the main route at Dalwhinnie and ran by means of a series of hair-raising zig-zags over the steep Pass of Corrieyairack to Fort Augustus.[41] The Highlands were still armed, and the great men of the region still held their extensive heritable jurisdictions, but something like a balance of power was created by this system, a balance which arguably protected the Highlanders from the political folly of another Jacobite rising, while leaving them with the means of self-defence against the more egregious follies of Westminster.

How, then, did Jacobitism contrive to survive in Scotland? Survive it certainly did, and between 1725 and 1739 survival was no mean achievement. Survival was not based on hope of an impending successful rebellion, for hope there was none. Rather was it the product of deep-seated intellectual attitudes and social structures which, protected to some extent by sheer distance from the metropolitan heart of Whig and Hanoverian authority, continued to exist and indeed develop in their own way, spinning a particularly important network of international contacts which enabled the exiled dynasty to keep in touch with its Scottish supporters and eventually to use that network to launch its last desperate fling for power. Complex as these phenomena were, it is possible to catch something of the general spirit pervading them by a study of the intellectual world of the more articulate Scottish Jacobites.

The social flavour of this world was strongly conservative. Learning, social order, the aristocratic graces, were all identified with Episcopal religion and Jacobite politics, while Presbyterian and Whig values were equated with the crass brutality of the hooligan mob. Dr Archibald Pitcairne, the noted Jacobite physician and poet, exemplifies this outlook. He was a fine flower of the aristocratic culture of Restoration Scotland, born in 1652; graduating M.A. at Edinburgh in 1671; studying law and medicine at Paris and becoming a founder member of the Royal College of Physicians in Edinburgh in 1681 before he held a chair of physics in Holland at the University of Leyden between 1692 and 1693. Until his death in 1713 he practised medicine with huge success in Edinburgh where he enjoyed a large circle of acquaintance. That he was a remarkable personality is attested by the fact that even the devout Presbyterian historian Robert Wodrow, though appalled by Pitcairne's minimal deistic religion, rabid Jacobitism, and frequent drunkenness, could not conceal his admiration for the man. Cultured Scots of the late seventeenth century faced a fragmented literary heritage. The old literary Scots of the fifteenth and sixteenth-century court poets disintegrated after 1603 into a series of dialects. Despite the use of the English Bible, standard English remained an alien tongue of little use for the expression of emotion. It was therefore natural for Pitcairne to express his deepest feelings in Latin verse, for Scotland had a magnificent heritage in this, the international vehicle for polite humanistic culture. Not that there is much of the polite in Pitcairne's verses. They seeth with a *saeva indignatio*, a fierce disdain, of the Presbyterian ascendancy under which the cultivation of the law, the classics, and the flowers of rhetoric all fell on evil days:

Jura silent, torpent classica, rostra vacant.

No word in Pitcairne's poetical vocabulary carries a heavier load of emotion than *vulgus*, the mob, always used with explicit connotation of the usage of the Roman poet Horace in the opening lines of the third book of his Odes:

Odi profanum vulgus et arceo . . .

(I hate the vulgar crowd and shun it.) Pitcairne's view of post-Revolution Scotland was '*Omnia vulgus erat*', the mob was everything. The poem in which this line occurs was entitled 'Deploratio status Regni Scotici' but there is a sense in which most of Pitcairne's Latin verse constitutes a lament for the state of Scotland. His views in no way died with him for he left behind a protégé in the shape of a Banffshire crofter's son, Thomas Ruddiman, who grew to become the greatest Scots Latinist of his day and Keeper of the Advocate's Library in Edinburgh. Best known as a grammarian, Ruddiman wrote a phenomenally successful textbook *Rudiments of the Latin Tongue* (1714) as well as a more detailed *Grammaticae Latinae Institutiones* (1725 and 1731). Episcopal in religion and Jacobite in sentiment, if not in action, Ruddiman was so much a champion of a Scottish classical and humanist tradition that he edited in two massive quarto volumes, published by his friend Robert Freebairn in 1715, the *Opera Omnia* of the great sixteenth-century Scots Presbyterian Latinist and radical, George Buchanan. Though Ruddiman had reservations about Buchanan's politics he was later to champion his Latin version of the Psalms against that of the seventeenth-century royalist Arthur Johnston.

Significant as this tradition of Scots Latinity was, there is no doubt that by the 1720s or 1730s it was losing its vitality outside such rugged strongholds as Aberdeen, where the last great figure in this apostolic succession of Latinists, Dr James Melvin, died as late as 1853.[42]

The scholarship of the Jacobite-inclined, though always socially conservative, was not necessarily intellectually conservative. Pitcairne's scientific ideas were trendily *avant-garde*, which is why his medical writings possessed no enduring value. Ruddiman, admittedly with very little confidence in his work, materially assisted the first stirrings of the revival of Scottish vernacular literature by printing the poems of Allan Ramsay and by editing Bishop Gavin Douglas's superb translation of Virgil's *Aeneid* into medieval Scots. Patriotic publishing in Scotland in the decades after the Union of 1707 was by no means confined to Jacobites, but Jacobites were very prominent in the field and certainly included the only two printers of any quality in early eighteenth-century Scotland, James Watson, who died in 1722, and Robert Freebairn who, despite an adventurous career, survived until 1747. Watson, the son of the 'Popish printer' set up in Holyroodhouse by James VII in 1686, was himself the author of a survey of Scottish printing which persistently identified disloyalty to the House of Stewart with decline in typographical standards. He not only published the works of seventeenth-century royalists like Drummond of Hawthornden and Mackenzie of Rosehaugh, but also much contemporary vernacular verse, and a deal of Scottish history.[43]

Robert Freebairn was the son of a deposed Episcopalian clergyman who turned to bookselling to earn a living after being ousted by the Presbyterians, and who died in 1739 as Bishop of Edinburgh. His children were raised on strong Jacobite principles which impelled both his surviving sons, James and Robert, to play an active role in the '15. James was an excise officer in Perthshire and like nearly all the excisemen in the county he joined the Pretender, thus showing that the new customs and excise system not only drove men into the arms of Jacobitism, but also failed to secure the loyalty of its own officials to the House of Hanover. Robert Freebairn was a friend of Archibald Pitcairne, both being members of that hotbed of sedition, the Royal Company of Archers, and he worked with Thomas Ruddiman, his brother Walter Ruddiman, and James Watson. The latter shared by 1714 with Robert Freebairn and three others the title and privileges of King's printer. This did not prevent Freebairn from participating in the plot to capture Edinburgh Castle and, when it failed, from fleeing into Mar's camp at Perth where he operated a press for the insurgent army, using equipment donated by the Jacobite rulers of Aberdeen.[44] After the débâcle Freebairn retired to the Continent but by 1722 he was back in Edinburgh and there he quietly resumed the title of King's Printer, to a monarch he held in the lowest esteem.

Because there was such a substantial Scottish Jacobite diaspora in Western Europe, there is no doubt that the Jacobite community was exceptionally exposed to the principal currents of contemporary European thought, and that this could have a deeply stimulating effect. One of the several very important books on Scottish history published in the early eighteenth century was Father Thomas Innes's *Critical Essay on the Ancient Inhabitants of the Northern Parts of Britain* (1729). It was compiled mainly from materials in the Advocates' Library where, under the supervision of Thomas Ruddiman, Innes, the Prefect of Studies of the Scots College in Paris, worked away surrounded by compatriots Whig and compatriots of his own Jacobite persuasion. That Jacobites made a significant contribution to the intellectual ferment which preceded the full flowering of the Scottish Enlightenment in the second half of the eighteenth century is obvious. To argue that they were the real progenitors of that Enlightenment is to push the case much too far.[45] They contributed to it, but did not make it, and much of their intellectual activity was stamped by a backward-looking quality quite at variance with the neo-classical but anglicized and infinitely worldly-wise culture of such men as the Reverend Principal Robertson, historian and Moderator of the General Assembly of the Kirk, and his friend the sceptical philosopher David Hume.

What was of vital importance to both the existence and future of Scottish Jacobitism was the network of contacts and routes between Scotland and Western Europe. Some of the most significant of these contacts, and not least for the origins of the '45, were financial. Despite the Act of Grace and the relatively lenient treatment of aristocratic rebels, the '15 was followed by lengthy periods of exile on the Continent for many Scotsmen of good family. A certain number could never hope to return home legally. Others did not want to. To those of noble birth the idea of taking a job, other than a military, diplomatic or ecclesiastical one, just did not occur, nor were such jobs easily come by on the part of uninfluential exiles in a period of comparative peace in Western Europe. Instead they lived on remittances from their relatives in Scotland, remittances normally handled by Scots merchants resident in France who were developing into private bankers. The most spectacular product of this strange world was John Law, the son of an Edinburgh goldsmith, who from 1705 endeavoured to have his novel ideas on banking and systematic credit-creation adopted by a series of governments including those of Scotland, England, Austria, and sundry Italian states. Gaining the ear of the Regent Orleans in France, he was allowed to create a precocious Banque Générale in 1716 and eventually to take control of French finances and create a vast monopolistic trading company, the Compagnie des Indes, in 1719. Law had strong Jacobite connections, but his manipulations created an inflationary speculative bubble which ruined him when it burst in 1720.[46]

By far the biggest stable example of Scottish private banking enterprise abroad was the bank founded in Holland by Archibald Hope in the seventeenth century. By the 1740s his family were 'pretty men, of great trade and reputation in the mercantile way' both in Amsterdam and Rotterdam. Among their activities was the task of procuring military commissions in the Dutch service for young Scotsmen. As Anabaptist Protestants, the Hopes were never likely to harbour Jacobite sympathies, but a surprisingly large proportion of Scottish private bankers did have Jacobite connections. Andrew Drummond, a goldsmith who came from a good Perthshire family of staunchly Jacobite opinions, settled in London in 1712 in Charing Cross, an area which contained the mansions of many of the wealthy Scots attracted to London after 1707. By 1717 he was active in banking, and indeed rose to be banker to George III.[47] In the earlier part of the eighteenth century there is no doubt that political affinities mattered in banking. The Jacobite Drummond was patronized mainly by Tories. In the same area of London a Whig banker from Scotland, John Campbell of the family of Ardkinglas, was patronized mainly by Whig nobles including the first two Dukes of Argyll. Ironically enough, the firm with which John Campbell was associated was eventually taken over from the 1750s by marriage by the Coutts family, merchants and bankers of Montrose and Edinburgh. The irony lay in the fact that the Montrose branch of the Coutts family had been in dire trouble after the '45 because of its active Jacobitism, and yet they too rose eventually to be bankers to their Britannic Majesties.[48] It had been widely alleged after the '15 that the Bank of Scotland had Jacobite sympathies. It certainly had the odd official who was strongly that way inclined. David Drummond, Treasurer of the Bank of Scotland 1700–1741 was notoriously a Jacobite and treasurer of the funds raised to assist the defence of the Jacobite prisoners. However, most Scottish institutions harboured influential Jacobites, and there is little doubt that so much was made of Drummond's case mainly in order to facilitate the granting of a bank charter to the very Whig Royal Bank of Scotland established in 1727 under the firm leadership of the Argyll interest.[49]

Just what all this implied in practical terms can be demonstrated by a glance at the papers of the Atholl family. The Jacobite 'Duke' William, exiled after the '15, blithely suggested to his Whig brother Duke James that the family funds should be placed under trustees to be nominated, of course, by the exile. Duke James was curiously unenthusiastic about this scheme. He doled out funds to his exiled brother on a scale sufficient to maintain him at a modest level, but the two men bickered endlessly over money, not surprisingly as they regarded one another in no charitable spirit. William thought James a parsimonious usurper. James thought William an irresponsible spendthrift who had done his best to ruin his family. More interesting than their endless rows is the list of bankers used to make the money transfers. They include Andrew Drummond of Charing Cross, William Law (brother of John Law) and, most significant of all, Aeneas Macdonald, banker, of Paris. This same Aeneas Macdonald, brother to Macdonald of Kinlochmoidart, was one of the companions of Prince Charles when that prince landed in Scotland in 1745.[50]

Apart from acting as a life-support system for a scattering of aristocratic exiles, the Jacobite communications network also connected the exiled court to specific communities and regions within Scotland where Jacobite principles were still dearly cherished. One such community, which was to prove strategically significant for the origins of the '45, was the Roman Catholic community, or if geographic be preferred to spiritual terms, the Roman Catholic communities, for they were small, dispersed and often remote. Therein lay part of the explanation for the survival, among mainland Highland Roman Catholics, of Jacobite militancy. They were far less exposed to punishment after the '15 than their co-religionists in the northern counties of England. There, in the three counties most affected by the rebellion, the laws against recusancy (normally torpid) were activated and the papers of the English Forfeited Estates Commission contains a list of Roman Catholics fined for that offence, grouped according to place of residence. Priests were harried. Many were arrested. Only one died in jail. The others were speedily released but their spiritual work was severely interrupted. Executions and widespread sequestration of their leaders, allied to new anti-Roman Catholic legislation not enforced but held over their heads as a perpetual threat, thoroughly cowed this once proud minority.[51]

By comparison Highland Roman Catholics, even on the mainland, were often remote from the reach of the Hanoverian regime. Amongst the several small clans into which the once imperial Clan Donald disintegrated after the final suppression of the Lordship of the Isles in 1493, the Macdonalds of Glengarry, Clanranald, and Keppoch remained Roman Catholic. By 1700 there were so many Macdonald priests that they were known jokingly as the priesthood of Aaron. They ran two schools for lay pupils, one at Arisaig and one at Strathavon, both much patronized by the Macdonald tacksmen, the gentry of the country. It is true that as a result of the '15 a small seminary on an island in Loch Morar in Keppoch's country had to be discreetly closed, but by 1717 another seminary had been opened in a remote site at Scalan in the Braes of Glenlivet in Banffshire.[52] The General Assembly of the Church of Scotland in the period around 1720 was much given to presenting memorials to the government about 'the growth of Popery'. On the whole, the detailed information in these documents was surprisingly accurate and sane, though the note of panic in the conclusion was uncalled for. The Assembly appreciated that the main pockets of Popery both on the mainland and in the Hebrides were places 'where the Reformation never yet had footing'. The islands of Barra, Benbecula, and South Uist were almost devoid of Protestants and served by local priests reinforced by colleagues from Ireland and France. In the north-east the powerful protection of the ducal House of Gordon enabled Roman Catholic life to flourish in traditional centres often served by schools in open rivalry with those of the Society for Propagating Christian Knowledge which was trying, not very successfully, to replace Romish error with Gospel light.

The Presbyterian Kirk insisted that Roman Catholic clergy were 'enemies of the Government and [of] our Religion'. Complaining that Roman Catholic missions were being amply financed from outside sources, the Presbyterians warned that 'everyone that is gained to Popery is infallibly a Jacobite'.[53] This was an over-simplification, but one which contained a substantial vein of truth. Roman Catholics were as capable of common prudence as any other Scottish community, so they were far from rushing into insurrection at the least opportunity, but their commitment to Jacobitism ran deeper than most. After all, the Holy See allowed both the exiled James VII and II, and his son James, the Old Pretender, admittedly reluctantly, to the end of the latter's days, the royal right to nominate to the senior posts in the Roman Catholic hierarchy in the British Isles. The bishops and archbishops of Ireland, as well as the vicars-apostolic who looked after the remnants of the faithful in England and Scotland, were all nominated by the Jacobite court. It was still true in 1740, as in 1715, that the bulk of active supporters for any Jacobite rising in Scotland were bound to be Episcopalians. Even in the north-east the activities of Jacobite Episcopal teachers were more significant politically than the much-resented seminary at Scanlan. The academics who scattered over the region in 1716 like William Smith, 'proffessor of Philosophy in the Marichell College of Aberdeen', who was being pursued by every variety of Hanoverian authority for treasonable practices, left an enduring mark on the areas which sheltered them.[54] William Meston, a notorious Jacobite, another refugee from Marischal College where he was a philosophy regent in 1714–15, was only the most inspired of the many Jacobite teachers who ran private academies all over the north-east. In the course of thirty years William Meston taught in Elgin, Turriff, Montrose, and Perth, often working in conjunction with his brother Samuel, a notable Greek scholar.[55]

Thus Jacobitism in Scotland between 1725 and 1739 was a paradoxical phenomenon. It quite failed to take advantage of the widespread and often violent demonstrations of disaffection towards the London government. Yet it survived as an ideology, especially amongst the gentry and Roman Catholic and Episcopal clergymen; as a network of communications between Scotland and western Europe; and in several isolated but intensely committed local communities. It is no accident that Prince Charles, on whom religion sat lightly, made his first landings on Scottish soil in areas which were overwhelmingly Roman Catholic. There he was at least safe. The ingredients for another national rising like the '15 were not to hand, but there was enough just, to launch that very different phenomenon, the '45.

10 The '45

There is little doubt that at the high noon of his greatness Sir Robert Walpole presided over a political system which left very little opportunity for the mounting of a serious Jacobite rebellion. As long as the Great Man (as he was sarcastically known) was in full control of the internal and external policies of His Britannic Majesty's government events were unlikely ever to stand in a favourable conjuncture for the Jacobites. Internally the regime was in many ways offensive. It was arrogant, blatantly corrupt, and gave grave offence to all those who believed that government ought to be primarily a moral activity. Jacobites, who generally stood well to the right on the political and religious spectrum, could share this conservative moralistic view of the function of political leadership with Protestant nonconformist groups well to the left. Neither could seriously shake a system which both appealed to the baser instincts of the political classes, and displayed a remarkable sense of its own limitations. In politicians who have reached the heights of power cynicism usually goes hand in hand with a burgeoning conceit which can easily lead on to megalomania and hubris. Not so in Walpole. He was cynical, corrupt, and vain, but he remained, at the apogee of his vanity, realistic about what was possible and what was desirable.

His central political principle when in office was to make sure that the fat cats of early Hanoverian Britain had plenty of cream. Taxation policies were consciously geared to this end. There were two main elements in the eighteenth-century British tax structure. One was taxation levied directly upon income and wealth of which the principal constituent was the land tax. Such taxation was generally 'progressive' in the sense that it was related to ability to pay, which is why it was so unpopular with a legislature representing primarily the wealthy and especially the landed class. Parliament resisted any increase in the land tax above two shillings in the pound except in war-time. Direct taxation had accounted for over 35 per cent of total revenue during Marlborough's wars in the first decade of the eighteenth century, but Walpole steadily reduced this proportion until in 1735, just before he began to lose control of events, it was down to 17 per cent. This, incidentally, was a far lower proportion of direct taxation than was typical of contemporary France, where a figure around 50 per cent was perfectly normal in the 1720s, 1730s and 1740s. To compensate for this progressive atrophy of direct taxation there had to be an increase in the incidence of indirect taxation. Its impact was mixed, but overall there is no doubt that indirect taxation was regressive in character, i.e. it hit the poor harder than the rich. This was because the big revenue-producing items were usually commodities like soap, candles, tobacco, beer, and salt, which were in mass demand. It was therefore a remarkable achievement on the part of the ruling élites of eighteenth-century Britain to persuade the bulk of their fellow-countrymen that they were better treated than a French population ground down by a reactionary and increasingly burdensome tax system. The truth was the reverse of this: French taxation was fairer and in the period 1715–85 grew very little compared with the substantial growth of the British tax load.[1]

One reason for the success of the British government's sleight of hand in matters fiscal was undoubtedly the oddly 'invisible' nature of much of the tax collection procedure. Walpole himself in 1732 described the land tax as 'partial and grievous', but at least it only affected some 400,000 proprietors of land, and that class assessed itself and taxed itself through representative groups of landowners acting as amateur, unpaid state administrators. There were no offensive privileged exemptions from taxation as in France and no elaborate internal customs dues. In Britain the bulk of customs revenue was levied at a few ports and the cost promptly became 'invisible', though of course it was passed on in the shape of increased prices. The inherent unpopularity of customs and excise in eighteenth-century Britain hinged precisely on the fact that it was a centralized system run by a paid bureaucracy. Scottish smuggling or the Glasgow Malt Tax riots were specific manifestations of an almost universal, and largely justified, suspicion of the central government. It was this suspicion which made it impossible for Walpole to carry a scheme for a general excise in 1733. The parliamentary opposition and the street mobs combined with the City of London to inflict on Sir Robert the first major political setback he had experienced since emerging as the ascendant minister of state. To the opposition it seemed a triumph, but the real victory was with Walpole. It was a victory over himself and with it he arguably scaled the peak of political achievement. He closely resembled some twentieth-century Prime Ministers in that he was a curiously isolated sort of figure, with no serious political ideology, sustaining himself on a combination of the arrogance of office and a deep sense of his own inherent reasonableness and rationality. Like his twentieth-century successors he relied heavily on a massive use of patronage to secure acquiescence in his will. Yet with the Crown behind him and total conviction of the rightness of his policy he sensed in 1733, however reluctantly, that victory would be pyrrhic. When Walpole gritted his teeth and told his intimates, 'This dance it will no further go', he showed that he understood the danger of creating in the political nation at large a feeling that Westminster knew nothing and cared less about its deepest emotion-respect for the autonomy of local élites. It was bad news for Jacobites.[2]

The sheer hopelessness of the Jacobite cause after the collapse of the '15 had for a long time tempted even the staunchest of Jacobites to come surreptitiously to terms with the House of Hanover. One of the most startling examples of how this could be done was the case of John Gordon of Glenbucket who as a boy of sixteen fought at Killiecrankie, as a man of forty-two at Sheriffmuir, and as an old man of seventy-two played an active role in the '45 from the first stirrings in Moidart to the fatal field of Culloden. He was the laird of the tiny estate of Glenbucket which is in Aberdeenshire near the Banffshire boundary. However, as bailie to the Duke of Gordon he was vastly more influential than the mere size of his property suggests and he has often been regarded as an example of a single-minded paladin of the cause of the exiled Stewarts. In fact for a very substantial part of the period between the '15 and the '45 he was a Hanoverian agent, being particularly thick with General Carpenter who secured his release from imprisonment in Carlisle in 1716 and who received regular intelligence reports from him during the '19 when the Jacobite commander, the Marquis of Tullibardine, fondly hoped that Glenbucket would rally to the Stewart standard.[3] The degree of 'canniness' exercised by Glenbucket was by no means unusual amongst leading Jacobites in the years when their cause lay in the doldrums. While it would be quite wrong to suggest that every Tory M.P. or peer at Westminster was a Jacobite, some were, and amongst the leaders of this last group can be found men who by the 1720s were playing the same game as Glenbucket had embarked on in 1716. After the exile of Atterbury in 1723 the Pretender's affairs in England were managed jointly by Lord Strafford, and two Tory M.P.s Lord Orrery and Charles Caesar. Yet at some point in 1727 the last two seem to have come to terms secretly with Walpole. Caesar did it in exchange for government support in his election for Hertfordshire. His finances had been ruined in the collapse of the South Sea Bubble and an M.P.'s privilege of immunity from arrest for debt was very important to him. Orrery sold his political soul for a pension which Walpole said 'he well earned'. By 1729 the incorruptible Jacobites led by William Shippen M.P. had rumbled Caesar and were cold-shouldering him, but his defection was a measure of their ineffectiveness.

The Pretender was clear enough about the only development which could breath life into his hopes. In 1730 he wrote a letter strongly urging his friends in the next session of Parliament to unite in opposition to the government 'even with those who oppose it for different views than theirs'.

In another memorandum he specially stressed the need to support any measure which was calculated to promote bad relations 'between the English Government and any foreign power, but most especially France'. The Jacobite M.P.s were naturally keen to secure a reduction in the regular army and in 1738 actually advanced towards this objective behind a verbal smokescreen consisting of a repeated insistence that this would be quite safe because of the virtual extinction of Jacobitism. Sir Robert Walpole crushed their bid with a speech which began with his usual smear that anyone who opposed the government was probably a crypto-Jacobite or fellow-traveller but which ended with a most able and sensible argument that it was essential to maintain a standing army capable of coping with a sudden descent by the striking force of five or six thousand men which could be carried on comparatively few ships and which might well, due to the quirks of weather and tides, be able to slip past the Royal Navy. Walpole's minimum establishment adequate to cope with such a menace was eighteen thousand men. He insisted that roughly one third of that number ought to be stationed around London, the nerve-centre of British government. Another third would have to be dispersed so as to guarantee tranquillity in those parts of Britain prone to disaffection, and the remaining third would form the mass of manoeuvre which could be hurled against any invading army. Provided the eighteen thousand men on the British establishment were predominantly seasoned troops, it must be said that Walpole's proposals for using them could hardly have been bettered.[4]

There was more likelihood that adequate forces would be retained for home defence in Britain in time of peace than in time of war. The diplomatic framework which engendered war or peace was, from the point of view of London, almost entirely a European structure, and war with another European power had a way of ending with a British commitment to find substantial forces for campaigns in Flanders or Germany. No Western European power other than France was likely to risk open conflict with Britain without first securing some indication that it would receive indirect or direct support from France. Thus the British were likely to have to duel, either as a principal or a second, with the might of the French army. Faced with the insatiable demands of army commanders for cannon fodder, British politicians usually succumbed to the temptation to strip the British military garrison to the bone, gambling on the ability of the Royal Navy to block any invasion. War was therefore the first requirement of the Jacobite cause. It came slowly, painfully, and with Spain.

That Walpole and the Duke of Newcastle, the Principal Secretary of State, were driven into belligerency by a mixture of commercial interests with grievances against Spanish commercial policy in the Americas, and an unscrupulous and factious group of opposition politicians led by Carteret and William Pitt, is well known. What is less often appreciated is that the negotiations between the British and Spanish governments which produced the famous preliminary agreement known as the Convention of the Pardo in January 1739 were perfectly sincere and might have led to a general Anglo-Spanish settlement and alliance. Both governments wanted peace. Spain was virtually bankrupt and in no fit state for war. The British ambassador, Benjamin Keene, reported that the first signs of an incipient settlement were greeted with universal joy in Spain except amongst the Pretender's supporters, but they amounted to a mere handful of hard-drinking Irish officers in the Spanish service. The eventual tragic rupture owed much to the intransigent and illegal behaviour of the South Sea Company which was too much and too shadily involved with the British government for Walpole to discipline it. It also derived to some extent from mounting British fears of an alliance between the two branches of the House of Bourbon which sat on the French and Spanish thrones.[5]

France and Spain had already signed the first of a series of Family Compacts in 1733, a fact of which the British were aware by early in the next year, but that treaty rapidly became waste paper. Cardinal Fleury, the master of French policy, was on appalling terms with Queen Elizabeth Farnese who, literally and metaphorically under her idle, uxorious and dotty husband Philip V, was the real ruler of Spain. Fleury was capable of firmness towards Britain. He warned the London government that it must not wage its Spanish war in a way calculated to harm French overseas interests, and he underlined his point by mobilizing the French fleet and dispatching a squadron to the West Indies. Nevertheless, Fleury did not want war, least of all with Britain. To the Jacobites who lobbied him relentlessly he offered only fair words, albeit with that silver-haired, benign almost saintly charm which always characterized the shrewd old double-crosser. By 1741, however, Fleury at the age of nearly ninety was losing control of French policy to powerful aristocratic and military groups led by Marshal Belle-Isle which were bent on a war of aggression in Germany against the traditional arch-enemy of France – the Habsburg rulers of Austria. Britain gave Maria Theresa, Empress of Austria, vital support against a ring of foes which included Prussia as well as France and her Bavarian satellites. Effectively, Britain and France were at war, but technically they were not; they were, strictly speaking, simply supporting opposite sides in the same war. This theory held up any formal rupture, even when British and French troops met in battle at Dettingen, where they were regarded as auxiliaries to the principal parties to the quarrel. That open war could not be indefinitely delayed became clearer and clearer. France responded to threats to her eastern boundaries by invading the Netherlands – an area of vital strategic importance to Britain. In 1743 Spain and France signed a second Family Compact and Philip V insisted that France must openly take his side in the war with England which had started in 1739. Above all, the death in January 1743 at the age of ninety of Cardinal Fleury was followed by a radical shift in French policy towards Britain.

No first minister was nominated to succeed him. In theory Louis XV assumed the reins of government in person. In practice that not very industrious mediocrity handed power to four Secretaries of State who waxed so potent that Frederick the Great of Prussia referred to them as 'the four kings of France'. These men were led by the Comte de Maurepas, Secretary of State for the Navy, and his colleagues were the Comte de Vignory, Comptroller General of Finances; the Comte d'Argenson, Secretary of State for War; and last and by all accounts least Amelot de Chaillou, Secretary of State for Foreign Affairs. The secretaries had disapproved of Belle-Isle's expensive and catastrophically unsuccessful onslaught on Austria. Looking around for more economical and effective ways of waging the war in which France was enmeshed, they became serious converts to the idea of a Stewart restoration. Novel as the gambit was in French policy, its justification was the usual cold-blooded calculation of the balance of advantages for France. That a close alliance with Britain was desirable, the secretaries accepted. Indeed they were very conscious of the benefits, especially the economic benefits, which had flowed from such an understanding since 1716. The crux of their argument was that the special relationship with the Hanoverian dynasty had been progressively collapsing since the late 1730s. Indeed, they were convinced that the endless meddling in European power politics, usually with an anti-French bias, which had characterized recent British foreign policy was rooted in the continental interests of the Elector of Hanover. A restored Stewart dynasty, dependent ultimately on French support, could be relied upon to liquidate the war with Spain and to withdraw from alliances aimed at France. The Habsburgs would thereby lose their main financial backer; Holland would be neutralized; the House of Savoy, which ruled the Kingdom of Sardinia, would cease to be an available component for anti-French coalitions and would have to come to terms with its overwhelmingly preponderant Gallic neighbours. So obvious and substantial would have been the gains to France if a Stewart restoration had worked out as the secretaries planned that the restoration was deemed an end in itself. There appear to have been no serious French designs on British territory or even on British colonies.[6]

What was envisaged was therefore something very like a re-run of the Glorious Revolution of 1688. By the end of November 1743 serious preparations for a French invasion of England, timed for January 1744, had begun. Louis XV informed Philip V that he was determined to set the Stewarts once more upon the British throne and he reinforced his words with an unwonted display of interest and energy. The detailed plan of invasion was hammered out in consultations between the French government, the Jacobite court, and representatives of the English Tories of Jacobite persuasion. Despite pressure for a separate expedition to Scotland under the Earl Marischal, the French were adamant that Scottish self-esteem should not be allowed to lead to a violation of the principle of the concentration of force. Ten thousand troops of the regular French Army were assembled for embarkation at Dunkirk. Naval cover was to be provided by a fleet based on Brest whose task was to neutralize the English Admiral Norris and his Channel Fleet. Maurice de Saxe, Marshal of France, a bastard son of the Saxon royal family who was providentially Protestant was to command, though he was to hand over to the Duke of Ormonde for political reasons as soon as was feasible. Originally the landing was to be made at Maldon near Colchester in Essex, because of the need to surprise the Royal Navy which did not patrol that stretch of coast. Maldon also had the advantage that from it London could be reached without crossing the Thames.

The Pretender's representative at the French court was Francis Lord Sempill, the son of a forfeited Scots Jacobite who had been created Baron Sempill in the Jacobite peerage by James Edward in 1723. He acted as courier between the French government and the English Jacobites and it was he who had carried to the French Secretary of State for Foreign Affairs in the spring of 1743 a request for intervention by the forces of His Most Christian Majesty. The request came from the Duke of Beaufort, Lord Orrery, Sir Watkin Williams Wynn, Sir John Hynde Cotton and Sir Robert Abdy. Apart from the dubious record of Orrery, these names represented straightforward Jacobitism on the part of substantial landed proprietors who were also Tories proscribed by a Whig vendetta from any of the fruits of office. Just how strong English Jacobitism was in the 1740s is a question to which only an impressionistic answer can be given. The Pretender's agents, anxious to please their master and to spur on the laggard court of France, had a vested interest in exaggerating the strength of their party in England. For example, they were given to asserting that they had substantial support in London where they argued that the hostility of such organizations as the Common Council of the City of London or the Independent Electors of the City of Westminster towards the Court Interest was rooted in 'their attachment to their rightful King'. To some historians it seems that the explanation of the situation is more convincing if reversed: significant sections of London opinion were so browned off with the nature and behaviour of the British government that they were even willing to flirt, verbally rather than in their hearts, with Jacobitism in order to express their spleen and frustration.

What is as plain as a pikestaff is that lists compiled by Jacobite agents of likely Jacobite sympathizers must be treated with extreme caution.

Even active participation in Jacobite plotting was no guarantee that a man would step forward to be counted when the Pretender's standard was in the field. The origins of the '45 in Scotland used to be traced back to 1739. In that year an association was formed as the result of the activities of Gordon of Glenbucket. In his old age that extraordinary and ambiguous character seems to have reverted to the underlying Jacobitism which was probably still there in the years when he was saving his skin by trafficking with the Hanoverians. In 1737 he sold his tiny property of Glenbucket for £700 and by January 1738 he was with the Pretender in Rome, having signally failed at an interview in Paris on the way to sell the idea of a Franco-Jacobite invasion of Britain to Cardinal Fleury. Returning with a major-general's commission in the phantom armies of the Pretender he exploited his contacts. Though scarcely even a laird, he was an impressive personality and his three daughters were married to significant Highland chiefs: Forbes of Skellater, Macdonald of Glengarry, and Macdonnell of Lochgarry. In 1739, more or less as a result of Glenbucket's Rome journey, a group of Jacobite personalities formed an association to forward the cause of the exiled Stewarts. The Associators, as they were known, were a curious and, on the whole, unimpressive crew. They were the Duke of Perth, described by an unkind critic as 'a foolish horse-racing boy'; his uncle Lord John Drummond of Fairntoun; Donald Campbell the younger of Lochiel, the Bayard of the Highlands; his uncle Sir John Campbell of Auchenbreck, who was a rarity among Campbell lairds for his Jacobitism as also for his, perhaps not unconnected, 'desperate fortune and little interest'; the Earl of Traquair (then Lord Linton); his brother the Honourable James Stewart; and Simon Fraser Lord Lovat. Of all of them only three actually served Prince Charles in the '45: Perth, Lochiel, and, after his fashion, Lovat.[7]

What would have been the response of English Tories to the arrival on English soil of an expeditionary force of 10,000 veterans under the baton of the first soldier of France remains an academic question, though the likeliest answer is surely that the Tories would have done very little until they saw the outcome of the battle for London. That battle de Saxe would have been very likely to win. Apart from his own scintillating military talents he could probably have counted on superiority in numbers of disciplined troops, for the garrison of England consisted of a mere 10,000 men, of whom it was reckoned only 7,000 could be concentrated in time to defend the capital. Given a French victory, the political situation was clearly such that there was every likelihood of widespread Tory support for, and even more widespread general acquiescence in, the overthrow of an unpopular minority Whig regime and its foreign dynasty. The political programme which the French secretaries rightly regarded as an essential part of the expedition was shrewd and appealing. Stress was to be laid on the fact that the restoration was unconditional and that the French troops would be withdrawn just as soon as they had performed their mission of counteracting the 'shoals of foreign mercenaries' with which the Elector of Hanover was wont to preserve his British throne. In December 1743 'King James' had signed a declaration largely drawn up by his English supporters and designed to be distributed when the landing occurred. It offered specific political alternatives as well as the usual Jacobite mysticism about the magic effects of the restoration of a rightful prince. Continental wars were to be wound up. This was a shrewd thrust, for even those who believed that 'the liberties of Europe' were menaced by France could hardly deny that Carteret's 'meddle and muddle' policy in Germany was an expensive failure. Convocation (the representative body for the bulk of the clergy of the Church of England), which had not been allowed to meet since the Hanoverian accession, was to meet again freely. Discrimination against Tories was to cease. Ormonde was ordered to pledge his word for the speedy repeal of the Septennial Act; the passing of an act designed rigorously to limit the number of government employees in the House of Commons; and the holding of free elections without improper government pressure.

Thus the invasion was geared to a mature political initiative, but was itself wholly dependent on speed and secrecy of execution. It was a disaster when, for various reasons, the English Jacobites started to call for delays and changes of plan. Hanoverian agents were everywhere from the post of principal cipher clerk to the Holy See in the Vatican to one of the senior clerkships in the French Foreign Office. From the latter source the British government obtained by February 1744 an account of French invasion plans. Charles Edward, the Jacobite 'Prince of Wales' was known to be in France waiting to embark with Maurice de Saxe. Indeed it was the refusal of France to expel the Young Pretender in accordance with her obligations under the Treaty of Utrecht which occasioned the formal declaration of war between Britain and France. The French government undoubtedly meant business, but the technical problems involved in transporting thousands of soldiers across the Channel were grave. Above all, the efficiency of the Royal Navy stood between the House of Hanover and nemesis. Whereas the navy of James II and Samuel Pepys in the late seventeenth century failed to prevent the invasions of both the Duke of Monmouth in 1685 and William of Orange in 1688, the Channel Fleet under Admiral Norris late in February 1744 was ready and waiting for the main French fleet from Brest. Off Dungeness the two lines of battle were formed within sight of one another when rain was followed by a roaring gale which tore the formations apart and blew straight into the harbour of Dunkirk where it played utter havoc with the transports on which were embarked the regiments of de Saxe and the hopes of Charles Edward

Stewart. Forty-eight hours later the gale was over but the game was up. The Brest fleet was gone. Norris with what he could salvage from his battered line of battle was still grimly at his post. There was no way of repairing damaged transports or replacing lost supplies before Dutch and other reinforcements poured into England.

Louis XV had always had doubts about the feasibility of the projected invasion. He was not, like William of Orange in 1688, already intimately involved in English politics and prepared to hazard the irreplaceable core of his military power. On the contrary, he knew full well that the expedition strained an already over-stressed military machine to breaking point. Feverishly he had sought to secure signed pledges of support from the English Tories. None were forthcoming. Such a signature might have proved suicidal and would certainly have ensured, in the event of the sort of miscarriage which occurred, that a signatory lived the rest of his life in the shadow of potential French blackmail. What followed the collapse of the 1744 invasion was in fact an object lesson in the duplicity and cool ruthlessness with which the Most Christian King's ministers could play with the lives and fortunes of British Jacobites.

So crooked were the paths trod by the French government, and so careful was it to cover its tracks, that the skein of evidence has only been unravelled in the twentieth century. Until recently Prince Charles, that darling of the romantic mind, has been given all the credit for initiating his immortal adventure. Sure it is that without that young man there would have been no '45. He was made for a rash enterprise as a sword for its sheath. Born at the very end of 1720 and very nominally blooded by being present at the siege of Gaeta (a small port situated about halfway between Rome and Naples) in 1734, he had developed into a hardy and handsome prince with gracious formal manners and a total belief in the rights and mission of his family. In the history of Jacobitism only perhaps the proto-martyr of the cause, Montrose, can match his brief career as a thunderbolt of war. Yet Charles was no Montrose, not just because he lacked the great Graham's military talents, but because he was a totally different personality. Montrose, with his black armour, his elemental violence, and his exalted final sacrifice, was a baroque character, if we accept that 'a cult of sensationalism lies at the root of baroque art'. His life, his death, nay even the rehabilitation of his desecrated bones were theatrical but deadly serious theatre. Charles, despite the bloodshed for which he was responsible, and the drink-sodden tragedy of his later years, was an altogether lighter character. If Montrose was baroque, Charles was rococo, a style which contrasts with the baroque from which it evolved by its lightness and surface quality. It is a style which in porcelain charms and surprises, and in all media it relies at its best on a subtle blend of the audacious, the skilful and the irresponsible.[8]

Audacity Charles had to the point of initiating the '45 with few resources and without his father's knowledge or blessing. Irresponsibility towards others, though masked by manners and superficial geniality, was basic to his egotistical personality. Skill was his with a gun or a horse, but never with a woman's heart or with the even more complex affairs of the world of high politics. The financial, political, and maritime expertise needed to launch the '45 was supplied by two shady groups – the French government and the privateer entrepreneurs of some northern French ports. It was the latter who, after the abandonment of the invasion, provided the main French war effort at sea in the shape of a relentless '*guerre de course*' against British shipping by fast heavily-armed privateers operating out of ports such as Dunkirk, Boulogne, St Malo and Nantes. Some of the men who organized and financed large-scale privateering were of Irish extraction. By the 1740s such men were usually French by birth or culture. There were plenty of genuine Irish merchant houses with a footing in France by 1740. They were particularly active in the brandy trade from Bordeaux, but they were to be found in most other important ports. However, they had to make a living in the Ireland of King George. Some of the most aggressive and successful of Irish mercantile groups like the 'Galway Mafia', a provincial landed merchant oligarchy, were far from committed to hazarding their all in the Jacobite cause. On the contrary, many of them conformed to the Protestant church of the Georgian Irish gentry, and although Galway firms can be found in Nantes from the 1690s they were not so foolish as to embark on naval warfare against their legal sovereign.[9] No similar compunction restrained the Franco-Irish privateering group to whom Prince Charles was introduced late in 1744 by Lord Clare, the commander of an Irish regiment in the service of Louis XV. Of these privateer bosses the most active Jacobite was Daniel D'Heguerty (or Hegarty), who had founded masonic lodges of a strongly Jacobite kind all over France. The most significant member of the privateer group turned out to be Antoine Walsh, a former officer in the French navy born in St Malo in 1703, the son of the Philip Walsh who had commanded the ship which carried James II to France after the Battle of the Boyne. Philip Walsh grew rich as a naval shipbuilder and slave trader. To a spectacular career in the family speciality of slaving, Antoine Walsh added the lucrative business of privateering. He was in truth one of the ablest, most active and voracious sharks cruising contemporary Atlantic waters. Also in the group were Richard Butler, Walsh's brother-in-law, a naturalized Frenchman operating out of St Malo, and Walter Ruttledge, banker and shipowner of Dunkirk, who had been born at St Germain.

That these men launched the '45 is clear. Their motives were a straightforward mixture of hereditary Jacobite loyalty and cold commercial calculation. Any disturbances in Scotland would compel the British government to withdraw naval units from convoy and patrol duties in the main sea approaches to England in order to try to seal off the Scottish coast. To the French privateers this would bring a happy time, for like all predatory animals they could not normally afford to accept serious damage when making any individual kill. What is more obscure at first sight is the degree of complicity on the part of the French government in the enterprise. After his return to France later in 1746 Prince Charles had a vested interest in insisting that the initiative was entirely his own, and this story was loyally propagated by his entourage. It added to the solitary grandeur of the hero Charles had become. Equally, the French government was committed to denying complicity in the origins of the '45 for two reasons. One was the fact that it had failed. The other was that whereas the invasion plan of 1744 was honourable and not impractical, the '45 was only too obviously an extremely disreputable device on the part of any European government which could be shown to have sponsored it. Regardless of how it developed, such an expedition could on rational grounds only be expected to act as a spoiling attack, tying down British forces at the cost of the certain ruin of those Scotsmen who rallied to it. In their different ways, neither Charles nor France had anything to lose.

Yet it is clear that the French government knew about the plan to transport Prince Charles to Scotland. Nearly three weeks before he embarked Charles wrote to Louis XV telling him all about his plans, but preserving the façade of French official non-participation. A very cursory investigation of the nature of the preparations required for the expedition shows how bogus that non-participation was. Charles reached Scotland aboard a handsome little frigate belonging to and commanded by Walsh, the *du Teillay*. However, he only reached Scottish waters because of the fighting power and sacrifice of a regular French 64-gun line of battle ship *L'Elisabeth* which fought H.M.S. *Lyon*, which intercepted the little Jacobite squadron, to a standstill. *L'Elisabeth* was on charter to Walsh, a perfectly normal arrangement between a leading privateer and the French Navy, but one which invariably implied absolute frankness about the proposed use of the vessel. There is just enough direct evidence to suggest that the Comte de Maurepas, Secretary of the Navy, was party to the D'Heguerty-Walsh group's plans, and if that evidence did not exist the indirect evidence would alone be damning. There was a volunteer company of French cadets aboard *L'Elisabeth*, a company which rejoiced in the title of the 'Compagnie Maurepas'. Even more significant was the fact that the substantial quantities of arms and ammunition aboard the two ships had been collected under the express authority of the Ministry of Marine and in the name of Louis XV. When the first exciting reports of the early successes of Prince Charles reached the French court at Versailles, the official line ascribed the whole business to the personal initiative of the young Stewart prince. Later Versailles openly aligned itself with and sent aid to the Jacobite army, but the natural deviousness of the bureaucratic mind when dealing with a potentially embarrassing issue remained a constant element in French handling of the '45.[10]

In the later part of 1745, for example, the French Secretary of State for Foreign Affairs lent his support to an extraordinary scheme for recruiting soldiers in Sweden, nominally for a Franco-Swedish unit in the French army, the Royal Swedish Regiment, and then diverting them, when they had been shipped out of Gothenburg on transport bought in Sweden, to Scotland to stiffen the Jacobite army. If successfully executed this stratagem would certainly have created a first-class diplomatic row of a three-cornered nature, between Britain, Sweden, and France. As it happened, British espionage secured reports of the plan at an early stage and the French mismanaged its details so badly that on the eve of Culloden it was still hanging fire when Louis XV, under pressure of events in Scotland, gave orders to cancel the plan for aid to the Jacobites from Sweden. It remains a classic illustration of the way in which the corporate mind of a great department of state can resemble nothing so much as that of an unsuccessful petty criminal.[11]

By themselves the Scottish Associators were unlikely to achieve anything. Their principal man of business and contact with Prince Charles in Paris epitomized the whole ramshackle non-movement. This was William Mac-Gregor or Drummond of Balhaldies, the son of a Jacobite baronet and son-in-law to Sir Ewen Cameron of Lochiel. A contemporary described him as 'the descendant of a cobbler, himself a broken butter and cheese merchant, a stickt doctor, a Jack of all trades, a bankrupt indebted to all the world, the awkwardest Porter-like fellow alive . . . master of as much bad French as to procure himself a whore and a dinner'. Apart from his mastery of basic French, he was suspected of having stolen from the Jacobite baggage train at Sheriffmuir, and of having fled the country 'in danger of being taken up for a Fifty Pound note'. From supporters like this funds were unlikely to be forthcoming on any scale. The purchase of arms appears in fact to have been funded by loans from Paris bankers. In the letter in which he told his father that he was embarking for Scotland, Charles acknowledged a debt of 180,000 livres to Waters and Son, a well-known Paris banking house. Charles was also helped financially by the banker who accompanied him to Scotland, Aeneas Macdonald. The debts to the Waters family were in due course repaid by the Old Pretender himself.[12] Though dependent on handouts from the papal and other well-disposed governments, James had built up financial reserves, partly by means of his miserably unhappy marriage. His two sons, Charles and Henry, were the principal assets which Clementina Sobieska gave to the Jacobite cause, but the jewels and cash of her dowry amounted to a very significant family asset which her cautious, not to say dull, spouse had never had any inclination to squander on riotous living.

If, then, the origins of the '45 stretch back a long way in time and space, the striking fact remains that the bulk of them were external to Scotland. Amongst the Jacobite agents moving between France and Scotland in the 1740s, probably the most intelligent was John Murray of Broughton, a younger son of Sir David Murray of Stanhope, a stoutly Jacobite laird from Peebleshire. Murray of Broughton acted as secretary to Prince Charles during the rising, was captured after Culloden, and saved his skin by turning King's Evidence against his former comrades in arms. Though arguably only Lovat lost his life as a result of evidence supplied by Murray, the act of betrayal attracted contempt and obloquy. From about 1757 Murray of Broughton wrote 'Memorials' which are both an account of his activities between 1740 and 1747 and an attempt to vindicate his conduct after Culloden. In them he alleges that he warned Prince Charles, when the latter threatened to come to Scotland 'though with a single footman', that he would be lucky to raise 4,000 men from a few clans in the Western Highlands and that the morale even of the handful of Highland magnates who could be relied upon to join him would be low indeed if he did not come with a body of troops.[13] Fortunately scraps of Murray of Broughton's papers contemporary with the period 1740–47 survive and they tend to substantiate his later story. There is little doubt that Scottish Jacobites such as Cameron of Lochiel and Lord Traquair were extremely unhappy at the thought of a rebellion unsupported by a substantial well-prepared French expeditionary force.[14] There was always a sense in which Charles Edward throughout his campaign remained encapsulated in that curious Franco-British exiled world which had launched him into the '45. His intimates tended to be Irish Jacobites from France, a fact which bred much bad blood between these men and the Scots who rallied to his standard. Even those Scots who were close to him tended to have strong connections with Jacobite circles in France. Murray of Broughton is a case in point, but a rather obscure Jacobite with whom Murray conferred in France, Charles Smith a banker and merchant of Boulogne, illustrates the point elegantly. Smith was at Linlithgow for a family wedding on the very day of Charles's first victory at Prestonpans. His wife was a daughter of Sir Hugh Patterson of Bannockburn, who acted as host to Charles during the unsuccessful Jacobite siege of Stirling Castle. Mrs Smith was also aunt to Clementina Walkinshaw, a ward of Sir Hugh Patterson and mistress to Prince Charles.[15]

The Franco-Scottish contacts which had been so important in conveying Charles to the Outer Hebrides were not enough to create an army for him. Aeneas Macdonald, the banker who was also an influential gentleman of the Clanranald, seems to have been totally unnerved by his failure to establish contact with his brother-in-law the chief of the Isle of Barra, and by the news that the government had arrested the chief of the Macleans of Mull, an active Jacobite plotter. Clanranald's own brother, Alexander Macdonald of Boisdale, met Charles on a rain-swept Isle of Eriskay and told him, very sensibly, to go home. Cajolery and threats failed to move a man who kept his head at the height of the rebellion's brief success and refused to allow Uist, his own principal area of responsibility in the Outer Hebrides, to become involved in what he saw as an act of irresponsible folly. That Charles ever reached the mainland of Scotland was as much accident as design. The Jacobite leaders aboard the *du Teillay* were quarrelling with all the bitterness of their similarly circumstanced pre-decessors of the '19. Only Charles and Walsh were for carrying on. Suddenly a common fear, misplaced but sharp, of Royal Navy patrols drove the divided company into taking refuge in the winding sea lochs which penetrated deep into the nearby mainland. Loch nan Uamh, which divides Arisaig from Morar, was where Charles first landed on the Scottish mainland. The weapons he had brought were unloaded a day or two later in the fjord-like fastnesses of Loch Ailort in Moidart. Here in Clanranald country the Young Pretender was perfectly safe. In the words of Alexander Macbain, Presbyterian Minister of Inverness, these Macdonalds were 'Popish but not so thievish as in Knoidart'.[16] It was a back-handed compli-ment for the Macdonalds of Knoydart, Glengarry's country, inhabited almost impenetrable terrain and had a vast contempt for a central govern-ment which could not reach them.

Support from the Macdonald chiefs of Morar, Glengarry, and Keppoch was absolutely predictable but hardly added up to the makings of a serious rising. When Keppoch drew first blood for the Jacobites by beating up and capturing two companies of the Royal Scots on the military road to Fort William he was not behaving much out of his ordinary fashion. Walsh had gone back to France. Had only 300 Macdonalds turned up for the raising of the Jacobite standard at Glenfinnan on 19 August, even Charles might have accepted the need to devise means of following him rapidly. That the adhesion of Cameron of Lochiel with his 700 fighting men turned a sensational incident into a rebellion is generally agreed, but this fact plunges the enquirer at once into the problem of the nature of the support for the '45. Was it the last stand of a dying civilization, the final armed protest of the uncommercialized Gael against the impact of an aggressive, money-grubbing Anglo-Saxon civilization?

Cameron of Lochiel alone knocks that idea on the head. 'Young' Lochiel was a brisk and enterprising business man very much involved in the most advanced and far-flung developments of his day. He managed his woods as a commercial asset, taking care that when he sold timber it was cut in a fashion which ensured the natural regeneration of the trees. For example in 1722 he sold to an Irishman called Murphy the birch and ash timber of several woods along with the oak bark (valuable for tanning) and alder of another. Murphy was obliged to stack his cut timber neatly in one place 'and to cull the same close to the ground for the benefit of the young growth'. Murphy was also a member of a copartnery for the carrying on of an iron work which bought the timber of several of Lochiel's woods in 1722, for the sake of the charcoal fuel which was vital for early iron furnaces, and promptly fell foul of the Cameron chieftain who alleged that they were culling his woods in a rambling and undisciplined way calculated to check regeneration.[17] The man of law consulted by Lochiel suggested a resort to a sheriff to secure an injunction against malpractices.[18]

Lochiel was a sophisticated man, socially and economically very much in touch with the contemporary Lowlands. His finances seem to have rested on a very complex net of bills of credit, a net which involved his uncle and business associate, the Jacobite agent Drummond of Balhaldie.[19] When Lochiel's brothers John and Sandy were to be sent abroad to earn their fortunes, Balhaldie's son Euan was consulted and seems to have gone abroad with them. Indeed, some fascinating letters survive from Euan to his father, written in Annapolis and New York. It is quite clear from them that Euan was speculating in American land, trying to secure profits by quick resale and returning money to his father and Lochiel by bills of exchange.[20] Lochiel's interests in the Americas were by no means confined to North America. He was involved in the West Indies trade. Other Highland chiefs contributed to the expansion of European settlement in the New World. In the 1730s Sir Alexander Macdonald of Sleat and Norman Macleod of Dunvegan can be found exporting labour across the Atlantic by the simple, if drastic, device of selling some of their own clansmen into slavery.[21]

The 'Gentle Lochiel' of the '45 was a hard man who ran his little territorial empire with an iron fist. It is far too easy, on the strength of a much-read passage in Adam Smith's *Wealth of Nations* published in 1776, to see him as the simple, just patriarch shepherding his people through life on a rent roll of a mere £700 per annum. He was in no position to rack rent them because his legal claims to his estates were disputed, and he needed their swords to defend the territorial base essential to his social prestige and business ventures. Social discipline he maintained ruthlessly. Men were hung for thieving, which fact no doubt added edge to Lochiel's threat to hang Allan Cameron of Callart when the latter tried to back out of the '45.[22] Even the vaunted solidarity of Clan Cameron concealed inner tensions and submerged groups. Probably 300 or more of the men whom Lochiel led so proudly to the royal standard in Glenfinnan did not think of themselves as Camerons. MacMartins were pretty well compelled to assume the name Cameron, as did more willingly 'broken men' who had migrated into Lochaber, but there were MacPhees of Glendessary and several other smaller groups whom outside commentators habitually confused with true Camerons.[23]

Jacobitism had never been incompatible with an interest in material improvement and by no means all Jacobites with such an interest were as inherently attractive characters as Macintosh of Borlum, the irascible old hero of the '15. Some of his comrades in arms of that rising would have been described as hard-faced bastards by their tenants. The Galloway family of the Dunbars of Baldoon, for example, were pioneers in really large-scale enclosure of land for commercial cattle grazing. Basil Hamilton of Baldoon who succeeded to the Dunbar inheritance through a female heiress was 'out' in '15, was captured at Preston, and was condemned to death and forfeiture. However, political pressure secured his life and his mother managed to keep control of most of his forfeited estates. When the local tenant farmers rose in 1723–5 in virtual rebellion against the evictions and seizures of land involved in the enclosures, they attacked the Baldoon estate dykes among others and did not fail to stress their own loyalty to Hanover and the Jacobitism of the Baldoon family. They were nevertheless crushed and by 1732 Basil Hamilton's attainder had been reversed.[24]

There were, of course, plenty of supporters of the '45 who were not particularly interested in improving their properties. Robertson of Struan is a prime example. Although a very old man and incapable of sustaining the rigours of the march to Derby, he showed his usual indomitable spirit and left nobody in any doubt where he stood. The government only established control over his estate, which was almost entirely in the Perthshire parish of Fortingall around Loch Rannoch, after his death. Its agents gave the old Jacobite a bad posthumous press, depicting him as an unenlightened rascal presiding over a thieves' kitchen many of whose knavish inhabitants had 'come to Ranoch not for building of kirks'. They reported 'a saying of the late Strouan's that be the roads never so bad, his friends would see him and he wanted no visits from his enemys', adding that 'very likely he had theeving in his view in this'. In particular it was alleged that Struan took 'a very fatherless care' of the valuable pine woods of the Black Wood of Rannoch, felling excessively and at random in such a way that scrub birch and alder encroached on the stands of Scots pine.[25] One would never imagine from these reports that the estate had a long history of highly commercial forestry, going well back into the seventeenth century. Sawmills converted pine logs into deals and in 1683 it was alleged that 176,000 deals had already been produced from local woods. Timber was floated along the considerable length of Loch Rannoch whence it found its way into the Rivers Tummel and Tay – a remarkable low-cost transit system. The problem of theft of floating timber was recognized by the Privy Council of Scotland in 1675 and 1683 when it empowered Alexander

Robertson, twelfth of Struan, to impose fines for such theft. Given the colossal cost of building roads to link Rannoch with the Lowlands, it must be said that the estate had made a totally rational choice of the only form of development likely to pay. No doubt the traumas in the life of Alexander, thirteenth of Struan and most persistent of Jacobites, undermined efficient forest management, but his estate, like his own curiously anglicized mind, was significantly geared to Lowland values.[26]

Struan was not the only chief whose early adhesion to Prince Charles owed something to a sense of security born of the extreme inaccessibility of his lair. The same was true of Keppoch and Glengarry, and indeed of the MacGregors. Rob Roy had been the only leading member of the nameless clan to fight for 'James VIII' in the '19, but despite the absence of any generally accepted chief quite a few MacGregors came in to fight under the Jacobite standard in 1745, coming from Glencarnaig to the west of the Braes of Balquidder under Robert MacGregor of Glencarnaig, or from the haunts of the Clan Dougal Ciar around Inversnaid, accessible only by tracks from the nearby Lowlands, under MacGregor of Glengyle. Compared with these Highland wolves the Hebridean chieftains were very exposed to the long arm and right hand of London, the Royal Navy. Early Highland adherents who were less securely placed than Struan or Keppoch and who had something to lose seem to have, very sensibly, taken security for their main assets before they were willing to commit themselves. The classic example is Cameron of Lochiel. His brother, John Cameron of Fassiefern, an astute if unscrupulous West India merchant and burgess of Glasgow, tried to dissuade him from even seeing Princes Charles. Fassiefern urged Lochiel to write a letter telling the young man to go home. Lochiel went to see Charles and succumbed, probably not so much to his charm as to his apparent sensibleness, his lavish assurances of coming French aid, and thinly-veiled threats. Even so Lochiel took full security from Prince Charles for the value of his estates, in the event of the rising proving abortive.

For once in his life Charles honoured one of the political promises with which he was so free. In exile Lochiel was given a French regiment worth more per annum than his Highland rent roll. If young Glengarry and Murray of Broughton were to be believed, Euan Macpherson of Cluny made a similar bargain as to his estate before he changed sides. Cluny held a commission in the Whig Lord Loudon's regiment. He was on his way home to raise his clan for King George when he fell into Jacobite hands and, after being a notably willing prisoner, threw in his lot with Prince Charles when the Jacobites reached Perth.[27] Precautions were reasonable, for when Charles marched from Glenfinnan his force was no more formidable than the rebel army of the '19, and it really should have had its brief light snuffed out as decisively as General Wightman had snuffed out the

'19. Three factors allowed the '45 to develop: the appalling state of the defences of Scotland; the military emasculation of Clan Campbell; and the desperate unpopularity of the British government, even amongst non-Jacobite Scotsmen.

Of the first of these factors Charles was undoubtedly well aware. He used many arguments to win over the hesitant but one of the most convincing was that it was relatively easy to seize control of Scotland. Government forces amounted to less than 4,000 men, and of these few were seasoned troops. There were three and a half infantry regiments of the line, of which only one had been raised before 1741. It alone had seen action. The infantry were not seriously strengthened by the presence of nine extra companies, recently raised for drafting into regiments already serving overseas, and all under strength. Equally unimpressive were the handful of weak companies of Lord Loudon's new regiment which was scarcely beginning to be recruited in the Highlands. The cavalry arm consisted of two dragoon regiments recruited in Ireland, unblooded in battle, with ill-disciplined troopers and horses young and untrained to gunfire. Though there were enough guns and mortars in Edinburgh Castle to equip a field force with an adequate artillery train, there was not a single trained royal artillery man in Scotland. Edinburgh Castle, like Stirling and Dumbarton Castles, was held by an 'invalid' garrison which has not been considered here because its men were by definition incapable of leaving the shelter of its walls.[28]

The situation was the usual scandalous one which had obtained in 1708 and to a lesser extent in 1715. Adequate forces had not been maintained in Scotland. Quite irresponsibly the Westminster government, despite the known French invasion plans of 1744, had stripped even the Highlands of the locally recruited infantry, known originally as the Independent Companies and embodied in 1740 into the 43rd Regiment, better known as the Black Watch. Assured originally that they would serve only in their native land, these stalwart warriors were marched south to England in 1743, with fair tales about a royal review. When they discovered that they were to be sent abroad, possibly to a lethally unhealthy posting in the West Indies, they mutinied, to little avail.[29] Duncan Forbes of Culloden, who had preached the necessity of raising soldiers in the Highlands to secure the area for Hanover for years to the deaf ears of his political masters, had by 1743 largely abandoned the subject and was working off some of his frustration in a neurotic fussing about the degrading effects of an excessive consumption of tea.

The absence of government troops during the critical early days of the rising was all the more telling because of the military disintegration of the great Whig clan – the Campbells. Curiously, it was 'Red John of the Battles', the second Duke of Argyll, who undermined the whole concept of clanship and vassalage, first in Kintyre from 1710, and from 1737, under the influence of Duncan Forbes, in his other lands. He deliberately set out to eliminate the tacksmen, the Campbell gentry, by letting farms directly to their former dependants. In the short run the policy was not even a great success financially for tenants, to secure farms, offered rents which they were incapable of paying. Militarily it was deadly. The tacksmen were Clan Campbell for all practical purposes. The third Duke of Argyll, a slippery and eccentric politician better known as the Earl of Islay, grasped the danger of his brother's policies and by 1744 was backtracking rapidly by telling the chamberlains who managed the major units of the Argyll empire to make sound politics rather than high bids the essential condition of tenancy. It was too late to recreate Clan Campbell as a ready fighting force in time for the '45.[30]

The incredible fact is that the army of Prince Charles conquered most of Scotland by the process of walking from Glenfinnan to Edinburgh. Some finesse was required to rush a city gate at the end of the long march, but nothing so crude as fighting interrupted the progression. Indeed the British government, by means of Wade's admirable military roads, did much to render the advance of the Jacobite army easier and more rapid than it might have otherwise been. Lieutenant-General Sir John Cope, Commander-in-Chief Scotland, had in fact marched into the Highlands to try to repeat the pattern of the '19. Charles was eager to grapple with him but no battle in Badenoch, the area where the armies were likely to collide, occurred. Instead Cope swung north by forced marches to Inverness. He then marched to Aberdeen whence he shipped his army south, landing at Dunbar to challenge a Prince Charles already ensconced in the Holyrood Palace of his ancestors. To explain such apparently bizarre manoeuvres it is necessary to look at the political situation within Scotland. Cope had arrived in Scotland in February 1744. While his own was a controversial appointment, he was to find that the executive officers of the Crown in Scotland were riven by faction and that the administration they represented enjoyed very little of that general support in the country which the politicians fondly fancied they had.

With the end of Walpole's rule in 1742, coalition government had become unavoidable at Westminster. The 'Old Corps' Whigs who had sustained his greatness were not cohesive enough to give his political heirs, Hardwicke and Newcastle in the Lords and Newcastle's brother Henry Pelham in the Commons, a reliable majority, so a section of the former opposition led by Lord Carteret and William Pulteney had to be brought into government. There was little love lost between the Pelhams and Carteret, not only because of personality clashes, but also because the Pelhams accused George II and Carteret of wanting to wage the ongoing war in a way calculated to protect Hanover rather than Britain. The

Scottish party system, excluding Jacobites, had remained frozen in its 1707 polarization between the Argyll faction, unpopular with George II but allied to the Pelhams, and the Squadrone, which contained most Scots magnates hostile to Argyll. Despite the fact that the Pelhams forced Carteret (now Earl Granville) out of office in 1743, splits in Westminster politics continued to be reflected in divisions within Scottish government appointments. On one side stood the Squadrone representative, the Secretary of State for Scotland, the Marquis of Tweeddale. Racked by gout, ignorant of Highland geography, and an advocate of economy at home to supply resources for foreign campaigns, Tweeddale was a disaster. He, of course, was based on London. Argyll, his rival, was also London-based but had the support of such key Scottish law officers as the Lord President of the Court of Session, Duncan Forbes, and the Lord Justice-Clerk, Andrew Fletcher of Milton, while Tweeddale could only rely on less important men like the Solicitor-General, Robert Dundas, younger of Arniston. On one point Argyll and Tweeddale agreed, for neither liked Cope, and both instructed their Scottish satellites to be correct but distant to him.[31]

From this bickering band of Hanoverian brothers a consensus emerged, even after the start of the rebellion, that it was not serious and that a mere show of government troops would suffice to crush it, with assistance from zealous Whig clans itching to get to grips with the Jacobites. Having done its best to disarm its subjects for fear that they might argue about politics, the British government, as usual, had left the loyal and peaceable inadequately protected against the armed and disloyal. Now, motivated by a mixture of self-righteous hope and a guilty conscience, Edinburgh and Westminster conspired to propel Cope, who was far more aware of the dangerous nature of the crisis than his political masters, into the Highlands lugging 1,500 spare stands of arms for Whig Highlanders. These last failed to materialize at all. At Crieff, Atholl and the Campbell heir to Breadalbane, Lord Glenorchy, met Cope and Loudon and blandly announced they could not raise a single man. At the same time a characteristically egregious dispatch from Tweeddale arrived ordering Cope to march his column of 2,000 raw, ill-disciplined men burdened with useless equipment straight north towards Prince Charles. After obeying orders and setting out with a view to forcing a passage to Fort Augustus, the central pivot of the Great Glen line of forts, Cope's nerve broke at Dalwhinnie. On that bleak upland he realized that he could not possibly force the dreaded seventeen zig-zags of the military road over the pass of Corrieyairack, already occupied by Prince Charles and his troops and between him and Fort Augustus. He could not stand fast due to lack of supplies. He would hardly retreat, for the vaunted 'Whig' areas had turned out sullenly hostile and had failed to provide vital scouting and flank protecting units. Inverness by forced marches to escape ambush was the best of a bad range of choices. Charles was presented with Scotland on a plate, through no merit of his own other than impudence.[32]

Deprived of its military screen, Edinburgh offered only token resistance. The future Reverend Doctor Alexander Carlyle, in 1745 a Whig divinity student and keen amateur soldier in a volunteer company, recorded that the Provost of Edinburgh was so unenthusiastic about arming the people 'that there was not a Whig in town who did not suspect that he favoured the Pretender's cause'. Attempts to convict the dignitary in question of treason after the '45 was over proved happily abortive, but whatever his private convictions there is no doubt that he did his civic duty. Even the venerable 'Dr William Wishart, Principle of the College' (i.e. Edinburgh University) regarded fighting as 'this rash enterprise . . . exposing the flower of the youth of Edinburgh, and the hope of the next generation, to the danger of being cut off, or made prisoners and maltreated, without any just or adequate object'.[33] Resistance inflicting serious casualties on an army storming the utterly inadequate city defences would certainly have been followed by pillage and just possibly by massacre, at least of armed defenders. The game was not worth the candle. Carteret and the Pelhams were not worth dying for.

By the time he reached Perth Charles had received a second wave of adherents which doubled his small Highland army and boosted it to a size more impressive than that which had failed in the '19, and also broadened, although not a great deal, the basis of his political support. On the way to Perth he had been entertained at Nairne House by the Dowager Lady Nairne, whose late husband had narrowly escaped execution after the '15, but the single most important recruit he received was the fiery old lady's nephew, Lord George Murray. With a heavy heart this younger brother of the Duke of Atholl threw in his lot with a cause for which he had fought in 1715 and 1719. His decision was unexpected. His eldest son, educated at Eton, held a commission in Loudon's regiment. His brother the Whig Duke James had just appointed him Sheriff-Depute of the Regality of Atholl. Lord George and his eldest brother, the Jacobite Duke William, were able to turn the structures of this mini-kingdom to the purposes of rebellion. Duke William, old in exile and shaken in health, was a fanatical royalist whose politics were obedience. There were others like him who rode in to the Jacobite standard in Perthshire, notably the Oliphants of Gask, that outrageously eccentric dynasty of lairds whose Episcopal religion went hand-in-hand with total devotion to the Roman Catholic Stewart monarchy, and whose convictions were impervious to all facts, including Culloden.

Lord George was very different, for he was a sophisticated, well-read and well-informed man. That he knew the price of failure is shown by the fact that ever afterwards his copy of *The Office and Authority of a Justice of the Peace* opened at the page which summarized the pains and penalties for high treason. His library catalogue confirms that he was very interested in the history, laws and constitution of both England and Scotland. He was not a wealthy man, and the very severe winter weather of early 1745 must have reduced his income as it reduced the productivity of all Highland agriculture, but he was a keen improver of agricultural methods, importing seed, cattle and sheep from England. Once a bitter foe of the Union, he had come to accept that measure, though he was convinced that it had been worked to the disadvantage of Scotland, and wanted a re-negotiation of its terms providing especially for an increased representation of the Scottish aristocracy in the House of Lords. In this he was not typical of the Jacobite ranks.[34] There is no doubt that one of the emotional supports of the '45 was a streak of unreconstructed Scottish nationalism. As Charles prepared to enter the palace of Holyrood there stepped out of the crowd assembled to witness his arrival the venerable and incorruptible anti-Unionist James Hepburn of Keith. Keith drew his sword and with arm held aloft preceded Charles up the steps. The gesture was as poignant as it was unmistakable.[35] Prince Charles did in fact abolish the Act of Union by decree in Edinburgh. He could scarcely have done less and expected to retain any serious support in Scotland. Lord George Murray was unusual in the Jacobite army in being disturbed at the unilateral nature of the gesture and its contempt for constitutional forms.

The rebellion recruited its strength from religious as well as nationalist sources, though of course a sharp distinction between the two categories would in many cases be absurd. Perhaps only in the brief moment of the '45 did Aberdeenshire and Banffshire stand out distinctive amongst Lowland regions by virtue of the unusual depth of their commitment to Jacobitism. To some extent this was undoubtedly the result of spiritual and educational developments peculiar to the region, and in the latter case largely the result of the consequences of the '15. Access to this source of strength was symbolized by the adherence to the Jacobite standard of the aged and saintly Alexander Forbes, fourth and last Lord Forbes of Pitsligo, always known simply as Lord Pitsligo. He was a central figure in those mystical circles so influential within the Episcopal community in the north-east. Born in 1678 and educated in France, he had been a personal friend of Archbishop Fénelon. He had withdrawn from the Scottish Parliament in 1707 in protest at the Act of Union and had joined his first cousin Mar in the '15. Fleeing abroad afterwards, he discovered that his name was not on the list of attainders, so he returned in 1720 to live quietly. Murray of Broughton started to correspond with him within a few weeks of the start of the rising, lacing his correspondence with those lies or half-truths about imminent and massive French aid under notable commanders with which both he and his royal master were only too lavish.[36] He need hardly have bothered, for when summoned to Edinburgh after the first Jacobite victory at Prestonpans, Pitsligo obeyed in a spirit of exalted and sacrificial loyalty beyond mere calculations of earthly success or failure. Recruiting vigorously among the Aberdeenshire lairds, Pitsligo led his troop of horse south from Aberdeen to Edinburgh with the words 'Oh Lord, Thou knowest our cause is just. Gentlemen, march.'

Roman Catholic support for Prince Charles came in its most vital form in the very early days of the rising, when the fact that he was in a Roman Catholic pocket on the mainland gave him the security he needed to negotiate for further support over a period of days. However, appropriately, at Perth itself Charles received the considerable addition to his following of James Drummond, third Duke of Perth in the Jacobite peerage, who brought with him a large number of men and was appointed Lieutenant-General, a rank later shared by Lord George Murray. Brave, self-effacing and fluent in French and old Court Scots but not English, Perth was a very rich young man who was passionately interested in the improvement of his extensive properties. Culturally he was a fossil from the brief reign of James VII between 1685 and 1688, of which his family had been so much a pillar that it had committed itself to the Roman Catholic faith of the royal circle. He was in the middle of a whole range of enterprises from 'the improvement and inlargement' of the town of Crieff to the widespread granting of leases to his tenants when he was summoned to war,[37] a war in which he was joined much later by his younger brother and successor Lord John Drummond. Both men had been brought up in France and Lord John arrived at the head of his own regiment in the French service, the Royal Scots. If in an odd way the Drummond brothers were more men of late seventeenth than of mid eighteenth-century Britain, there were plenty less exotic representatives of the Roman Catholic community in the ranks of the rebel army. Their clergy had to minister to them when possible, which may help explain why fifteen Roman Catholic priests were arrested after the rebellion. Some had been military chaplains like Bishop Hugh Macdonell, who had blessed the standard at Glenfinnan, or Father Allan Macdonald, a Clanranald man, who rode down the line blessing the men at the Battle of Falkirk. The attitude of the Roman Catholic authorities in Scotland seems in fact to have been one of some embarrassment from the start to the finish of the '45, which their keener minds expected to fail, but which they could hardly ignore.[38] These clergymen were treated far more leniently after Culloden than the more exposed and committed non-juring Episcopalians. Even Bishop Macdonnell escaped with his life after capture. Whatever the '45 was, it was not primarily a Roman Catholic rising.

Indeed the '45 was never a very big rising. When Cope finally landed his forces east of Edinburgh and Charles marched to meet him at Preston-pans, both armies were tiny – 2,500 men apiece. The battle itself, as distinct from the pursuit, lasted not more than quarter of an hour. It was decided by two factors. One was local knowledge obtained from Robert Anderson through Hepburn of Keith, knowledge which enabled the Jacobites to cross a bog and send in their charge against Cope over dry ground, not to say a tramway leading from local coal pits to the harbour of Prestonpans. The other, and decisive, factor was the way Cope's untried troops panicked and ran away. It was a fluke victory. The Highland line wavered at the single discharge unleashed by Cope's artillery before it was abandoned, so fine was the balance of morale.

Inevitably Prestonpans decided some fence-sitters, but it is worth stressing that no really great Scottish magnate ever committed himself to the '45. Seaforth, out in the '15 and '19 with his Mackenzies, refused to move in the '45. The reigning Duke of Atholl was hostile, though Lord George Murray and 'Duke William' mobilized many of his men. In much the same way, though less effectively, Lord Lewis Gordon, third son of Alexander, second Duke of Gordon, was used to try to rally the considerable interest of the ducal house of Gordon to the Jacobite side. Lord Lewis was under twenty-one when Prince Charles appointed him Lord-Lieutenant of Aberdeenshire and Banffshire. He was a lieutenant in the Royal Navy, and his mother Henrietta Duchess of Gordon had agreed after the death of her husband Alexander, second Duke of Gordon, to bring up her family of four sons and eleven daughters in the Protestant faith. From 1735 to 1745 she received a government pension of £1,000 per annum in exchange for so doing. Her husband had been tainted with Jacobitism in the '15, though she herself, the daughter of an English earl, was Whig. Though not very active in the '45, she clearly sympathized with Lord Lewis, to the point of forfeiting her pension after Culloden. Lord Lewis's brother, the third Duke of Gordon, played an equivocal role until November 1746, when he definitely disavowed the Jacobite cause and aligned himself with men like Lord Braco, Lord Banff, Lord Findlater, and the latter's son-in-law Ludovick Grant of Grant, in the regional Hanoverian party, a party which in Banffshire at any rate was probably a minority one amongst the landed classes.[39] In the Highlands active Jacobites were a distinct minority. Partly due to the influence of Lord President Duncan Forbes of Culloden, the major Skye chiefs, Macleod of Macleod and Macdonald of Sleat, refused to stir in the interest of Prince Charles. In Skye only Mackinnon of Mackinnon came out and he was an exceptional case as a son-in-law of the martyred Archbishop Sharp of St Andrews.[40]

Committed Hanoverians outside Argyll country tended to be equally thin on the ground. Only the small clan of the Monroes joined Cope on his march to Inverness, but the clans of the north-western Highlands beyond the Great Glen, such as the Mackays and Sutherlands, remained stolidly Whig in their allegiance. There was a great deal of hedging of bets amongst Jacobites during the '45 and many a son was sent out to fight with all or part of the family following while his father sat unctuously at home. The Earl of Airlie, an active Jacobite in 1715 and a refugee in France until pardoned in 1725, did not risk his hand openly again in 1745. He sent his heir, the young and very dashing David, Lord Ogilvy, to lead the Airlie tenants in the Jacobite army. Lord Ogilvy went the more willingly in that he had since late in 1743 been pursuing military studies in France, where he had, inevitably, been drawn into the circle of Prince Charles. The fourth Earl of Airlie undoubtedly applied severe pressure to his tenants to offer themselves as recruits for the regiment which Lord Ogilvy raised on the family estates, saying that 'They maun dae* or be destroyed'.[41] At the same time he managed to behave in such a fashion that no legal action was ever taken against him, while Lord Ogilvy was exiled until 1778 and only fully pardoned in 1788. Lord Ogilvy was not the only son so used by his father. He at least was willing, but the unfortunate eldest son of Simon Fraser Lord Lovat was propelled into the rebellion at the head of his father's clansmen in defiance of his own good sense and basic Whiggism. In his own bizarre way Simon Fraser was an affectionate father to his heir, whom he referred to as the Brigadier or 'the Brig.' for short, but he had always subjected him to the domineering blast of his own personality, insisting that he be 'absolutely under my Command' and reinforcing the point with wild threats to 'renounce him as my son and send him to Glenstrathfarrar to be a cow herd with John McDougall', all in tones which were far from jesting.[42]

Marginality is in fact the keynote of the support which Prince Charles received. It was marginal in size. His army was always barely adequate for operations. After Prestonpans it was reckoned that, partly due to desertion and departures to beat up recruits, he could hardly have scraped together 1,500 men for the march to Berwick he was so keen on. A lot of support was ambiguous. Great men did not commit themselves. For the few men of sense and substance like Lochiel and Lord George the decision to rebel was clearly difficult. A significant proportion of Jacobite supporters were patently marginal members of the ruling class by virtue of want of wit or want of funds. The Earl of Kilmarnock, for example, was no enthusiast for any political theory. He was just broke and desperate. In the end he was executed, but not before he had told the Duke of Argyll that 'for the two Kings and their rights, I cared not a farthing which prevailed; but I was starving, and, by God, if Mahommed had set up his standard in the High-

* They had better do so.

lands I had been a good Mussulman for bread, and stuck close to the party, for I must eat.'[43] Alexander, fifth Earl of Kellie, was not quite so hard up, but he was poor and his intelligence was commonly acknowledged to be so low that he was subsequently treated as if he had the diminished responsibility of a mental defective for his decision to join the rebellion. Amongst the Edinburgh literary coteries who had indulged so freely in Jacobite sentiment before 1745, discretion proved much the better part of valour when it came to the crunch. Virtually none of them joined the army of Prince Charles except the poet William Hamilton of Bangour, a wild man of strongly nationalist convictions described by a hostile Whig as 'the nationall poetic good for nothing lad'.[44]

Charles could not raise a regiment in Edinburgh. Other major towns in Scotland were hostile or in Whig hands. Glasgow he only occupied in December 1745 after his retreat from England and even he admitted that the citizens had no enthusiasm for him at all. Inverness was held for the government by a motley force composed mainly of independent companies raised by Whig chiefs under the influence of Forbes of Culloden and latterly commanded by Lord Loudon. As soon as Charles marched out of Edinburgh to invade England the Whigs moved back in and took over control, which they never lost again. Only early in 1746 did the retreating Jacobite forces occupy Inverness and capture Fort Augustus, though not Fort William. On the eve of Culloden Jacobite forces were campaigning against the remnants of independent companies north of Inverness, chasing them eventually into Skye. Whereas in 1715 the Jacobites were able to hold elections to confirm their grip on the east-coast burghs north of the Tay, in the '45 Charles had to simply appoint governors for the major burghs. Even so, on 30 October 1745, the birthday of George II, Hanoverian mobs besieged Oliphant of Gask, depute governor of Perth, in his residence, and chased the governor of Dundee, David Fotheringham, out of town.[45]

The Presbyterian clergy were totally hostile to the '45 and they carried with them the overwhelming bulk of Lowland opinion, at least to the point of ensuring that Prince Charles received little positive assistance. With the burghs unenthusiastic about his cause, and only a minority of Highland chiefs committed to it, Charles was straining every nerve to put together the 5,500 men he led into England on that astonishing six-week foray in November and December 1745. If its leaders were atypical of the ruling class as a whole, its rank and file undoubtedly contained a very high percentage of men who had been forced out. The evidence accumulated for legal purposes after the '45, even allowing for anxiety to exaggerate the unwillingness of many men to join the Jacobites, is overwhelming in this respect and shows that female Jacobite supporters like Mrs Robertson of Lude, a spitfire daughter of the House of Nairne, could be as ruthless in forcing men out as their male counterparts. The correspondence of Lord

Lewis Gordon as Lord-Lieutenant of Aberdeenshire and Banffshire in late 1745 and 1746 shows quite clearly that the normal Jacobite technique for beating up recruits in the later stages of the rebellion was to threaten local landlords that their estates would be ravaged with fire and sword if they did not produce a set quota of men. This was also the standard method of collecting provisions and the cess or tax which was so vital for the hand-to-mouth finances of the rebellion.[46] Charles had virtually no money left when he first reached Perth, and by March 1746 his financial and man-power crises were becoming intolerable.

The fact that the Highland army reached Derby before it turned back was due to two sets of factors. The first was the sheer quality and drive of Lord George Murray's generalship, especially when contrasted with the funereal pace at which such aged Hanoverian commanders as Marshal Wade responded to his moves. The second was political and legal. Hanoverian Britain was a law-bound society with an unpopular, divided and irresponsible political class, and in the '45 the result of this state of affairs was near-paralysis. Due to political feuds at Westminster which made agreements about appointments impossible, many Scottish counties were without Lord-Lieutenants in 1745. In England, where Lord-Lieutenants existed there were very genuine doubts as to whether they had the power to see to the security of their counties by mustering the militia without some further specific statutory warrant, which was not forthcoming. Army transport was hamstrung by severe legal restrictions on commandeering men, horses and vehicles. So conditioned by their political system to obedience to central authority were the English that the Jacobites, usurping that authority as they went, were able to collect such public moneys as excise, to use it to pay for their keep, and to maintain an admirable discipline which put the Hanoverian armies to shame.[47]

Charles proceeded throughout on the bland assumption that all troops sent against him would always run away without fighting. It was an idiotic assumption and only on it could a decision to advance from Derby to London be justified. Most of his advisers had not wanted to leave Scotland. They invaded England because Charles insisted that he would receive massive support there. Whatever the private mouthings of Jacobite phrases by English Tories, the fact is that they did not stir as Charles advanced. Even the Lancashire Roman Catholics had reverted, very wisely after their experience in the '15, to their traditional political passivity. Manchester was a very partial exception to all this. The few hundred recruits who came in there seem to have been drawn mainly from the local unemployed. Embodied in the tragically-fated Manchester Regiment, they were commanded by Francis Townley, scion of a landed Roman Catholic family whose commission in the French army failed in the end to save him from the scaffold.

The absence of any other English support seems to have been, rightly, decisive at the Jacobite council of war at Derby. At the highest level, the Hanoverian regime was not panic-stricken. George II had a remarkably sane understanding of the extreme weakness of the Jacobite army. He knew their grip on Scotland was uncertain and like Lord George Murray he regarded the absence of any English rising as fatal to Prince Charles. Three armies, two of them much larger than the Highland army, were converging on Prince Charles. Wade was bearing down on his rear. George II's unpleasant but competent younger son the Duke of Cumberland was to the west of Lichfield, and between Charles and London stood the Brigade of Guards, which had sworn neither to give nor receive quarter.[48] French aid to the rebellion had been minimal. It consisted of little more than Lord John Drummond and his regiment plus detachments of fifty men each from the Irish regiments in French service. An emissary of dubious diplomatic status, the Marquis d'Eguilles, hardly ranked as more than a psychological crutch. It is true that with Charles deep in England French troops had been rushed to Channel ports, but the English Channel Fleet under Admiral Vernon, gaining information from prizes, identified the embarkation port and kept so strict a blockade that even Charles's brother Henry, Jacobite Duke of York, despaired of a crossing.[49] After Derby the Jacobites won a skirmish at Clifton near Penrith and a lucky victory in Scotland at Falkirk, when the brutal General Hawley's troops lost their nerve in action, but it was absolutely fitting that the final action at Culloden, where the harsh realities of power eventually asserted themselves, was precipitated by a blockage of French funds. Charles needed money to keep his army in the field. Incapable of raising funds as he lost control of Scotland, he had to have French gold. When the French sloop *Le Prince Charles*, which was carrying £12,000 in English gold guineas, was intercepted trying to reach Inverness, the game was up. Charles had to stand and fight though he chose a stupid place to do so. It was the end not so much of a mass rising as of an abortive French-sponsored *coup d'état*.

Although, as is well-known, the remnants of the Jacobite army reassembled at Ruthven in Badenoch a few days after their crushing defeat at Culloden, there was never any serious prospect of the continuation of organized resistance to the victorious forces of the British government. We have a dramatic account by the Jesuit Guilio Cesare Cordara of an appeal to Prince Charles by the arrogant young commander of his Life Guards, David Lord Elcho, who as they fled the field urged his leader to betake himself to the mountains of Lochaber and Badenoch. Escape to France on the part of their prince, Elcho cried, would merely dishearten the countless brave men ready still to lay down their lives for the Stewart cause. Sir Thomas Sheridan told Elcho not to be a fool. Elcho was incandescent with rage, but Sheridan was right. Sustained irregular warfare against Cumberland was impractical. Guerrilla warfare as the twentieth century was to know it was utterly inconceivable in 1746. The suicidal nature of the '45 ensured that its committed supporters were far from being a representative cross-section of the contemporary Scottish ruling class. Many were marginal or eccentric members of that class, and one or two were just plain mad, but the strength of the Jacobite movement still lay in the support given it by a limited number of nobles, lairds, and burghal patricians. Such privileged propertied individuals were in no position to wage the sort of guerrilla wars which two centuries later, under favourable conditions, could indefinitely frustrate modern war machines and sap the will to victory of their political masters. Nor did the favourable circumstances necessary for a successful struggle of this kind exist in the mid eighteenth-century Highlands. There was no adjacent land frontier with a friendly or studiously ambiguous state ready to act as a refuge and springboard. Nor was there a mass political consciousness below the level of the gentry.[1]

A mere 1,500 men rallied to Lord George Murray at Ruthven. Among them the Macpherson and Ogilvy regiments were virtually intact, but the remainder were the leaderless wreckage of shattered units. Nearly all the Highland chiefs were 'a-missing', usually for the best of reasons. To take only the two outstanding clan leaders of the rebellion: Lochiel had been severely wounded in both ankles by grapeshot at Culloden, and had been fortunate to escape the field, while the dauntless Keppoch had fallen with his brother Donald in a last heroic charge against the triumphant Hanoverian line of battle. Some contemporaries expected Lord George Murray, who clearly neither expected nor deserved mercy from the government after his third act of rebellion, to be for holding out, not in the hope of victory, but to secure terms. Certainly Lord George had wanted to retreat into the hills for a summer campaign. However, this policy was an alternative to an early pitched battle like Culloden, not something feasible after it. Supplies and ammunition captured by Cumberland in Inverness should have been moved into the mountains weeks before to enable a Highland campaign to be fought.[2] As it was, the 1,500 at Ruthven could not be held together for more than a few days. There was no money to pay the men, few of whom were strictly volunteers, and the commanders were enraged when Prince Charles, who had sent what little money he had to Ruthven to be distributed to the troops, recalled it for his own personal use. Worse still was the harsh reality of food shortage. Due to a bad harvest, oatmeal, the basic food grain of the Highlands, was scarce and dear in the winter and spring of 1746. There were endless worries about feeding the loyally Hanoverian Campbell militia as it concentrated around Inveraray,[3] so the choice before the beaten Jacobite remnant at Ruthven was disperse, or starve.

Thus the first consequence of the '45 was the complete removal of the normal balance between the Westminster government and those armed and distant Scottish Highlands for which the Hanoverian regime really cared so very little. A powerful Hanoverian army had been drawn into the Highland area, and the countervailing strength of the Jacobite clans had been decisively broken. If the consequences of the '45 can be grouped for convenience under three headings – military, legal and political – it is the military aspect which must first be examined, for the military situation was unprecedented. After Culloden the Duke of Cumberland established himself in the very heart of the Highlands at Fort Augustus where he coordinated widespread mopping up and counter-insurgency operations. At his disposal for these purposes were not only the regular soldiers of his army, but also the many units of the Royal Navy concentrated in western Highland waters, and two substantial militia forces commanded by Lord Loudon and Major-General John Campbell of Mamore. Against this array there could be no defence. For the first time the Highlands and Islands were at the mercy of the British government.

Drastic punitive action against Jacobite areas was quite inevitable, not because of any breakdown in military discipline, but because the demand for this action in leading political circles was irresistible. Cumberland was ever ready to use the noose or the lash on his own troops to punish unauthorized plundering. Such savagery as occurred was therefore the product of deliberate policy, and was justified mainly by the failure of the Highland population to respond to the Duke of Cumberland's proclamation summoning those who had taken part in the rebellion to bring in their weapons and surrender themselves to the king's mercy. Predictably, that proclamation was attended with little success, the Macphersons alone, as a clan, surrendering their weapons. The Duke of Newcastle, who combined in one personality an amiable twitterer and an astute political manager, had stressed early in March 1746, before Culloden, that the power of the Highlands must be 'absolutely reduced' to ensure that France did not sponsor annual Jacobite risings. The recipient of his letter, Lord Chesterfield, the Lord Lieutenant of Ireland, was much more explicit. He was for genocide. Chesterfield urged a naval blockade to ensure that food supplies did not reach the starving Highlands. A price was to be put on chiefs' heads while Cumberland was urged to massacre the peasantry. Chesterfield usually goes down in the history books as a man of letters and an early example of the Good European, for he sponsored the legislation which brought the British calendar into line with the Gregorian system of Western Europe. That irascible fellow-Englishman Dr Samuel Johnson summed Chesterfield up more realistically. He had indeed the manners of a dancing master, and the morals of a whore.

What made Chesterfield's bloody-mindedness so outstanding was the fact that he carried it into practice, in so far as he could. At the height of the rebellion, with General Campbell desperate for meal for his militia, Chesterfield had banned the export of as much as an oatcake from Ireland. He made no bones about his readiness to 'starve the loyal with the disloyal'.[4] Other politicians equally addicted to projecting an image of themselves as moderate and reasonable men, like the Duke of Richmond, were in private consumed with a blood-lust quite as great as that of Chesterfield, if blessedly less capable of practical expression. Richmond made it clear to Newcastle in March 1746 that he would much prefer the rebellion to culminate in a heavy slaughter than in a tame surrender, for in Richmond's view the more corpses Cumberland climbed over on his way to the reduction of the Highlands, the better. Cumberland had already begun to ravage the estates of Jacobite noblemen during his march north to Culloden. In early February 1746 he reported to Newcastle from Crieff, on the southern edge of the Perthshire Highlands, that he had let his troops loose on 'some of the Drummond's, Strathallan's and other disaffected persons' estates'. What followed after Culloden was wider in scope and ruthless in method. Lieutenant-Colonel Whitefoord, in a letter of July 1746, tabulated clinically the destruction of the basis of life in many humble communities living at the best of times near the margin of survival. Rebels found in arms were, of course, shot out of hand. Those who absconded had their homes plundered and burned, their cattle driven away, and their ploughs and other utensils smashed.[5]

Those who were active in this distasteful work, which Newcastle told Cumberland was more important than Culloden itself, always insisted that ordinary rebels who surrendered and handed in their arms were released with a certificate to ensure that they were not in future molested by Crown forces. In fact it is clear that this was not always so. Sixteen Grants of Glenmoriston and sixty-eight of Glenurquhart who surrendered in May 1746 to Sir Ludovic Grant and gave up their arms to him were promptly marched to Inverness as prisoners, along with James Grant of Sheuglie and the Reverend John Grant. At Inverness, in blatant violation of the promise under which they had surrendered, they were all handed over to the tender mercies of the Duke of Cumberland for punishment by due legal process. There is little doubt that these men were victims of the suspicions and hostility of their own chief Ludovic Grant of Grant. Most of them were humble farmers and a high proportion of them appear to have been very reluctant conscripts forced into the Jacobite army. It availed them naught. They were unimportant. They could make little interest on their own behalf, so they were transported. One at least, Donald Grant of Blairy Glenmoriston, late of Glengarry's Regiment, managed to return from Barbados in 1750. The more important men like Sheuglie and his son, and John Grant 'Minister of the Gospel in Urquhart', were able to put up a stiff legal struggle in the course of which they indignantly insisted that they had been actively Hanoverian in sympathy during the rising. Sheuglie died of fever in prison at Tilbury. Grudgingly, after the discomfort of prison in Inverness and London, not to mention the expense and agony of mind, the other two were discharged.[6] In the witch-hunt which follows most unsuccessful rebellions private vendettas flourish. Many a Highland peasant gazing down from the high ridge on the flames and smoke marking the site of his home must have reckoned he had made the best of a bad choice.

Lowland Scots were undoubtedly prominent amongst the subordinate commanders who enforced Cumberland's orders with a degree of harshness which exceeded even that of the royal duke himself. Captain John Fergussone of H.M.S. *Furnace*, for example, earned an evil name for the indiscriminate ruthlessness of the amphibious operations which he conducted off the west coast and in the islands. He burned the laird's house on Raasay, ravaged the island of Eigg, and in a series of operations in the districts of Arisaig and Morar burned not only the big houses of known Jacobite leaders, but a large number of humble villages as well. His activities in Morar were crowned by the capture of that slippery rascal Lord Lovat, along with a mass of incriminating correspondence which helped send him to the scaffold. Captain Caroline Scott, the soldier who successfully defended Fort William against a Jacobite siege, was a man of the same kidney. Troops under his command had scoured with sadistic zeal the lands of Appin and Lochaber. On an expedition from Fort William to burn the house of Macdonald of Keppoch in June 1746, Scott spiced this well-merited act of retribution with the wanton hanging, with the ropes of a salmon net, of three unfortunate peasants on their way to surrender their arms in accordance with Cumberland's proclamation. Other examples of Scots or English officers behaving in a similar fashion are easy to come by, but in the last analysis these were Cumberland's men, indeed his favourites, picked out, commended and promoted by the interest of that hard young commander.[7] To describe Cumberland as arrogant and brutal is to differentiate him little from a very large proportion of the contemporary political and military élite of Hanoverian Britain. It is the indiscriminate and unintelligent nature of the savagery which he licensed which is so depressing.

It is very dubious whether these horrors served any useful purpose, apart from creating a fund of resentment in the Highlands from which the last Jacobite rebellion was to draw much of its retrospective justification. The best heads in the Highlands counselled moderation. Lord President Duncan Forbes was strongly in favour of disarming the Highlands and of swift, firm justice on the aristocratic leaders of the rising, but he thought that to proceed to extremes against the Jacobite rank and file would merely arouse compassion and resentment. Indeed Cumberland wrote sneeringly that Forbes was 'as arrant Highland mad as Lord Stair or Crawford', and that all three seemed to regard the Highlanders after Culloden as being harmless as a dispersed London mob.[8] The analogy was probably a good one, yet there was no chance that the government would accept it. So far from comprehending the niceties of social structure and social control in the Highlands, official English opinion tended to work on the assumption that all Scots were Jacobites.

Intelligent Lowlanders of a Whig persuasion had been afraid that this would be an inevitable result of the rebellion from an early stage in its progress and had been at pains in communications to English friends to emphasize that three-quarters of the Scottish population at least were bitterly hostile to the Jacobite cause. So they probably were, but it made no difference. At the end of 1746 an anonymous pamphlet entitled *Old England* summed up the views of many Englishmen, of both low and high estate, when it declared that, 'A Scot is a natural hereditary Jacobite, and incurable by acts of lenity, generosity, and friendly dealing.' A reply was forthcoming in 1747 from the pen of a young Scot, William Murray M.P., later the silver-tongued Lord Mansfield, Lord Chief Justice of England from 1756. William Murray entitled his piece *The Thistle* and in it he rebutted the absurd notion that the vast majority of Scots were other than loyal to the Protestant Succession. However, the pessimism of the Ayrshire Whig and Lord of Session Lord Kilkerran about the effect of the '45 on the Scottish image in England was nearer the mark, and was shared by so intelligent an English correspondent as Dr Philip Doddridge, the greatest Dissenting schoolmaster of his day. To an eminent Hanoverian Englishman like the Archbishop of York it seemed obvious that the feats of the Jacobite army were only possible because it was sustained by the general national sentiment of Scotland.[9]

There is no question but that Cumberland shared the crudest and crassest of contemporary anti-Scottish prejudices. It was therefore an act of breath-taking impudence on the part of his best-known biographer to endeavour to shift responsibility for post-Culloden atrocities from his hero's shoulders on to those of the commanders of the independent companies or Highland militia, Lord Loudon and General Campbell.[10] In fact those public-spirited and humane Campbell magnates, whilst obeying to the letter their orders to take action against the persons and property of known Jacobites, also showed a sympathy for the innocent victims of misfortune which lends lustre to the name they bore. Responsibility for the profoundly unsatisfactory state of the Highlands after Culloden must be borne by Cumberland and the man who after his departure was gazetted Commander-in-Chief Scotland on 23 August 1746, William Anne Keppel, second Earl of Albemarle.

The son of a Dutch favourite of William of Orange, Albemarle had accompanied Cumberland to Scotland in the capacity of a volunteer. He had extensive experience of campaigning on the Continent, especially in Flanders, and he commanded the first line of Cumberland's army at Culloden. Albemarle was unenthusiastic about the prospect of his new command on the ground that it would leave him bereft of family and friends:

> split upon the rocks that has in different ways undone four of my predecessors, and be left to the mercy of these people [i.e. the Scots], who never want Lyes or malice to ruin a man that wishes well to the King and his interest, and it is absolutely impossible for the person that commands here to do his Duty like an honest man and be well with the people and their present Minister at Court, who wee hear begins already to skreen some of these Rebellious rascals.[11]

Clearly Albemarle reflected all too accurately views prevalent in Cumberland's intimate circle. Law and order were to be imposed on an ungrateful and untrustworthy people with an iron hand. Iron it certainly was, but whether it produced law and order may be doubted. Into military dispatches originally preoccupied with the whereabouts of 'the Pretender's

Son' or 'Rebells' there crept increasingly references to 'the Highland Thieves'.

Major-General Bland, writing to Albemarle from Stirling on 27 August 1746, discussed the siting of a chain of outposts of regular troops on the southern confines of the Highlands designed 'to catch the Rebell or Thieving Highlanders' and reverted to the recurring official pipe-dream of a blockade of vital food supplies. In memorable words he enthused that:

> If the Officers Commanding the Several Posts now forming the Chain follow their instructions, the Rebells in the Highlands can't be supplied with Victual, as they call Meal, from this Country, unless the Justices of the Peace and the Ministers are accessory to it by granting Certificates for that purpose; nor will I answer for their not doing it from a mistaken notion of Christian Charity, now they think the Rebellion, in a manner, over.[12]

Yet in the very same letter Bland had to refer to thieves, as distinct from Jacobites, and to report that when two droves of black cattle had passed through Stirling on their way from Macleod country in Skye to the great cattle tryst or fair at Falkirk, they had been escorted by armed men bearing official documents, issued by the military authorities, which exempted them from the general ban on the carrying of weapons. Such exemptions were essential because of the disturbed state of the Highlands. Men moving north to buy cattle needed arms for their security every bit as much as when driving their assembled herds south. A safe-conduct issued by the Sheriff-Depute of Argyll on 11 December 1746 permitted James Macnab, drover in Craig of Glenorchy, who was going with two servants to buy cattle in Kintail and Skye, 'to pass to and from these countries with their arms alwise behaving themselves as Loyall subjects of His Majesty'. Drovers had in fact to be exempted from both the Disarming Act of 1716 and that of 1748.

Cattle thieving by such marginal groups in Highland society as the Macgregors or the Macdonalds of Keppoch or Glencoe had always been a problem. Larger groups such as the Mackenzies were marginally prone to the crime, and dealing with the problem was something which exercised the minds of both General Wade and the Jacobite Mackintosh of Borlum, who published in 1742 a work largely devoted to the need to put down the depredations of cattle thieves. Borlum saw the problem as mainly concentrated in the western part of Inverness, and the northern parts of Argyll, Perthshire, and Stirlingshire, but there was also the problem of Highland cattle raids into such exposed and adjacent parts of the Lowlands as the north-east, Kincardineshire, and the Angus glens.[13] The whole business has to be kept in proportion. Armed drovers with their dogs were a formidable deterrent to rustlers. At no time did thieving seriously threaten the almost continuous expansion of the black cattle trade after 1660, and one would expect a flow of mobile wealth to attract parasites. By way of comparison, it is worth noting that in the London docks at the end of the eighteenth century it was estimated that some £350,000 worth of goods were stolen annually by a swarm of meticulously sub-divided and specialized water thieves with such splendid names as Night Plunderers, Light Horsemen, Mudlarks and Scuffle Hunters. Ten to eleven thousand people were said to either participate in, or connive at this orgy of larceny. Private maritime police forces had to be organized after 1798, but even this scale of plundering was not enough to blight the expansion of London's trade.[14]

If anything, the situation in the Highlands in the years immediately after Culloden was more disturbed than usual. On top of the normal deterrents to successful prosecution of thieves, like reluctance of witnesses to testify and the cost of proceedings to relatively poor victims of theft, was heaped a great deal of social instability due to fear and hatred of the military, not to mention the collapse of ancient patterns of jurisdiction and control. There were many 'masterless men' like 'that nest of Rogues who still keep in Arms and plunder that part of the Country' who moved the Hanoverian Graham of Gartmore to appeal to Major-General Bland at Stirling for a detachment of thirty soldiers to be stationed at Gartmore, on the southern edge of the Highlands, to hold their depredations in check.[15] Hanoverian commanders like Major-General Blakeney were perfectly prepared to use torture to extract information during their sweeps through the Highlands,[16] and the severities of the Cumberland 'search and destroy' tactics were in no way relaxed under the Albemarle regime, but pacification proved as illusory as it usually does under such methods. Intelligence reports in Albemarle's hands by late 1746 indicated that the spirits of the men of Morven had survived undaunted the burning of many of their townships by amphibious government operations. They had preserved most of their cattle by hiding them, had plenty of weapons, some French and Spanish gold, and were nursing their wrath whilst rebuilding their houses and talking of a French landing in the spring. Their Papist compatriots in Moydart were given to harping on that theme. Short of meal and fuel, they had plenty firearms and enough rum and brandy to keep the inner man warm. Albemarle was informed that, 'There are great thefts committed all over Moydart, Morven and Sounart and about Strontian.'[17]

All of these circumstances may have contributed to the decidedly sour note on which Albemarle ended 1746. In September of that year he informed the Duke of Newcastle that he was convinced that the only way to restore peace and quietness to Scotland was to devastate its northern counties and deport most of their inhabitants. After a particularly impudent Jacobite attempt to organize celebrations in Edinburgh on 20

December 1746, 'the Birthday of the Pretender's Son', an exasperated Albemarle begged Newcastle, 'Au Nom de Dieu retire moy d'icy.'[18] Just why Albemarle was so ready to invoke the name of the Almighty to facilitate his escape from Scotland may also be partly explained by the fact that his intelligence appraisals were preaching to him in much the same vein as his predecessor Lord Carpenter had felt obliged to preach to the London politicians of the day after the '19. The ability of lumbering regular units to disarm determined and disaffected Highlanders, let alone capture their chiefs, was very small.[19] The recurring fantasies about mass deportation which passed through the minds of men like Cumberland and Albemarle were the product of bigotry and frustration, but any attempt to implement them would have turned a chaotic situation into a politically dangerous one. As it was, even Jacobite gentlemen in the Highlands were bound, in the long run, to favour a return to normality.

They had no interest in endemic unrest with undertones of social instability. Indeed in December 1747 the Lord Justice Clerk wrote to the Duke of Newcastle with an enclosure which illustrated the point. The main letter was really a continuation of correspondence about Justices of the Peace, for the Justice Clerk was trying to purge Jacobites from this office. He knew that in a county like Inverness this would leave so weak a bench that it would have to be stiffened by the appointment of army officers. However, the enclosure was a report from an informant, 'Mr Douglas, store-keeper at Fortwilliam', to the effect that Lochiel's brother John Cameron of Fassiefern had just convened a meeting of the Cameron gentry, not to plot treason, but to discuss measures against 'the great Theft of Cattle that has been practised by the Commonality (more of late than formerly)'. Fassiefern disapproved of, and refused to assist, the Jacobite rebellion in which his brother was so prominent but on the subject of 'the Commonality', Hanover and Stewart were as one.[20]

Arguably, if Cumberland and his immediate successors in command of the Hanoverian forces in the Highlands had been less heavy-handed and more discriminating in their use of the power at their disposal, stability would have come much more rapidly to the area. Virtually all the Jacobite gentry believed that they had been misled by Prince Charles, with his constant talk of massive French intervention on his side. For the sake of their self-respect Highland Jacobites, like the Jacobites of the north-eastern parts of England immediately after the '15, adopted in public an aggressively defiant attitude. They repeatedly said that if the French landed in strength, they would be ready to join them. In view of the events of the '45, this was a face-saving admission of defeat. Albemarle escaped into Flanders from his bondage in Scotland in March 1747. His successor as Commander-in-Chief Scotland, General Bland, continued to display the blind hostility to the Scottish upper classes which characterized Cumberland's circle. Bland felt very foreign in a country where 'the Law and Custome are so different from ours'.[21] He was convinced that nobody in Scotland could be trusted since 'Sheriffs, Deputy Sheriffs, Justices of the Peace, and the other Civil Officers throughout the Kingdom are very remiss in their duty, and unwilling to seize any of the attainted Rebels, or those who harbour them and abett their causes.' This Commander-in-Chief's' correspondence with the Lord Justice Clerk is peppered with demands that Provosts of Lowland burghs be prosecuted for anything from taking a light view of the probably drunken remarks of a local baker (remarks which consigned King George to the nether regions), to holding an idiosyncratic interpretation of the Disarming Act. Bland was sure that the civil magistrates of Scotland needed to be subjected to exemplary discipline lest their tendency to dispense with the laws encouraged anarchy and confusion in the land.[22]

Political views of infantile over-simplicity have tended to be a hallmark of distinguished General officers in the British Service from the eighteenth to the twentieth century. These gallant gentlemen seem to derive mental solace from inhabiting a black-and-white world of 'them' and 'us' which incidentally provides justification for the maintenance of a large regular army of the most unimaginatively conventional kind. The London politicians who in early 1746 clearly shared the paranoid categories of thought characteristic of their generals in Scotland, seem gradually to have moved towards more realistic positions. Their faith in the judgement of the military must have been shaken by the extraordinary events which disgraced the evening of 1 August 1746 in Aberdeen. The Earl of Ancram, who had recently arrived to take command of the troops there, decided to mark the first of August as a day of rejoicing on the ground that it was the accession day of the late King George I, and 'consequently of the present Establishment'. Ancram asked the magistrates of the city to arrange for the citizens to illuminate their windows by placing candles in them, as was the normal custom. However, this particular anniversary was one not usually celebrated in Scotland. After firing sundry volleys, the military were annoyed to see many windows unilluminated. Openly urged on by some of their officers, the soldiers indulged in an orgy of smashing unlighted windows. This army hooliganism was too much for the Whig magistrates of Aberdeen, who mobilized their legal resources and their political influence to make life difficult for the officers who had behaved with such wanton arrogance. Even Albemarle had to eat humble pie; for him an unaccustomed diet.[23]

By 1752 the alarmism of the regular army mind was a joke amongst politicians concerned with the day-to-day realities of the Highlands. Commissioner Campbell, writing to Lord Milton, the law lord who was still principal man of business to the Argyll interest in Scotland, remarked in

June of that year that he was sending the military reports forwarded by General Bland to him to London by a separate cover from an official report which he had just finished compiling. He explained that 'the Army Informations have no evidence to support them, and are otherwise so trivial and ridiculous that wee did not think it proper to sully our report with them.' Campbell could not resist offering Milton the pick of Bland's bouquet of nonsenses. This concerned 'one Bethune a Tidesman (i.e. customs officer) at Inverness and Said to be a Highland Poet'. Campbell went on to the effect that 'This Genius is informed against for being suspected for author of ane Irish Ballad in praise of the Clans at the Battle of Culloden.' Beyond the faded handwriting the titter in the writer's voice is still audible.[24]

Certain very substantial pieces of military engineering commissioned in the immediate aftermath of the '45 continued to be ongoing projects for another generation. The Highland forts had fared badly, Fort William apart, during the rebellion and Cumberland urgently asked the government to replace Fort Augustus and Fort George at Inverness Castle by modern structures more capable of defence than their predecessors had proved. It was eventually decided not to waste money on so inherently weak a position as Fort Augustus, which was merely patched up. Disputes over land values at Inverness drove the government to a far better, if bleaker, site at Ardersier, a peninsula jutting into the Moray Firth nine miles east of Inverness. There between 1748 and 1769 one of the great bastion and ravelin-defended artillery forts of Europe was constructed. Its geometrical functionalism and neo-classical embellishment still impress, but by the time it was complete it was already recognized as a white elephant. The military road system was greatly enlarged until by 1767 there was over a thousand miles of it. A road from Blairgowrie to Fort George was built in 1749–54 and in 1748–50 two traditional tower-house castles on its route were converted into small barracks at Corgarff and Braemar. By the 1760s doubts were arising about both the necessity and expense of the military road network.[25]

It is true that in the long run military patrols mounted by small scattered outposts of regular troops did help to put an end to the ancient pattern of raiding by Highlanders into the richer lands of Morayshire, Aberdeenshire, and the Angus glens. The basic technique used was to try to exercise surveillance over the passes which were the key bottlenecks through which stolen eastern cattle had to be driven west.[26] However, had the Highland aristocracy been actively hostile the Hanoverian posts would have been ineffective. As it was, neither Cumberland nor Albemarle nor Bland could effect the arrest of such notorious Jacobites as Euan Macpherson of Cluny, who lurked for years in his own country until he chose to go abroad, and Alexander Robertson of Struan, who died in his bed and in effective possession of his estate. The fundamental explanation for the taming of the Highlands, apart from the fact that their wildness before 1745 has been ridiculously exaggerated, is the will of their own ruling classes. The Reverend Mr Patrick Stuart, incumbent of the parish of Killin in north-western Perthshire, provided in the late eighteenth century a retrospective but revealing summary of the process of pacification, which he ascribed to the wise policy of the Breadalbane family, 'superiors of the country'. Mr Stuart continued:

> A Sheriff-substitute was got to Killin for settling differences; a check was given to knavery; the sober and industrious among the people were supported and encouraged; and the turbulent and irregular expelled the country, to which they were so much attached, that it was reckoned no small punishment by them. These means, together with the happy change in the times, have had very good effects. The people of Breadal-bane are now sober, regular, and industrious.[27]

Though clearly over-simplified, and reeking of incense, the statement is significant.

The centrality of disaffection amongst members of the contemporary ruling élites to the whole Jacobite saga is underlined by an examination of the second category of consequences which flowed from the '45 – the immediate legal consequences. These were always likely to be more draconian than those which followed the '15. Though no complete Jacobite army was captured as at Preston in the earlier rebellion, pockets of rebels such as the doomed garrison of Carlisle were picked up, and there was a far more serious and sustained hunt for rebels after the disintegration of what was left of the Jacobite army than had been the case in 1716. By the nature of the case, we are never likely to have a definitive total for Jacobite prisoners, but painstaking research on reasonably abundant records has identified 3,471 men, women and children who were taken prisoner, and that figure is probably close to the correct total. Technically a very high percentage of these people had been guilty of high treason and lay in the shadow of a possible death sentence. Official and popular opinion were inflamed against them, so the way they were processed is all the more revealing.

There was, of course, no intention of trying prisoners in Scotland other than deserters from the British army who, after drum-head court martial, were summarily executed. A meeting of the Privy Council held at New-castle House on 15 May 1746 gave preliminary consideration to the treatment of prisoners. In attendance were the Duke of Argyll, the Earl of Harrington, Henry Pelham (the head of the ruling ministry), and his brother the Duke of Newcastle. They reached a series of decisions of which the first was 'That all the Rebel Prisoners in Scotland be tried at Carlisle or Newcastle'. The local authorities in Newcastle promptly besieged the government with requests that they be spared the dubious distinction of having to mount treason trials. Amongst the arguments which eventually prevailed was the compelling one that 'we have not proper places for their security'. Transport ships laden with prisoners from Inverness were actually in the Tyne when Westminster relented. The ships were diverted to the Thames where 300 of the prisoners were decanted into Tilbury Fort as an emergency measure. The remainder were left literally to rot aboard ships which were already stinking, typhus-ridden slums. The unfortunate rebels died like flies.[28]

The next move was to revive a procedure originally authorized by an Order in Council of 1715. To modern eyes it is a very strange procedure, for it provided for the selection of prisoners for trial, amongst those in English jails or aboard prison ships, by lot. A new Order in Council of 23 July 1746 said that 'the said Prisoners, not being Gentlemen or Men of Estates, or such as shall appear to have distinguish'd themselves by any Extraordinary Degree of Guilt' were 'to draw Lots', so that every twentieth prisoner should go forward to trial and due punishment. The arbitrary nature of the proceedings served two purposes. It drastically reduced the backlog of formal trials whilst also hopefully awakening feelings of awe and gratitude in the lucky majority. The 'luck' of the latter was of a strictly relative nature. They were regarded as at the disposal of such 'Mercy' as the Crown chose to extend. Almost all were transported to the North American or West Indian colonies as indentured (i.e. virtually slave) labourers for life. Ironically, this was precisely the same fate as that which overtook the great majority of their brothers in misfortune whose lot it was to be tried for their lives. They went through the farcically predictable process of being tried, condemned to death, and then pardoned on condition of transportation as indentured labour to the colonies. The authorities were worried about the possibility that some of them might contrive to return from the Americas, as a few, though only a few, did. The problem was commonplace, and had indeed induced the legislature to pass two Transportation Acts in 1719, one of which imposed severe penalties on any 'returned transport' while the other offered a £40 reward for the arrest of such criminals. Many of the rogues employed in the criminal gangs of Jonathan Wild, 'Thief-Taker General' and master-crook of early Georgian London, who was himself hanged in 1725, were 'returned transports'.[29] To prevent Jacobite prisoners who were to be transported from returning in large numbers the Crown Solicitor, Philip Carteret Webb, seriously suggested in September 1746 that they should all be branded on the face before transportation, and that it should be made a hanging offence for them to return at all. Branding was one of the savage mutilating penalties used by early modern criminal law systems, which were, of course, plagued by their inability to identify malefactors. In the Netherlands branding survived as a punishment into the middle of the nineteenth century,[30] but the prospect of branding the best part of a thousand prisoners as a precaution was obviously too much for the British government in 1746. No more was heard of the proposal.

If the treatment of the lower orders amongst the prisoners was casually brutal in its use of transportation, it was also basically contemptuous. What the government was determined to underline was that pleas that men had been 'forced out' to serve in the rebel army by their social superiors would only be accepted if resistance to forced enlistment could be shown to be violent, well-attested, and sustained, in the sense that the unwilling soldier seized every chance to try to desert. It was a formidable requirement, which only a few could meet. Despite the fact that the trials of rebels produced a great deal of convincing evidence to the effect that force had been widely employed to compel men into the Jacobite ranks, most of the victims of that violence were transported. The odd individual was just unlucky or was arbitrarily selected for an example and suffered the supreme penalty despite his inherent obscurity. Unluckiest of all, perhaps, was James Reid, a piper in Lord Ogilvy's regiment. Taken at Carlisle, he was tried at York. It was pointed out that he was only a piper and he was recommended to mercy, but the court ruled that since Highlanders never marched without a piper, his bagpipe must, in the eyes of the law, rank as an instrument of war. Poor Reid was executed at York, having unwittingly done much for the honour of his instrument.[31] The only group in the Jacobite army which the British government pursued with relentless severity regardless of social rank were the members of the Manchester Regiment. Precisely because this was the only English unit raised for the service of Prince Charles, its members were marked or rather doomed men. One of the few consolations available to the ministers of George II was the thought that their humiliation had been due to Scottish disloyalty. All the greater, then, was their wrath against this tragic Manchester unit.

The bulk of the prisoners were subjected to a rough-and-ready process of social classification, with a view to winnowing out, for particular attention, the socially more significant groups. Scottish prisons were combed for important prisoners, but we know more about the grading procedures of Mr John Sharpe, Solicitor to the Treasury, in English prisons. He separated the Jacobite prisoners into four classes: (1) 'really gentlemen'; (2) 'not properly gentlemen, but above the rank of common men'; (3) 'a lower degree than the preceding'; and (4) 'common men'. Quite clearly his categories were far from precise. Members of substantial merchant families or well-established professional men seem to have joined the landed in the first class. The second was inhabited mostly by younger men in the early stages of professional or business training. The third class was conspicuously vague, while the fourth was by far the biggest. Gentlemen, so defined, along with other prominent fish in the Hanoverian net, such as peers, were then subjected to the cruel but not necessarily hopeless game which was always played in eighteenth-century England when men became liable to the death penalty. It must be remembered that amongst ordinary felons in the eighteenth century, roughly half of those condemned to death never went to the gallows, but were pardoned, usually with a lesser penalty.

The prerogative of mercy was an important part of the social structure of Hanoverian Britain, for it was activated primarily by those chains of interest, dependence, and kinship which were the very sinews of the power of the ruling class. Any condemned man automatically asked himself whether he could make enough interest to escape the scaffold, and, of course, preserve his property from forfeiture if he was a man of substance. At a very early stage in the legal proceedings against the more important rebels, Jacobite sympathizers were lobbying people like the wife of Lord President Forbes to ask her to intercede for clemency. It was taken for granted that condemned gentlemen would normally ask for a royal pardon, and that 'they must try every method to enforce it'. The Edinburgh legal fraternity was naturally consulted as to ways and means of averting forfeiture of estates. This was deemed a duty to one's family, but by November 1748 doubts were being expressed as to whether the halcyon days of legal obstruction which had followed the '15 would be tolerated. By early 1749 condemned gentlemen were mobilizing support for petitions for mercy. Informed opinion reckoned that a certain number of the condemned were marked for exemplary punishment and that their case was hopeless, but that the rest might well escape death 'though the petitioning signifies nothing unless some Great Man patronise and support it'. In short, escape could only be obtained by a penitent and humble prisoner capable of inserting himself in one of those vertical chains of patronage which held Hanoverian Britain together. Specimen petitions were circulated. Great play was made with ties of blood or marriage with men of consequence in good standing with the government.[32]

If only to bid defiance to France, which pulled out all the stops in a diplomatic offensive designed to save Jacobite lives, the British government was clearly determined to find a fair number of victims for the axe and the noose. Peers were by far the best-publicized victims of this policy, though in fact only a limited number of them suffered the supreme penalty. The Earls of Kilmarnock and Cromartie and Lord Balmerino were brought up for trial together in Westminster Hall before the House of Lords in July 1746 and were all condemned to death on 1 August. Kilmarnock and Balmerino were beheaded on 18 August, the latter meeting his end like the hero and Scottish patriot he was. Cromartie, a Mackenzie who had been routed and captured by the Earl of Sutherland's levies a couple of days before Culloden when he was returning from a vain attempt to recover the gold on *Le Prince Charles*, was reprieved. The representations of his friends saved his life and he was kept under open arrest in England until he died in dire poverty in London in 1766. The nice balance between severity and mercy in eighteenth-century English justice is well illustrated by the fates of these three men.

Lovat, whose shiftiness and endless chicanery had exasperated all parties, and surely indicates that he was not quite right in the head, was captured and brought to the Tower of London on 15 August 1746. Interestingly the London government was anxious, for propaganda reasons, to have him indicted of high treason by a Grand Jury in his native county, but they were advised by the Lord Advocate and the Lord Justice Clerk that it was probable that any conceivable Grand Jury in Inverness-shire would refuse to indict him, regardless of the evidence. Impeached by the House of Commons and condemned for treasonable intercourse with the Jacobites by the Lords on the evidence of Murray of Broughton and that of his own ex-secretary Hugh Fraser, Lovat grovelled assiduously, even to Cumberland, in hopes of a reprieve. Once he knew there was no hope, his finest hour came and he who had lived like a fox died under the axe with the courage of a lion.[33] A particular defiance to France was the execution of Charles, Jacobite Earl of Derwentwater, whose elder brother had been a martyr to the same cause after the '15. The younger brother was also attainted and condemned but he escaped and fled to France. Captured with other French officers aboard a ship carrying reinforcements for Prince Charles, the *de jure* Earl of Derwentwater was executed under his old attainder. He was a marginal case. Jacobite officers holding regular French commissions who were captured were usually safe, regardless of their original nationality, because of the hostages for their lives held by the French government in the shape of British officer prisoners of war. An exchange was inevitable.

Altogether 120 men, including the four peers, seem to have been executed. These included thirty-eight deserters from the British army and two spies, all summarily executed. No less than twenty-four officers and men of the Manchester Regiment were put to death for 'High treason and levying War'. Forty men from other Jacobite units suffered, as well as twelve whose units are not stated, or who were on the staff, or who were civilians. Judiciously spread over England from London to York and Carlisle, the executions made their point and cannot be said to constitute a holocaust. Most contemporary European governments would have sought at least as bloody a revenge for the act of rebellion. Many more Jacobites died of diseases contracted in prison than on the scaffold, one of these latter being Thomas Ruddiman, junior, the son of the great

Jacobite printer-scholar of the same name. The Ruddimans ran a not very aggressively Jacobite Edinburgh thrice-weekly newspaper, the *Caledonian Mercury*. Thomas Ruddiman, like his partner John Grant, was in fact arrested because he had helped to print Jacobite proclamations, but the Hanoverian authorities hardly took a serious view of the matter. Another printer prisoner whose case demonstrates the importance of influence and arbitrary extensions of clemency in the contemporary legal scene was James Gedd, a captain in the Duke of Perth's regiment captured at Carlisle. His father William, an Edinburgh goldsmith and jeweller, had invented a process for stereotyping or taking a cast of a set-up page of type. Ruined by trade hostility when he tried to capitalize on his invention in London, he retired to Scotland, but his dealings with the ancient English universities saved his son's life after Culloden. James Gedd 'Printer or typefounder' was condemned to death but pardoned unconditionally in 1748 through the influence of friends, including the Master of Trinity College, Oxford, and in recognition of his father's invention. He emigrated to Jamaica.

In short, however bloody-minded most Hanoverian generals and many Westminster politicians may have been early in 1746, the legal processes which followed the '45 can be seen as the start of the rehabilitation and reintegration into the political nation of that not at all representaatic minority of families who had fostered the rising. However casually brutal the treatment of the humbler prisoners, many of whom were clearly very unwilling recruits in the Jacobite ranks, and who were often transported mainly for the grave crime of not having influential friends, people who mattered were handled with some discrimination. Originally this probably owed more to the ingrained tendency of legal procedures to work in certain ways, than to self-conscious moderation. Necessary examples were made, to warn France against further meddling and to underline the intolerable nature of the episode. A good many well-connected prisoners who could have been executed were banished or granted conditional pardons or even, in a certain number of cases and usually after a lapse of time, unconditional pardons. The most extraordinary case of all was probably that of William Sharp, son of Sir Alexander Sharp, Bt, of Scotscraig in Fife, and a great-grandson of Archbishop Sharp. This seventeen-year-old son of a merchant laird pleaded guilty to treason at York and was condemned to death. However his teachers at St Leonard's College, the most eccentric of the colleges of St Andrews University, appealed on his behalf. He was reprieved and confined at Carlisle while the Attorney General pondered his case. The decision to pardon him had been taken when, unaware of it, he escaped, fled abroad and rose to high rank in the Portuguese Army. Pardoned by Royal Warrant in 1769 he returned home, succeeding in 1770 to the family baronetcy of Scotscraig.[14]

One of the most striking differences between the '45 and the '15 was the absence of any successful obstruction of the inevitable forfeitures which followed attainder for high treason in 1746. Such forfeiture was, of course, not limited to landed men who fell into the hands of the government and were condemned after trial. An Act of Attainder was passed in 1746 listing the more prominent Jacobites, including many not yet or never to be prisoners, and rendering them liable to the penalties of treason if they failed to surrender by 12 July 1746. The conspiracy of the legal profession which had so clogged the machinery of forfeiture after the earlier rebellion only reasserted itself briefly on behalf of the venerable Lord Pitsligo. While he was in hiding after Culloden, the Court of Session accepted the plea that because he was referred to in the Act of Attainder as 'Lord Pitsligo' when the name should have been 'Lord Forbes of Pitsligo', the attainder was invalid. By early 1750 the House of Lords had reversed this decision. The worldly wisdom of men like Lord Airlie, who had stayed at home even if he had sent his son out, was amply justified. Marginal cases like Macdonald of Glengarry, who had given open assistance to Prince Charles after he landed, but who in the end stayed at home, sending his men out under his sons and Macdonald of Lochgarry, were given a thorough fright before they were allowed to save their skins and estates. Glengarry was arrested, exempted from a general Act of Indemnity passed in 1747, and only released after petitioning after 'wrongeous' imprisonment in 1749. In 1747 Parliament decreed that the estates of the attainted be 'discovered, known, described and ascertained, and that Rents, Issues and Profits be brought for the Use of His Majesty'. These forfeited estates were to be administered by the Barons of the Exchequer in Scotland. A few men managed to save their properties by legal quibbles but a large collection of estates, ranging from the vast properties of the Duke of Perth, to very humble holdings indeed were thus vested in the Lord Chief Baron and his colleagues.

Other measures passed at this time were perhaps not as significant as has often been thought. The Disarming Act of 1746 provided for stiffer penalties and more effective enforcement than had been the case with its predecessors, but no Hanoverian commander in the Highlands by 1750 believed it was really possible to totally disarm Highlanders who did not want to be disarmed. Equally, the banning of Highland dress, largely a furious reaction to the provocative behaviour of the Jacobite commanders in clothing all their infantry, Lowland and Highland alike, in Highland dress, was a sad rather than an epoch-making event, and was in any case a difficult measure to enforce in remoter parts. Influential Whigs could soon safely be painted in the traditional garb of the Highland gentlemen. What was epoch-making was the most underrated consequence of the '45 – the abolition of the heritable jurisdictions.

Those jurisdictions had, broadly speaking, been in decline since 1707. There were about 160 courts of regality surviving at the time of abolition, ranging from the regality of Kilwinning, which covered two parishes, to very large jurisdictions like the regality of Atholl. Since 1707 the central courts in Edinburgh, without any legislative authority, had been receiving appeals from regalian jurisdictions even though technically only high treason could be taken out of a regality for royal justice. There were of course many other hereditary jurisdictions, the basic one being that of the baron court. A very large number of royal jurisdictions had become hereditary in noble hands. A great many sheriffdoms fell into this category including all Border sheriffdoms, but other royal jurisdictions from bailiaries to stewartries, carrying powers short of regalian, had been granted away in this fashion. The Stewarts had never been happy about the scale of heritable jurisdictions in Scotland and had tried to curb them by legislation of 1455, 1494, 1540, 1555, 1587, 1633 and 1662. Forfeitures after the 1715 had marginally affected the structure of the heritable jurisdictions, as when the regality of Falkirk was downgraded to a barony after the attainder of the Earl of Linlithgow and Callendar, who had fought as a brigadier-general in Mar's army at Sheriffmuir. The only generally effective piece of legislation was the last one, the Heritable Jurisdictions (Scotland) Act of 1747 (20 Geo. II c. 43) which abolished most of the jurisdictions from 25 March 1748. Arguably this is a date which should rank with the Union of the Crowns in 1603 and the Union of the Parliaments of 1707 in the slow destruction of the traditional Scottish polity.

The principal author of the Heritable Jurisdictions (Scotland) Act was Lord Hardwicke, the great Lord Chancellor of England. His measure was opposed feebly by the English Tories and with some vigour by many Scotsmen, including not a few Whigs. After all, the legislation was in direct violation of the twentieth article of the Act of Union which guaranteed 'all heritable Offices, Superiorities, heritable Jurisdictions, Offices for life, and Jurisdictions for life . . . notwithstanding of this Treaty'. On this ground, as well as on grounds of inherent impracticability, the Court of Session in Scotland refused to co-operate in drawing up a list of the jurisdictions with a view to their abolition. Hardwicke was a firm believer in the unrestrained absolutism of the legislature. However, with practised ease he employed all the self-righteous humbug of the political lawyer to prove, to his own satisfaction in the House of Lords, that when the twentieth article of the Treaty of 1707 set out to guarantee heritable rights its true intent was to prepare the way for their elimination.[35] After the word-twisting, the practical difficulties remained. From the start the government knew that it had to offer substantial financial compensation to holders of the jurisdictions. After the refusal of the Lords of Session to draw up a list of relevant jurisdictions, the only possible way of proceeding was to invite people to file claims for compensation, and to test these judicially. In the event 157 claims were filed with demands for compensation coming altogether to £582,990. The government looked to the Court of Session to reduce both the number and value of these claims significantly, but was depressed by the thought of the delays likely to be incurred by the testing of so many titles.[36]

The Court of Session was in fact notably businesslike in coping with the problem. Duncan Forbes, the Lord President, owed his position to Lord Hardwicke, as the high sycophancy rate in his correspondence with the English legal luminary demonstrates,[37] so he drove his colleagues to as efficient a discharge of their duties as possible. At the same time, even those Scots most obsessed with the desirability of total uniformity with England in all matters realized that Scots M.P.s who supported the abolition of the heritable jurisdictions would suffer at the next election if the legislation was not seen to be moderate and reasonable both in form and effect.[38] On 15 December 1747 the Court of Session issued an Act of Sederunt designed 'for the more speedy Dispatch of the Claims entered into Court anent the Heretable Jurisdictions'. They ruled that there was to be no repeated arguing of the same point of law with successive claims. A point of principle once established was to be a permanent guide. Furthermore interlocking titles from the same district, or which had originally formed part of one jurisdiction, were to be tested as to their general validity before individual units were formally valued.[39]

The records of the claims are quite fascinating. All the significant claimants had printed claims made out on their behalf by Edinburgh lawyers, and obviously nobody underestimated either the extent or the value of his jurisdictions. On the other hand, the government lawyers were only too anxious to challenge virtually every claim to jurisdiction on various grounds. Specimen records had to be submitted to show that the jurisdiction was actually being exercised. Once over that hurdle, a claim could be challenged on the grounds that there was lacking totally satisfactory and continuous documentation of the grant of the rights, or as a last resort obsolete and ineffective Stewart legislation of previous centuries could be cited to vitiate the whole concept of heritable jurisdictions. Some of the claims clearly were bogus. Others raised tricky points of law, an example being the claim of James, Earl of Morton, for compensation for the fact that he was 'infeft by Charter under the Great Seal, proceeding on a British Act of Parliament, in the Earldom of Orkney and Lordship of Zetland, with the hereditary Offices of Justiciary, Sheriffdom or Stewartry'. Just what these words implied depended on an analysis of the very complex jurisdictional and legal history of the Northern Isles, though Morton was sure that they amounted to regalian rights. On 22 January 1748 the Lords of Session finally ruled that this was not so. They decided that the justiciary was not distinct from the stewartry or sheriffdom and that all three terms implied simply a sheriff's authority, and not the regality which Morton did in fact manage to establish as the status of smaller jurisdictions which he held elsewhere in Scotland.

Particularly irritating must have been the experience of Sir Andrew Agnew of Lochnaw, last of the hereditary sheriffs of Wigtown. He was a remarkable man who had defended Blair Castle in early 1746 with success against no less a foe than Lord George Murray. Admittedly Lord George's two four-pound cannon had little chance of smashing the castle's seven foot walls, but Sir Andrew put up a spirited performance, coping with a hail of red-hot shot with great aplomb, whilst displaying a truly volcanic temper towards any of his officers who breathed the thought of surrender. Blair was held for Hanover mainly because its garrison was much more frightened of the peerless baronet who commanded them than of the Jacobite besiegers. Sir Andrew's next campaign was the vexing rearguard action necessary to receive less than he thought his due for a jurisdiction held by his family since 1330. By 18 March 1748 the Court of Session had completed its task. As one of its members said, 'it was our wish to proceed impartially, and neither to load the public unreasonably nor to lay the seeds of discontents among the subjects.'[40] They had nevertheless reduced the bill to His Majesty's Government to a manageable £164,232 16s. 0d. The last success of Duncan Forbes of Culloden, who died early in December 1747, was the preservation to the baron courts of a modest but meaningful jurisdiction comprising not only recovery of rent and the keeping of the peace at fairs and markets but also civil cases concerning disputes up to 40 shillings in value. Forbes was convinced that only thus could cheap, swift and accessible justice be made available to the average Scots country-man.[41]

Politically inevitable and socially significant though it was, the abolition of the heritable jurisdictions was not as relevant as most assumed. Keppoch and Lochiel, arch rebels both, had no regalities, the Whig Duke of Argyll, who sulked publicly at the passing of the legislation despite being much the biggest beneficiary from compensation, had a vast regality covering 500 square miles. The direct consequences of the '45 were in fact more para-doxical than is generally realized. Although legislation abolishing ward-holding – a form of military tenure peculiar to the Highlands – was like so much else inevitable, it scarcely altered the price of green cheese in the sense that the débâcle in which the rising culminated spelled the end of Jacobite rebellion as a conceivable option in the Highlands. A worried government, passing through an evanescent spasm of interest in matters Scottish, embodied its hopes for an anti-Jacobite reconstruction of High-land society in programmes of action which mostly turned out to be total, not to say hilarious, failures.

The government obviously expected that the principal instrument for socio-economic change in the Highlands would be the power which for-feiture of many estates placed in the hands of the Crown. Indeed in the circle of the Duke of Cumberland in August 1749 there, were thoughts of adding by purchase estates which had not been forfeited, 'as would form a Chain betwixt Inverness and the Western Seas, whether under For-feiture, or not'. The surveyor sent to examine the feasibility of such ideas was also to see if the law could be put into effect against 'Popish Priests'. Cumberland himself had some inklings of the staggering potential costs, at least to the point of fussing about the debt burden which many of the estates were known to carry.[42] Financial and other considerations ensured that most of the forty-one estates forfeited were sold by the Barons of the Exchequer by public auction to pay creditors. However thirteen of the forty-one were by an Annexing Act of March 1752 inalienably annexed to the Crown and managed as a public enterprise between 1752 and 1784 under unpaid Commissioners charged with using the rents of the estates to promote 'the Protestant Religion, good Government Industry and Manu-factures, and the Principles of Duty and Loyalty to His Majesty'. In practice lowish rents to encourage loyalty acted as a disincentive to eco-nomic change even in agriculture, while the establishment of manufactures in the Highlands was an uphill struggle, as the Board of Trustees for Fisheries and Manufactures in Scotland had learned in the course of their own efforts since 1727. Though Commissioners were unpaid, administra-tive expenses were high, and attempts to colonize Highland moors with settlements of ex-soldiers merely proved that a well-developed taste for loafing and liquor could not easily be shaken off when a man left the regular army. Some good was done by shrewd investment in communica-tions, mainly roads and bridges, but the lawyer Commissioner Lord Kames had to admit at the end of the day that much of the government money spent in the Highlands had been 'no better than water spilt on the ground'.[43]

There was nothing unusual about the experience of the Commissioners. In the second half of the eighteenth century the Highlands of Scotland were the object of a great many proposals aimed at inducing rapid economic development. They all breathed optimism, and they all came to grief on the bitter realities of a poorly-endowed and remote region. It is a measure of the sagacity of the father of modern economics, Adam Smith, that his great work *An Inquiry into the Nature and Causes of the Wealth of Nations*, published in 1776, is deafeningly silent about the problem of the contemporary Highland economy.[44] Virtually no attempt at social reconstruction north of the Highland Line since 1745 has produced the results originally aimed at. The odd field where government objectives were achieved can usually be shown to have been largely untouched by government policy. Thus Highland Protestantism was indeed revitalized and given a new confidence and appeal, by 1800, but by a handful of Evangelical clergymen assisted by devout groups of laymen known as the 'Men' rather than by state sponsorship.[45]

Conclusion

Between the triumphant downhill charge of Dundee's Highland infantry at Killiecrankie in July 1689 and the despairing, desperate and unsuccessful onslaught of the centre and right of the Jacobite line at Culloden in April 1746, lie the best part of sixty eventful years. The clansmen who lay in bloody broken swathes under Cumberland's guns as the tartan tide ebbed on Drummossie Moor beside Culloden House had died for 'James VIII' as their forbears had fought and died for James VII and II, but the content and meaning of the phenomenon we call Jacobitism had shown no such constancy. It was the product not only of a relatively static ideology but also of constantly changing social, economic and political circumstances. Each Jacobite rising was unique in nature. It is not reasonable to suggest that the bulk of the Jacobite rank and file on any battle-field had a very sophisticated understanding of why they stood where they did. A great many would clearly have preferred to have been almost anywhere else, having been recruited by threats of violence against themselves or their families. Those in the ranks impelled primarily by loyalty often focused their loyalty on their immediate leader, be he landlord, clan chief, or the usual ambiguous mixture of the two. As Angus Ban helped to carry his dying father, Macdonald of Keppoch, off the battlefield of Culloden, a wounded Macdonald leaning on his own son's shoulder told his youngster to go help Keppoch as his first duty was to his chief, not to his father. Many a Jacobite faced terrible judicial death sustained by religious faith, more often than not faith of a Scots Episcopal or High Anglican variety. Some may even have been motivated to join a rebellion mainly by religious loyalty, and here one thinks of the unfortunate Lancashire Roman Catholics of the '15. Confusion, not clarity is the mark of minds under shearing, contradictory pressures. The historian has, or should have, the privilege of intellectual detachment, however strong his natural sympathies.

What seems clear is that Claverhouse's rebellion was the end of an epoch, the dying spasm of an abandoned political order, rather than the dawning of the Jacobite era. The Restoration regime in Scotland rested on the solid conservatism of the nobility and gentry. They disliked Parliaments, which the Crown only summoned when it needed money grants or wanted to ram, generally unpalatable, legislative proposals down the throat of the political nation. They preferred the 'good old form of Government by his Majesty's Privy Council', on which they took it for granted they would be adequately represented. Equally, they disliked a Scottish standing army, which the country could hardly afford, and in 1663 persuaded Charles II to dispense with most of his regular forces in exchange for the establishment of a Scottish militia, organized on a county basis and usually commanded by the great nobles. Militia units were the crucial underpinning of Stewart power in late seventeenth-century Scotland.[1] They held down the Campbell lands for James VII after Argyll's unsuccessful 1685 rising. When no great man rallied to Claverhouse, when only two and a half thousand fighting men could be assembled to fight for Scotland's rightful king, the regime was clearly dead. In England James fell in some ways like a comic-opera villain, his uncomprehending wooden arrogance changing under pressure into complete nervous prostration. In Scotland, where politics were more bitter, more blood was shed, but the cause of the collapse of the government was the same as in England – withdrawal of support by the outraged conservative aristocratic classes, both landed and urban.

The death of Claverhouse was remembered, if only to help people to forget the shameful final rout of the Jacobite army. It reinforced an ideology of royalism and sacrifice assiduously built up around the memory of the Great Marquis of Montrose by the Restoration regime itself. However, such an ideology could only inspire action after James VII and II had become an object of affection for his former subjects, and to achieve that it was necessary to remove him from their immediate view. At St Germain the pious exile benefited from all the resentment roused by the new Continental entanglements into which William of Orange led his British kingdoms, and by the zeal with which that prince strove to retain as much as he could of his predecessor's high-handed political system. In Scotland in particular the reign of Dutch William was the seedbed of much future trouble. Politics were unstable, corrupt and soured by William's evident lack of interest in the realm. Reconciliation in the ecclesiastical field was impossible because of *odium theologicum*, while the funds which had rendered the sixteenth-century Scottish Reformation such a surprisingly untraumatic and good-humoured affair, by massively cushioning those clergymen on the losing side, were simply not available. Episcopalian bitterness and insecurity sharpened Episcopalian Jacobitism. Clergymen shamelessly and habitually sold down the river by sovereigns who despised them between the first Indulgence offered to their Presbyterian enemies in 1669 and 1688, became articulate spokesmen for the dynasty which had so often betrayed them. This was change indeed from the 'Kirk invisible' of Claverhouse's rising.

When asked to do something about the problem of a rapidly rising temperature, the professional politician's first instinct is always to tamper with the thermometer, and it was in this spirit that William urged Union with Scotland on his deathbed. He wanted to solve the problem of resentments he had done much to create by eliminating the Scottish Parliament, the principle vehicle through which those resentments could be expressed. In practice Union was off the political agenda as an urgent issue until the mounting and mismanaged crisis in Anglo-Scottish relations restored its priority in the eyes of English politicians in 1704. The pre-arranged package which was pushed through the Scottish Parliament in 1707 to achieve the abolition of that body was perhaps the biggest single political gift ever handed to the Jacobite cause in Scotland. That the Union was profoundly unpopular in the northern kingdom was the one point on which its enemies and, in private, its supporters, were agreed. The latter hoped to render it irreversible by a classic piece of forced polarization of opinion. Most Scots were to be made to swallow something they did not want by being told that the alternative – Jacobitism – was even worse.

The old tradition of radical Presbyterian nationalism, a tune whose last notes had been trumpeted defiantly by Fletcher of Saltoun and Lord Belhaven, was emasculated after 1707. The great majority of Presbyterian divines became what they have, by and large, been ever since – willing prisoners of an English political and social Establishment which viewed them at best with patronizing amusement. What shook the Union to its foundations was the willingness of laymen touched by the Fletcher of Saltoun tradition to use Jacobitism as the tool for their nationalist aspirations. When the diarist and biographer James Boswell met the old Jacobite exile, the Earl Marischal, in Berlin in 1764, that veteran 'talked against the Union' and gave Boswell a copy of Barbour's *Brus*, the epic poem of Scotland's medieval War of Independence. Talking to Jean-Jacques Rousseau, the French writer and philosopher, in 1764 Boswell discovered that the Earl Marischal had asked Rousseau to write a life of Fletcher of Saltoun.[2] Having fought in the '15 and the '19 George Keith, tenth and last Earl Marischal of Scotland, entered the service of Frederick the Great of Prussia, along with his brother James, a service in which both died. Although he did what he could, which was very little, to persuade the French government to give adequate backing to the '45, it is clear that the Earl Marischal did not approve of, or expect success to attend, the adventure. Aeneas Macdonald, the banker who was captured after Culloden and turned King's Evidence, then said that:

the doctrine of the most sensible people even of that party (such as Lord

Marischal) looked upon any such attempt (though concerted with some forethought) as unlawful without the Consent of the Nation, and I do much detest such mad flights.[3]

By 1759 the Earl Marischal had been pardoned by George II and allowed to inherit property, though his attainder was not reversed.

In 1708, however, the scandalous lack of an adequate garrison in Scotland and the temper of the nation would probably have enabled the Old Pretender to re-possess his 'Ancient Kingdom' with very little fighting had he only been able to persuade the French naval and military commanders of his expedition to do their duty. Abortive as the '08 was, it brings out three major themes of later Jacobite history. One is the ambiguous attitude of the Court of France, an attitude sensed all too clearly by contemporaries. The second is the strange but important relationship between the exiled dynasty and the French privateering industry, a relationship going back to the earliest years of James VII and II in exile at St Germain when that monarch had commissioned privateers to sail under his own flag against English and Scots shipping, and had obtained French commissions for many more.[4] The third is the way in which the meaning of Jacobitism had changed with the death of James VII and II. He was by instinct and conviction an autocrat distinguished all his life by a deep and sincere lack of interest in any personality or opinions other than his own. His son had to offer his prospective subjects political options attractive to them, or there was no chance of turning his shadowy kingship into a reality. To the Scots he had to stand for repeal of the Union which his own ancestors from James VI and I to Charles II had intermittently tried to bring about. The change ran much deeper than this one issue. It was a theme of Jacobite proganda by such writers as the Chevalier Andrew Michael Ramsay (1686–1743) that the new Jacobite claimant to the British thrones had no 'ambition of absolute government'. The Chevalier Ramsay, an intriguing man introduced to mystical religion in Scotland by George Garden, converted to not very orthodox Roman Catholicism by Archbishop Fénelon in France, and a confidant of that remarkable mystic Madame Guyon, even used his *Life of Fénelon* to stress that James had been educated to believe in balanced government where royal authority was moderated by the advice of the wisest and most experienced subjects.[5]

Though not an inspiring leader, James Edward might have made rather a good constitutional monarch had he reached a throne. The risings of 1715 should have gained him three, for they were deep-rooted in profound economic, social, and political discontent, and not just in Scotland. In 1711 no less a person than that ferocious Irish Tory, Jonathan Swift, argued that Queen Anne was 'in the full peaceable Possession of Her

Kingdoms, and of the Hearts of her People; among whom, hardly one in five hundred are in the Pretender's Interest'.[6] It does seem to have been the accession of George I and the establishment of a rabidly partisan minority ascendancy in Whig hands which alienated so large a proportion of the English political nation as to render the whole British political fabric susceptible to revolution. Particular complexes of grievances triggered off rebellious activity in Scotland, the north-eastern part of England, and Lancashire, but it is clear that had dynamism and success marked the early stages of the rising, there would have been an immense reservoir of sympathy to draw on as the Jacobite armies swept down on London. To Mar's incompetence as a man of action the House of Hanover owed an immeasurable debt.

After 1716 the real problem of Jacobite history is why there ever was another major rebellion. The '19 was a nonsense from the start. It was a mere diversionary force which even its crazily unrealistic Spanish sponsors did not think capable of major achievement. After the guts were hammered out of it by mortar fire and grenades in Glen Shiel the whole episode redounded to the discredit of the exiled Stewarts, both because of its miserable failure and because it showed the Old Pretender as little more than a marionette in the hands of anti-British foreign politicians. Of course, George I and George II, ably and unscrupulously seconded by Walpole, continued the policy of total proscription of the Tories, probably the natural majority party in the political nation of the time, while the exiled line was prolonged by the birth of the Pretender's sons, but the sands were steadily running out for the Jacobite cause. However much James Edward might have graced a throne, he possessed none of the talents needed to seize one.

The '45 cannot in fact be explained in the same positive terms as the '15. It was the product of French intrigue, the survival of Jacobite ideology amongst a minority of Scots, and the known inadequacy of Hanoverian home defence precautions. Two other factors were crucial. One was the obstinate, insensitive egotism of Prince Charles which drove the rebellion relentlessly to its bloody climax, and the other was the massive apathy of the British peoples towards their arrogant, unrepresentative, and appallingly incompetent government. What Charles could never grasp was that most Scots and a majority of Englishmen still reckoned that he was marginally the worst of two evils. Positive support he could not rouse after he crossed the English border. The private huffing of frustrated Tory M.P.s proved worthless to him. He had no contact with them. After he retreated they counted for so little that the Pelhams unhesitatingly engineered a major political crisis at Westminster early in February 1746 in order to coerce George II.

Lord George Murray, than whom few men thought more highly of Lord

George Murray's military talents, knew well that the run of Jacobite victories in the field from Prestonpans to Falkirk owed a vast amount to luck. Highland charges had smashed home against inadequate defensive firepower mainly because the Jacobites, until Culloden, never faced a well-served field artillery. Drilled to move like clockwork, good gunners could fire a field piece once every fifteen seconds by 1746. Indeed outstanding gun crews could fire for brief periods at twelve-second intervals, faster than an individual could fire a musket, and infinitely more lethal against massed targets. Guns fired 'grape', which was clusters of iron balls roughly the size of golf balls, at short range and 'case', which was bagged musket shot the size of marbles, when the enemy was at the muzzles of the fieldpieces. The result was indescribable.[7] Against a well-equipped and disciplined army like that of Cumberland, only guerrilla tactics made sense, but Charles had not come to be a king in the heather. Many of his leading followers were on the verge of bankruptcy before the rebellion, as the sale of such a large proportion of the forfeited estates to satisfy creditors demonstrated, but by Culloden most of them were bitterly aware that they had been tricked into committing themselves to a prince with the temper of a despot by insincere assurances about massive French aid.

There is no evidence that France was ever prepared to support the '45 with a significant proportion of her naval and military resources. The invasion planned for early 1744 was a serious proposition. Its political programme was shrewd and appealing. Implemented, it would have produced a government in London incapable of any strong initiatives, either domestically or in foreign affairs, because it would have lacked the means to control the legislature. However, it is at least arguable that as well as being clearly in the interests of the French, such a situation was desirable from the point of view of the British peoples. The '45 was quite different. Whereas in 1744 the French had a promising plan foiled by the Royal Navy, the '45 was an irresponsible gamble which the French did not even back to the extent they could have without seriously straining themselves. Eventually there was a heavy concentration of Royal Navy ships in Scottish waters. The last battle of the '45 was a determined and bloody naval action in Loch nan Uamh on 3 May 1746 between British warships and two big French privateers from Nantes. Earlier in the rising it would have been easy for the French to slip into Scotland significantly greater quantities of men, arms, and money than they actually dispatched. Losses would have occurred, but they would have been a small price to pay for breaking a weak blockade. Even at the very end of the crisis, after Culloden had been fought, a sum of 35,000 gold louis d'ors was successfully run into the west coast of the Highlands. Louis XV no doubt expected it to be used to pay troops. In practice this money, known to history as the Lochar-kaig treasure, was partly misappropriated by men like Murray of

Broughton, but mostly disbursed under the supervision of Macpherson of Cluny for the very reasonable purpose of alleviating suffering among families who had lost almost everything for the Jacobite cause.[8]

Absolutely central to the long-term pacification of the Highlands was the reconciliation and reintegration into the existing political system of the Jacobite section of the Highland ruling class. As in the north-eastern parts of England after the '15, economic decline eliminated a fair number of Jacobite families in the Highlands after 1746, but there remained a hard core of former Jacobite houses which were still locally significant. Such was the scale of disillusionment with France and with Prince Charles in these circles that the process of reconciliation could have started to gather serious momentum earlier than it did. The principal obstacle to this development was the violence of anti-Scottish feeling amongst the contemporary English Establishment, a violence which naturally tended to fade with time, but not universally. Cumberland retained a venomous dislike of Scots in general, despite the fact that their most ancient university had fallen over itself with eagerness to invite him in February 1746 to become its Chancellor. St Andrews University, desperate to bury memories of former Jacobite peccadilloes, even enclosed the seal on the Instrument of Cumberland's election in a gold box, which the university could not afford but whose cost was loaned to them by 'Mr John Craigie of Dumbarney, Regent in St Leonard's College'. Dr John Pringle, a former student at St Andrews and currently a physician on Cumberland's staff, suggested that it would be appropriate also to bestow a Doctorate of Laws on Sir Everard Fawkener, Postmaster-General of Great Britain and Secretary at War to the Duke of Cumberland. The doctorate was bestowed.[9] The university next agreed to light bonfires and ring bells to celebrate the birthday of its new Chancellor.[10] It was the start of a long career of boot licking and worse to the London Establishment, though outsiders may derive consolation from the thought that the material rewards have always tended to fall well below the university's hopes.

A glance at the huge correspondence which Sir Everard organized so meticulously for Cumberland is very revealing about the origins of his royal master's sustained Scotophobia. A host of penurious Presbyterian clergymen bombarded Cumberland with fawning requests for everything from a kirk to a royal almonership or chaplaincy, or indeed for the Principalship of St Andrews University. Their letters to the man to whom 'under Providence we owe our Deliverance' tended to grossly exaggerate the strength and universality of Jacobitism in order to stress the need for the government to cosset its friends in North Britain.[11] Cumberland was not particularly responsive. He was enmeshed in arguments about compensating Hanoverian loyalists like Lord Sutherland for expenses incurred during the rebellion. Cumberland had been deeply unimpressed by the performance of Sutherland's men who, in truth, showed extreme reluctance to stand and fight during the skirmishes in the northern Highlands.[12] The early 1750s saw the duke still calling for more attainders; for a ruthless purge of 'Jacobite sympathizers' ranging from Andrew Fletcher Lord Milton, Argyll's man of business, to professors in Glasgow university; and for action against magistrates who refused, as many did, seriously to enforce the laws against Highland dress. The last problem may well have hinged on the fact that the legislation which condemned a man to six months in prison if he wore a kilt did not specify who was to pay for his upkeep there.[13]

Nevertheless, by 1763 the pardoned Earl Marischal had taken the oaths to the *de facto* government and was negotiating, a little nervously, for the re-purchase of his ancestral estates. In February 1764 he did indeed buy the Keith portion of the estate for £31,320, with nobody bidding against him. Lord Lovat's eldest son elicited official sympathy early on, but in 1748 Baron Edlin could write that it was still safer to give him a pension to ten times the annual value of his ancestral lands than restore them. By 1774 Major-General Simon Fraser of Lovat was so distinguished a servant of the British Crown that the restoration of his estates in that year was universally applauded. He had not only raised the Fraser Highlanders but had also led them on to the Plains of Abraham outside Quebec in late 1759 to help General Wolfe, against whom he had fought in the '45, deal a lethal blow to French Canada by the victory which won Quebec but cost him his life. After 1774 the restoration of the other forfeited annexed estates was merely a question of time. It was vital that none of the heirs of the forfeiting Jacobites had encouraged armed resistance to the new regime on their confiscated properties. The slightest hint of agrarian violence by the tenantry deeply alarmed the Hanoverian authorities,[14] and it seems clear that James Stewart in Aucharn was hung in 1752 after the fatal shooting of Colin Campbell of Glenure, Crown factor on the forfeited estate of Stewart of Ardsheal, less because his trial proved him guilty of the deed than as a warning to a restive district.[15] The American War of Independence, when the heirs of men who bled at Culloden, at least in some measure for Scottish independence, flocked to raise regiments to sustain the claim of Westminster to ultimate authority over the American colonies, was the final test. In 1784, with America lost, the estates were disannexed. The wheel had come full cycle.

The Jacobite risings were an integral part of British politics. They were never primarily a culture clash. Those conservative Gaelic bards in the Highlands of Scotland who, from Killiecrankie to Culloden, persisted in regarding Jacobitism as a celtic crusade were suffering from a professional myopia which made them poor guides to the realities of a complex situation, and indeed often put them at odds with their own more sophisticated chiefs.[16] That Jacobite leaders were not as a group after 1707 particularly backward-looking is clear. John Holker, a Lancashire manufacturer who as a Roman Catholic Jacobite felt impelled to accept a lieutenancy in the Manchester Regiment in 1745, may serve as a last-ditch example. Escaping (blessedly, given the fate of his comrades) from Newgate to France, he became a pioneer of a mechanized, factory-organized French cotton industry.[17] English and Lowland Scots attitudes towards Gaelic civilization were usually unenlightened and the Jacobite rebellions made them briefly even more so, but by 1765 the Society in Scotland for Propagating Christian Knowledge and for Spreading the Gospel Among the Indians in America was promoting a Gaelic New Testament, and shortly afterwards was using the language in its schools. This belligerently Protestant and pro-Hanoverian body, with its splendid name, became one of the vehicles for an extraordinary metamorphosis in attitudes towards Gaelic-speaking Highlanders. Long dreaded by many of their Lowland compatriots as semi-savage denizens of an internal frontier region, they were, once their capacity to harm was broken, incorporated in the Scottish national self-image in the same way that Americans to some extent built their self-image on the safely dead savages of their own bigger frontier.[18] Men like Holker were conveniently forgotten. The loyal, uncomplaining tartan-clad clansmen of Culloden entered national mythology.

Yet there is more to the Jacobite risings than that mythology, however potent. They are an index of just how unsatisfactory a great many contemporaries found the historically much-lauded ruling cliques of Hanoverian Britain. After 1746 the antics of the exiled Stewarts were seen to be increasingly irrelevant. The family acknowledged this when Henry, the brother of Prince Charles, very sensibly accepted a cardinal's hat and an ecclesiastical career in 1747. Prince Charles was marginally less attractive in 1745 to most informed uncommitted opinion than George II, and vastly less attractive than George III, whose accession in 1760 marked the end of the proscription of what was left of the Tories. In these facts, as the last Earl Marischal might have said (but did not), lay the true tragedy of Culloden. Intellectually, Jacobitism was an emasculating experience for opposition to Westminster. The future lay with the radicals in America.

Notes

I THE PRE-HISTORY OF JACOBITISM

1. W. Bray (ed.), *Diary and Correspondence of John Evelyn, F.R.S.* (London, n.d.), p. 233.
2. A. H. Woolrych, 'The Collapse of the Great Rebellion', *History Today*, vol. VIII, no. 9 (September 1958), pp. 606–15.
3. M. Ashley, *General Monck* (London, 1977), chs. 12–15.
4. J. N. Figgis, *The Divine Right of Kings*, 2nd edn (Cambridge, 1914).
5. C. V. Wedgwood, *The Trial of Charles I* (London, 1964).
6. For an excellent survey of the triumphant phase of the Covenanting Revolution in Scotland see D. Stevenson, *The Scottish Revolution 1637–1644* (Newton Abbot, 1973). H. L. Rubinstein, *Captain Luckless: James, First Duke of Hamilton 1606–1649* (Edinburgh and London, 1975), fails to make the most of what case can be made for Hamilton.
7. C. E. Mallet, *A History of the University of Oxford* (London, 1924), vol. II, p. 448.
8. A. Clark (ed.), *The Life and Times of Anthony Wood, antiquary, of Oxford, 1632–1695 described by Himself. Vol. III: 1682–1695* (Oxford, 1894), pp. 63–4.
9. D. Ogg, *England in the Reigns of James II and William III*, paperback edn (O.U.P., 1969), p. 139.
10. R. Nicholson, *Scotland: The Later Middle Ages* (Edinburgh, 1974), pp. 184–5.
11. Quoted in G. Donaldson, *Scotland: James V – James VII* (Edinburgh, 1971), p. 380.
12. H. N. Paul, *The Royal Play of Macbeth* (New York, 1950).
13. A. Lang, *Sir George Mackenzie* (London, 1909), pp. 278–81.
14. Monro to Mackenzie of Delvine, 23 December 1691, printed in 'Letters To John Mackenzie Of Delvine Advocate, One Of The Principal Clerks Of Session From The Revd. Alexander Monro, D.D. Sometime Principal Of The University Of Edinburgh 1690 to 1698', in W. K. Dickson (ed.), *Miscellany of the Scottish History Society: Fifth Volume*, Scottish History Society, third series, vol. XXI (Edinburgh, 1933), pp. 219–21.
15. C. Hill, *The Intellectual Origins of the English Revolution* (Panther, 1972), pp. 179–81.
16. W. G. Scott-Moncrieff (ed.), *Narrative of Mr James Nimmo*, Scottish History Society, first series, vol. VI (Edinburgh, 1889), p. 92.
17. G. Davies, *The Oxford History of England: The Early Stuarts 1603–1660*, 2nd edn (Oxford, 1959), p. 159.
18. J. Buchan, *Montrose* (London, 1931), pp. 367–78.
19. For an account of the writing of Buchan's *Montrose*, its impact, and the way in which it was part of 'a confession of faith' by the author, see J. Buchan, *Memory Hold-The-Door* (London, 1940), pp. 197–9. Among recent biographies R. Williams, *Montrose: Cavalier in Mourning* (London, 1975) is a good example of the enduring attraction of the Buchan view of Montrose. A more astringent

and detached interpretation may be found in the writings of E. J. Cowan, and especially his 'Montrose and Argyll' in G. Menzie (ed.), *The Scottish Nation* (B.B.C., 1972), pp. 118–32, and *Montrose: For Covenant and King* (London, 1977).

20. Extracts from the contemporary *Mercurius Caledonius* edited by Thomas Saintserf and giving detailed accounts of the proceedings in both Aberdeen and Edinburgh were printed by Mark Napier in his *Memoirs of the Marquis of Montrose: Volume 2* (Edinburgh, 1856), pp. 825–37.

21. W. R. Kermack, 'Lord Lyon Sir Alexander Durham of Largo', *The Scottish Genealogist*, vol. XVII, no. 1 (March 1970), pp. 1–3.

22. J. C. Robbie, 'The Embalming Of Montrose', *The Book of the Old Edinburgh Club*, vol. I (1908), p. 37.

23. Sir Walter Scott, *Letters on Demonology and Witchcraft*, 2nd edn (London, 1885), p. 139.

24. P. Hume Brown (ed.), *The Register of the Privy Council of Scotland*, third series, vol. I, 1661–1664 (Edinburgh, 1908), p. 388.

25. Sir Thomas Innes of Learney, *Scots Heraldry*, 2nd edn (Edinburgh and London, 1956), pp. 77–80.

26. R. Kirk, *St Andrews* (London, 1954), ch. 5.

27. D. Fraser, *Discovering East Scotland* (Montrose, 1974), pp. 226–7.

28. A. and H. Tayler, *John Graham of Claverhouse* (London, 1939), p. 224.

29. C. S. Terry, *John Graham of Claverhouse, Viscount of Dundee 1648–1689* (London, 1905), pp. 45–8 and 85–101.

30. The relevant passage from R. Patten, *The History of the Late Rebellion*, 2nd edn (London, 1717) is reprinted in C. S. Terry, *The Jacobites and the Union* (Cambridge, 1922), p. 197.

31. 'Reasons for appointing and observing a day of Solemn Fasting and Humiliation etc.', National Library of Scotland (hereafter N.L.S.), MS. 1012. The writer has added notes stating that it was in great part drafted by Dr James Garden and that he, the writer, read it in the New Church, Aberdeen.

32. 'The Speech of Mr James Bradshaw', reprinted in *The Lyon In Mourning*, collected by Bishop Robert Forbes and edited by Henry Paton, Scottish History Society, vols. 20–22 (Edinburgh, 1895–6), vol. I, p. 50.

33. 'The Speech of David Morgan, Esquire', ibid., vol. I, p. 43.

34. 'The Speech of the Right Honourable Arthur Lord Balmerino, faithfully transcribed from his lordships own handwrit', ibid., vol. I, p. 54.

35. Atholl Muniments, Blair Castle, Box 50/I, 28–33, consists of a bundle of last speeches before execution of Lord Balmerino (two copies in different hands), the Reverend Thomas Coppoch, Major Donald Macdonald of Tiendrish, Thomas Deacon, James Bradshaw and James Dawson. The bundle seems to date from 1746. Biographical details of these and all other prisoners of the '45 may conveniently be found in Sir Bruce Gordon Seton and Jean Gordon Arnot (eds.), *The Prisoners of the '45*, Scottish History Society, third series, vols. XIII–XV (Edinburgh, 1928–9).

36. Archibald Cameron's last statements are reprinted in *The Lyon In Mourning*, vol. III, pp. 132–42.

2 THE GLORIOUS REVOLUTION AND THE FIRST JACOBITE REBELLION

1. V. G. Kiernan, 'Foreign Mercenaries and Absolute Monarchy', in T. Aston (ed.), *Crisis In Europe 1560–1660*, paperback edn (London, 1974), p. 136.

2. A. Joly, *Un Converti de Bossuet: James Drummond Duc De Perth 1648–1716* (Lille, 1934).
3. Sir Archibald Geikie, *The Founders of Geology* (London, 1905), pp. 53–4.
4. For Sibbald's career see F. P. Hett (ed.), *The Memoirs of Sir Robert Sibbald* (Oxford, 1932).
5. W. Ferguson, *Scotland: 1689 to the Present* (Edinburgh and London, 1968), pp. 1–2.
6. E. W. M. Balfour Melville (ed.), *An Account of the Proceedings of the Estates in Scotland 1689–1690*, 2 vols., Scottish History Society, third series, vol. XLVI (Edinburgh, 1954), vol. 1, p. 5.
7. Ibid., p. 11.
8. ibid., pp. 17, 24, 27, 46–7.
9. H. Hazlett, 'The Recruitment and Organisation of the Scottish Army in Ulster, 1642–9', in H. A. Cronne, T. W. Moody, and D. B. Quinn (eds.), *Essays in British and Irish History in Honour of James Eadie Todd* (London, 1949), pp. 107–33.
10. Melville (ed.), *An Account of the Proceedings of the Estates*, vol. 1, p. 29.
11. The best account of the battle is still that in C. S. Terry, *John Graham of Claverhouse* (London, 1905), ch. XVI. It is followed by A. and H. Tayler in their *John Graham of Claverhouse* (London, 1939).
12. J. P. Kenyon, 'The Revolution of 1688: Resistance and Contract', in N. McKendrick (ed.), *Historical Perspectives: Studies – in honour of J. H. Plumb* (London, 1974), pp. 43–69.
13. G. M. Straka, 'The Final Phase of Divine Right Theory in England 1688–1702', *English Historical Review*, LXXVII (1962), pp. 638–58, does not quite prove the importance of his theme.
14. C. S. Terry, *A History of Scotland* (Cambridge, 1920), p. 465.
15. R. Mousnier, *The Assassination of Henry IV*, English edn (London, 1973), pp. 283–7.
16. J. P. Kenyon, *Revolution Principles: The Politics of Party 1689–1720* (Cambridge, 1977).
17. W. Wilson, *The House of Airlie*, 2 vols. (London, 1924), vol. II, p. 91.
18. C. R. Boxer, 'Some Second Thoughts On The Third Anglo-Dutch War, 1672–1674', in *Transactions of the Royal Historical Society*, fifth series, vol. 19 (1969).
19. Lyon King Sir Charles Erskine to Lord Lauderdale, 26 Nov. 1672, National Library of Scotland, MS. 98, no. 15.
20. W. Wilson, *The House of Airlie*, vol. II, pp. 108–9.
21. W. Mackay, 'The Highland Host (1678)', *Transactions of the Gaelic Society of Inverness*, vol. 32 (1924–5), p. 67.
22. J. R. Elder, *The Highland Host of 1678* (Aberdeen, 1914), p. 31.
23. Lady Murray to Lord John Murray, 14 Jan. 1689, Atholl MSS., Blair Castle, Box 29, I(5)96.
24. Marchioness of Atholl to Lord John Murray, 5 Jan. 1689, Atholl MSS., Box 29, I(5)93.
25. Duke of Hamilton to Lord John Murray, 3 June 1689, Atholl MSS., Box 29, I(5)118.
26. Same to same, 30 May 1689, Atholl MSS., Box 29, I(5)116.
27. W. Wilson, *The House of Airlie*, vol. II, pp. 109–10.
28. A. Philip, *The Parish of Longforgan* (Edinburgh, 1895), pp. 121–8; A. H. Millar (ed.), *Glamis Book of Record*, Scottish History Society, vol. 9 (Edinburgh, 1890), pp. 94–5.

29. Lord James Murray to Lady Murray, 11 Aug. 1689, Athol MSS., Box 29, I(5)173.
30. See M. Ashley, *The Glorious Revolution of 1688* (Panther, 1968).
31. G. Donaldson, *Scotland: James V–James VII*, p. 382.
32. Dundee Town Council Minutes, vol. VI, 1669–1707, entry for 27 May 1684, Dundee District Archives, City Chambers, Dundee.
33. ibid., 19 August, 18 Sept., 30 Dec. 1684.
34. ibid., 22 June 1685.
35. ibid., 23 and 29 June 1686.
36. ibid., 2 Dec. 1686.
37. A. Keith, *A Thousand Years of Aberdeen* (Aberdeen, 1972), pp. 271–2.
38. W. Stephen, *The Story of Inverkeithing and Rosyth* (Edinburgh and London, 1938), pp. 64–5.
39. T. C. Smout, 'The Glasgow merchant community in the seventeenth century', *Scottish Historical Review*, vol. XLVII (1968), pp. 56, 67.
40. G. Stewart, *Curiosities of Glasgow Citizenship* (Glasgow, 1881), pp. 3–5.
41. 'Unto His Illustrious Highness William Prince of Orange The address of the Provost Bailies and Council of the City of Glasgow, Jan. 29, 1689', N.L.S., MSS. 2617, fol. 8.
42. A. D. Murdoch (ed.), *The Grameid*, Scottish History Society, vol. 3 (Edinburgh, 1888), pp. ix–xlviii.
43. The roll-call of the Jacobite army will be found in ibid., pp. 118–70, along with very full scholarly discussion in footnotes.
44. W. R. Kermack, *The Clan MacGregor* (Edinburgh and London, 1953).
45. I. Moncreiffe, *The Robertsons* (Edinburgh and London, 1954), p. 16.
46. J. Prebble, *Glencoe* (London, 1966), pp. 36–8.
47. I. Moncreiffe, *The Robertsons*, p. 15.
48. Notably Audrey Cunningham in her distinguished study, *The Loyal Clans* (Cambridge, 1932).
49. 'Extracts from the Instructions left by James II for his Son, 1692' are conveniently printed as Appendix I of Sir Charles Petrie, *The Jacobite Movement*, 3rd edn (London, 1959).
50. Sir James Balfour Paul (ed.), *The Scots Peerage*, 9 vols. (Edinburgh, 1904–14), vol. 1, pp. 475–6.
51. Lord James Murray to Lord John Murray, 5 Sept. 1689, Atholl MSS., Box 29, I(5)184.
52. W. Ferguson, *Scotland's Relations with England: a Survey to 1707* (Edinburgh, 1977), pp. 170–72.

3 THE GROWTH OF JACOBITE SENTIMENT
FROM THE REVOLUTION TO 1704

1. C. Petrie, *The Jacobite Movement*, 3rd edn, pp. 118–19.
2. W. Baird, *George Drummond An Edinburgh Lord Provost of the Eighteenth Century* (Edinburgh, 1912), pp. 49–50. This book is a limited edition of twenty copies reprinted from the 4th volume of *The Book of the Old Edinburgh Club*.
3. P. Haffenden, 'The Crown and the Colonial Charters 1675–1688', Parts I and II, *The William and Mary Quarterly*, vol. XV, nos. 3 and 4 (July and October 1958), pp. 297–311 and 452–66.
4. A. L. Murray, 'The Scottish Treasury 1667–1708', *The Scottish Historical Review*, vol. 45 (1966), p. 104.

5. A. Cunningham, 'The Revolution Government in the Highlands', ibid., vol. 16 (1919), p. 29.

6. J. Prebble, *Glencoe*, pp. 312–18.

7. D. C. MacTavish (ed.), *The Commons of Argyll: Name Lists of 1685 and 1692* (Lochgilphead, 1935).

8. E. Carpenter, *The Protestant Bishop* (London, 1956), pp. 162–3, 172–5 and 177–81.

9. C. S. Terry, *A History of Scotland* (Cambridge, 1920), pp. 473–4.

10. W. Mackay, 'A Famous Minister of Daviot, 1672–1726', *Transactions of the Gaelic Society of Inverness*, vol. XII (1885–6), pp. 244–56.

11. D. Maclean, 'Highland Libraries in the Eighteenth Century', ibid., vol. XXI (1922–4), pp. 69–97.

12. D. Maclean, 'Life and Literary Labours of the Reverend Robert Kirk, of Aberfoyle', ibid., pp. 328–66.

13. A revealing collection of documents relating to Robert Kirk can be found in the Scottish Record Office G.D.50/75. The collection includes the marriage contract between Kirk and Isabel Campbell; a subsequent bond thereanent between Kirk and Campbell of Carwhin; a bond by the Earl of Menteith to Kirk and a draft bond by Kirk to Menteith, as well as a bond from James Campbell of Glendaruel to Robert Kirk. The bulk of the collection consists of letters from Robert Kirk to Colin Campbell of Carwhin, mostly on the subject of debts, but containing occasional references to other matters.

14. D. B. Smith, 'Mr Robert Kirk's Note-book', *The Scottish Historical Review*, vol. XVIII, no. 72 (July 1921), pp. 237–48.

15. W. Christie, 'The History of the Episcopal Church in the Diocese of Brechin 1688–1875', University of Dundee, unpublished Ph.D. Thesis (1967), ch. 3.

16. A. Mackay, *Three Scots Bishops* (Peterhead, 1918), pp. 9–27.

17. Transcript of the Register of the Presbytery of Dunkeld 1706–1717', S.R.O., R.H.2/1/69, entry for 28 January 1707. This particular transcript was made by the Reverend John Hunter B.D., Minister of Rattray 1894–1915, and is now in the Scottish Record Office in Edinburgh.

18. ibid., entry for 25 February 1707. The standard source for the Jacobite peerage and gentry is Melville Henry Massue, Marquis de Ruvigny and Raineval, *The Jacobite Peerage, Baronetage, Knightage, and Grants of Honour*. A facsimile of the original 1904 edition has recently been issued with a new Introduction by Roger Ararat (London and Edinburgh, 1974). For an interesting statement that Roman Catholicism in the area of Perthshire around Stobhall was no more ancient than the entourage of the fourth Earl of Perth see Sir Arthur Mitchell (ed.), *Macfarlane's Geographical Collections*, Scottish History Society, 3 vols. (Edinburgh, 1906–8), p. 128.

19. 'Transcript of Presbytery of Dunkeld 1706–1717', entries for 5 August 1707; 23 December 1707; 21 January 1708; and 4 May 1708.

20. ibid., entry for 21 January 1708; and entry for 17 February 1708.

21. Archbishop Sharp to David second Earl of Wemyss, 22 January 1678, printed in Sir William Fraser, *Memorials of the Family of Wemyss of Wemyss* (Edinburgh, 1888), p. 137. The other pieces of correspondence between Sharp and the Earl which appear in this book show just how closely they worked together.

22. 'Transcript of Presbytery of Dunkeld 1706–1717', entries for 25 March 1707; 15 July 1707; 29 October 1707; and 23 December 1707.

23. ibid., entry for 7 May 1713.

24. Information on the Edwards is derived from Hew Scott (ed.), *Fasti Ecclesiae*

Scoticanae, vol. V, New Edition (Edinburgh, 1925), as is the biographical material later adduced in connection with Henry Christie and William Spens.

25. For a recent study of Sir William Bruce see H. Fenwick, *Architect Royal* (Kineton, 1970).

26. *The Register of the Privy Council of Scotland*, third series, vol. XVI, A.D. 1691 (Edinburgh, H.M.S.O., 1970), pp. 134–7.

27. *A Description of the County of Angus Translated from the Original Latin of Robert Edward Minister of Murroes* (Dundee, printed by T. Colville, 1793). This pamphlet was reprinted by the Forfar and District Historical Society in 1967.

28. C. Findlay, 'Brechin Castle, Angus', *Scottish Field* (December 1970), pp. 19–23.

29. There is an excellent entry for King in the *Dictionary of National Biography*.

30. E. Carpenter, *The Protestant Bishop* (London, 1956), ch. XVI.

31. The 1690 act is conveniently reprinted as the first document in D. J. Withrington, 'Lists of schoolmasters teaching Latin', *Miscellany X*, Scottish History Society, fourth series, pp. 131–2.

32. R. G. Cant, *The University of St Andrews*, 2nd edn (London and Edinburgh, 1970), pp. 77–80. I have benefited in this area from the learning and generosity of Mr Robert Smart, Archivist and Keeper of Muniments to the University of St Andrews.

33. *Deputati commissionis parliamenti ad visitandas academias et scholas etc.* This is a folio broadside of nineteen lines set within a border of type ornaments. Its date is undoubtedly late 1690, though no date is given on the broadside. This is probably the most extraordinary single sheet of paper ever printed relating to the universities of the British Isles. One copy is known. It was Item 34 on Catalogue 110 of Messrs Richardson of 26 Charing Cross Road, W.C.2.

34. R. S. Rait, *The Universities of Aberdeen* (Aberdeen, 1895), p. 171.

35. For the Revolution Settlement in Glasgow University see J. D. Mackie, *The University of Glasgow 1451–1951* (Glasgow, 1954), chs. IX and X.

36. D. B. Horn, *A Short History of the University of Edinburgh 1556–1889* (Edinburgh, 1967), p. 36.

37. St Andrews University Senate Minutes, 16 March, 9 April, and 30 May 1696; St Andrews University Muniments.

38. ibid., 11 May, 4 July, 20 July, 25 December 1696; 27 May, 29 October 1697.

39. ibid., 16 August 1697; 6 January 1698.

40. King's College Minutes, 5 February, 21 February, 12 March, 17 March, 7 May 1711; 11 February and 2 March 1712; Aberdeen University Library MS. KC40.

41. T. M. Devine, 'The Cromwellian Union and the Scottish Burghs: the case of Aberdeen and Glasgow, 1652–60', in J. Butt and J. T. Ward (eds.), *Scottish Themes* (Scottish Academic Press, 1976), pp. 1–16.

42. The best introduction to Scotland's late seventeenth-century economic crisis is T. C. Smout, *Scottish Trade on the Eve of the Union* (Edinburgh and London, 1963), pp. 244–53.

43. B. Seton, 'A Seventeenth Century Deal in Corn', *Scottish Historical Review*, vol. 18 (1921), pp. 253–6.

44. E. E. B. Thomson, *The Parliament of Scotland, 1690–1702* (St Andrews University Publications no. 29, Oxford University Press, 1929), pp. 74–5.

45. The best summary of the incredible life of Simon Fraser, Lord Lovat, is still W. C. Mackenzie, *Lovat of the Forty-Five* (Edinburgh and London, 1934).

46. Bishop Burnet, *History of his own Time*, vol. V, p. 133, quoted in P. Hume Brown, *History of Scotland*, vol. III (Cambridge, 1909) p. 92.

47. B. Lenman, *An Economic History of Modern Scotland* (London, 1977), pp. 46–7.
48. The two outstanding books on the Darien episode are G. P. Insh, *The Company of Scotland* (London, 1932) and J. Prebble, *The Darien Disaster* (London, 1968). The definitive study of the murder of Green is Sir Richard Temple, *New Light on the Mysterious Tragedy of the 'Worcester' 1704–5* (London, 1930).
49. H. S. K. Kent, *War and Trade in Northern Seas* (Cambridge, 1973), pp. 114–29.
50. H. Gordon Slade, 'The House of Fettermear: a history and a description', *Proceedings of the Society of Antiquaries of Scotland* (hereinafter P.S.A.S.), vol. 103 (1970–71), p. 181.
51. J. B. Wolf, *Louis XIV* (Panther edn) pp. 620–21.
52. 'Réflections sur le métier du Roi' (1679). There is a translation of the passage cited in O. and P. Ranum, *The Century of Louis XIV* (London, 1973), p. 71.
53. P. Goubert, *Louis XIV and Twenty Million Frenchmen* (London, 1970), p. 212.

4 THE UNION, THE '08 AND POST-UNION DISILLUSIONMENT

1. G. Donaldson, 'Foundations of Anglo-Scottish Union', in S. T. Bindoff, J. Hurstfield, and C. H. Williams (eds.), *Elizabethan Government and Society: Essays presented to Sir John Neale* (London, 1961), pp. 282–314.
2. W. Ferguson, *Scotland's Relations with England to 1707*, chs. 10–14. This is, despite an unnecessarily combative tone, much the best modern analysis of these complex events.
3. 'Sir Daniel Fleming's Description of Cumberland, Westmoreland and Furness, 1671', printed in E. Hughes (ed.), *Fleming-Senhouse Papers* (Cumberland County Council Record Series, vol. II, Carlisle, 1961), pp. 54–5.
4. R. K. Marshall, *The Days of Duchess Anne* (London, 1973).
5. Lord Tarbat, 'Characters of Families', in P. Hume Brown (ed.), *Letters Relating to Scotland in the Reign of Queen Anne*, Scottish History Society, second series, vol. XI (Edinburgh, 1915), p. 130.
6. B. Duckham, *A History of the Scottish Coal Industry Volume I: 1700–1815* (Newton Abbot, 1970), ch. 9.
7. B. Lenman, *An Economic History of Modern Scotland 1660–1976* (London, 1977), pp. 23–4, 96.
8. There is an account of Hamilton's crucial *volte face* in Joseph Taylor, *A Journey To Edenborough In Scotland*, ed. W. Cowan (Edinburgh, 1903), p. 117. The correspondence between Baillie of Jerviswood, Roxburgh and Secretary Johnstone is printed in *Correspondence of George Baillie of Jerviswood 1702–1708*, Bannatyne Club, vol. 72 (Edinburgh, 1842). The evidence as it relates to Hamilton is perceptively discussed in P. H. Scott, *1707: The Union of Scotland and England* (Edinburgh, 1979), p. 35–8.
9. A. I. Dunlop, *William Carstares* (Edinburgh, 1967), p. 115.
10. A. M. Carstairs, 'Some Economic Aspects of the Union of Parliaments', *Scottish Journal of Political Economy*, vol. 2 (1955), pp. 64–72.
11. W. F. MacArthur, *History of Port Glasgow* (Glasgow, 1932), pp. 34–5.
12. Seafield to Godolphin, 21 September 1705, *Letters Relating to Scotland in the Reign of Queen Anne*, p. 91.
13. I have drawn heavily in this section on work done by my colleague Dr Geoffrey Parker and myself, with financial assistance from the Social Science Research Council, in connection with a survey of archival resources for the study of criminality in Early Modern Scotland.

14. G. S. Pryde, *The Treaty of Union of Scotland and England 1707* (Edinburgh, 1950), p. 26.

15. A. Fletcher, *An Historical Account of the Ancient Rights and Power of the Parliament of Scotland* (Aberdeen, 1823 edn), 'Dedication', p. 6.

16. Extracts from Hooke's writings are conveniently assembled in C. S. Terry, *The Jacobites and the Union* (Cambridge, 1922), pp. 7–27.

17. There are accounts of the Jacobite attempt of 1708 in A. and H. Tayler, *The Old Chevalier* (London, 1934), ch. 2; C. S. Terry, *The Jacobites and the Union*, ch. 1; and G. M. Trevelyan, *England Under Queen Anne: Ramillies and the Union with Scotland* (Fontana edn, 1965), ch. 17.

18. R. Chambers, *Domestic Annals of Scotland Vol. 3* (Edinburgh, 1861), p. 345.

19. P. W. J. Riley, *The English Ministers and Scotland 1707–1727* (London, 1964), pp. 103–6.

20. W. C. Mackenzie, *Andrew Fletcher of Saltoun* (Edinburgh, 1935), pp. 294–8.

21. John, seventh Duke of Atholl (ed.), *Chronicles of the Atholl and Tullibardine Families* (5 vols., privately printed Edinburgh, 1908), vol. II, p. 20.

22. Marquis of Tullibardine to Duchess of Atholl, 27 Jan. 1704, in ibid., pp. 21–2.

23. ibid., pp. 24–5.

24. Godolphin to Atholl, 28 July 1704, ibid., p. 33.

25. Atholl to Godolphin, Oct. 1704, ibid., p. 36.

26. Atholl to Seafield, 20 Nov. 1704, ibid., p. 39.

27. ibid., pp. 43–8.

28. Scott to Atholl, 5 July 1706; Duchess of Atholl to Scott, 13 July 1706, ibid., pp. 57–8.

29. The documents relating to this protracted pantomime are printed in ibid., pp. 86–100.

30. P. W. J. Riley, *The English Ministers and Scotland 1707–1727* (London, 1964), pp. 87–99.

31. The text of the 1609 act establishing Justices of the Peace is largely printed in W. C. Dickinson and G. Donaldson, *A Source Book of Scottish History Volume Three 1567 to 1707*, 2nd edn (Edinburgh, 1961), pp. 278–81, along with some significant excerpts from *Basilikon Doron*.

32. C. A. Malcolm (ed.), *The Minutes of the Justices of the Peace for Lanarkshire 1707–1723*, Scottish History Society, third series, vol. XVII (Edinburgh, 1931), pp. xxx–xxxii.

33. ibid., pp. 72–6, 80–81.

34. Robert Wodrow to George Serle, 30 May 1706, in L. W. Sharp (ed.), *Early Letters of Robert Wodrow 1698–1709*, Scottish History Society, third series, vol. XXIV (Edinburgh, 1937), p. 291.

35 G. Menary, *The Life and Letters of Duncan Forbes of Culloden* (London, 1936), p. 310.

36. R. Dudley Edwards, 'Ireland, Elizabeth I and the Counter-Reformation', in S. T. Bindoff, J. Hurstfield, C. H. Williams (eds.), *Elizabethan Government and Society* (London, 1961), pp. 334–5.

37. G. S. Holmes, 'The Hamilton Affair of 1711–1712: A Crisis in Anglo-Scottish Relations', *English Historical Review*, vol. LXXVII (1962), pp. 257–82.

38. Mar to Oxford, 10 June 1711, in *Report on the Manuscripts of the Earl of Mar and Kellie*, Historical Manuscripts Commission (London, 1904), p. 490.

39. P. Hume Brown, *History Of Scotland, Vol. III* (Cambridge, 1909), pp. 152–3.

40. A. Maxwell, *The History of Old Dundee* (Dundee, 1884), p. 474.

41. R. Davis, 'The Rise of Protection in England, 1689–1786', *Economic History Review*, second series, vol. XIX (1966).

42. Notariele Archieven, Gemeentearchief Amsterdam, no. 2157, 1st packet, fols. 54–5 (Notary Joannes d'Amour). For a brief summary of the careers of the Wedderburns of Blackness see A. H. Millar, *Glimpses of Old and New Dundee* (Dundee, 1925), p. 39.

43. W. R. Scott (ed.), *The Records of a Scottish Cloth Manufactory at New Mills, Haddingtonshire 1681–1703*, Scottish History Society, vol. XLVI (Edinburgh, 1905), Introduction; and C. Gulvin, *The Tweedmakers* (Newton Abbot, 1973), ch. 1.

44. L. Cullen, *An Economic History of Ireland since 1660* (London, 1972), pp. 40–41.

45. Board to Collector, 10 Aug. 1708, Board to Collector 2/1 (1708–1749), Customs House Records, Dundee.

46. Same to same, 18 March 1708, ibid.

47. Same to same, 18 June 1712, ibid.

48. Same to same, 5 Aug. 1708, ibid.

49. A. G. Thomson, *The Paper Industry in Scotland 1590–1861* (Edinburgh, 1974), p. 4.

50. Board to Collector, 4 April, 14 May, 4 July, and 8 Aug. 1713, Board to Collector 2/1 (1707–1724), Customs House Records, Montrose.

51. Same to same, 10 June 1714, and 6 July 1715, ibid.

52. Same to same, 14 May 1713, ibid.

53. Same to same, 26 May 1714, ibid.

54. J. A. Inglis, 'The Last Episcopal Minister of Moneydie', *Scottish Historical Review*, vol. 13 (1916), pp. 229–43. A convenient survey of the general ecclesiastical history of the period can be found in A. L. Drummond and J. Bulloch, *The Scottish Church 1688–1843* (Edinburgh, 1973), chs. 1–2.

55. H. See and A. A. Cormack, 'An Aberdeen Trader Two Hundred Years Ago', *The Aberdeen University Review*, vol. XV (1927–8), pp. 32–6.

56. W. Ferguson, 'Imperial crowns: a neglected facet of the background to the Treaty of Union of 1707', *Scottish Historical Review*, vol. LIII (1974), pp. 22–44.

57. 'Copie of an Address or Petition to the King Representing the grievances of the Union and desyring the Dissolution of the same, 1715', Atholl MSS., Box 42/I(i) 62.

5 ROOTS OF REBELLION I – THE 1715 IN ENGLAND

1. H. C. B. Rogers, *The British Army of the Eighteenth Century* (London, 1977), ch. 1.

2. J. Erskine of Carnock, *Principles of the Law of Scotland* (20th edn by J. Rankine, Edinburgh, 1903), pp. 602–6.

3. Mar to Justice Clerk, 27 December 1711, in *Report on the Manuscripts of the Earl of Mar and Kellie*, Historical Manuscripts Commission (London, 1904), pp. 489–90.

4. Quoted in J. P. Kenyon, *Revolution Principles* (Cambridge, 1977), pp. 175–6.

5. J. H. Plumb, *The Growth of Political Stability in England, 1675–1725* (London, 1967).

6. C. Cox to J. Gellibrand, 24 February 1705, in G. S. Holmes and W. A. Speck (eds.), *The Divided Society: Party Conflict in England 1694–1716* (London, 1967), p. 102

7. G. Holmes, *British Politics in the Age of Anne* (London, 1967), pp. 92–4.

8. On Queen Anne's attitudes see the trenchant and convincing article by E Gregg, 'Was Queen Anne A Jacobite?', *History*, vol. 57, no. 191 (October 1972), pp. 358–75.

9. The extensive literature on the Tory ministry of 1710–14 is well summarized in S. Biddle, *Bolingbroke and Harley* (London, 1975).

10. There is a very full account of Charles Leslie (with a shorter one of his father) in S. Lee (ed.), *Dictionary of National Biography*, vol. XXXIII (London, 1893).

11. G. V. Bennett, *The Tory Crisis in Church and State, 1688–1730* (Oxford, 1975), pp. 181–92.

12. D. Defoe, *The History of the Union of Great Britain* (Edinburgh, 1709), Sig. *T1ʳ⁻ᵛ 'Minutes of the Parliament of Scotland, with Observations thereon', pp. 73–4.

13. A. McInnes, *Robert Harley, Puritan Politician* (London, 1970).

14. W. A. Speck, 'The General Election of 1715', *The English Historical Review*, vol. XC (1975), pp. 507–22.

15. *Dictionary of National Biography*, vol. XLVII, has a lengthy account of John Radcliffe.

16. R. Arnold, *Northern Lights: The Story of Lord Derwentwater* (London, 1959), pp. 50–52.

17. W. A. Speck, *Stability and Strife: England 1714–1760* (London, 1977), pp. 79–80.

18. W. Cotesworth (nephew) to W. Cotesworth, 12 July 1715, Cotesworth MSS. CP/3/44, Gateshead Public Library.

19. H. Liddell to W. Cotesworth, 18 January 1715 and 25 January 1715, Ellison MSS. A36/28–9, Gateshead Public Library.

20. H. Liddell to W. Cotesworth, 26 October 1714, Ellison MSS. A36/19, Gateshead Public Library.

21. E. Hughes, *North Country Life in the Eighteenth Century: The North-East 1700–1750* (London, 1952).

22. J. V. Beckett, 'English Landownership in the Later Seventeenth and Eighteenth Centuries: The Debate and the Problems', *The Economic History Review*, second series, vol. XXX (1977), pp. 567–81.

23. R. Arnold, *Northern Lights*, provides a good survey of Northumberland in 1715.

24. W. Cotesworth to W. Cotesworth (son), 23 May 1716, Ellison MSS. A36/37, Gateshead Public Library.

25. E. Hughes, *North Country Life in the Eighteenth Century: The North-East 1700–1750*, Appendix A, 'William Cotesworth and the Fifteen'; W. Cotesworth (nephew) to W. Cotesworth, 6 September 1716, Cotesworth MSS. CP/3/7, Gateshead Public Library.

26. W. Cotesworth (son) to W. Cotesworth, 2 June 1716, copy, Cotesworth MSS. CP/3/22, Gateshead Public Library.

27. Earl of Carlisle to Deputy Lieutenants for Cumberland and Westmoreland, 25 October 1715, in R. C. Jarvis (ed.), *The Jacobite Risings of 1715 and 1745*, Cumberland County Council Record Series, vol. I (1954), pp. 161–2.

28. R. C. Jarvis's 'Introduction' to *The Jacobite Risings of 1715 and 1745* is a mine of precise information on events in Cumberland and Westmoreland.

29. W. Beamont (ed.), *The Jacobite Trials at Manchester in 1694*, Chetham Society, vol. XXVIII (1853). The remarks of Mr Justice Eyre to the acquitted can be found on p. 103.

30. S. H. Ware (ed.), *Lancashire Memorials of the Rebellion 1715*, Chetham Society, vol. V (1845), pp. 16–19.

31. ibid., pp. 192–201, 115–36.

32. W. Cotesworth (son) to W. Cotesworth, 2 June 1716, copy, Cotesworth MSS. CP/3/22, Gateshead Public Library.

6 ROOTS OF REBELLION II – THE 1715 IN SCOTLAND

1. The best general guide to the '15 is probably A. and H. Tayler, *1715: The Story of the Rising* (London, 1936), though the coverage of English events is inadequate and the British political context of the rising is seriously misrepresented.
2. A. Cunningham, *The Loyal Clans* (Cambridge, 1932).
3. G. P. Insh, *The Scottish Jacobite Movement* (Edinburgh, 1952).
4. See G. Donaldson, 'Scotland's Conservative North in the Sixteenth and Seventeenth Centuries', *Transactions of the Royal Historical Society*, fifth series, vol. 16 (1966), pp. 65–79.
5. G. D. Henderson (ed.), *Mystics of the North-East* (Aberdeen, The Third Spalding Club, 1934), Introduction.
6. Dr James Keith to Lord Deskford, 4 August 1715, ibid., pp. 102–3.
7. M. K. and C. Ritchie (eds.), 'An Apology For The Aberdeen Evictions', *The Miscellany of the Third Spalding Club Volume III* (Aberdeen, The Third Spalding Club, 1960), pp. 57–95.
8. D. McRoberts and C. Oman, 'Plate Made By King James II and VII for the Chapel Royal of Holyroodhouse in 1686', *The Antiquaries Journal*, vol. XLVIII, Part II (1968), pp. 285–95. The surviving vessels were in 1967 deposited on loan in the National Museum of Antiquities of Scotland.
9. There is an account of Nisbet's life and works in Sir James Fergusson's *Lowland Lairds* (London, 1949), ch. 4.
10. Sir Ian Moncreiffe of that Ilk and D. Hicks, *The Highland Clans* (London, 1967), p. 21.
11. D. Fraser, *Highland Perthshire* (Montrose, 1969), pp. 77–9.
12. B. Catton, *This Hallowed Ground* (London, Book Society edn, 1957), p. 256.
13. Henderson, *Mystics of the North-East*, p. 36.
14. H. Tayler, 'John, Duke of Argyll and Greenwich', *Scottish Historical Review*, vol. XXVI (1947), pp. 64–74.
15. A. J. Warden, *Angus Or Forfarshire*, 5 vols. (Dundee, 1880–5), vol. I, pp. 367–71.
16. ibid., vol. I, pp. 400–402
17. G. G. Simpson, *Scottish Handwriting 1150–1650* (Edinburgh, 1973), pp. 36–7.
18. Warden, *Angus Or Forfarshire*, vol. I, pp. 432–3.
19. A. and H. Tayler, *Jacobites of Aberdeenshire and Banffshire in the Rising of 1715* (London, 1934), p. 79.
20. L. Melville, *The Fair Land of Gowrie* (Coupar Angus, 1939), pp. 119–21.
21. A. Keith, *A Thousand Years of Aberdeen* (Aberdeen, 1972), p. 273.
22. J. T. Findlay, *A History of Peterhead* (Peterhead, 1933), pp. 105–8.
23. G. Hay, *History of Arbroath* (Arbroath, 1876), pp. 165–7.
24. Warrant of John, Duke of Argyll, General and Commander-in-Chief of His Majesty's Forces in North Britain, 3 February 1716, in J. Thomson, *The History of Dundee* (Dundee, 1846), p. 94.
25. R. W. Munro, *Highland Clans and Tartans* (London, 1977), pp. 14–17.
26. J. Dunlop, *The Clan Gordon* (Edinburgh, 1955).
27. G. W. S. Barrow, *The Kingdom of the Scots* (London, 1973), ch. 13.
28. See J. Cameron (ed.), *The Justiciary Records of Argyll and the Isles*, vol. I 1664–1705, and J. Imrie (ed.), vol. II 1705–1742, Stair Society, vols. 12 and 25 (Edinburgh, 1949 and 1969).
29. B. Lenman, 'History', in *The History and Heritage of Pitlochry and District* (Pitlochry Tourist Association, 1974), pp. 26–38; Sir Ian Moncreiffe of that Ilk, *The Atholl Highlanders* (Derby, n.d.), pp. 1–4.

30. D. Defoe, *A Tour through the Whole Island of Great Britain* (London, Everyman's Library, 1974), p. 423.
31. C. I. Fraser of Reelig, *The Clan Cameron*, 2nd edn (Edinburgh, 1963).
32. Sir Ian Moncreiffe of that Ilk and D. Hicks, *The Highland Clans* (London, 1967).
33. The Marquess of Huntly, *The Cock O' The North* (London, 1935), chs. IX and X.
34. J. Baynes, *The Jacobite Rising of 1715* (London, 1970), pp. 61–2.
35. I. F. Grant, *The Macleods: The History of a Clan 1200–1956* (London, 1959), pp. 383–8.
36. G. Menary, *Duncan Forbes of Culloden* (London, 1936), pp. 22–5.
37. J. Stewart (Lord Advocate) to Marquis of Atholl, 19 Oct. 1697, Atholl MSS., 29I(9)360. This letter contains a reference to 'the unaccountable insolence of Beaufort and his son'.
38. The efforts of the Atholls to bring Beaufort to justice may be traced in such correspondence as Marquis of Atholl to Earl of Tullibardine, 31 August 1697; and in Patrick Murray of Dollery to Earl of Tullibardine, 18 Nov. 1697, Atholl MSS., 29I(9)297 and 439 respectively. The reference to the difficulty of apprehending Beaufort by force, because so many in the north are favourable to him, is to be found in P. Murray of Dollery to Earl of Tullibardine, 23 Nov. 1697, Atholl MSS., 29I(9)451.
39. I. J. Murray, 'Letters of Andrew Fletcher of Saltoun and his family 1715–1716', printed in *Miscellany X*, Scottish History Society, fourth series, vol. 2 (Edinburgh, 1965), pp. 143–73.
40. W. Duke, *Lord George Murray and the Forty-Five* (Aberdeen, 1927), ch. 2.
41. The best introduction to this extraordinary man, his clan, and its country is a visit to the Clan Donnachaidh Museum, Bruar Falls, Blair Atholl, Perthshire.
42. *Poems, On Various Subjects and Occasions, By the Honourable Alexander Robertson of Struan, Esq.* (Edinburgh, printed for Ch. Alexander, 1751?) is a rare book, but there is a handy *Selected Poems of Alexander Robertson of Struan* (Edinburgh, The Tragara Press, 1971), with an Introduction by John Vladimir Price.
43. Amongst the extensive literature see J. H. Burton, *The Scot Abroad* (Edinburgh, 1881); G. Donaldson, *The Scot Overseas* (London, 1966), whose bibliography is comprehensive. For specific points see I. Grimble, *Chief of Mackay* (London, 1965); and J. W. Barnhill and P. Dukes, 'North-east Scots in Muscovy in the seventeenth century', *Northern Scotland*, vol. 2 (1976–7), pp. 49–63.
44. 'Notes from dictates of Mr Alexander Grant, Regent of St Leonard's College', St Andrews University MS. 36225.
45. J. L. Carvel, *One Hundred Years In Coal* (Edinburgh, 1944), ch. 1.
46. J. A. Symon, *Scottish Farming: Past and Present* (Edinburgh, 1959), p. 303.
47. J. Laver, *The House of Haig* (Markinch, 1958), pp. 12–14.
48. I. Hay, *The Royal Company of Archers 1676–1951* (Edinburgh, 1951), pp. 7–9.
49. Warrender to Stanhope and Townshend, 10 Sept. 1715, in W. K. Dickson (ed.), *Warrender Letters*, Scottish History Society, third series, vol. XXV (Edinburgh, 1935), pp. 88–90.
50. Mayor of Berwick to Warrender, 27 Sept. 1715, and enclosed William Cotesworth to Warrender, 26 Sept. 1715, ibid., pp. 98–9.
51. Warrender to magistrates of Edinburgh, 30 April 1715, ibid., pp. 26–7.
52. Duke of Montrose to Lord Advocate, 28 Sept. 1714, and same to same 7 Oct. 1714, Dalquharran Papers, Scottish Record Office, GD 27/5/5 and 27/5/7.
53. Accounts of evidence given before the Lord Advocate and dated Leith, 3 Oct.

1715 can be found in the Ogilvy of Inverquharity Papers in the Scottish Record Office. The reference is G.D.205, portfolio 8.

54. H. Tayler, *Lady Nithsdale and her Family* (London, 1939), ch. 2.
55. R. Hatton, *Diplomatic Relations Between Great Britain and the Dutch Republic 1714–21* (London, 1950), p. 239.

7 THE AFTERMATH OF THE '15

1. N. Rogers, 'Popular Protest In Early Hanoverian London', *Past and Present*, no. 79 (May 1978), pp. 70–100.
2. S. Ware (ed.), *Lancashire Memorials of 1715*, Chetham Society, vol. V (1845), pp. 218–34.
3. D. Marshall, *Eighteenth Century England* (London, 1962), pp. 84–6.
4. J. F. Nayler (ed.), *The British Aristocracy and the Peerage Bill of 1719* (London, 1968).
5. J. H. Plumb, *Sir Robert Walpole: The Making of a Statesman* (London, 1956), pp. 218–20.
6. Robert Cotesworth (son) to William Cotesworth, 26 May 1716; and William Cotesworth (son) to William Cotesworth, 2 June 1716, Cotesworth MSS. CP/3/21 and 22, Gateshead Public Library.
7. J. Baynes, *The Jacobite Rising of 1715* (London, 1970), pp. 195–8.
8. J. S. Cockburn (ed.), *Crime In England 1550–1800* (London, 1977), chs. 10 and 11. Dr E. Cruickshanks has drawn my attention to contemporary allegations that Jacobite prisoners who escaped from Newgate did so with the collusion of the sheriff and/or the Lord Mayor of London under whose jurisdiction the prison lay (see *Secret History of Rebels in Newgate*, London, 1717).
9. Lady Nithsdale to Lucy Herbert (sister), n.d., in H. Tayler, *Lady Nithsdale and her Family*, p. 47.
10. *The Records of the Forfeited Estates Commission*, Public Record Office Handbooks, no. 12 (London, 1968), Introduction.
11. *A Report From The Commissioners Appointed to Enquire of the Estates of Certain Traitors, etc. In that Part of Great Britain Called Scotland* (London, 1717), p. 4.
12. 'Memorial and Letters of the Commissioners of Enquiry to the Right Honourable Charles Lord Viscount Townshend', ibid., Appendix, p. 3.
13. ibid., main text, p. 5.
14. Commissioners to Lord Advocate, 19 December 1716, and Lord Advocate to Commissioners, 19 December 1716, ibid., Appendix, pp. 21–2.
15. The careers of this extraordinary legal dynasty may be traced in the *Dictionary of National Biography*, vol. XIII (London, 1888).
16. *A Report From The Commissioners . . . etc.*, Appendix, pp. 41–8.
17. D. Murray, *The York Buildings Company*, 2nd edn (Edinburgh, 1973).
18. See draft authority February 1716 (day in date not filled in) To Patrick Strachan of Glenkindy, Surveyor Generall, and his Clerk, and Appriser, in Forfeited Estates Papers 1715, Scottish Record Office, E603/7/1–13. I am most grateful to Mr John Imrie, Keeper of the Records of Scotland, for making the 1715 papers available to me. They are currently being catalogued by Dr Annette Smith of Dundee University and individual items were not numbered at time of consultation in St Andrews University Library. E603/7/1–13, for example, refers to a single manilla folder with 13 items in it.
19. Surveyor General to Commissioners, 21 Nov. 1716, ibid.
20. H. Baillie to Commissioners, 15 Feb. 1717, ibid.

21. 'Directions about valuing Statues and Pictures', ibid.
22. Surveyor General to Commissioners, 11 May 1717, ibid.; *The Memoirs Of The Insurrection In Scotland in 1715 By John, Master of Sinclair*, were printed, with Notes by Sir Walter Scott, by the Abbotsford Club (Edinburgh, 1858). Sir Walter Scott presented to the Roxburghe Club an edition of *Proceedings In The Court Martial Held Upon John, Master Of Sinclair* (Edinburgh, 1828, reprinted S.R. Publishers, 1969).
23. 'Extract of a letter from Lieutenant General Carpenter to Coll. Murray Commanding att Inverness dated att Edinburgh the 9 of May 1717', Forfeited Estates Papers, 1715, ibid.
24. 'Judiciall Account or Rentall of the Reall Estate which belonged to Alexander Mackenzie Late of Applecross in Tarradale Taken ... this Seventh day of October 1718 years', among Rentals of Applecross E611/1/1–3, Forfeited Estates Papers 1715.
25. 'Applecross: List of Claims upon said estate', along with the detailed documents supporting all the individual claims, can be found in E611/2, Forfeited Estates Papers 1715.
26. The Earl Marischal estate final settlement can be found in a ledger entitled 'Forfeited Estates: List Of Claims Sustained, Rebellion 1715', where it is the second major item listed.
27. 'Translation and Assignation of Claims 1723–4: Applecross', E611, Forfeited Estates Papers 1715.
28. Returns by Thomas Crisp, Esq., High Sheriff of the County Palatine of Lancaster, 1. These are preserved with the rest of the material from the English Forfeited Estates Commissioners in the London Public Record Office. The reference for these Returns is PRO/FEC2/120.
29. ibid., 41.
30. See the examples in ibid., 27–38.
31. ibid., 45.
32. C. Slaughter to Commissioners for Forfeited Estates, 9 Dec. 1716, PRO/FEC1/C75/2/27/1.
33. Same to same, 4 Jan. 1716, PRO/FEC1/C75/2/27/2.
34. Same to same, 8 Jan. 1716, PRO/FEC1/C75/2/27/3.
35. Same to same, 13 Jan. 1716, PRO/FEC1/C75/2/27/4.
36. Same to same, 17 Feb. 1716, PRO/FEC1/C75/2/27/8.
37. Same to same, 13 Jan. 1716, PRO/FEC1/C75/2/27/4.
38. H. Liddell to Wm. Cotesworth, 26 March 1715, 'Jacobite Letters 1715–1716', Newcastle University Library, Miscellaneous MS. 30, fol. 3. This collection was presented to the library in 1947 by Major Carr-Ellison.
39. Same to same, 22 Sept. 1715, ibid., fol. 9.
40. Same to same, 6 Oct. 1715, ibid., fol. 11.
41. Same to same, 4 Jan. 1716, ibid., fol. 33.
42. Same to same, 18 Oct. 1715, ibid., fol. 16.
43. Same to same, 'Queen Bess's Day' (17 November) 1715, ibid., fol. 25.
44. Same to same, 24 Dec. 1715, ibid., fol. 32.
45. 'Register of Appeals to the Honourable the Commissioners nominated and appointed . . . to Inquire of the Estates of certain Traitors and of Popish Recusants and of Estates given to superstitious uses', 1–8, PRO/FEC2/53.
46. C. Slaughter to Commissioners, 5 Feb. 1716, PRO/FEC1/C75/2/27/6.
47. E. Hughes, *North Country Life in the Eighteenth Century: The North East 1700–1750* (London, 1952), ch. 1.
48. J. Steven Watson, *The Reign of George III 1760–1815* (Oxford, 1960), p. 51, footnote.

49. W. E. McCulloch, *Viri Illustres Universitatum Abredonensium* (Aberdeen, 1923), p. 58.

50. T. Blackwell to Lord Hardwicke, 13 March 1749, and accompanying 'Memorial concerning the North of Scotland', Hardwicke Papers, British Library, 35,447, fols. 5–7.

51. I am very grateful for the permission which Elizabeth K. Carmichael gave me to read her unpublished 1977 Glasgow Ph.D. thesis, 'The Scottish Commission of the Peace, 1707–1760', though both the Introduction and documents in C. A. Malcolm (ed.), *The Minutes of the Justices of the Peace for Lanarkshire 1707–1723*, Scottish History Society, third series, vol. 17 (Edinburgh, 1931) remain a fundamental source of information on this subject.

52. D. Murray, *The York Buildings Company* (Edinburgh, Bratton edn, 1973).

53. Anonymous, 'Memorial As To The State Of The Prisoners On Account Of The Late Rebellion, 1715', *The Spottiswoode Miscellany*, vol. II (Edinburgh, 1845), pp. 473–80.

8 A DECADE OF DISASTERS – JACOBITISM 1717–27

1. D. B. Horn, *Great Britain and Europe in the Eighteenth Century* (Oxford, 1967), ch. 3.

2. J. Klaits, *Printed Propaganda Under Louis XIV* (Princeton, 1976), pp. 171–83.

3. For the faction struggles at St Germain in 1709–10 see G. H. Jones, *Charles Middleton: The Life and Times of a Restoration Politician* (Chicago, 1967), pp. 286–90.

4. J. C. Rule, 'France and the Preliminaries to the Gertruydenberg Conference, September 1709 to March 1710', in R. Hatton and M. S. Anderson (eds.), *Studies in Diplomatic History: Essays in memory of David Bayne Horn* (London, 1970), pp. 97–115.

5. W. Mediger, 'Great Britain, Hanover and the Rise of Prussia', in ibid., pp. 199–213.

6. H. S. K. Kent, *War and Trade in Northern Seas* (Cambridge, 1973), ch. 1.

7. John Steuart to Alexander Andrew (Rotterdam), 24 Sept. 1715, in W. Mackay (ed.), *The Letter-Book of Bailie John Steuart Of Inverness 1715–1752*, Scottish History Society, second series, vol. 9 (Edinburgh, 1915), p. 12.

8. Same to same, 27 April 1716, ibid., pp. 17–18.

9. Same to same, 27 Oct. 1716; and J. Steuart to Messrs Marjoribancks and Coutts (Danzig), 27 Oct. 1716, ibid., pp. 29–30.

10. J. Steuart to A. Andrew (Rotterdam), 11 Jan. 1718, ibid., p. 63.

11. ibid., Introduction, *passim*.

12. Henry Liddell to William Cotesworth, 17 Jan. 1717, Ellison MSS., A36/54, Gateshead Public Library.

13. E. Hughes, *North Country Life in the Eighteenth Century: The North-East 1700–1750* (London, 1952), p. 19.

14. J. J. Murray, *George I, The Baltic and the Whig Split of 1717* (London, 1969), chs. XI and XII.

15. T. V. Bulpin, *Islands in a Forgotten Sea*, 2nd edn (Cape Town, 1969), chs. 7–9.

16. 'Memorandum' by Johan Friedrich Osthoff, MS. 992, National Library of Scotland. There was certainly a Jacobite captain called William Morgan working for Ormonde in 1722, when he commanded a flotilla of three ships in the port of Cadiz. The 'Osthoff' memorandum seems to be a mixture of muddle, propaganda, and basic fact.

17. T. Borenius, 'Sweden and the Jacobites', *Scottish Historical Review*, vol. XXIII (1926), pp. 238–40.
18. There seems to be no doubt that Charles died by 'an honest enemy bullet'. Contemporary allegations of assassination cannot be sustained. See R. Hatton, *Charles XII of Sweden* (London, 1968), Book 7, ch. 4.
19. M. S. Anderson, *Europe in the Eighteenth Century 1713–1783* (London, 1961), pp. 222–5.
20. Aylmer Valance, *The Summer King* (London, 1956). The best summary of the events of the '19 is the Introduction to W. K. Dickson (ed.), *The Jacobite Attempt of 1719*, Scottish History Society, vol. 19 (Edinburgh, 1895).
21. Alberoni to Ormonde, 4 April 1719, ibid., pp. 222–3. The dates of correspondence originating on the Continent of Europe, like this letter, are in the so-called New Style or Gregorian Calendar. The Old Style or Julian Calendar date used in Britain and Russia may be obtained by subtracting eleven days.
22. Ormonde to Alberoni, by the Earl Marischal, 13 Feb. 1719, ibid., pp. 60–61.
23. J. Craggs to Stair, 16 March 1719, ibid., pp. 237–8. New Style, this letter would be dated 27 March.
24. 'To the Laird of Brolus', 26 Feb. 1719, ibid., p. 70.
25. Tullibardine to Mar, 16 June 1719, ibid., pp. 269–73.
26. Major-General Wightman to Charles Delafaye, 17 Sept. 1719, ibid., pp. 285–6.
27. Same to same, 29 Sept. 1719, ibid., pp. 290–92.
28. Lord Carpenter to Charles Delafaye, 7 July and 21 July 1719, ibid., pp. 278–80.
29. Abbé Dubois to J. Craggs, 8 March 1719, ibid., pp. 224–7.
30. J. H. Plumb, *Sir Robert Walpole Vol. 2: The King's Minister* (London, Penguin Press, 1972), pp. 40–49.
31. P. S. Fritz, *The English Ministers and Jacobitism between the Rebellions of 1715 and 1745* (Toronto, 1975), ch. 10.
32. James Francis Edward Stewart to Duke of Mar, 15 May 1722, H. Tayler (ed.), *The Jacobite Court at Rome in 1719*, Scottish History Society, third series, vol. 31 (Edinburgh, 1938), p. 215 and footnote.
33. Mar to King (i.e. James), 6 March 1724, ibid., p. 220.
34. G. V. Bennett, *The Tory Crisis in Church and State 1688–1730* (Oxford, 1975), ch. 15.

9 FAILURE AND SURVIVAL – SCOTTISH JACOBITISM 1725–39

1. *Dictionary of National Biography*, vol. XXXI (London, 1892), pp. 167–70.
2. C. Winslow, 'Sussex Smugglers', in D. Hay *et al.*, *Albion's Fatal Tree: Crime and Society in Eighteenth-Century England* (London, 1975), pp. 156–7.
3. When no other source is given material on Duncan Forbes is drawn from G. Menary, *The Life and Letters of Duncan Forbes of Culloden Lord President of the Court of Session 1685–1747* (London, 1936).
4. D. Forbes to Secretary of State, 26 June 1725, Scottish Record Office, RH 2/4 (317) fols. 226–9. This RH series comprises xerox copies of Home Office records relevant to Scotland. The originals are in the London Public Record Office. I have consulted the copies in the Scottish Record Office.
5. C. Erskine to Secretary of State, 26 June 1725, S.R.O., RH 2/4 (317) fols. 222–4.
6. B. Fairfax to Duke of Newcastle, 26 June 1725, S.R.O., RH 2/4 (317) fols. 230–31.
7. Daniel Campbell to Duncan Campbell, 5 March 1695, Campbell of Shawfield Papers, Sh I, fol. 56, Mitchell Library, Glasgow.

8. J. Campbell to Caleb Chapman, 21 Oct. 1693, Sh I, fol. 43, Mitchell Library.
9. 'Memorandum' dated 23 July 1706, Sh I, fol. 301, Mitchell Library.
10. Papers relating to the case before the Barons of the Exchequer will be found in Sh II, fols. 479 and 481, Mitchell Library.
11. Campbell, Jarratt and Dobson (Stockholm) to D. Campbell, 10 June 1714, Sh I, fol. 502, Mitchell Library.
12. M. H. Norry to D. Campbell, 25 June 1711, Sh I, fol. 506 (r. and v.), Mitchell Library.
13. The best brief biographical introduction to Daniel Campbell of Shawfield will be found in a series of articles in the *Glasgow Herald* of 1, 2 and 3 June 1959.
14. D. Campbell to Lord Townshend, 1 July 1725, S.R.O., RH 2/4 (317) fols. 266–9.
15. General Wade to Duke of Newcastle, 26 June 1725, S.R.O., RH 2/4 (317) fols. 232–9.
16. Sir J. Scrope to Secretary of State, 12 July 1725, plus enclosed Resolution of the Convention of Royal Burghs, 12 July 1725, and copy of *The Daily Courant*, no. 7407, Tuesday, 13 July 1725, S.R.O., RH 2/4 (317) fols. 322–31.
17. General Wade to Duke of Newcastle, 29 June 1725, S.R.O., RH 2/4 (317) fols. 241–2.
18. Same to same, 17 July 1725, S.R.O., RH 2/4 (317) fols. 355–6.
19. Same to same, 20 July 1725, S.R.O., RH 2/4 (317) fols. 358–9.
20. *A Letter From a Gentleman in Glasgow, to his Friend in the Country, Concerning the late Tumults which happened in that City*, printed in the year 1725, S.R.O., RH 2/4 (319) fol. 18 for a copy of this 20-page pamphlet.
21. Major Wansborough to General Wade, 27 June 1725, and enclosed dispatch from M. Macleod, S.R.O., RH 2/4 (317) fols. 249–52.
22. General Wade to Duke of Newcastle, 12 July 1725, S.R.O., RH 2/4 (317) fols. 318–20.
23. Same to same, 14 July 1725, S.R.O., RH 2/4 (317) fols. 341–3.
24. D. Daiches, *Charles Edward Stuart* (London, 1973), pp. 79–81.
25. C. Chenevix Trench, *George II* (London, 1973), pp. 149 and 134.
26. These remarks are based on a host of references in the Dundee Customs House Records, Board to Collector 2/1 series.
27. Board to Collector, 26 Nov. 1728, ibid.
28. Collector to Board, 28 May 1728, Collector to Board 1/1 (1724–31), Customs House Records, Montrose.
29. Same to same, 25 April 1728, and 1 May 1728, ibid.
30. Same to same, 8 May 1728, ibid.
31. Same to same, 11 Oct. 1728, ibid.
32. Same to same, 13 Oct. 1728, ibid.
33. Same to same, 8 Jan. 1731, Collector to Board 1/2 (1731–8), Customs House Records, Montrose.
34. Same to same, 13 May 1732, and 28 Sept. 1732, ibid.
35. Same to same, 1 May 1733, ibid.
36. Same to same, 10 Jan. 1736, ibid.
37. G. Menary, *The Life and Letters of Duncan Forbes of Culloden* (London, 1936), p. 106.
38. ibid., ch. VI, for a general description of the Porteous Riot and its sequelae.
39. Lord President Forbes to Duke of Argyll, 6 Oct. 1738, *Culloden Papers* (London, 1815), p. 150.
40. C. S. Terry, *A History of Scotland* (Cambridge, 1920), pp. 548–9.
41. J. B. Salmond, *Wade In Scotland* (Edinburgh, 1934).

42. D. Duncan, *Thomas Ruddiman* (Edinburgh, 1965). There is a convenient sketch of Melvin's life in D. Masson, *Memories Of Two Cities: Edinburgh and Aberdeen* (Edinburgh, 1911), ch. X.

43. I. Ross and S. Scobie, 'Patriotic Publishing as a Response to the Union', in I. Rae (ed.), *The Union of 1707: Its Impact on Scotland* (Glasgow, 1974), pp. 94–119.

44. W. J. Couper, 'The Pretender's Printer', *Scottish Historical Review*, vol. 15 (1918), pp. 106–23.

45. H. R. Trevor-Roper, 'The Religious Origins of the Enlightenment', in *Religion, the Reformation and Social Change*, 2nd edn (London, 1972), pp. 231–2.

46. P. Roberts, *The Quest for Security 1715–1740* (New York, Harper Torchbook edn, 1963), pp. 78–9 and 88–90.

47. S. G. Checkland, *Scottish Banking: A History, 1695–1973* (Glasgow, 1975), pp. 70–71.

48. For the history of the Coutts family see E. H. Coleridge, *The Life of Thomas Coutts, Banker* (London, 1920), vol. 1; R. M. Robinson, *Coutts: The History of a Banking House* (London, 1929); and Sir W. Forbes, *Memoirs of a Banking House*, 2nd edn (Edinburgh, 1860).

49. N. Munro, *The History of the Royal Bank of Scotland 1727–1927* (Edinburgh, 1928).

50. These remarks are based on financial correspondence relating to the exiled William Marquis of Tullibardine, usually referred to as 'William Kateson' in the letters, but by Jacobites often called after his father's death in 1724 'Duke William'. The letters dated from January 1724 to June 1742 and are preserved in the Atholl MSS., Box 45A, I(1).

51. P. Purcell, 'The Jacobite Rising of 1715 and the English Catholics', *English Historical Review*, vol. XLIV (1929), pp. 418–32.

52. I. Mackay, 'Clanranald's Tacksmen of the Late Eighteenth Century', *Transactions of the Gaelic Society of Inverness*, vol. XLIV (1964–6), pp. 61–93.

53. 'Additional Memorial Concerning the Growth of Popery' (c. 1720), Taylor Coll., National Library of Scotland, N.L.S., MS. 68.

54. Warrant for the arrest of 'Mr. Wm. Smith proffessor Philosophy in The Marichell College of Aberdeen', 14 March 1716, Warding and Liberation Books of Edinburgh Tolbooth, S.R.O., HH 11/11.

55. D. J. Withrington, 'Education and Society in the Eighteenth Century', in N. T. Phillipson and R. Mitchison (eds.), *Scotland in the Age of Improvement* (Edinburgh, 1970), pp. 188–9, and footnote 60 on p. 199.

10 THE '45

1. P. Mathias and P. O'Brien, 'Taxation in Britain and France, 1715–1810', *The Journal of European Economic History*, vol. 5 (1976), pp. 601–50.

2. J. H. Plumb, *Sir Robert Walpole Vol. II* (London, 1960), ch. VII.

3. H. Tayler, 'John Gordon of Glenbucket', *Scottish Historical Review*, vol. 27 (1948), pp. 165–75.

4. R. Sedgwick, *The History of Parliament: The House of Commons 1715–1754*, vol. I (London, 1970), ch. V.

5. H. W. V. Temperley, 'The Causes of the War of Jenkins' Ear, 1739', originally read to the Royal Historical Society in 1909 and reprinted in I. R. Christie (ed.), *Essays in Modern History* (London, 1968), pp. 196–233.

6. I am deeply indebted to Dr Eveline Cruickshank for her kindness in making available to me a proof copy of her book *Political Untouchables: The Tories*

and the '45 (London, 1979), which among other virtues contains by far the most satisfactory account of French government policy towards the House of Stewart in the years 1743–5.

7. W. Duke, *Prince Charles Edward and the Forty-Five* (London, 1938), pp. 31–2.
8. For a discussion of the baroque mind as a unifying force in the centrifugal civilization of seventeenth-century Europe see C. J. Friederich, *The Age of the Baroque* (New York, Harper Torchbook edn, 1962). For a brilliant brief discussion of the rococo and its relationships with baroque and neo-classicism see the Introduction by Ralph Edwards to *English Taste in the Eighteenth Century from Baroque to Neo-Classic* (Catalogue for the Winter Exhibition, 1955–1956, Royal Academy of Arts, London).
9. L. M. Cullen, 'Merchant Communities Overseas: the Navigation Acts and Irish and Scottish Responses', in L. M. Cullen and T. C. Smout (eds.), *Comparative Aspects of Scottish and Irish Economic and Social History 1600–1900* (Edinburgh, 1976), pp. 169–70.
10. J. S. Gibson, *Ships of the '45* (London, 1967), ch. I.
11. Goran Behre, 'Sweden and the rising of 1745', *The Scottish Historical Review*, vol. LI (1972), pp. 148–71.
12. D. Daiches, *Charles Edward Stuart* (London, 1973), pp. 102–3.
13. R. F. Bell (ed.), *Memorials of John Murray of Broughton Sometime Secretary to Prince Charles Edward 1740–1747*, Scottish History Society, vol. XXVII (Edinburgh, 1898), p. 93.
14. 'Papers of John Murray of Broughton Found After Culloden', in W. B. Blaikie (ed.), *Origins of the 'Forty-Five*, Scottish History Society, second series, vol. II (Edinburgh, 1916), p. 5.
15. ibid., p. 11.
16. 'Memorial Concerning The Highlands Written by Alexander Macbean, A. M. Minister Of Inverness', in ibid., p. 81.
17. There are summaries of these contracts prepared for legal use in the Balhaldie Papers, National Library of Scotland, MS. 3186, fol. 172.
18. The legal opinion is in ibid., fols. 173–4.
19. Donald Cameron of Lochiel to Balhaldie, 30 Sept. 1718, and 3 March 1719, ibid., fols. 85 and 89–90.
20. Cameron of Lochiel to Balhaldie, 22 Aug. 1719; Euan Drummond to Drummond of Balhaldie, 1720, and 15 Nov. 1722, ibid., fols. 97, 97–100, and 104 respectively.
21. J. Hunter, *The Making of the Crofting Community* (Edinburgh, 1976), p. 8.
22. S. Macmillan, *Bygone Lochaber* (Glasgow, 1971), p. 122.
23. ibid., ch. V.
24. P. H. McKerlie, *History of the Lands and their Owners in Galloway, Vol. II* (Paisley, 1906), pp. 224–5. The point about the 'Levellers' I owe to an excellent lecture delivered to the Scottish Economic Historians Conference held in Strathclyde University in December 1978 by Mr John W. Leopold.
25. J. Small's report on the annexed estate of Struan Robertson printed in V. Wills (ed.), *Reports on the Annexed Estates 1755–1769* (Edinburgh, H.M.S.O., 1973), pp. 30–36. The quotations are on p. 33.
26. H. M. Steven and A. Carlisle, *The Native Pinewoods of Scotland* (Edinburgh, 1959), pp. 139–40.
27. W. Duke, *Prince Charles Edward and the Forty-Five*, p. 61.
28. K. Tomasson and F. Buist, *Battles of the '45* (London, 1962), p. 25.
29. J. Prebble, *Mutiny* (London, 1975), ch. I.
30. E. Cregeen, 'The Changing Role of the House of Argyll in the Scottish High-

lands', in N. T. Phillipson and R. Mitchison, *Scotland in the Age of Improvement* (Edinburgh, 1970), pp. 5–23.

31. R. Mitchison, 'The Government and the Highlands, 1707–1745', ibid., pp. 24–6.
32. R. C. Jarvis, *Collected Papers on the Jacobite Risings*, vol. I (Manchester, 1971), ch. I.
33. *Autobiography of the Rev. Dr Alexander Carlyle Minister of Inveresk*, 2nd edn (Edinburgh, 1860), pp. 112 and 118.
34. K. Tomasson, *The Jacobite General* (Edinburgh, 1958), pp. 19 and 60.
35. D. Daiches, *Charles Edward Stuart* (London, 1973), p. 132.
36. J. Murray to Lord Pitsligo, 2 Sept. 1745; and 29 Sept. 1745 A. and H. Tayler (eds.), *Jacobite Letters to Lord Pitsligo 1745–1746* (Aberdeen, 1930), pp.31–3.
37. 'Report By John Campbell of Barcaldine, Factor upon The Annexed Estates of Perth', *Reports on the Annexed Estates 1755–1769*, pp. 21–3.
38. Sir Bruce Seton and J. G. Arnot (eds.), *The Prisoners of the '45*, vol. I, pp. 223–4; P. F. Anson, *Underground Catholicism In Scotland* (Montrose, 1970), pp. 144–50.
39. A. and H. Tayler, *Jacobites of Aberdeenshire and Banffshire in the Forty-Five* (Aberdeen, 1928).
40. W. B. Blaikie, *Origins of the 'Forty-Five*, p. 80.
41. W. Wilson, *The House of Airlie*, vol. II, p. 171.
42. Simon Fraser to Simon Fraser (son), 21 Aug. 1739; and Simon Fraser to Donald Fraser, 16 Oct. 1740, printed in W. Mackay (ed.), 'Unpublished Letters By Simon Lord Lovat', *Transactions of the Gaelic Society of Inverness*, vol. XIII (1886–1887), pp. 142–3 and 169–70.
43. Quoted in Sir Charles Petrie, *The Jacobite Movement*, 3rd edn (London, 1959), p. 396.
44. N. S. Bushnell, *William Hamilton of Bangour* (Aberdeen, 1957), p. 73.
45. E. Charteris (ed.), *A Short Account of the Affairs of Scotland* (London, 1907), p. 306.
46. These remarks are based on a series of remarkable transcripts of the correspondence of Lord Lewis from December 1745 to April 1746 in the Walter Blaikie Collection in the National Library of Scotland, MS. 298, fols. 5–15.
47. The study of the grass-roots realities during the Jacobite rebellions has been revolutionized by the brilliant work of Rupert C. Jarvis available in his *Collected Papers on the Jacobite Risings*, 2 vols. (Manchester, 1971–2).
48. C. Chenevix Trench, *George II*, pp. 233–4.
49. E. Cruickshank, *Political Untouchables*, ch. 6.

11 THE AFTERMATH OF THE '45

1. For a good introduction to the problems of modern guerrilla war see E. R. Wolf, *Peasant Wars of the Twentieth Century* (London, Faber paperback, 1973).
2. K. Tomasson, *The Jacobite General* (Edinburgh, 1958), ch. XIV.
3. Sir James Fergusson, *Argyll in the Forty-Five* (London, 1951), pp. 41 and 64.
4. ibid., pp. 87–8 and 119–20.
5. The best source for British government attitudes and policy towards the daunting of the Highlands in 1746 is still E. Charteris, *William Augustus Duke of Cumberland: His Early Life and Times (1721–1748)* (London, 1913), chs. XX and XXI.
6. Sir Bruce Gordon Seton and J. G. Arnot (eds.), *The Prisoners of the '45*, Scottish History Society, third series, vols. XIII–XV (Edinburgh, 1928–9), vol. I, p. 313; and vol. II, pp. 248–65.

7. Fergusson, *Argyll in the Forty-Five*, chs. XIII and XIV.

8. G. Menary, *The Life and Letters of Duncan Forbes of Culloden*, ch. XVI.

9. Sir James Fergusson, *John Fergusson 1727–1750: An Ayrshire Family and the Forty-Five* (London, 1948), *passim*. For the views of the Archbishop of York see 'Thomas Ebor' to Colonel Yorke, 13 March and 29 March 1746, Hardwicke Papers, British Library, Ad. MS. 35431, fols. 57–9.

10. E. Charteris, op. cit., p. 283.

11. Earl of Albemarle to Duke of Richmond, 17 June 1746, in C. S. Terry (ed.), *The Albemarle Papers: Being the Correspondence of William Anne, Second Earl of Albemarle Commander-in-Chief in Scotland 1746–1747*, 2 vols. (Aberdeen, The New Spalding Club, 1902), vol. I, p. 6.

12. Major-General Bland to Earl of Albemarle, 27 Aug. 1746, ibid., pp. 181–4.

13. A. R. B. Haldane, *The Drove Roads of Scotland* (London, 1952), pp. 25–6 and 118–20.

14. C. Northcote Parkinson (ed.), *The Trade Winds* (London, 1948), p. 52.

15. Major-General Bland to Major Roper, 29 Aug. 1746, *The Albemarle Papers*, vol. I, pp. 191–2.

16. Major-General Blakeney to Earl of Albemarle, 27 Aug. and 30 Aug. 1746, ibid., pp. 178–9 and 195–6.

17. Intelligence enclosure in Earl of Albemarle to Duke of Newcastle, 15 Dec. 1746, ibid., pp. 329–40.

18. Earl of Albemarle to Duke of Newcastle, 24 Dec. 1746, ibid., pp. 347–50 (two letters, the first endorsed 'private').

19. Enclosures I and II in Earl of Albemarle to Duke of Newcastle, 11 Feb. 1747, ibid., pp. 368–74.

20. Lord Justice Clerk to Duke of Newcastle, 20 Oct. 1747, and 19 Dec. 1747, with enclosure, ibid., vol. II, pp. 462–3 and 505–6. For Fassiefern's record during the '45 see Campbell of Glenorchy to Colonel Yorke, 29 March 1746, Hardwicke Papers, British Library, Ad. MS. 35431, fols. 61–3.

21. General Bland to Major Wilson, 5 Dec. 1747, 'Letter Book of General Bland 1747–1754', Blaikie Collection, National Library of Scotland, N.L.S., MS. 304.

22. General Bland to Lord Justice Clerk, 26 Jan. 1749, and General Bland to Captain Hamilton, 12 Dec. 1747, ibid.

23. A great deal of correspondence relating to this episode will be found in *The Albemarle Papers*, vol. I, pp. 28, 30, 31, 41, 42, 56, 89, 105, 108, 116, 123, 133, 185, 193, 197, 210; and vol. II, pp. 401 and 407.

24. Commissioner Campbell to Lord Milton, 11 June 1752, Saltoun Papers, National Library of Scotland, N.L.S., S.C.174, fols. 210–11.

25. I. MacIvor, *Fort George* (Edinburgh, H.M.S.O., 1970).

26. A. R. B. Haldane, *The Drove Roads of Scotland*, pp. 118–20.

27. *The Statistical Account of Scotland 1791–99 Edited by Sir John Sinclair: Vol. XII, North and West Perthshire*, with a new introduction by B. Lenman (Ilkley, E.P., 1977), p. 487.

28. There is an admirable survey of the treatment of the prisoners in vol. I of Sir Bruce Gordon Seton and J. G. Arnot (eds.), *The Prisoners of the '45*.

29. G. Howson, *Thief-Taker General: The Rise and Fall of Jonathan Wild* (London, 1970), pp. 91–2.

30. C. L. Ten Cate, *Tot glorie der gerechtigheid: De geschiedenis van het brandmerken als lyfstraf in Nederland* (Amsterdam, 1975).

31. Seton and Arnot, *The Prisoners of the '45*, vol. III, p. 267.

32. These remarks are based on a collection of 'Petitions etc. connected with the rising of 1745 Presented by Captain A. J. Campbell, Edinburgh, 1933' which

can be found in the National Library of Scotland, N.L.S., MS. 1004, fols. 6–19. Most of these letters and other documents are anonymous. Those that are dated run from 22 Oct. 1748 (a letter addressed to Jane Forbes, first wife of John Forbes, son of Lord President Duncan Forbes of Culloden) to 18 Feb. 1749 (copy of a letter to 'Mr D. F.'). From internal evidence, all the documents are roughly contemporary.

33. W. C. Mackenzie, *Lovat of the Forty-Five* (Edinburgh, 1934), p. 172.
34. Heavy use has been made of Seton and Arnot, *The Prisoners of the '45* in this section. The best account of the Gedds, father and son, is in the *Dictionary of National Biography*.
35. Lord Hardwicke, *Two Speeches in the House of Lords: I, On the Bill for Abolishing the Heritable Jurisdictions in Scotland; II, On the Militia Bill* (London, 1770 edn), pp. 2–29.
36. W. Grant to Lord Hardwicke, 19 Nov. 1747, Hardwicke Papers, British Library, Ad. MS. 35446, fol. 218.
37. D. Forbes to Lord Hardwicke, 27 Dec. 1737, and many other letters in British Library, Ad. MS. 35446, demonstrate the point.
38. James Erskine of Grange to Lord Hardwicke, 24 April 1747, ibid., fols. 166–7.
39. These remarks are based on a remarkable collection of printed and MS. materials relating to claims for compensation on the abolition of the heritable jurisdictions which are in the Scottish Record Office, which are referenced CS 4/8–12 and which are currently (1979) stored in the Historical Search Room, General Register House, in the cupboard marked 'T'. Use has also been made of a substantial collection of similar material in the Atholl MSS. at Blair Castle in Box 50 of the collection.
40. C. Erskine (Lord Tinwald) to Lord Hardwicke, 18 March 1748, Hardwicke Papers, British Library, Ad. MS. 35446, fol. 260.
41. G. Menary, *The Life and Letters of Duncan Forbes*, ch. 18.
42. 'Instructions to D. Bruce', Aug. 1749; and Col. Robert Napier to R. Stone, 21 Aug. 1749, Cumberland Papers, Box 43/292 and 301 respectively. The Cumberland Papers are in the Royal Archives at Windsor Castle. I have worked from a microfilm in St Andrews University Library.
43. A. M. Smith, 'The administration of the Forfeited Annexed Estates, 1752–1784', in G. W. S. Barrow (ed.), *The Scottish Tradition: Essays in honour of Ronald Gordon Cant* (Edinburgh, 1974), pp. 198–210. See also Dr Smith's unpublished 1974 St Andrews Ph.D. thesis, 'The Forfeited Estates Papers, 1745 – A Study of the work of the Commissioners for the Forfeited Annexed Estates, 1755–1784, with particular reference to their contribution to the development of communications in Scotland'.
44. A. J. Youngson, *After the Forty-Five: The Economic Impact on the Scottish Highlands* (Edinburgh, 1973).
45. J. MacInnes, *The Evangelical Movement in the Highlands of Scotland 1688 to 1800* (Aberdeen, 1951).

CONCLUSION

1. A. Robertson, *The Life of Sir Robert Moray* (London, 1922), pp. 119–22.
2. J. Adam Smith, 'Some Eighteenth-Century Ideas of Scotland', in N. T. Phillipson and R. Mitchison (eds.), *Scotland in the Age of Improvement*, p.114.
3. For the life of the Earl Marischal see E. E. Cuthell, *The Scottish Friend of Frederic the Great*, 2 vols. (London, 1915). The quotation is in vol. I, p. 220.
4. J. S. Bromley, 'The Jacobite Privateers in the Nine Years War', in A. Whiteman,

J. S. Bromley and P. G. M. Dickson (eds.), *Statesmen, Scholars and Merchants: Essays in Eighteenth-Century History presented to Dame Lucy Sutherland* (Oxford, 1973), pp. 17–43.

5. There is a good life of Ramsay: G. D. Henderson, *Chevalier Ramsay* (London, 1952). James Francis Stewart visited Cambrai in 1709–10 and his conversations with Fénelon, noted down by Ramsay, were the basis of the *Essai Philosophique sur le gouvernement civil* which Ramsay published in London in 1721. See A. M. Ramsay, *History of the Life of Fénelon* (Paisley, translated by D. Cuthbertson, 1897), p. 211 and note A², 275–6.

6. C. B. Wheeler (ed.), *The Conduct of the Allies by Jonathan Swift* (Oxford, 1916), p. 30.

7. S. Bidwell, *Swords For Hire* (London, 1971), p. 8.

8. M. F. Hamilton (ed.), 'The Locharkaig Treasure', *Miscellany of the Scottish History Society Volume VII*, Scottish History Society, third series, vol. XXXV (Edinburgh, 1941), pp. 131–68.

9. Entries in the St Andrews University Senate Minutes vol. V, 4, 14, 17 and 26 Feb. 1746. I am grateful to Mr Robert Smart, Keeper of the Muniments, for help in consulting these.

10. ibid. entry for 10 April 1746.

11. Rev. D. Blair to Sir Everard Fawkener, 4 May 1749; T. Maculloch to same, 16 May 1749; Rev. J. Jardine to same, 21 Aug. 1749; Rev. T. Reid to same, 27 Aug. 1749, Cumberland Papers, Box 43/229, 248, 300, 305 respectively.

12. 'Remarks of the Honourable Sir Everard Fawkener, and Lieutenant General Bland on the Accounts of Disbursements of the Right Honourable the Earl of Sutherland in His Majesty's Service during the late Rebellion in the years 1745 and 1746', and Earl of Sutherland to Sir Everard Fawkener, 26 June 1749, Cumberland Papers, Box 43/233 and 275. The best modern account of the campaign in which Sutherland was involved is R. J. Adam, 'The Northern Campaign of the '45: The Story of a Little War', *History Today*, vol. VIII, no. 6 (June 1958), pp. 413–20.

13. 'Copy of Captain Hughe's Report, Aug. 12, 1749', marked 'to H.R.H.'; 'Extracts of some letters etc. from Scotland for the consideration of His Grace the Duke of Newcastle from Sir Everard Fawkener by order of His Royal Highness the Duke sent to Mr Stone, Sept. 26, 1749'; 'Some few of the Instances where Jacobites or Non-Jurors have been provided for since the rebellion', n.d. but probably 1749; 'Delivered to His Royal Highness, Mar. 20, 1752 – Extracts of His Royal Highness the Duke's Letter to His Grace the Duke of Newcastle, May 19, 1746, from Inverness', Cumberland Papers, Box 43/307 and 316, and Box 44/231 and 232 respectively.

14. See the 'Reports of the Commander at Loch Arkaig and the posts depending', 16 Sept. to 15 Oct. 1751, in Cumberland Papers, Box 44/196.

15. Sir James Fergusson, 'The Appin Murder Case', in *The White Hind and other discoveries* (London, 1963), pp. 133–73.

16. W. Matheson (ed.), *The Blind Harper: The Songs of Roderick Morison and his Music* (Edinburgh, Scottish Gaelic Texts Society, 1970). For magisterial pioneering scholarship in this field, but not of course my interpretation, see J. L. Campbell, *Highland Songs of the Forty-Five* (Edinburgh, 1933).

17. W. O. Henderson, *Britain and Industrial Europe 1750–1870* (Leicester, 1965), pp. 14–24.

18. I owe this point to a splendid unpublished 1974 Aberdeen M.Litt. thesis ' "Wilderness" and "Civilization" in Eighteenth-Century Scotland and America' by Linda Spencer.

Index